.4.95

SO-BRU-851

Readings in
BASIC MARKETING

KLINCK MEMORIAL LIBRARY
Concordia College
River Forest, IL 60305

Readings in
BASIC MARKETING

E. JEROME McCARTHY
Michigan State University

JOHN F. GRASHOF
Temple University

ANDREW A. BROGOWICZ
University of Illinois at Chicago Circle

KLINCK MEMORIAL LIBRARY
Concordia College
River Forest, IL 60305

 1975

RICHARD D. IRWIN, INC.   Homewood, Illinois   60430
Irwin-Dorsey International   London, England   WC2H 9NJ
Irwin-Dorsey Limited   Georgetown, Ontario   L7G 4B3

© RICHARD D. IRWIN, INC., 1975

All rights reserved. No part of this publication may be
reproduced, stored in a retrieval system, or transmitted,
in any form or by any means, electronic, mechanical,
photocopying, recording, or otherwise, without the prior
written permission of the publisher.

First Printing, February 1975

ISBN 0-256-01568-6
Library of Congress Catalog Card No. 74-24449
Printed in the United States of America

142430
G

Preface

Just another readings book? No!

This collection of articles is intended as an educational tool to help enhance the beginning student's understanding of marketing. It has been designed to parallel the topical development of most introductory marketing books and, in particular, E. J. McCarthy's *Basic Marketing, A Managerial Approach.* The articles contained in this collection were not selected just because they are popular, because their authors are popular, or because they happen to relate to the topical area. Rather, each potential article was evaluated with the following criteria in mind:

1. The article should amplify or illustrate concepts introduced in the beginning marketing course, with an emphasis on *deepening* the student's understanding of these concepts rather than exposing him or her to more new concepts.
2. The article should be concise, readable, and within the scope of the beginning marketing student.
3. The article should make a specific contribution to the collection as a whole.
4. The article should provide a basis for class discussion.

Applying these criteria led to the selection of a variety of articles from more than a dozen different sources, whose authors provide a wide diversity of views and insights. The readings range from relatively theoretical selections from the *Journal of Marketing* to more pragmatic selections from sources such as *Business Week* and *Sales Management*. Some of the articles have become classics in the marketing literature while others, to our knowledge, have never been reprinted before; two were written especially for this collection. Together, these articles offer what we hope will be an interesting and fruitful educational experience for the beginning marketing student.

The articles have been grouped into five major sections:

1. "Introduction to Marketing."
2. "Selecting Target Markets."
3. "Developing Marketing Mixes."
4. "Marketing Management in Action."
5. "Marketing Reappraised."

To help guide the student through the readings, each major section begins with a short introduction which presents an overview of the topics covered in that section. In addition, each article is preceded by a brief introduction to help the reader focus on important aspects of the article.

Each reading in the collection is followed by a set of discussion questions that can serve as a check on the reader's understanding of key points contained in the article, while also providing a basis for class discussion. Most questions can be answered from the material contained in the article. Some questions, however—those indicated by an asterisk (*)—are broader in scope and try to relate concepts introduced in that one article to concepts discussed in one or more other articles. This integration of concepts from different readings can result not only in a deeper understanding of these concepts, but also in a heightened appreciation of the interrelationships among marketing variables.

The editors gratefully acknowledge the cooperation of the authors and journals who graciously consented to our reprinting their material. Most of the articles appear in their original versions. Occasionally, however, space constraints have made it necessary to shorten articles somewhat in order to expose the student to a broader array of authors, issues, and ideas. Where articles have been edited, we have tried to maintain the emphasis of the original article without distorting the meaning of an author's words. Of course, the original authors cannot be held fully accountable for the edited version of their work which appears here. Interested readers are strongly encouraged to refer to the original article for complete exposure to an author's views and insights.

The concept underlying this collection of readings evolved over a period of several years. The contribution of Alan Kelman to that evolution was significant.

We hope the collection proves useful to both faculty and students. We do encourage your comments and suggestions. Responsibility for editorial errors or failure to accomplish our objective is ours.

January 1975   E. J. McCarthy

J. F. Grashof

A. A. Brogowicz

Contents

1

Introduction to marketing

MARKETING IS currently undergoing a reexamination of its role within the firm and its role within society. Scholars are examining the critical role which marketing plays within an economy, the influence which marketing techniques can have on nonprofit institutions, and the social responsibility which marketers should show.

Most of the readings in this section were selected to illustrate current thought about marketing and its many roles. The articles present various points of view about marketing and its relationship to the firm and to society. All of these readings lay the groundwork for understanding the managerial approach to the study of marketing, which will be the focus of most of the readings in the remaining sections of this collection. In particular, the concept of strategy and the importance of marketing strategy to the survival of the firm are discussed by several of the authors.

The final reading in this section discusses the impact of the environment on marketing activities. Concerned with energy and pollution, it emphasizes that marketers do not operate in a vacuum. Rather, their activities are bounded by many kinds of pressures, including the desires of society, the restraints of the economic system, and the constraints imposed by government regulation.

1

What are the role(s) of marketing in our society? Lazer contends that marketing is a social institution which has a role that includes but also extends beyond the marketing activities of a firm. Recognition of this societal role provides a new perspective for examining the role of marketing tasks within a firm. Similarly, environmental factors such as changing life styles and social norms can have considerable impact on the firm's marketing activities.

1. MARKETING'S CHANGING SOCIAL RELATIONSHIPS*

William Lazer

MARKETING IS NOT an end in itself. It is not the exclusive province of business management. Marketing must serve not only business but also the goals of society. It must act in concert with broad public interest. For marketing does not end with the buy-sell transaction—its responsibilities extend well beyond making profits. Marketing shares in the problems and goals of society and its contributions extend well beyond the formal boundaries of the firm.

The purpose of this article is to present some viewpoints and ideas on topics concerning marketing's changing social relationships. The author hopes to stimulate discussion and encourage work by others concerned with the marketing discipline, rather than to present a definitive set of statements. He first presents a brief discussion of marketing and our life style, and marketing's role beyond the realm of profit. This is followed by the development of some ideas and viewpoints on marketing and consumption under conditions of abundance, with a particular focus on changing consumption norms. The last section is concerned with changing marketing boundaries and emerging social perspectives.

Marketing and life style

Recent developments in such areas as consumer safety and protection, product warranties, government investigations, and a host of urban issues, including air and water pollution, and poverty, are stimulating

* Reprinted with permission from the *Journal of Marketing,* published by the American Marketing Association, vol. 33, January 1969, pp. 3–9. At the time of writing, the author was Professor of Marketing at Michigan State University.

thoughtful executives and academicians to pay increasing attention to marketing's fundamental interfaces with society. They highlight the fact that marketers are inevitably concerned with societal norms and life styles of both our total society and societal segments. Since the American economy is a materialistic, acquisitive, thing-minded, abundant market economy, marketing becomes one of the cores for understanding and influencing life styles: and marketers assume the role of taste counselors. Since American tastes are being emulated in other parts of the world such as Europe, Japan, and Latin America, the impact of our values and norms reverberate throughout a broad international community.

Yet a basic difference exists between the orientation of the American life style, which is interwoven with marketing, and the life style of many other countries, particularly of the emerging and lesser-developed countries, although the differences are blurring. American norms include a general belief in equality of opportunity to strive for a better standard of living; the achievement of status and success through individual initiative, sacrifice, and personal skills; the provision and maintenance of a relatively open society with upward economic and social movement; the availability of education which is a route for social achievement, occupational advancement, and higher income. Yet, there are contradictory and conflicting concepts operating within this value system. One contradiction is seen in the conflict between concepts of equality for all on the one hand and the visible rank and status orderings in society. Another conflict much discussed today concerns the conflicts between the coexisting values of our affluent society and the pockets of poverty in the United States.

In their scheme of norms the majority of Americans, even younger Americans, exude optimism in the materialistic productivity of our society. They feel confident that the economic future will be much better than the present, that our standard of living and consumption will expand and increase, that pleasures will be multiplied, and that there is little need to curb desires. They are certain that increasing purchasing power will be made available to them.

This is not to deny the existence of discontent in our economy of plenty, or the challenging and questioning of values. There is evidence that some younger members are critical of our hedonistic culture, of our economic institutions and achievements. Questions have been raised about priorities of expenditures, and authority has been challenged. Various marketing processes and institutions have been attacked. But, by and large, there exists a general expectation of increasing growth, the availability of more and more, and a brighter and better future. As a result of this perspective, economic opportunities and growth are perceived not so much in terms of curbing consumer desires as is the case in many other societies, particularly in underdeveloped economies, but in increasing desires; in attempting to stimulate people to try to realize themselves to the fullest extent of their resources and capabilities by acquiring complementary goods and symbols. Whereas other societies have often hoped that tomorrow will be no worse than today, we would certainly be dismayed if present expectations did not indicate that tomorrow will be much better than today. Similarly, the emerging nations now have rising economic expectations and aspiration levels, and their life style perspectives are changing. They expect to share in the economic abundance achieved by highly industrialized economies.

The growth orientation which reverberates throughout the American society has its impact on our norms and on marketing practices. It is reflected in such marketing concepts and techniques as product planning, new product development, installment credit, pricing practices, advertising campaigns, sales promotion, personal selling campaigns, and a host of merchandising activities.

Beyond the realm of profit

One of the next marketing frontiers may well be related to markets that extend beyond mere profit considerations to intrinsic values—to markets based on social concern, markets of the mind, and markets concerned with the development of people to the fullest extent of their capabilities. This may be considered a macro frontier of marketing, one geared to interpersonal and social development, to social concern.

From this perspective one of marketing's roles may be to encourage increasing expenditures by consumers of dollars and time to develop themselves socially, intellectually, and morally. Another may be the direction of marketing to help solve some of the fundamental problems that nations face today. Included are such problems as the search for peace, since peace and economic progress are closely intertwined; the renewal of our urban areas which is closely related to marketing development and practices, particularly in the area of retailing; the reduction and elimination of poverty, for marketing should have a major role here; the preservation of our natural resources; the reshaping of governmental interfaces with business; and the stimulation of economic growth. To help solve such problems, in addition to its current sense of purpose in the firm, marketing must develop its sense of community, its societal commitments and obligations, and accept the challenges inherent in any institution of social control.

But one may ask whether social welfare is consonant with the bilateral transfer characteristics of an exchange or market economy, or can it be realized only through the unilateral transfer of a grants economy? This is a pregnant social question now confronting marketing.

Business executives operating in a market economy can achieve the degree of adaptation necessary to accept their social responsibilities and still meet the demands of both markets and the business enterprise.

At the very least, the exchange economy will support the necessary supplementary grants economy. Currently we are witnessing several examples of this.[1] The National Alliance for Businessmen composed of 50 top business executives is seeking jobs in 50 of our largest cities for 500,000 hard-core unemployed; the Urban Coalition, composed of religious, labor, government, and business leaders, as well as several individual companies, is actively seeking ways of attacking the problem of unemployment among the disadvantaged; and the insurance companies are investing and spending millions for new housing developments in slum areas. It even seems likely that business executives, operating in a market environment, stimulated by the profit motive, may well succeed in meeting certain challenges of social responsibility where social planners and governmental agencies have not.

Governmental agencies alone cannot meet the social tasks. A spirit of mutual endeavor must be developed encompassing a marketing thrust. For marketing cannot insulate itself from societal responsibilities and problems that do not bear immediately on profit. Marketing practice must be reconciled with the concept of community involvement, and marketing leaders must respond to pressures to accept a new social role.[2]

The development of the societal dimensions of marketing by industry and/or other institutions is necessary to mold a society in which every person has the opportunity to grow to the fullest extent of his capabilities, in which older people can play out their roles in a dignified manner, in which human potentials are recognized and nurtured, and in which the dignity of the individual is accepted. While prone to point out the undesirable impact of marketing in our life style (as they should), social critics have neglected to indicate the progress and the contributions that have been made.

In achieving its sense of broad community interest and participation, marketing performs its social role in two ways. First, marketing faces social challenges in the same sense as the government and other institutions. But unlike the government, marketing finds its major social justification through offering product-service mixes and commercially unified applications of the results of technology to the marketplace for a profit.

[1] For a discussion of this point see Robert J. Holloway, "Total Involvement in Our Society," in Changing Marketing Systems, Reed Moyer, ed. (Washington, D.C.: American Marketing Association 1967 Winter Conference Proceedings, December 1967), pp. 6–8; Robert Lekachman, "Business Must Lead the Way," Dun's Review, vol. 91 (April 1968), p. 11; and Charles B. McCoy, "Business and the Community," Dun's Review, vol. 91 (May 1968), pp. 110–11.

[2] Among the recent articles discussing management's new social role are "Business Must Pursue Social Goals: Gardner," Advertising Age, vol. 39 (February 1968), p. 2; B. K. Wickstrum, "Managers Must Master Social Problems," Administrative Management, vol. 28 (August 1967), p. 34; and G. H. Wyman, "Role of Industry in Social Change," Advanced Management Journal, vol. 33 (April 1968), pp. 70–4.

Second, it participates in welfare and cultural efforts extending beyond mere profit considerations, and these include various community services and charitable and welfare activities. For example, marketing has had a hand in the renewed support for the arts in general, the increasing demand for good books, the attendance at operas and symphony concerts, the sale of classical records, the purchase of fine paintings through mail-order catalogues, and the attention being given to meeting educational needs. These worthy activities, while sometimes used as a social measure, do not determine the degree of social concern or the acceptance of social responsibility.

A fundamental value question to be answered is not one of the absolute morality or lack of problems in our economic system and marketing activities, as many critics suggest. Rather, it is one concerning the *relative* desirability of our life style with its norms, its emphasis on materialism, its hedonistic thrust, its imperfections, injustices, and poverty, as contrasted with other life styles that have different emphases. Great materialistic stress and accomplishment is not inherently sinful and bad. Moral values are not vitiated (as many critics might lead one to believe) by substantial material acquisitions. Increasing leisure time does not automatically lead to the decay and decline of a civilization. In reality, the improvement of material situations is a stimulus for recognition of intrinsic values, the general lifting of taste, the enhancement of a moral climate, the direction of more attention to the appreciation of arts and esthetics. History seems to confirm this; for great artistic and cultural advancements were at least accompanied by, if not directly stimulated by, periods of flourishing trade and commerce.

Marketing and consumption under abundance

American consumers are confronted with a dilemma. On the one hand, they live in a very abundant, automated economy that provides a surplus of products, an increasing amount of leisure, and an opportunity for a relative life of ease. On the other hand, they have a rich tradition of hard physical work, sweat, perseverance in the face of adversity, earning a living through hard labor, being thrifty, and "saving for a rainy day." There is more than token acceptance of a philosophy that a life of ease is sinful, immoral, and wrong. Some consumers appear to fear the abundance we have and the potential life style that it can bring, and are basically uncomfortable with such a way of life.

Yet, for continued economic growth and expansion, this feeling of guilt must be overcome. American consumers still adhere to many puritanical concepts of consumption, which are relevant in an economy of scarcity but not in our economy of abundance. Our society faces a task of making consumers accept comfortably the fact that a life style of relative leisure and luxury that eliminates much hard physical labor and drudgery, and permits us to alter unpleasant environments, is actually one of the major accomplishments of our age, rather than the indication of a sick, failing, or decaying society. Those activities resulting in the acquisition of more material benefits and greater enjoyment of life are not to be feared or automatically belittled, nor is the reduction of drudgery and hard physical tasks to be regretted.

Some of the very fundamental precepts underlying consumption have changed. For example, consumption is no longer an exclusive home-centered activity as it once was; consumption of large quantities of many goods and services outside the home on a regular basis is very common. Similarly, the hard work and drudgery of the home is being replaced by machines and services. The inherent values of thrift and saving are now being challenged by the benefits of spending and the security of new financial and employment arrangements.[3] In fact, the intriguing problems of consumption must now receive the attention previously accorded to those of physical production.

In essence, our consumption philosophy must change. It must be brought into line with our age of plenty, with an age of automation and mass production, with a highly industrialized mass-consumption society. To do so, the abundant life style must be accepted as a moral one, as an ethical one, as a life which can be inherently good. The criteria for judging our economic system and our marketing activities should include opportunity for consumers to develop themselves to the fullest extent, personally and professionally; to realize and express themselves in a creative manner; to accept their societal responsibilities; and to achieve large measures of happiness. Abundance should not lead to a sense of guilt stemming from the automatic declaration of the immorality of a comfortable way of life spurred on by marketing practices.

In our society, is it not desirable to urge consumers to acquire additional material objects? Cannot the extension of consumer wants and needs be a great force for improvement and for increasing societal awareness and social contributions? Is it not part of marketing's social responsibility to help stimulate the desire to improve the quality of life—particularly the economic quality—and so serve the public interest?

In assessing consumption norms, we should recognize that consumer expenditures and investments are not merely the functions of increased income. They stem from and reflect our life style. Thus, new consumption standards should be established, including the acceptance of self-indulgence, of luxurious surroundings, and of non-utilitarian products. Obviously, products that permit consumers to indulge themselves are not "strict necessities." Their purchase does not, and should not, appeal to a "utilitarian rationale." For if our economic system produced only

---

[3] Some aspects of the economic ambivalence of economic values are discussed by David P. Eastburn, "Economic Discipline and the Middle Generation," *Business Review*, Federal Reserve Bank of Philadelphia (July 1968), pp. 3–8.

"utilitarian products," products that were absolute necessities, it would incur severe economic and social problems, including unemployment. — NO —

Yet some very significant questions may be posed. Can or should American consumers feel comfortable, physically and psychologically, with a life of relative luxury while they are fully cognizant of the existence of poverty in the midst of plenty, of practice of discrimination in a democratic society, the feeling of hopelessness and despair among many in our expanding and increasingly productive economy, and the prevalence of ignorance in a relatively enlightened age? Or, on a broader base, can or should Americans feel comfortable with their luxuries, regular model and style changes, gadgetry, packaging variations, and waste while people in other nations of the world confront starvation? These are among the questions related to priorities in the allocation of our resources, particularly between the public and private sectors and between the national and international boundaries that have been discussed by social and economic commentators such as Galbraith[4] and Toynbee.

These are not easy questions to answer. The answers depend on the perspective adopted (whether macro or micro), on the personal philosophy adhered to (religious and otherwise), and on the social concern of individuals, groups, and nations. No perfect economic system has or will ever exist, and the market system is no exception. Economic and social problems and conflicts will remain, but we should strive to eliminate the undesirable features of our market system. And it is clear that when abundance prevails individuals and nations can afford to, and do, exercise increasing social concern.

Toynbee, in assessing our norms and value systems (particularly advertising), wrote that if it is true that personal consumption stimulated by advertising is essential for growth and full employment in our economy (which we in marketing believe), then it demonstrates automatically to his mind that an economy of abundance is a spiritually unhealthy way of life and that the sooner it is reformed, the better.[5] Thus, he concluded that our way of life, based on personal consumption stimulated by advertising, needs immediate reform. But let us ponder for a moment these rather strong indictments of our norms and the impact of marketing on our value systems and life style.

When economic abundance prevails, the limitations and constraints on both our economic system and various parts of our life style shift. The most critical point in the functioning of society shifts from physical production to consumption. Accordingly, the culture must be reoriented: a producers' culture must be converted into a consumers' culture. Society

---

[4] John K. Galbraith, "The Theory of Social Balance," in *Social Issues in Marketing*, Lee E. Preston, ed. (Glenview, Illinois: Scott, Foresman and Company 1968), pp. 247–52.

[5] "Toynbee vs. Bernbach: Is Advertising Morally Defensible?" *Yale Daily News* (Special Issue 1963), p. 2.

must adjust to a new set of drives and values in which consumption, and hence marketing activities, becomes paramount. Buckminster Fuller has referred to the necessity of creating regenerative consumers in our affluent society.[6] The need for consumers willing and able to expand their purchases both quantitatively and qualitatively is now apparent in the United States. It is becoming increasingly so in Russia, and it will be so in the future among the underdeveloped and emerging nations. Herein lies a challenge for marketing—the challenge of changing norms and values to bring them into line with the requirements of an abundant economy.

Although some social critics and observers might lead us to believe that we should be ashamed of our life style, and although our affluent society is widely criticized, it is circumspect to observe that other nations of the world are struggling to achieve the stage of affluence that has been delivered by our economic system. When they achieve it, they will be forced to wrestle with similar problems of abundance, materialism, consumption, and marketing that we now face.

Consumption activities and norms

The relative significance of consumers and consumption as economic determinants has been underemphasized in our system.[7] Consumption should not be considered an automatic or a happenstance activity. We must understand and establish the necessary conditions for consumption to proceed on a continuing and orderly basis. This has rich meaning for marketing. New marketing concepts and tools that encourage continuing production rather than disruptive production or the placement of consumer orders far in advance, or new contractual obligations, must be developed.[8] To achieve our stated economic goals of stability, growth, and full employment, marketing must be viewed as a force that will shape economic destiny by expanding and stabilizing consumption.

To date the major determinant of consumption has been income. But as economic abundance increases, the consumption constraints change. By the year 2000 it has been noted that the customer will experience as his first constraint not money, but time.[9] As time takes on greater utility, affluence will permit the purchase of more time-saving products and services. Interestingly enough, although time is an important by-

---

[6] Buckminster Fuller, *Education Automation: Freeing the Scholar to Return to His Studies* (Carbondale, Ill.: Southern Illinois University Press, 1961).

[7] George Katona, "Consumer Investment and Business Investment," *Michigan Business Review* (June 1961), pp. 17–22.

[8] Ferdinand F. Mauser, "A Universe-in-Motion Approach to Marketing," in *Managerial Marketing—Perspectives and Viewpoints,* Eugene J. Kelley and William Lazer, eds. (Homewood, Illinois: Richard D. Irwin, Inc., 1967), pp. 46–56.

[9] Nelson N. Foote, "The Image of the Consumer in the Year 2000," Proceedings, Thirty-Fifth Annual Boston Conference on Distribution, 1963, pp. 13–18.

product of our industrial productivity, many consumers are not presently prepared to consume time in any great quantities, which in turn presents another opportunity for marketing. The manner in which leisure time is consumed will affect the quality of our life style.

In other ages, the wealthy achieved more free time through the purchase of personal services and the use of servants. In our society, a multitude of products with built-in services extend free time to consumers on a broad base. Included are such products as automobiles, jet planes, mechanized products in home, prepared foods, "throw-aways," and leased facilities. Related to this is the concept that many consumers now desire the use of products rather than mere ownership. The symbolism of ownership appears to take on lesser importance with increasing wealth.[10]

We live in a sensate culture, one which stresses materialism and sensory enjoyment. Consumers desire and can obtain the use of products and symbols associated with status, achievement, and accomplishments. Material values which are visible have become more important to a broader segment of society, and marketing responds to and reinforces such norms. But our basic underlying value system is not merely the result of the whims of marketers—it has its roots in human nature and our cultural and economic environments.

The concept of consumption usually conjures a false image. Consumption generally seems to be related to chronic scarcity. It is associated with hunger, with the bare necessities of life, and with the struggle to obtain adequate food, shelter, and clothing.[11] It is associated with the perception of economics as the "dismal science," with the study of the allocation of scarce resources.

But, it has been noted that in the future consumption and consuming activities will occur in a society suffering from obesity and not hunger; in a society emerged from a state of chronic scarcity, one confronting problems of satiation—full stomachs, garages, closets and houses.[12] Such an environment requires a contemporary perspective and concept of consumption and consumers. It requires a recognition and appreciation of the importance of stimulating the consumption of goods. For consumers will find that their financial capabilities for acquiring new products are outstripping their natural inclinations to do so.

But what happens to norms and values when people have suitably gratified their "needs"? What happens after the acquisition of the third automobile, the second color television set, and three or four larger and more luxurious houses? Maslow has noted that consumers then become motivated in a manner different from that explained by his hierarchy of motives. They become devoted to tasks outside themselves. The

[10] Same reference as footnote 8.

[11] Same reference as footnote 9.

[12] Same reference as footnote 9.

differences between work and play are transcended; one blends into the other, and work is defined in a different manner. Consumers become concerned with different norms and values reflected in metamotives or metaneeds, motives or needs beyond physical love, safety, esteem, and self-actualization.[13]

The tasks to which people become dedicated, given the gratification of their "needs," are those concerned with intrinsic values. The tasks are enjoyed because they embody these values. The self then becomes enlarged to include other aspects of the world. Under those conditions, Maslow maintains that the highest values, the spiritual life, and the highest aspirations of mankind become proper subjects for scientific study and research. The hierarchy of basic needs such as physical, safety, and social is prepotent to metaneeds. The latter, metaneeds, are equally potent among themselves.

Maslow also makes a distinction between the realm of being, the "B-realm," and the realm of deficiencies, the "D-realm,"—between the external and the practical. For example, in the practical realm of marketing with its daily pressures, executives tend to be responders. They react to stimuli, rewards, punishments, emergencies, and the demands of others. However, given an economy of abundance with a "saturation of materialism," they can turn attentions to the intrinsic values and implied norms—seeking to expose themselves to great cultural activities, to natural beauty, to the developments of those "B" values.

Our society has reached the stage of affluence without having developed an acceptable justification for our economic system, and for the eventual life of abundance and relative leisure that it will supply. Herein lies a challenge for marketing: to justify and stimulate our age of consumption. We must learn to realize ourselves in an affluent life and to enjoy it without pangs of guilt. What is required is a set of norms and a concept of morality and ethics that corresponds to our age. This means that basic concepts must be changed, which is difficult to achieve because people have been trained for centuries to expect little more than subsistence, and to gird for a fight with the elements. They have been governed by a puritanical philosophy, and often view luxurious, new, convenient products and services with suspicion.

When we think of abundance, we usually consider only the physical resources, capabilities, and potentialities of our society. But abundance depends on more than this. Abundance is also dependent on the society and culture itself. It requires psychological and sociological environments that encourage and stimulate achievement. *In large measure, our economic abundance results from certain institutions in our society which affect our pattern of living, and not the least of these institutions is marketing.*

---

[13] Abraham Maslow, "Metamotivation," *The Humanist* (May–June 1967), pp. 82–84.

Advertising is the institution uniquely identified with abundance, particularly in America. But the institution that is actually brought into being by abundance without previous emphasis or existence in the same form is marketing.[14] It is marketing expressed not only through advertising. It is also expressed in the emphasis on consumption in our society, new approaches to product development, the role of credit, the use of marketing research and marketing planning, the implementation of the marketing concept, the management of innovation, the utilization of effective merchandising techniques, and the cultivation of mass markets. Such institutions and techniques as self-service, supermarkets, discount houses, advertising, credit plans, and marketing research are spreading marketing and the American life style through other parts of the world.

Marketing is truly an institution of social control in a relatively abundant economy, in the same sense as the school and the home. It is one of the fundamental influences of our life style. It is a necessary condition of our high standard of living. It is a social process for satisfying the wants and needs of our society. It is a very formative force in our culture. In fact, it is impossible to understand fully the American culture without a comprehension of marketing. But, unlike some other social institutions, marketing is confronted with great conflicts that cloud its social role.

Changing marketing boundaries

We may well ask, what are the boundaries of marketing in modern society? This is an important question that cannot be answered simply. But surely these boundaries have changed and now extend beyond the profit motive. Marketing ethics, values, responsibilities, and marketing-government relationships are involved. These marketing dimensions will unquestionably receive increasing scrutiny by practitioners and academicians in a variety of areas, and the result will be some very challenging and basic questions that must be answered.

We might ask, for example, can or should marketing, as a function of business, possess a social role distinct from the personal social roles of individuals who are charged with marketing responsibilities?[15] Does the business as a legal entity possess a conscience and a personality whose sum is greater than the respective attributes of its individual managers and owners? Should each member of management be held

---

[14] David M. Potter, "People of Plenty" (Chicago, Ill.: The University of Chicago Press, 1954), p. 167.

[15] For a discussion of the social responsibilities of executives see James M. Patterson, "What are the Social and Ethical Responsibilities of Marketing Executives?" *Journal of Marketing*, vol. 30 (July 1936), pp. 12–15, and K. Davis, "Understanding the Social Responsibility Puzzle," *Business Horizons*, vol. 10 (Winter 1967), pp. 45–50.

personally accountable for social acts committed or omitted in the name of the business? Answers to such questions change with times and situations, but the trend is surely to a broadening recognition of greater social responsibilities—the development of marketing's social role.

Few marketing practitioners or academicians disagree totally with the concept that marketing has important social dimensions and can be viewed as a social instrument in a highly industrialized society. Disagreement exists, however, about the relative importance of marketing's social dimensions as compared to its managerial or technical dimensions.

The more traditional view has been that marketing management fulfills the greater part of its responsibility by providing products and services to satisfy consumer needs profitably and efficiently. Those adopting this view believe that as a natural consequence of its efficiency, customers are satisfied, firms prosper, and the well-being of society follows automatically. They fear that the acceptance of any other responsibilities by marketing managers, particularly social responsibilities, tends to threaten the very foundation of our economic system. Moot questions about who will establish the guidelines, who will determine what these social responsibilities should be, and who will enforce departures from any standards established, are raised.

However, an emerging view is one that does not take issue with the ends of customer satisfaction, the profit focus, the market economy, and economic growth. Rather, its premise seems to be that the tasks of marketing and its concomitant responsibilities are much wider than purely economic concerns. It views the market process as one of the controlling elements of the world's social and economic growth. Because marketing is a social instrument through which a standard of living is transmitted to society, as a discipline it is a social one with commensurate social responsibilities that cannot merely be the exclusive concern of companies and consumers.

Perhaps nowhere is the inner self of the populace more openly demonstrated than in the marketplace; for the marketplace is an arena where actions are the proof of words and transactions represent values, both physical and moral. One theologian has written, "the saintly cannot be separated from the marketplace, for it is in the marketplace that man's future is being decided and the saintly must be schooled in the arts of the marketplace as in the discipline of saintliness itself."[16]

In this context, marketing's responsibility is only partially fulfilled through economic processes. There is a greater responsibility to consumers and to the human dignity that is vital to the marketplace—the concern for marketing beyond the profit motive.

Academicians and executives will be forced to rethink and reevaluate such situations in the immediate future just by the sheer weight of

---

[16] Louis Finkelstein in Conference on the American Character, Bulletin Center for the Study of Democratic Institutions (October 1961), p. 6.

government concern and decisions if by nothing else.[17] In the last year, there have been governmental decisions about safety standards, devices for controlling air pollution, implied product warranties, packaging rules and regulations, the relationship of national brands to private labels, pricing practices, credit practices, and mergers. There have been discussions about limiting the amount that can be spent on advertising for a product, about controlling trading stamps, about investigating various promotional devices and marketing activities. Such actions pose serious questions about marketing's social role. If we do not answer them, others will; and perhaps in a manner not too pleasing, or even realistic.

There need be no wide chasm between the profit motive and social responsibility, between corporate marketing objectives and social goals, between marketing actions and public welfare. What is required is a broader perception and definition of marketing than has hitherto been the case—one that recognizes marketing's societal dimensions and perceives of marketing as more than just a technology of the firm. For the multiple contributions of marketing that are so necessary to meet business challenges, here and abroad, are also necessary to meet the nation's social and cultural problems.

QUESTIONS

1. Identify the several roles, or potential roles, assigned to marketing by Lazer.

2. What are the dominant social norms and values of the U.S. and what demands do they place on the marketing system?

3. If businesses accepted Lazer's ideas, what specific changes might we expect in firms' marketing activities? How would profit be affected?

4. Should (and if so, how should) Lazer's analysis be modified if our young people must now live in and adjust to a world of shortages and growing austerity?

5. Should marketing accept the challenge suggested by Lazer: changing norms and values to bring them into line with the requirements of an abundant economy?

---

[17] The reader can gain some insight into government concern from such articles as "Consumer Advisory Council: First Report," in *Social Issues in Marketing*, Lee E. Preston, ed. (Glenview, Ill.: Scott, Foresman and Company, 1968), pp. 282–94; Betty Furness, "Responsibility in Marketing," in *Changing Marketing Systems* . . . , Reed Moyer, ed. (Washington, D.C.: American Marketing Association 1967 Winter Conference Proceedings. December 1967), pp. 25–27; Galbraith, same reference as footnote 4; Richard H. Holton, "The Consumer and the Business Community," in *Social Issues in Marketing*, Lee E. Preston, ed. (Glenview, Ill.: Scott, Foresman and Company, 1968), pp. 295–303; George H. Koch, "Government-Consumer Interest: From the Business Point of View," in *Changing Marketing Systems* . . . , Reed Moyer, ed. (Washington, D.C.: American Marketing Association 1967 Winter Conference Proceedings, December 1967), pp. 156–60.

Changing life styles, social norms and technology may affect the survival of the firm. In the following edited version of his well-known article, Levitt shows that the result of failing to recognize such changes can be failure of the firm or industry. He emphasizes that long run survival requires (1) a clear understanding of the nature of the firm's business and (2) top management ability to recognize and deal with change.

2. MARKETING MYOPIA*

Theodore Levitt

EVERY MAJOR INDUSTRY was once a growth industry. But some that are now riding a wave of growth enthusiasm are very much in the shadow of decline. Others which are thought of as seasoned growth industries have actually stopped growing. In every case the reason growth is threatened, slowed, or stopped is *not* because the market is saturated. It is because there has been a failure of management.

FATEFUL PURPOSES

The failure is at the top. The executives responsible for it, in the last analysis, are those who deal with broad aims and policies. Thus:

The railroads did not stop growing because the need for passenger and freight transportation declined. That grew. The railroads are in trouble today not because the need was filled by others (cars, trucks, airplanes, even telephones), but because it was *not* filled by the railroads themselves. They let others take customers away from them because they assumed themselves to be in the railroad business rather than in the transportation business. The reason they defined their industry wrong was because they were railroad-oriented instead of transportation-oriented; they were product-oriented instead of customer-oriented.

---

* Reprinted by permission of the publishers from Edward C. Bursk and John F. Chapman, eds., *Modern Marketing Strategy* (Cambridge, Mass: Harvard University Press), © 1964 by the President and Fellows of Harvard College, pp. 24–48. At the time of writing, Theodore Levitt was Professor of Marketing at the Harvard Business School.

Hollywood barely escaped being totally ravished by television. Actually, all the established film companies went through drastic reorganizations. Some simply disappeared. All of them got into trouble not because of TV's inroads but because of their own myopia. As with the railroads, Hollywood defined its business incorrectly. It thought it was in the movie business when it was actually in the entertainment business. "Movies" implied a specific, limited product. This produced a fatuous contentment which from the beginning led producers to view TV as a threat. Hollywood scorned and rejected TV when it should have welcomed it as an opportunity—an opportunity to expand the entertainment business.

Today TV is a bigger business than the old narrowly defined movie business ever was. Had Hollywood been customer-oriented (providing entertainment), rather than product-oriented (making movies), would it have gone through the fiscal purgatory that it did? I doubt it. What ultimately saved Hollywood and accounted for its recent resurgence was the wave of new young writers, producers, and directors whose previous success in television had decimated the old movie companies and toppled the big movie moguls.

There are other less obvious examples of industries that have been and are now endangering their futures by improperly defining their purposes. I shall discuss some in detail later and analyze the kind of policies that lead to trouble. Right now it may help to show what a thoroughly customer-oriented management *can* do to keep a growth industry growing, even after the obvious opportunities have been exhausted; and here there are two examples that have been around for a long time. They are nylon and glass—specifically, E. I. duPont de Nemours & Company and Corning Glass Works:

Both companies have great technical competence. Their product orientation is unquestioned. But this alone does not explain their success. After all, who was more pridefully product-oriented and product-conscious than the erstwhile New England textile companies that have been so thoroughly massacred? The DuPonts and the Cornings have succeeded not primarily because of their product or research orientation but because they have been thoroughly customer-oriented also. It is constant watchfulness for opportunities to apply their technical know-how to the creation of customer-satisfying uses which accounts for their prodigious output of successful new products. Without a very sophisticated eye on the customer, most of their new products might have been wrong, their sales methods useless.

Aluminum has also continued to be a growth industry, thanks to the efforts of two wartime-created companies which deliberately set about creating new customer-satisfying uses. Without Kaiser Aluminum & Chemical Corporation and Reynolds Metals Company, the total demand for aluminum today would be vastly less than it is.

Error of analysis

Some may argue that it is foolish to set the railroads off against aluminum or the movies off against glass. Are not aluminum and glass naturally so versatile that the industries are bound to have more growth opportunities than the railroads and movies? This view commits precisely the error I have been talking about. It defines an industry, or a product, or a cluster of know-how so narrowly as to guarantee its premature senescence. When we mention "railroads," we should make sure we mean "transportation." As transporters, the railroads still have a good chance for very considerable growth. They are not limited to the railroad business as such (though in my opinion rail transportation is potentially a much stronger transportation medium than is generally believed). What the railroads lack is not opportunity, but some of the same managerial imaginativeness and audacity that made them great. Even an amateur like Jacques Barzun can see what is lacking when he says: "I grieve to see the most advanced physical and social organization of the last century go down in shabby disgrace for lack of the same comprehensive imagination that built it up. [*What is lacking is*] the will of the companies to survive and to satisfy the public by inventiveness and skill."[1]

SHADOW OF OBSOLESCENCE

It is impossible to mention a single major industry that did not at one time qualify for the magic appellation of "growth industry." In each case its assumed strength lay in the apparently unchallenged superiority of its product. There appeared to be no effective substitute for it. It was itself a runaway substitute for the product it so triumphantly replaced. Yet one after another of these celebrated industries has come under a shadow. Let us look briefly at a few more of them, this time taking examples that have so far received a little less attention:

Dry cleaning. This was once a growth industry with lavish prospects. In an age of wool garments, imagine being finally able to get them safely and easily clean. The boom was on.

Yet here we are 30 years after the boom started and the industry is in trouble. Where has the competition come from? From a better way of cleaning? No. It has come from synthetic fibers and chemical additives that have cut the need for dry cleaning. But this is only the beginning. Lurking in the wings and ready to make chemical dry cleaning totally obsolescent is that powerful magician, ultrasonics.

Electric utilities. This is another one of those supposedly "no-substi-

---

[1] Jacques Barzun, "Trains and the Mind of Man," *Holiday*, February 1960, p. 21.

tute" products that has been enthroned on a pedestal of invincible growth. When the incandescent lamp came along, kerosene lights were finished. Later the water wheel and the steam engine were cut to ribbons by the flexibility, reliability, simplicity, and just plain easy availability of electric motors. The prosperity of electric utilities continues to wax extravagant as the home is converted into a museum of electric gadgetry. How can anybody miss by investing in utilities, with no competition, nothing but growth ahead?

But a second look is not quite so comforting. A score of nonutility companies are well advanced toward developing a powerful chemical fuel cell which could sit in some hidden closet of every home silently ticking off electric power. The electric lines that vulgarize so many neighborhoods will be eliminated. So will the endless demolition of streets and service interruptions during storms. Also on the horizon is solar energy, again pioneered by nonutility companies.

Who says that the utilities have no competition? They may be natural monopolies now, but tomorrow they may be natural deaths. To avoid this prospect, they too will have to develop fuel cells, solar energy, and other power sources. To survive, they themselves will have to plot the obsolescence of what now produces their livelihood.

Grocery stores. Many people find it hard to realize that there ever was a thriving establishment known as the "corner grocery store." The supermarket has taken over with a powerful effectiveness. Yet the big food chains of the 1930's narrowly escaped being completely wiped out by the aggressive expansion of independent supermarkets. The first genuine supermarket was opened in 1930, in Jamaica, Long Island. By 1933 supermarkets were thriving in California, Ohio, Pennsylvania, and elsewhere. Yet the established chains pompously ignored them. When they chose to notice them, it was with such derisive descriptions as "cheapy," "horse-and-buggy," "cracker-barrel storekeeping," and "unethical opportunists."

The executive of one big chain announced at the time that he found it "hard to believe that people will drive for miles to shop for foods and sacrifice the personal service chains have perfected and to which Mrs. Consumer is accustomed."[2] As late as 1936, the National Wholesale Grocers convention and the New Jersey Retail Grocers Association said there was nothing to fear. They said that the supers' narrow appeal to the price buyer limited the size of their market. They had to draw from miles around. When imitators came, there would be wholesale liquidations as volume fell. The current high sales of the supers was said to be partly due to their novelty. Basically people wanted convenient neighborhood grocers. If the neighborhood stores "cooperate with their suppliers, pay attention to their costs, and improve their

---

[2] For more details see M. M. Zimmerman, *The Super Market: A Revolution in Distribution* (New York, McGraw-Hill Book Company, Inc., 1955), p. 48.

service," they would be able to weather the competition until it blew over.[3]

It never blew over. The chains discovered that survival required going into the supermarket business. This meant the wholesale destruction of their huge investments in corner store sites and in established distribution and merchandising methods. The companies with "the courage of their convictions" resolutely stuck to the corner store philosophy. They kept their pride but lost their shirts.

Self-deceiving cycle

But memories are short. For example, it is hard for people who today confidently hail the twin messiahs of electronics and chemicals to see how things could possibly go wrong with these galloping industries. They probably also cannot see how a reasonably sensible businessman could have been as myopic as the famous Boston millionaire who 50 years ago unintentionally sentenced his heirs to poverty by stipulating that his entire estate be forever invested exclusively in electric streetcar securities. His posthumous declaration, "There will always be a big demand for efficient urban transportation," is no consolation to his heirs who sustain life by pumping gasoline at automobile filling stations.

Yet, in a casual survey I recently took among a group of intelligent business executives, nearly half agreed that it would be hard to hurt their heirs by tying their estates forever to the electronics industry. When I then confronted them with the Boston streetcar example, they chorused unanimously, "That's different!" But is it? Is not the basic situation identical?

In truth, *there is no such thing* as a growth industry, I believe. There are only companies organized and operated to create and capitalize on growth opportunities. Industries that assume themselves to be riding some automatic growth escalator invariably descend into stagnation. The history of every dead and dying "growth" industry shows a self-deceiving cycle of bountiful expansion and undetected decay. There are four conditions which usually guarantee this cycle:

1. The belief that growth is assured by an expanding and more affluent population.
2. The belief that there is no competitive substitute for the industry's major product.
3. Too much faith in mass production and in the advantages of rapidly declining unit costs as output rises.
4. Preoccupation with a product that lends itself to carefully controlled scientific experimentation, improvement, and manufacturing cost reduction.

---

[3] Ibid., pp. 45–47.

I should like now to begin examining each of these conditions in some detail. To build my case as boldly as possible, I shall illustrate the points with reference to three industries—petroleum, automobiles, and electronics—particularly petroleum, because it spans more years and more vicissitudes. Not only do these three have excellent reputations with the general public and also enjoy the confidence of sophisticated investors, but their managements have become known for progressive thinking in areas like financial control, product research, and management training. If obsolescence can cripple even these industries, it can happen anywhere.

POPULATION MYTH

The belief that profits are assured by an expanding and more affluent population is dear to the heart of every industry. It takes the edge off the apprehensions everybody understandably feels about the future. If consumers are multiplying and also buying more of your product or service, you can face the future with considerably more comfort than if the market is shrinking. An expanding market keeps the manufacturer from having to think very hard or imaginatively. If thinking is an intellectual response to a problem, then the absence of a problem leads to the absence of thinking. If your product has an automatically expanding market, then you will not give much thought to how to expand it.

One of the most interesting examples of this is provided by the petroleum industry. Probably our oldest growth industry, it has an enviable record. While there are some current apprehensions about its growth rate, the industry itself tends to be optimistic. But I believe it can be demonstrated that it is undergoing a fundamental yet typical change. It is not only ceasing to be a growth industry, but may actually be a declining one, relative to other business. Although there is widespread unawareness of it, I believe that within 25 years the oil industry may find itself in much the same position of retrospective glory that the railroads are now in. Despite its pioneering work in developing and applying the present-value method of investment evaluation, in employee relations, and in working with backward countries, the petroleum business is a distressing example of how complacency and wrongheadedness can stubbornly convert opportunity into near disaster.

One of the characteristics of this and other industries that have believed very strongly in the beneficial consequences of an expanding population, while at the same time being industries with a generic product for which there has appeared to be no competitive substitute, is that the individual companies have sought to outdo their competitors by improving on what they are already doing. This makes sense, of course, if one assumes that sales are tied to the country's population strings, because the customer can compare products only on a feature-by-feature basis. I believe it is significant, for example, that not since John D. Rockefeller sent free kerosene lamps to China has the oil industry done anything really outstanding to create a demand for its product. Not even in product improvement has it showered itself with eminence. The greatest single improvement, namely, the development of tetraethyl lead, came from outside the industry, specifically from General Motors and DuPont. The big contributions made by the industry itself are confined to the technology of oil exploration, production, and refining.

* * *

Idea of indispensability

The petroleum industry is pretty much persuaded that there is no competitive substitute for its major product, gasoline—or if there is, that it will continue to be a derivative of crude oil, such as diesel fuel or kerosene jet fuel.

There is a lot of automatic wishful thinking in this assumption. The trouble is that most refining companies own huge amounts of crude oil reserves. These have value only if there is a market for products into which oil can be converted—hence the tenacious belief in the continuing competitive superiority of automobile fuels made from crude oil.

This idea persists despite all historic evidence against it. The evidence not only shows that oil has never been a superior product for any purpose for very long, but it also shows that the oil industry has never really been a growth industry. It has been a succession of different businesses that have gone through the usual historic cycles of growth, maturity, and decay. Its over-all survival is owed to a series of miraculous escapes from total obsolescence, of last-minute and unexpected reprieves from total disaster reminiscent of the Perils of Pauline.

Perils of petroleum

I shall sketch in only the main episodes:
First, crude oil was largely a patent medicine. But even before that fad ran out, demand was greatly expanded by the use of oil in kerosene lamps. The prospect of lighting the world's lamps gave rise to an extravagant promise of growth. The prospects were similar to those the industry now holds for gasoline in other parts of the world. It can hardly wait for the underdeveloped nations to get a car in every garage.

In the days of the kerosene lamp, the oil companies competed with each other and against gaslight by trying to improve the illuminating characteristics of kerosene. Then suddenly the impossible happened. Edison invented a light which was totally nondependent on crude oil. Had it not been for the growing use of kerosene in space heaters, the incandescent lamp would have completely finished oil as a growth industry at that time. Oil would have been good for little else than axle grease.

Then disaster and reprieve struck again. Two great innovations occurred, neither originating in the oil industry. The successful development of coal-burning domestic central-heating systems made the space heater obsolescent. While the industry reeled, along came its most magnificent boost yet—the internal combustion engine, also invented by outsiders. Then when the prodigious expansion for gasoline finally began to level off in the 1920's, along came the miraculous escape of a central oil heater. Once again the escape was provided by an outsider's invention and development. And when that market weakened, wartime demand for aviation fuel came to the rescue. After the war the expansion of civilian aviation, the dieselization of railroads, and the explosive demand for cars and trucks kept the industry's growth in high gear.

Meanwhile centralized oil heating—whose boom potential had only recently been proclaimed—ran into severe competition from natural gas. While the oil companies themselves owned the gas that now competed with their oil, the industry did not originate the natural gas revolution, nor has it to this day greatly profited from its gas ownership. The gas revolution was made by newly formed transmission companies that marketed the product with an aggressive ardor. They started a magnificent new industry, first against the advice and then against the resistance of the oil companies.

By all the logic of the situation, the oil companies themselves should have made the gas revolution. They not only owned the gas; they also were the only people experienced in handling, scrubbing, and using it, the only people experienced in pipeline technology and transmission, and they understood heating problems. But, partly because they knew that natural gas would compete with their own sale of heating oil, the oil companies pooh-poohed the potentials of gas.

The revolution was finally started by oil pipeline executives who, unable to persuade their own companies to go into gas, quit and organized the spectacularly successful gas transmission companies. Even after their success became painfully evident to the oil companies, the latter did not go into gas transmission. The multibillion dollar business which should have been theirs went to others. As in the past, the industry was blinded by its narrow preoccupation with a specific product and the value of its reserves. It paid little or no attention to its customers' basic needs and preferences.

❉   ❉   ❉

Uncertain future

Management cannot find much consolation today in the rapidly expanding petrochemical industry, another oil-using idea that did not originate in the leading firms. The total United States production of petrochemicals is equivalent to about 2% (by volume) of the demand for all petroleum products. Although the petrochemical industry is now expected to grow by about 10% per year, this will not offset other drains on the growth of crude oil consumption. Furthermore, while petrochemical products are many and growing, it is well to remember that there are nonpetroleum sources of the basic raw material, such as coal. Besides, a lot of plastics can be produced with relatively little oil. A 50,000-barrel-per-day oil refinery is now considered the absolute minimum size for efficiency. But a 5,000-barrel-per-day chemical plant is a giant operation.

Oil has never been a continuously strong growth industry. It has grown by fits and starts, always miraculously saved by innovations and developments not of its own making. The reason it has not grown in a smooth progression is that each time it thought it had a superior product safe from the possibility of competitive substitutes, the product turned out to be inferior and notoriously subject to obsolescence. Until now, gasoline (for motor fuel, anyhow) has escaped this fate. But, as we shall see later, it too may be on its last legs.

The point of all this is that there is no guarantee against product obsolescence. If a company's own research does not make it obsolete, another's will. Unless an industry is especially lucky, as oil has been until now, it can easily go down in a sea of red figures—just as the railroads have, as the buggy whip manufacturers have, as the corner grocery chains have, as most of the big movie companies have, and indeed as many other industries have.

The best way for a firm to be lucky is to make its own luck. That requires knowing what makes a business successful. One of the greatest enemies of this knowledge is mass production.

PRODUCTION PRESSURES

Mass-production industries are impelled by a great drive to produce all they can. The prospect of steeply declining unit costs as output rises is more than most companies can usually resist. The profit possibilities look spectacular. All effort focuses on production. The result is that marketing gets neglected.

John Kenneth Galbraith contends that just the opposite occurs.[4] Output is so prodigious that all effort concentrates on trying to get rid of it. He says this accounts for singing commercials, desecration of the countryside with advertising signs, and other wasteful and vulgar prac-

---

[4] *The Affluent Society* (Boston, Houghton Mifflin Company, 1958), pp. 152–60.

tices. Galbraith has a finger on something real, but he misses the strategic point. Mass production does indeed generate great pressure to "move" the product. But what usually gets emphasized is selling, not marketing. Marketing, being a more sophisticated and complex process, gets ignored.

The difference between marketing and selling is more than semantic. Selling focuses on the needs of the seller, marketing on the needs of the buyer. Selling is preoccupied with the seller's need to convert his product into cash; marketing with the idea of satisfying the needs of the customer by means of the product and the whole cluster of things associated with creating, delivering, and finally consuming it.

In some industries the enticements of full mass production have been so powerful that for many years top management in effect has told the sales departments, "You get rid of it; we'll worry about profits." By contrast, a truly marketing-minded firm tries to create value-satisfying goods and services that consumers will want to buy. What it offers for sale includes not only the generic product or service, but also how it is made available to the customer, in what form, when, under what conditions, and at what terms of trade. Most important, what it offers for sale is determined not by the seller but by the buyer. The seller takes his cues from the buyer in such a way that the product becomes a consequence of the marketing effort, not vice versa.

Lag in Detroit

This may sound like an elementary rule of business, but that does not keep it from being violated wholesale. It is certainly more violated than honored. Take the automobile industry:

Here mass production is most famous, most honored, and has the greatest impact on the entire society. The industry has hitched its fortune to the relentless requirements of the annual model change, a policy that makes customer orientation an especially urgent necessity. Consequently the auto companies annually spend millions of dollars on consumer research. But the fact that the new compact cars are selling so well in their first year indicates that Detroit's vast researches have for a long time failed to reveal what the customer really wanted. Detroit was not persuaded that he wanted anything different from what he had been getting until it lost millions of customers to other small car manufacturers.

How could this unbelievable lag behind consumer wants have been perpetuated so long? Why did not research reveal consumer preferences before consumers' buying decisions themselves revealed the facts? Is that not what consumer research is for—to find out before the fact what is going to happen? The answer is that Detroit never really researched the customer's wants. It only researched his preferences between the kinds of things which it had already decided to offer him.

For Detroit is mainly product-oriented, not customer-oriented. To the extent that the customer is recognized as having needs that the manufacturer should try to satisfy, Detroit usually acts as if the job can be done entirely by product changes. Occasionally attention gets paid to financing, too, but that is done more in order to sell than to enable the customer to buy.

As for taking care of other customer needs, there is not enough being done to write about. The areas of the greatest unsatisfied needs are ignored, or at best get stepchild attention. These are at the point of sale and on the matter of automotive repair and maintenance. Detroit views these problem areas as being of secondary importance. That is underscored by the fact that the retailing and servicing ends of this industry are neither owned and operated nor controlled by the manufacturers. Once the car is produced, things are pretty much in the dealer's inadequate hands. Illustrative of Detroit's arm's-length attitude is the fact that, while servicing holds enormous sales-stimulating, profit-building opportunities, only 57 of Chevrolet's 7,000 dealers provide night maintenance service.

Motorists repeatedly express their dissatisfaction with servicing and their apprehensions about buying cars under the present selling setup. The anxieties and problems they encounter during the auto buying and maintenance processes are probably more intense and widespread today than 30 years ago. Yet the automobile companies do not *seem* to listen to or take their cues from the anguished consumer. If they do listen, it must be through the filter of their own preoccupation with production. The marketing effort is still viewed as a necessary consequence of the product, not vice versa, as it should be. That is the legacy of mass production, with its parochial view that profit resides essentially in low-cost full production.

✸   ✸   ✸

Product provincialism

The tantalizing profit possibilities of low unit production costs may be the most seriously self-deceiving attitude that can afflict a company, particularly a "growth" company where an apparently assured expansion of demand already tends to undermine a proper concern for the importance of marketing and the customer.

The usual result of this narrow preoccupation with so-called concrete matters is that instead of growing, the industry declines. It usually means that the product fails to adapt to the constantly changing patterns of consumer needs and tastes, to new and modified marketing institutions and practices, or to product developments in competing or complementary industries. The industry has its eyes so firmly on its own specific product that it does not see how it is being made obsolete.

The classical example of this is the buggy whip industry. No amount of product improvement could stave off its death sentence. But had the industry defined itself as being in the transportation business rather than the buggy whip business, it might have survived. It would have done what survival always entails, that is, changing. Even if it had only defined its business as providing a stimulant or catalyst to an energy source, it might have survived by becoming a manufacturer of, say, fanbelts or air cleaners.

What may some day be a still more classical example is, again, the oil industry. Having let others steal marvelous opportunities from it (e.g., natural gas, as already mentioned, missile fuels, and jet engine lubricants), one would expect it to have taken steps never to let that happen again. But this is not the case. We are now getting extraordinary new developments in fuel systems specifically designed to power automobiles. Not only are these developments concentrated in firms outside the petroleum industry, but petroleum is almost systematically ignoring them, securely content in its wedded bliss to oil. It is the story of the kerosene lamp versus the incandescent lamp all over again. Oil is trying to improve hydrocarbon fuels rather than to develop *any* fuels best suited to the needs of their users, whether or not made in different ways and with different raw materials from oil.

☼   ☼   ☼

Management might be more likely to do what is needed for its own preservation if it thought of itself as being in the energy business. But even that would not be enough if it persists in imprisoning itself in the narrow grip of its tight product orientation. It has to think of itself as taking care of customer needs, not finding, refining, or even selling oil. Once it genuinely thinks of its business as taking care of people's transportation needs, nothing can stop it from creating its own extravagantly profitable growth.

☼   ☼   ☼

DANGERS OF R&D

Another big danger to a firm's continued growth arises when top management is wholly transfixed by the profit possibilities of technical research and development. To illustrate I shall turn first to a new industry—electronics—and then return once more to the oil companies. By comparing a fresh example with a familiar one, I hope to emphasize the prevalence and insidiousness of a hazardous way of thinking.

Marketing shortchanged

In the case of electronics, the greatest danger which faces the glamorous new companies in this field is not that they do not pay enough attention to research and development, but that they pay *too much* attention to it. And the fact that the fastest growing electronics firms owe their eminence to their heavy emphasis on technical research is completely beside the point. They have vaulted to affluence on a sudden crest of unusually strong general receptiveness to new technical ideas. Also, their success has been shaped in the virtually guaranteed market of military subsidies and by military orders that in many cases actually preceded the existence of facilities to make the products. Their expansion has, in other words, been almost totally devoid of marketing effort.

Thus, they are growing up under conditions that come dangerously close to creating the illusion that a superior product will sell itself. Having created a successful company by making a superior product, it is not surprising that management continues to be oriented toward the product rather than the people who consume it. It develops the philosophy that continued growth is a matter of continued product innovation and improvement.

A number of other factors tend to strengthen and sustain this belief:

1. Because electronic products are highly complex and sophisticated, managements become top-heavy with engineers and scientists. This creates a selective bias in favor of research and production at the expense of marketing. The organization tends to view itself as making things rather than satisfying customer needs. Marketing gets treated as a residual activity, "something else" that must be done once the vital job of product creation and production is completed.

2. To this bias in favor of product research, development, and production is added the bias in favor of dealing with controllable variables. Engineers and scientists are at home in the world of concrete things like machines, test tubes, production lines, and even balance sheets. The abstractions to which they feel kindly are those which are testable or manipulatable in the laboratory, or, if not testable, then functional, such as Euclid's axioms. In short, the managements of the new glamour-growth companies tend to favor those business activities which lend themselves to careful study, experimentation, and control—the hard, practical, realities of the lab, the shop, the books.

What gets shortchanged are the realities of the *market*. Consumers are unpredictable, varied, fickle, stupid, shortsighted, stubborn, and generally bothersome. This is not what the engineer-managers say, but deep down in their consciousness it is what they believe. And this accounts for their concentrating on what they know and what they can control, namely, product research, engineering, and production. The emphasis on production becomes particularly attractive when the product can be made at declining unit costs. There is no more inviting way of making money than by running the plant full blast.

Today the top-heavy science-engineering-production orientation of so many electronics companies works reasonably well because they are

142430

pushing into new frontiers in which the armed services have pioneered virtually assured markets. The companies are in the felicitous position of having to fill, not find markets; of not having to discover what the customer needs and wants, but of having the customer voluntarily come forward with specific new product demands. If a team of consultants had been assigned specifically to design a business situation calculated to prevent the emergence and development of a customer-oriented marketing viewpoint, it could not have produced anything better than the conditions just described.

❈   ❈   ❈

Beginning & end

The view that an industry is a customer-satisfying process, not a goods-producing process, is vital for all businessmen to understand. An industry begins with the customer and his needs, not with a patent, a raw material, or a selling skill. Given the customer's needs, the industry develops backwards, first concerning itself with the physical *delivery* of customer satisfactions. Then it moves back further to *creating* the things by which these satisfactions are in part achieved. How these materials are created is a matter of indifference to the customer, hence the particular form of manufacturing, processing, or what-have-you cannot be considered as a vital aspect of the industry. Finally, the industry moves back still further to *finding* the raw materials necessary for making its products.

The irony of some industries oriented toward technical research and development is that the scientists who occupy the high executive positions are totally unscientific when it comes to defining their companies' over-all needs and purposes. They violate the first two rules of the scientific method—being aware of and defining their companies' problems, and then developing testable hypotheses about solving them. They are scientific only about the convenient things, such as laboratory and product experiments. The reason that the customer (and the satisfaction of his deepest needs) is not considered as being "the problem" is not because there is any certain belief that no such problem exists, but because an organizational lifetime has conditioned management to look in the opposite direction. Marketing is a stepchild.

I do not mean that selling is ignored. Far from it. But selling, again, is not marketing. As already pointed out, selling concerns itself with the tricks and techniques of getting people to exchange their cash for your product. It is not concerned with the values that the exchange is all about. And it does not, as marketing invariably does, view the entire business process as consisting of a tightly integrated effort to discover, create, arouse, and satisfy customer needs. The customer is somebody "out there" who, with proper cunning, can be separated from his loose change.

Actually, not even selling gets much attention in some technologically minded firms. Because there is a virtually guaranteed market for the abundant flow of their new products, they do not actually know what a real market is. It is as if they lived in a planned economy, moving their products routinely from factory to retail outlet. Their successful concentration on products tends to convince them of the soundness of what they have been doing, and they fail to see the gathering clouds over the market.

CONCLUSION

Less than 75 years ago American railroads enjoyed a fierce loyalty among astute Wall Streeters. European monarchs invested in them heavily. Eternal wealth was thought to be the benediction for anybody who could scrape a few thousand dollars together to put into rail stocks. No other form of transportation could compete with the railroads in speed, flexibility, durability, economy, and growth potentials. As Jacques Barzun put it, "By the turn of the century it was an institution, an image of man, a tradition, a code of honor, a source of poetry, a nursery of boyhood desires, a sublimest of toys, and the most solemn machine—next to the funeral hearse—that marks the epochs in man's life."[5]

Even after the advent of automobiles, trucks, and airplanes, the railroad tycoons remained imperturbably self-confident. If you had told them 60 years ago that in 30 years they would be flat on their backs, broke, and pleading for government subsidies, they would have thought you totally demented. Such a future was simply not considered possible. It was not even a discussable subject, or an askable question, or a matter which any sane person would consider worth speculating about. The very thought was insane. Yet a lot of insane notions now have matter-of-fact acceptance—for example, the idea of 100-ton tubes of metal moving smoothly through the air 20,000 feet above the earth, loaded with 100 sane and solid citizens casually drinking martinis—and they have dealt cruel blows to the railroads.

What specifically must other companies do to avoid this fate? What does customer orientation involve? These questions have in part been answered by the preceding examples and analysis. It would take another article to show in detail what is required for specific industries. In any case, it should be obvious that building an effective customer-oriented company involves are more than good intentions or promotional tricks; it involves profound matters of human organization and leadership. For

---

[5] Op. cit., p. 20.

the present, let me merely suggest what appear to be some general requirements.

Visceral feel of greatness

Obviously the company has to do what survival demands. It has to adapt to the requirements of the market, and it has to do it sooner rather than later. But mere survival is a so-so aspiration. Anybody can survive in some way or other, even the skid-row bum. The trick is to survive gallantly, to feel the surging impulse of commercial mastery; not just to experience the sweet smell of success, but to have the visceral feel of entrepreneurial greatness.

No organization can achieve greatness without a vigorous leader who is driven onward by his own pulsating *will to succeed.* He has to have a vision of grandeur, a vision that can produce eager followers in vast numbers. In business, the followers are the customers. To produce these customers, the entire corporation must be viewed as a customer-creating and customer-satisfying organism. Management must think of itself not as producing products but as providing customer-creating value satisfactions. It must push this idea (and everything it means and requires) into every nook and cranny of the organization. It has to do this continuously and with the kind of flair that excites and stimulates the people in it. Otherwise, the company will be merely a series of pigeonholed parts, with no consolidating sense of purpose or direction.

In short, the organization must learn to think of itself not as producing goods or services but as *buying customers,* as doing the things that will make people *want* to do business with it. And the chief executive himself has the inescapable responsibility for creating this environment, this viewpoint, this attitude, this aspiration. He himself must set the company's style, its direction, and its goals. This means he has to know precisely where he himself wants to go, and to make sure the whole organization is enthusiastically aware of where that is. This is a first requisite of leadership, for *unless he knows where he is going, any road will take him there.*

If any road is okay, the chief executive might as well pack his attaché case and go fishing. If an organization does not know or care where it is going, it does not need to advertise that fact with a ceremonial figurehead. Everybody will notice it soon enough.

QUESTIONS

1. What, exactly, does Levitt feel business leaders are myopic about? How could you avoid falling into this "trap"?

2. What does Levitt mean about having a "visceral feel of greatness"? Who should have this feel? What relevance would this have to someone just looking for a permanent job?

3. In the examples cited by Levitt, which industries failed because of social change and which failed because of technological improvements? Cite two more examples of firms that failed because of one or the other of these types of changes? Explain.

4. Select a current social, economic or technological change. What industries are apt to suffer because of this change? Are there industries that will benefit, or perhaps be created, by this change?

General Electric pioneered in the development and application of the "marketing concept" and Mr. McKitterick was right in the midst of this effort. In this classic article, he explains how the concept evolved and discusses the basic changes in business philosophy that it implies.

---

3. WHAT IS THE MARKETING MANAGEMENT CONCEPT?*

J. B. McKitterick

THE PAPERS PRESENTED here provide intensive discussion of the implications of the marketing concept to top management decisions, to organization structure and to market strategy. From this one would infer that the marketing concept itself is an unequivocal thing, certainly as explicit as the turbo aire ride, the filter that leaves the taste in and the woman who is every inch a female—to mention three of its most recent manifestations. Yet one of the most charming attributes of this tireless conference subject is its sturdy resistance to onslaughts of definition and prescription. Indeed, to be asked to define the marketing concept can almost be accepted in the spirit of a challenge—because it is probably impossible—or if you have already tried and know it is impossible, then such a request can be passed off as spoken in jest—or more morbidly, considered as an insult. In view of the great amount of attention already being given to the definitions of the marketing concept, it seems to me that it would be timely to look into the general

---

* Reprinted with permission from Frank M. Bass, ed., *The Frontiers of Marketing Thought and Science* (Chicago: American Marketing Association, 1957), pp. 71–81. At the time of writing, Mr. McKitterick was with the General Electric Company.

economic developments that have accompanied this heightened interest in marketing. So rather than present the views of General Electric on this subject, it is my intention to speak somewhat more freely about the relationship between the evolution of business philosophy and the style of competition that characterizes modern markets. If in this manner we can develop a clearer understanding of why we are increasingly formulating business policy in terms of market considerations, we will have a better starting point for this discussion of means of implementation.

Anyone who gets a new idea bearing on business philosophy and who then takes the trouble to scan corresponding utterances of preceding generations will return to this thought with increased awareness of its apparent lack of originality. In an attempt to locate the historic significance of this marketing concept that we are going to discuss today, I started reading the 1930 and 1940 issues of the *Journal of Marketing* and the *Harvard Business Review*. To my surprise, I found that many of the viewpoints expressed and the stances advocated on business philosophy bear striking resemblance to current writings. Indeed, what really seems to have changed are the phenomena—the goings on—that the authors cite to validate the importance and rationale of their message. So we have here a not unfamiliar problem in the social sciences; namely that words change their meaning much more slowly than the things to which they refer. This is particularly true of concepts such as profit, overhead, productivity and marketing orientation—which deal not so much with things that happen as with ways of thinking about them.

In order to map changing meanings, it frequently is helpful to superimpose on a history of thought some crude scheme of classification which takes its definitions from the present. If we do this in the case of the marketing concept, we will notice that over the last thirty years the preoccupation of businessmen with the customer increasingly has been formulated in terms of an end rather than in terms of a means. Correspondingly, the conception of profit as the end objective in business seems to have declined, with a tendency to view it more as a basic condition that must be satisfied. To be sure, thirty years ago businessmen admonished each other to keep the customer's interests in mind, but they usually connected this focus merely with their own need to adjust prices and volume of production to what the market would accept. Indeed, if we read between the lines, we find that the customer used to be the chap that you sent the bill to—frequently a distributor, agent or dealer, but very rarely the actual end user. And sales tactics were conceived in terms of exploiting some scheme that would permit dealing with these trade institutions on a semi-exclusive basis. There was almost no mention of the idea that the manufacturer should focus his attention on the end user, and base his competitive footing on some superiority of value that matched with the needs of a particular group of these users. And it was obvious that few manufacturers felt that they had ability to look at the trade structure as a group of institutions for hire, to be selected and employed to perform specific functions that this end user needed. On the contrary, the trade structure was regarded as an impenetrable barrier—it *was* the market, and this fellow we have been calling the end user was the exclusive problem of the dealer, and no concern of the manufacturer.

Occasionally someone like Oswald Knauth, who has always been a bit ahead of his time, would remind the manufacturer that packaging and product styling had better be customer oriented. But by comparison to these occasional warnings to the man at the helm to keep his eye on what the customer was doing, there were urgent exhortations to the man in the engine room to get more output with less input. Indeed, the problem of winning out over competition seemed to be conceived essentially in terms of subtracting from the costs of production, and delivering an equivalent product at a lower price. So it was quite fitting that in the 1930's manufacturers studied the economies of scale, economists explored marginal concepts for setting the volume of production, and the government tried to prevent the large and efficient firm from sinking its smaller adversaries with the torpedo of lower price. In a short body of remarks it is out of scale to put a generalization such as this to adequate test, yet I cannot entirely resist some elaboration, because the social implications of what we call the marketing concept in the end are going to be of much greater importance than its bearing on management theory.

If we examine the 1920–1940 period, we find that it witnessed great gains in productivity, but not all of these gains were distributed to the labor force. The installed horsepower per production worker almost doubled, and the output per worker more than doubled. However, the average hourly wage in these twenty years increased only from 50¢ to 66¢—not quite a third, and the number of production workers stayed almost constant at around 8½ million members in a population that actually grew by over 20%. So, with rising productivity only to a limited degree passed on to the static body of production workers in the form of wage increases, consumer prices fell steadily until in 1940 they were only 70% of the 1920 level, and unemployment in a growing population was a serious and long continuing problem. During this same period, the design and manner of use of most products changed only slowly, and the gross national product increased a scant 14%.

To sum it up, the business ideology of producing the same product for less cost scarcely turned out to be an adequate driving force for economic growth. While a great deal of criticism was directed at the imperfections of markets organized around administered prices, subsequent events suggest that the real trouble was that most consumers had inadequate income and inadequate reason to buy. In short, productivity gains unevenly accompanied by innovation of new products and broad distribution of purchasing power resulted in a condition of chronic underconsumption.

Starting around 1940, the threat of war and the sponsorship of government combined to introduce a basic transformation in the business process which has had far reaching consequences. In a nutshell, business discovered research. On the eve of this revolution the total research outlay of businessmen stood at perhaps 100 million dollars. Today, these outlays are somewhere around four billions, and for the first time over 50% of all the research done in this country is being paid for by industry out of its own pocket. If we throw in the defense effort which the government pays for, the total research outlay rises to about 7½ billions. However, our interest here is not so much in the growth of this new industry or the sheer size of its burden, which seems likely to surpass the total cost of all advertising; rather we are concerned to learn what research did to the growth of the economy and to the problems of designing and managing an enterprise.

Where the pre-1940 period was preoccupied with trying to make the same product cheaper, the postwar period saw a new dimension added to competition, in which the focus was to try and make the old product better, or even more bold, to try and launch a new product. And as the research-equipped manufacturer looked around for applications for his new found creative power, he frequently discovered them in markets that he heretofore had not entered. The petroleum refinery began to turn out chemicals; the rubber plant, plastics; new alloys challenged older metals; electronics cast its shadows over hydraulics; and soon, everyone's research and competitive endeavor was attacking someone else's status quo. Established concepts of industry alignment began to obliterate, schemes narrowly conceived to defend market position in terms of price advantage proved inadequate; and managements began to contend with problems of uncertainty that had multiple dimensions. A labor plentiful economy overnight became a labor short economy, and even though the number of employee and production workers had grown 50% since 1940, and their productivity probably another 50%, still the demand for their services has grown even faster, and wages have gone up some 70% in constant dollars. So here we had a reversal of the conditions of the preceding 20 years; worker income rose more rapidly than productivity, competition was focused on using research to obsolete old ways of doing things, a flood of new products poured forth to meet the rising discretionary spending power, and we became so impressed with the results of focusing on what would be better for the customer rather than merely cheaper that we invented a now familiar phrase—"the marketing concept"—to describe this triumph of innovation over productive capacity.

If we look back on these basic changes in the economy, we find clues to many of the problems which have concerned management science over the last ten years. I refer especially to the constant search for means of planning and control that can contend with these rapidly changing marketing conditions. For example, many businessmen have complained that the problem of predicting the customer's behavior has been greatly complicated both by his rapidly rising discretionary income and by his growing control over the use of leisure time. Mink coats and motor cars, buying things and buying experiences all have begun to interact, and the passing fad and the more slowly changing style of life of which it is a part have become very difficult to diagnose and distinguish. And as we already have noted, the industrial customer with his multiple raw material and process alternatives, and his possibilities of sub-contracting entire operations, swimming all the while in his own competitive sea of changing functions and market alignments, presents an equally fickle target for prediction.

At the same time both the need for and difficulty of business planning have been heightened by technological trends in the production and distribution process. The long term commitments required by automated plants, guaranteed wages, basic research, and multi-million dollar national promotions imply not only irreversible decisions, but also greater lead time, because the assumptions in planning have to hold good over a longer and longer period as the separation between decision and implementation grows apace. The annual budget in many companies has been supplemented with the five year and even the twenty year plan. The very considerable risks entailed in these large resource commitments, combined with the increasing hazards posed by the caprice of the customer and the research efforts of an undefined arena of prospective competitors, have resulted in a powerful urge for diversification. Few businesses today seem to be able to undertake the risk of staying in a single market with a single product. Indeed, observing the pell-mell flight to add new products and markets, one might say that the most characteristic response of modern corporations to uncertainty is to refuse to choose. As new product applications emerge, as new categories of customers come into the market, as new technologies compete to answer the old need, the corporation is inclined to embrace each in turn, forfeiting no opportunity, straddling all risks.

In due course, the organization structure begins to gow like a Christmas tree as the work of decision making is subdivided to take advantage of the specialized information and skills required. The sales executive is joined by the service manager, the product development manager, the advertising manager, the distribution planning manager, the market research director, and the whole team is duplicated anew as further lines are added. Many decisions become difficult to deal with in such a structure because they straddle the responsibilities of individuals. And when it comes to prepare purposive plans, the business is troubled by its inability to bring its own identity into view—to see entirely its unique resources, skills and commitments, and the whole market environment of which they are a part.

Finally, in analyzing this planning problem and its bearing on the marketing concept, something probably should be said about the decline of the owner-manager. The great size of modern enterprise, the progressive tax structures, and the new found affluence of even the most lowly worker all have combined to lessen the inclination and ability of individuals to undertake an entrepreneurial role in many markets. Fortunately, the very economic growth which rules out individual enterprise in one area opens up an opportunity for it somewhere else—as in the service industries. But it is my impression that the passing of the entrepreneur, where it has occurred, has removed an important element in the planning process, because he supplied the reason for planning in the sense that he specified the objectives to be attained. Indeed, this entrepreneur made planning easy—if at the same time fickle—by telling people what he wanted to accomplish, and the whole matter was scarcely less personal or more complicated than his choice of a necktie for the day. In the modern corporation we have replaced the owner-manager with a hired management accountable in concept to a diffuse and rapidly changing body of shareholders, but actually in performance quite sensitive to the appraisal of multiple audiences among customers, suppliers, labor, financial institutions, government and the public at large. By degrees, therefore, the decline of perfect competition and the decline of the entrepreneur with his simple conception of objectives are not unrelated events. Today's complex markets with many dimensions of competition have been accompanied by a corresponding multiplication of the values to be reconciled in the policies of modern enterprises.

So to summarize, business management has very difficult planning decisions to make, requiring that it foresee and analyze many alternate developments relating to its customers, competitors, and its own resources, and management must get these decisions made by people who are organized in an enormously complex structure, in which they are aware of the interrelationships of their part and the business, but unable to adequately see the whole business and its environment, and the ends to be served by all these forecasts and decisions are becoming increasingly diffuse and uncertain. It is in this sort of setting that the marketing concept was born, and it is my belief, after reflecting both on the background of the movement and the many statements of the case which businessmen have set forth, that what this really represents is a search for a management philosophy—a primacy of decision values—that can restore order and manageability out of what threatens to seem like chaos. Indeed, at the risk of introducing controversy, I would speculate that looking back on this development twenty years hence, the marketing concept belatedly will be recognized as an appropriate voicing of the basic purpose of corporate institutions grown too large to be adequately guided by the profit interests of a single compact group of owners. Certainly, anyone who carefully subtracts out of the total expenses of a modern business all of the sums expended on preparation for the future—ranging from research and advertising to new plant and training of personnel—is bound to discover that profit is a feeble measure of the current day's battle with competition, and is certainly meaningless if not considered with reference to accompanying changes in market position. With many companies today operating in conditions of oligopoly, it is small wonder that enlargement of the market and competitive share held in that market have become matters of management concern at least equal if not prerequisite to profit.

Now I want to turn from the general economic conditions and management problems which accompanied the emergence of the marketing concept to a discussion of its implications for business practices. Necessarily, this will be a highly personal statement because it is next to impossible to synthesize into a single theme what others have already set forth on this subject. It does seem to me, however, that the real distinction of the marketing concept which leads to the conclusion "this company has it" or "this one doesn't," is not so much a matter of organization structure or day-to-day tactics as it is a matter of what the management is trying to accomplish.

A moment ago I referred to the shifting focus of objectives that has characterized the evolution of modern business enterprise—first, from a focus on profit for the owner to a striving for market position and success against competition, and most recently to a focus on growth in which there is a continuing planned effort to enlarge the size of the market. It seems to me that the crux of the marketing concept is expressed in the latter orientation. When a company sets out to increase its sales, not by depriving its historic competitors of the market position which they already have captured, but by the application of research and insight to the task of creating new markets—indeed, new businesses—then we know that we are dealing with a management that has fully embraced the marketing concept. To be sure, as already has been brought out rather fully, any such endeavor is not without its economic repercussions in other markets and industries, but the very extent of these effects, reaching as they do to far and foreign places, confirms that something more than a minor improvement in the lot of the customer must have occurred. So to say it precisely, a company committed to the marketing concept focuses its major innovative effort on enlarging the size of the market in which it participates by introducing new generic products and services, by promoting new applications for existing products, and by seeking out new classes of customers who heretofore have not used the existing products.

In all cases the word "new" means more then just new to the company in question. It means "new," period. This is a somewhat more rigorous definition than to merely say that the business must constantly think of the customers' best interests or put supremacy in marketing functions foremost. And I might add that the rigor is deliberate, because only thinking of the customer and mere technical proficiency in marketing both turn out to be inferior hands when played against the company that couples its thoughts with action and actually comes to market with a successful innovation. To be sure, the business that seeks to apply its research and mass production and national promotion prowess to such ambitious notions as doing really new things is going to have to be knowledgeably benign with respect to the customer, and it certainly will reduce its risks to the degree that it is experienced and skillful in its marketing organization. But if the product and the service and the way they are sold are fundamentally in the customer's best interests, a great deal of amateurism in marketing tactics can be tolerated without serious consequences. Turning the issue around, if business enterprises are to compete successfully in the quicksilver of modern markets, something more than sophistication in means of doing marketing work is going to be required. Indeed, to plan at all, and think adequately of what competition might do and its possible effects before committing multi-million dollar resources, requires knowledge of the customer which penetrates to the level of theory. *So the principal task of the marketing function in a management concept is not so much to be skillful in making the customer do what suits the interests of the business as to be skillful in conceiving and then making the business do what suits the interests of the customer.* As Frank Knight observed some years ago, in conditions of real uncertainty, the outcome of a venture will be controlled much more by the entrepreneurial decision on what major course of action to undertake than by expert practice in implementation.[1] Thus, the central meaning of the marketing concept to the decision structure of a business in that the major purpose of the venture is taken from the need to solve some problem in the outer environment—some betterment for the customer—and all subsidiary decisions dealing with the acquisition and allocation of resources within the business are bent to that objective. In this light, certain tests can be applied to our daily business practices which sharpen the distinction between the marketing concept and the mere awareness in management that superiority in the marketing function is beginning to be of greater strategic importance than superiority in the production function.

---

[1] Frank H. Knight, *Risk, Uncertainty, and Profit* (Boston: Houghton Mifflin Company, 1921).

For example, we might ask, is the service of customers or defense against competition the main focus of the creative search for better courses of action? Is the business in the habit of undertaking tactics which pay their way in added sales volume, but which in prompt imitation by competition fail to add to profit? If so, is the overall marketing effort really adding consumable value for the customer, or only adding cost—as for instance, advertising expenditures which seek to make like products seem unlike, and product redesign which attempts to produce obsolescence without adding to the functions performed by the product? Is the business constantly exhausting itself, trying to hold back changes introduced by its competitors—as when it refuses to recognize a new product technology, a new service, or a new sales channel which the customer seems to prefer? Is foolish pride—as the songwriter puts it—causing the management to reject the verdict of the marketplace? Is the business trying to be all things to all customers when their requirements and interests in the product are so fragmenting that some forfeiture of clientele and specialization of customer alignment obviously are needed? Is what the business considers a good salesman essentially a customer oriented man or is he a loyal "company" man, intent on making the customer understand his employer's policies? And finally, is the business using its resources and ability to innovate on tasks that smaller competitors with less overhead can handle better, or is it taxing its capacities to the fullest in undertakings that really challenge it?

These are fairly direct questions, but the answers turn on rather subtle differences in the marketing posture of a company. By and large, it is my observation that concerns which are in an active growth phase will pass this sort of test; those that have slowed down and see themselves as digging in for a defense against younger, more vigorous competitors in time will fail the test. Certainly, anyone who examines the turnover in rankings of the hundred largest corporations, or the turnover in the leadership position in even the smallest markets, cannot fail to see that the graveyards of business are full of those who conceived their obligations to the customer too narrowly.

Now, one might ask, how can the active growth phase of a company be infinitely prolonged? In the end, will not the constant adding of new products, new applications and new users lead to a loss of identity and a nomad-like wandering over the entire market terrain? And how does a company so oriented—or disoriented—respond to the attack of competition? Must every action pass the test of what is truly in the customer's interests? To be sure, these are important questions. But much of the difficulty is removed if we remember that it often is in the interests of both the customer and the company that it abandon a market, that it forego an existing product line and forfeit some present clientele to competition.

Where two groups of product users have different requirements in either the product or the services that go with it, the constant temptation is to suppress these differences, to force homogenization of the requirements, and we all are familiar with examples of the skillful use of price policy, engineering standards, advertising, and product design to such ends. Yet when such an unnatural marriage is challenged by a competitor who selects only one of the two user groups as his intended clientele, a competitor who aligns all his decisions in the interests of that single group and who brings to it a specially designed product, then the profit position of the company that is straddling the issue is likely to become quite untenable. In the same way, a company may choose to deal with two unrelated markets in a manner that is dictated by the desire to apply some common technology or shared resource of production or distribution. The endeavor in each market being limited by the requirements of the opposite market, this company, too, is vulnerable to a competitor that specializes in only one of these undertakings. So I submit, it is no prescription of dogma but the hard facts of competition that argue for coupling a program of innovation and growth with a sharp pruning knife to cut out the commitments that threaten to compromise the marketing concept. If we all freely admitted our mistakes and were prompt in forfeiting a losing battle to competition, a great deal of pointless advertising could be turned into profit, and a substantial improvement could be worked in sales to other markets where efforts have been less than customer oriented due to the conflicts that have been baked in. Indeed, it is precisely because of this constant need for pruning that companies which were guided by pre-war notions of production efficiency, and which grew along lines of by-product diversification and vertical integration are in the gravest sort of difficulty today. Hence the most cogent argument for designing an industrial enterprise from the customer backward into the factory, rather than from the production process forward, so to speak, is that the success of the venture is becoming much less dependent on its production efficiency and much more dependent on its flexibility in adjusting to the risks posed by the changing requirements of its customers.

QUESTIONS

1. What did the "marketing concept" mean to Mr. McKitterick?
2. Discuss why firms such as G.E. have evolved towards the marketing concept.
°3. Discuss McKitterick's view that the crux of the marketing concept is a "continuing planned effort to enlarge the size of the market" in relation to Levitt's view (Reading 2) that too many firms have "marketing myopia."

> *Marketing is an activity that goes considerably beyond the selling of toothpaste, soap, and steel. The authors explain the value of the marketing concept for nonbusiness organizations and illustrate the application of marketing principles in such organizations. This article is placed here to help deepen (as well as broaden) your understanding of the marketing concept, as it applies to both business and nonbusiness organizations.*

4. BROADENING THE CONCEPT OF MARKETING*

Philip Kotler and Sidney J. Levy

THE TERM "MARKETING" connotes to most people a function peculiar to business firms. Marketing is seen as the task of finding and stimulating buyers for the firm's output. It involves product development, pricing, distribution, and communication; and in the more progressive firms, continuous attention to the changing needs of customers and the development of new products, with product modifications and services to meet these needs. But whether marketing is viewed in the old sense of "pushing" products or in the new sense of "customer satisfaction engineering," it is almost always viewed and discussed as a business activity.

It is the authors' contention that marketing is a pervasive societal activity that goes considerably beyond the selling of toothpaste, soap, and steel. Political contests remind us that candidates are marketed as well as soap; student recruitment by colleges reminds us that higher education is marketed; and fund raising reminds us that "causes" are marketed. Yet these areas of marketing are typically ignored by the student of marketing. Or they are treated cursorily as public relations or publicity activities. No attempt is made to incorporate these phenomena in the body proper of marketing thought and theory. No attempt is made to redefine the meaning of product development, pricing, distribution, and communication in these newer contexts to see if they have

---

* Reprinted with permission from the *Journal of Marketing*, published by the American Marketing Association, vol. 33, January 1969, pp. 10–15. At the time of publication of this article, Drs. Kotler and Levy were both Professors of Marketing at Northwestern University.

a useful meaning. No attempt is made to examine whether the principles of "good" marketing in traditional product areas are transferable to the marketing of services, persons, and ideas.

The authors see a great opportunity for marketing people to expand their thinking and to apply their skills to an increasingly interesting range of social activity. The challenge depends on the attention given to it; marketing will either take on a broader social meaning or remain a narrowly defined business activity.

THE RISE OF ORGANIZATIONAL MARKETING

One of the most striking trends in the United States is the increasing amount of society's work being performed by organizations other than business firms. As a society moves beyond the stage where shortages of food, clothing, and shelter are the major problems, it begins to organize to meet other social needs that formerly had been put aside. Business enterprises remain a dominant type of organization, but other types of organizations gain in conspicuousness and in influence. Many of these organizations become enormous and require the same rarefied management skills as traditional business organizations. Managing the United Auto Workers, Defense Department, Ford Foundation, World Bank, Catholic Church, and University of California has become every bit as challenging as managing Procter and Gamble, General Motors, and General Electric. These nonbusiness organizations have an increasing range of influence, affect as many livelihoods, and occupy as much media prominence as major business firms.

All of these organizations perform the classic business functions. Every organization must perform a financial function insofar as money must be raised, managed, and budgeted according to sound business principles. Every organization must perform a production function in that it must conceive of the best way of arranging inputs to produce the outputs of the organization. Every organization must perform a personnel function in that people must be hired, trained, assigned, and promoted in the course of the organization's work. Every organization must perform a purchasing function in that it must acquire materials in an efficient way through comparing and selecting sources of supply.

When we come to the marketing function, it is also clear that every organization performs marketing-like activities whether or not they are recognized as such. Several examples can be given.

The police department of a major U.S. city, concerned with the poor image it has among an important segment of its population, developed a campaign to "win friends and influence people." One highlight of this campaign is a "visit your police station" day in which tours are conducted to show citizens the daily operations of the police department, including the crime laboratories, police lineups, and cells. The police department also sends officers to speak at public schools and carries out a number of other activities to improve its community relations.

Most museum directors interpret their primary responsibility as "the proper preservation of an artistic heritage for posterity."[1] As a result, for many people museums are cold marble mausoleums that house miles of relics that soon give way to yawns and tired feet. Although museum attendance in the United States advances each year, a large number of citizens are uninterested in museums. Is this indifference due to failure in the manner of presenting what museums have to offer? This nagging question led the new director of the Metropolitan Museum of Art to broaden the museum's appeal through sponsoring contemporary art shows and "happenings." His marketing philosophy of museum management led to substantial increases in the Met's attendance.

The public school system in Oklahoma City sorely needed more public support and funds to prevent a deterioration of facilities and exodus of teachers. It recently resorted to television programming to dramatize the work the public schools were doing to fight the high school dropout problem, to develop new teaching techniques, and to enrich the children. Although an expensive medium, television quickly reached large numbers of parents whose response and interest were tremendous.

Nations also resort to international marketing campaigns to get across important points about themselves to the citizens of other countries. The junta of Greek colonels who seized power in Greece in 1967 found the international publicity surrounding their cause to be extremely unfavorable and potentially disruptive of international recognition. They hired a major New York public relations firm and soon full-page newspaper ads appeared carrying the headline "Greece Was Saved From Communism," detailing in small print why the takeover was necessary for the stability of Greece and the world.[2]

An anti-cigarette group in Canada is trying to press the Canadian legislature to ban cigarettes on the grounds that they are harmful to health. There is widespread support for this cause but the organization's funds are limited, particularly measured against the huge advertising resources of the cigarette industry. The group's problem is to find effective ways to make a little money go a long way in persuading influential legislators of the need for discouraging cigarette consumption. This group has come up with several ideas for marketing anti-smoking to Canadians, including television spots, a paperback book featuring pictures of cancer and heart disease patients, and legal research on company liability for the smoker's loss of health.

What concepts are common to these and many other possible illustrations of organizational marketing? All of these organizations are con-

---

[1] This is the view of Sherman Lee, Director of the Cleveland Museum, quoted in *Newsweek*, vol. 71 (April 1, 1968), p. 55.

[2] "PR for the Colonels," *Newsweek*, vol. 71 (March 18, 1968), p. 70.

cerned about their "product" in the eyes of certain "consumers" and are seeking to find "tools" for furthering their acceptance. Let us consider each of these concepts in general organizational terms.

Products

Every organization produces a "product" of at least one of the following types:

Physical products. "Product" first brings to mind everyday items like soap, clothes, and food, and extends to cover millions of *tangible* items that have a market value and are available for purchase.

Services. Services are *intangible* goods that are subject to market transaction such as tours, insurance, consultation, hairdos, and banking.

Persons. Personal marketing is an endemic *human* activity, from the employee trying to impress his boss to the statesman trying to win the support of the public. With the advent of mass communications, the marketing of persons has been turned over to professionals. Hollywood stars have their press agents, political candidates their advertising agencies, and so on.

Organizations. Many organizations spend a great deal of time marketing themselves. The Republican Party has invested considerable thought and resources in trying to develop a modern look. The American Medical Association decided recently that it needed to launch a campaign to improve the image of the American doctor.[3] Many charitable organizations and universities see selling their *organization* as their primary responsibility.

Ideas. Many organizations are mainly in the business of selling *ideas* to the larger society. Population organizations are trying to sell the idea of birth control, and the Women's Christian Temperance Union is still trying to sell the idea of prohibition.

Thus the "product" can take many forms, and this is the first crucial point in the case for broadening the concept of marketing.

Consumers

The second crucial point is that organizations must deal with many groups that are interested in their products and can make a difference in its success. It is vitally important to the organization's success that it be sensitive to, serve, and satisfy these groups. One set of groups can be called the *suppliers. Suppliers* are those who provide the management group with the inputs necessary to perform its work and develop its product effectively. Suppliers include employees, vendors of the materials, banks, advertising agencies, and consultants.

---

[3] "Doctors Try an Image Transplant," *Business Week,* no. 2025 (June 22, 1968), p. 64.

The other set of groups are the *consumers* of the organization's product, of which four sub-groups can be distinguished. The *clients* are those who are the immediate consumers of the organization's product. The clients of a business firm are its buyers and potential buyers; of a service organization those receiving the services, such as the needy (from the Salvation Army) or the sick (from County Hospital); and of a protective or a primary organization, the members themselves. The second group is the *trustees or directors,* those who are vested with the legal authority and responsibility for the organization, oversee the management, and enjoy a variety of benefits from the "product." The third group is the active *publics* that take a specific interest in the organization. For a business firm, the active publics include consumer rating groups, governmental agencies, and pressure groups of various kinds. For a university, the active publics include alumni and friends of the university, foundations, and city fathers. Finally, the fourth consumer group is the *general public.* These are all the people who might develop attitudes toward the organization that might affect its conduct in some way. Organizational marketing concerns the programs designed by management to create satisfactions and favorable attitudes in the organization's four consuming groups: clients, trustees, active publics, and general public.

Marketing tools

Students of business firms spend much time studying the various tools under the firm's control that affect product acceptance: product improvement, pricing, distribution, and communication. All of these tools have counterpart applications to nonbusiness organizational activity.

Nonbusiness organizations to various degrees engage in product improvement, especially when they recognize the competition they face from other organizations. Thus, over the years churches have added a host of nonreligious activities to their basic religious activities to satisfy members seeking other bases of human fellowship. Universities keep updating their curricula and adding new students services in an attempt to make the educational experience relevant to the students. Where they have failed to do this, students have sometimes organized their own courses and publications, or have expressed their dissatisfaction in organized protest. Government agencies such as license bureaus, police forces, and taxing bodies are often not responsive to the public because of monopoly status; but even here citizens have shown an increasing readiness to protest mediocre services, and more alert bureaucracies have shown a growing interest in reading the user's needs and developing the required product services.

All organizations face the problem of pricing their products and services so that they cover costs. Churches charge dues, universities charge tuition, governmental agencies charge fees, fund-raising organizations send out bills. Very often specific product charges are not sufficient to meet the organization's budget, and it must rely on gifts and surcharges to make up the difference. Opinions vary as to how much the users should be charged for the individual services and how much should be made up through general collection. If the university increases its tuition, it will have to face losing some students and putting more students on scholarship. If the hospital raises its charges to cover rising costs and additional services, it may provoke a reaction from the community. All organizations face complex pricing issues although not all of them understand good pricing practice.

Distribution is a central concern to the manufacturer seeking to make his goods conveniently accessible to buyers. Distribution also can be an important marketing decision area for nonbusiness organizations. A city's public library has to consider the best means of making its books available to the public. Should it establish one large library with an extensive collection of books, or several neighborhood branch libraries with duplication of books? Should it use bookmobiles that bring the books to the customers instead of relying exclusively on the customers coming to the books? Should it distribute through school libraries? Similarly the police department of a city must think through the problem of distributing its protective services efficiently through the community. It has to determine how much protective service to allocate to different neighborhoods; the respective merits of squad cars, motorcycles, and foot patrolmen; and the positioning of emergency phones.

Customer communication is an essential activity of all organizations although many nonmarketing organizations often fail to accord it the importance it deserves. Managements of many organizations think they have fully met their communication responsibilities by setting up advertising and/or public relations departments. They fail to realize that *everything about an organization talks.* Customers form impressions of an organization from its physical facilities, employees, officers, stationery, and a hundred other company surrogates. Only when this is appreciated do the members of the organization recognize that they all are in marketing, whatever else they do. With this understanding they can assess realistically the impact of their activities on the consumers.

CONCEPTS FOR EFFECTIVE MARKETING MANAGEMENT IN NONBUSINESS ORGANIZATIONS

Although all organizations have products, markets, and marketing tools, the art and science of effective marketing management have reached their highest state of development in the business type of organization. Business organizations depend on customer goodwill for survival and have generally learned how to sense and cater to their needs effectively. As other types of organizations recognize their marketing roles, they will turn increasingly to the body of marketing principles worked out by business organizations and adapt them to their own situations.

What are the main principles of effective marketing management as they appear in most forward-looking business organizations? Nine concepts stand out as crucial in guiding the marketing effort of a business organization.

Generic product definition

Business organizations have increasingly recognized the value of placing a broad definition on their products, one that emphasizes the basic customer need(s) being served. A modern soap company recognizes that its basic product is cleaning, not soap; a cosmetics company sees its basic product as beauty or hope, not lipsticks and makeup; a publishing company sees its basic product as information, not books.

The same need for a broader definition of its business is incumbent upon nonbusiness organizations if they are to survive and grow. Churches at one time tended to define their product narrowly as that of producing religious services for members. Recently, most churchmen have decided that their basic product is human fellowship. There was a time when educators said that their product was the three R's. Now most of them define their product as education for the whole man. They try to serve the social, emotional, and political needs of young people in addition to intellectual needs.

Target groups definition

A generic product definition usually results in defining a very wide market, and it is then necessary for the organization, because of limited resources, to limit its product offering to certain clearly defined groups within the market. Although the generic product of an automobile company is transportation, the company typically sticks to cars, trucks, and buses, and stays away from bicycles, airplanes, and steamships. Furthermore, the manufacturer does not produce every size and shape of car but concentrates on producing a few major types to satisfy certain substantial and specific parts of the market.

In the same way, nonbusiness organizations have to define their target groups carefully. For example, in Chicago the YMCA defines its target groups as men, women and children who want recreational opportunities and are willing to pay $20 or more a year for them. The Chicago Boys Club, on the other hand, defines its target group as poorer boys within the city boundaries who are in want of recreational facilities and can pay $1 a year.

Differentiated marketing

When a business organization sets out to serve more than one target group, it will be maximally effective by differentiating its product offerings and communications. This is also true for nonbusiness organizations. Fund-raising organizations have recognized the advantage of treating clients, trustees, and various publics in different ways. These groups require differentiated appeals and frequency of solicitation. Labor unions find that they must address different messages to different parties rather than one message to all parties. To the company they may seem unyielding, to the conciliator they may appear willing to compromise, and to the public they seek to appear economically exploited.

Customer behavior analysis

Business organizations are increasingly recognizing that customer needs and behavior are not obvious without formal research and analysis; they cannot rely on impressionistic evidence. Soap companies spend hundreds of thousands of dollars each year researching how Mrs. Housewife feels about her laundry, how, when, and where she does her laundry, and what she desires of a detergent.

Fund raising illustrates how an industry has benefited by replacing stereotypes of donors with studies of why people contribute to causes. Fund raisers have learned that people give because they are getting something. Many give to community chests to relieve a sense of guilt because of their elevated state compared to the needy. Many give to medical charities to relieve a sense of fear that they may be struck by a disease whose cure has not yet been found. Some give to feel pride. Fund raisers have stressed the importance of identifying the motives operating in the marketplace of givers as a basis for planning drives.

Differential advantages

In considering different ways of reaching target groups, an organization is advised to think in terms of seeking a differential advantage. It should consider what elements in its reputation or resources can be exploited to create a special value in the minds of its potential customers. In the same way Zenith has built a reputation for quality and International Harvester a reputation for service, a nonbusiness organization should base its case on some dramatic value that competitive organizations lack. The small island of Nassau can compete against Miami for the tourist trade by advertising the greater dependability of its weather; the Heart Association can compete for funds against the Cancer Society by advertising the amazing strides made in heart research.

Multiple marketing tools

The modern business firm relies on a multitude of tools to sell its product, including product improvement, consumer and dealer advertising, salesman incentive programs, sale promotions, contests, multiple-size offerings, and so forth. Likewise nonbusiness organizations also can reach their audiences in a variety of ways. A church can sustain the interest of its members through discussion groups, newsletters, news releases, campaign drives, annual reports and retreats. Its "salesmen" include the religious head, the board members, and the present members in terms of attracting potential members. Its advertising includes announcements of weddings, births and deaths, religious pronouncements, and newsworthy developments.

Integrated marketing planning

The multiplicity of available marketing tools suggests the desirability of overall coordination so that these tools do not work at cross purposes. Over time, business firms have placed under a marketing vice-president activities that were previously managed in a semi-autonomous fashion, such as sales, advertising, and marketing research. Nonbusiness organizations typically have not integrated their marketing activities. Thus, no single officer in the typical university is given total responsibility for studying the needs and attitudes of clients, trustees, and publics, and undertaking the necessary product development and communication programs to serve these groups. The university administration instead includes a variety of "marketing" positions such as dean of students, director of alumni affairs, director of public relations, and director of development; coordination is often poor.

Continuous marketing feedback

Business organizations gather continuous information about changes in the environment and about their own performance. They use their salesmen, research department, specialized research services, and other means to check on the movement of goods, actions of competitors, and feelings of customers to make sure they are progressing along satisfactory lines. Nonbusiness organizations typically are more casual about collecting vital information on how they are doing and what is happening in the marketplace. Universities have been caught off guard by underestimating the magnitude of student grievance and unrest, and so have major cities underestimated the degree to which they were failing to meet the needs of important minority constituencies.

Marketing audit

Change is a fact of life, although it may proceed almost invisibly on a day-to-day basis. Over a long stretch of time it might be so fundamental as to threaten organizations that have not provided for periodic reexaminations of their purposes. Organizations can grow set in their ways and unresponsive to new opportunities or problems. Some great American companies are no longer with us because they did not change definitions of their businesses, and their products lost relevance in a changing world. Political parties become unresponsive after they enjoy power for a while and every so often experience a major upset. Many union leaders grow insensitive to new needs and problems until one day they find themselves out of office. For an organization to remain viable, its management must provide for periodic audits of its objectives, resources, and opportunities. It must reexamine its basic business, target groups, differential advantage, communication channels, and messages in the light of current trends and needs. It might recognize when change is needed and make it before it is too late.

IS ORGANIZATIONAL MARKETING A SOCIALLY USEFUL ACTIVITY?

Modern marketing has two different meanings in the minds of people who use the term. One meaning of marketing conjures up the term selling, influencing, persuading. Marketing is seen as a huge and increasingly dangerous technology, making it possible to sell persons on buying things, propositions, and causes they either do not want or which are bad for them. This was the indictment in Vance Packard's *Hidden Persuaders* and numerous other social criticisms, with the net effect that a large number of persons think of marketing as immoral or entirely self-seeking in its fundamental premises. They can be counted on to resist the idea of organizational marketing as so much "Madison Avenue."

The other meaning of marketing unfortunately is weaker in the public mind; it is the concept of sensitively *serving and satisfying human needs.* This was the great contribution of the marketing concept that was promulgated in the 1950s, and that concept now counts many business firms as its practitioners. The marketing concept holds that the problem of all business firms in an age of abundance is to develop customer loyalties and satisfaction, and the key to this problem is to focus on the customer's needs.[4] Perhaps the short-run problem of business firms is to sell people on buying the existing products, but the long-run prob-

---

[4] Theodore Levitt, "Marketing Myopia," *Harvard Business Review,* vol. 38 (July–August 1960), pp. 45–56. (See Reading 2.)

lem is clearly to create the products that people need. By this recognition that effective marketing requires a consumer orientation instead of a product orientation, marketing has taken a new lease on life and tied its economic activity to a higher social purpose.

It is this second side of marketing that provides a useful concept for all organizations. All organizations are formed to serve the interest of particular groups: hospitals serve the sick, schools serve the students, governments serve the citizens, and labor unions serve the members. In the course of evolving, many organizations lose sight of their original mandate, grow hard, and become self-serving. The bureaucratic mentality begins to dominate the original service mentality. Hospitals may become perfunctory in their handling of patients, schools treat their students as nuisances, city bureaucrats behave like petty tyrants toward the citizens, and labor unions try to run instead of serve their members. All of these actions tend to build frustration in the consuming groups. As a result some withdraw meekly from these organizations, accept frustration as part of their condition, and find their satisfactions elsewhere. This used to be the common reaction of ghetto Negroes and college students in the face of indifferent city and university bureaucracies. But new possibilities have arisen, and now the same consumers refuse to withdraw so readily. Organized dissent and protest are seen to be an answer, and many organizations thinking of themselves as responsible have been stunned into recognizing that they have lost touch with their constituencies. They had grown unresponsive.

Where does marketing fit into this picture? Marketing is that function of the organization that can keep in constant touch with the organization's consumers, read their needs, develop "products" that meet these needs, and build a program of communications to express the organization's purposes. Certainly selling and influencing will be large parts of organizational marketing; but, properly seen, selling follows rather than precedes the organization's drive to create products to satisfy its consumers.

CONCLUSION

It has been argued here that the modern marketing concept serves very naturally to describe an important facet of all organizational activity. All organizations must develop appropriate products to serve their sundry consuming groups and must use modern tools of communication to reach their consuming publics. The business heritage of marketing provides a useful set of concepts for guiding all organizations.

The choice facing those who manage nonbusiness organizations is not whether to market or not to market, for no organization can avoid marketing. The choice is whether to do it well or poorly, and on this necessity the case for organizational marketing is basically founded.

QUESTIONS

1. Explain how your college could use the author's nine concepts to improve its effectiveness. Be specific.
2. What is the basic difference between business and nonbusiness organizations? How would nonbusiness organizations choose among attractive alternatives when applying the marketing concept?
3. If marketing techniques do lead to unnecessary consumption, as some have contended, then is it appropriate to use these tools in an even broader set of circumstances?
*4. Would Levitt (Reading 2) consider Kotler and Levy "myopic," i.e., have they lost sight of what marketing is about? Explain.

Marketers often seek a "differential advantage" over their competitors. Wroe Alderson helped popularize this term among marketing people, showing that it had theoretical relevance not only for business planning but also for public policy. Alderson moved easily between micro and macro concerns, as the following portion of his chapter on "Competition for Differential Advantage" demonstrates.

---

5. COMPETITION FOR DIFFERENTIAL ADVANTAGE*

Wroe Alderson

THE ECONOMICS OF DIFFERENTIAL ADVANTAGE

The functionalist or ecological approach to competition begins with the assumption that every firm must seek and find a function in order to maintain itself in the market place. Every business firm occupies a position which is in some respects unique. Its location, the products it sells, its operating methods, or the customers it serves tend to set it off in some degree from every other firm. Each firm competes by making the most of its individuality and its special character. It is con-

---

* Reprinted with permission of the publisher from Wroe Alderson, *Marketing Behavior and Executive Action* (Homewood, Ill.: Richard D. Irwin, Inc., 1957), pp. 101–9. Wroe Alderson was Professor of Marketing at the Wharton School of the University of Pennsylvania and a consultant to many corporations.

stantly seeking to establish some competitive advantage. Absolute advantage in the sense of an advanced method of operation is not enough if all competitors live up to the same high standards. What is important in competition is differential advantage, which can give a firm an edge over what others in the field are offering.

Differential advantage and dynamic competition

It is the unending search for differential advantage which keeps competition dynamic. A firm which has been bested by competitors according to certain dimensions of value in products or services always has before it the possibility of turning the tables by developing something new in other directions. The company which has the lead is vulnerable to attack at numerous points. Therein is a strong incentive for technical innovation and other forms of economic progress, both for the leader who is trying to stay out in front and for others who are trying to seize the initiative.

Departures from previous product designs or patterns of practice will not be successful unless they appeal to needs or attitudes of the buyer. Differentiation by the seller is an adaptation to differences in taste and requirements among consumers. Demand is radically heterogeneous or diversified and quite independent of the actions of the seller. Supply also breaks down into heterogeneous segments according to differences in location, raw materials, plant equipment, and the skills of management and labor. The process of exchange in the market place are directed toward matching up segments of supply and demand to provide the best fit.

This conception of an economics of differential advantage has important consequences for the analysis of monopoly and competition and for the choice of criteria to determine the degree of competitiveness in a given industry. New firms enter a field because of an expectation of enjoying differential advantage. Their chance for survival depends on whether their expectations were realistic in the first place and whether the original advantage is maintained or wrested from them by others. The profit incentive provides the drive for vigorous competition, but this drive is directed toward differential advantage because of the fundamentally heterogeneous character of markets. The enterpriser accepts the risks of innovation in his search for differential advantage. Success may be rewarded by profits until other enterprises overtake him. Later sections will develop further implications of this view for both market structure and market behavior.

The term "differential advantage" is currently being used by J. M. Clark, who developed the concept of workable competition. It is adopted here as the term which best characterizes the dynamics of competitive advantage. Much of the underlying analysis was developed by E. H.

Chamberlin, who inaugurated a new era in the theory of the firm something over twenty years ago.

Differential advantage and monopolistic competition

In his formulation of the theory of monopolistic competition, Chamberlin was applying to a wider field and developing with a greater elegance methods of analysis which, in their essentials, are already to be found in earlier economists such as Walras and Marshall. The roots of the economics of differential advantage go back still further, to the treatment of the division of labor and regional specialization by Adam Smith and Ricardo. J. M. Clark makes a fresh start by dealing directly with the struggle for differential advantage as the essence of competition. Chamberlin reaches a similar position in his later discussions of monopolistic competition by beginning with the traditional concepts of monopoly and pure competition and showing how they are usually blended in concrete situations.

Not a few economists join with Chamberlin in the advancement of a theory blending monopoly and competition. Arthur R. Burns in 1936 wrote: "The elements of monopoly . . . can no longer be regarded as occasional and relatively unimportant aberrations from competition. They are such an organic part of the industrial system that it is useless to hope they can be removed by law." W. A. Joehr points out that bilateral monopolies and oligopolies form a part of the competitive system. "Thus even if the existing structure of the present market economy could be called a 'world of monopolies,' its system of coordination could nevertheless be termed a competitive mechanism." It is the opinion of another contemporary, Kurt Rothschild, that the more realistic models of competition advanced by Chamberlin and Joan Robinson seemed to destroy the last nimbus which the idea of competition had managed to save through all the years of skepticism and criticism, by showing that so many adverse features were not occasional blemishes but were part and parcel of the way competition works in our world.

Such terms as "pure competition" and "pure monopoly" have little relevance except for tracing the transition from an atomistic model to what is essentially an ecological view of the competition among business firms. If Chamberlin had been the first major student of the subject, he might have moved more directly toward the creation of an appropriate theory. That would have meant starting with a recognition that markets are radically heterogeneous on both the supply side and the demand side. Under this approach, pure competition is nothing more than a limiting case in which there is a tendency to approach homogeneity. It is only an analytical reference point; and the true norm is effective competition, or that state of affairs which will facilitate the flow of goods in heterogeneous markets.

The fact that Chamberlin started from the traditional view led him to apply the slightly invidious term of "monopolistic competition" to what he recognized as the normal situation.

Preoccupied as they were with the problem of resource allocation, economists of the classical school devised an ingenious framework for the solution of the allocative problem. In the classical system, market structures were classified under either of two mutually exclusive categories, pure monopoly or perfect competition. In capsule form, a perfectly competitive market situation is one in which large numbers of atomistic buyers and sellers exchange an identical product. Since by assumption the quantities purchased or offered by any one buyer or seller do not represent a significant portion of the total amount being exchanged, no individual has an appreciable influence on the selling price. And since in any market the product is homogeneous, buyers are indifferent as to the source of their supply. It is assumed, moreover, that all productive resources are completely mobile and will move promptly to industrial sectors where money rewards are highest. Finally, in a perfectly competitive market all buyers and sellers and productive services are fully informed of available alternatives.

The functionalist approach

Within these assumptions (and taking the distribution of income as given), the allocation of resources will be "ideal." Consumer want-satisfaction will be maximized. All productive services will be compensated according to their contribution to the national income. Business firms will be compelled to produce at lowest costs per unit of output in the short run and to adopt the most efficient size of plant in the long run. Should an innovation create economic rents (excess profits), additional resources will flow into the industry until the rents are dissipated. In brief, under static conditions, changes in demand or costs will set in motion adjustments which will bring about a new position of equilibrium.

BUSINESS EXPECTATIONS IN HETEROGENEOUS MARKETS

Chamberlin formulated the principle that the market for every competitor is in some degree unique, thus initiating a drastic revision in competitive theory. This "market uniqueness" he believed to be due mainly to the phenomenon known as "product differentiation," a concept involving both monopoly and competition. Grether and his associates, pursuing this lead from a marketing viewpoint, have suggested the equally helpful concept of enterprise differentiation which is implicit in the present treatment. Chamberlin writes that ". . . a general class of product is differentiated if any significant basis exists for distinguishing the goods (or services) of one seller from those of another." The basis may be real or fancied, so long as it is of any importance to buyers and leads to a preference for one variety of the product over another. The market for each seller is unique, for ". . . where such differentiation exists, even though it be slight, buyers will be paired with sellers, not by chance and at random as under pure competition, but according to their preferences."

Product differentiation

Product differentiation takes various forms. It may be based upon certain characteristics of the product itself: patented features; trade-marks; trade names; peculiarities of the package or container; singularity in quality, design, color, or style. Product differentiation may also exist with respect to the conditions surrounding its sale. Examples of this are convenience of the seller's location, reputation and good will of the seller, services provided by the seller, and various other links which attach the customers to the seller. Product differentiation, broadly interpreted, represents a control over supply in the sense that only one seller offers a product of that exact name and identity. The seller offering a product different from others actually does occupy a monopoly position in that limited sense. A seller in a particular location is a monopolist in more ways than merely the obvious sense that two physical bodies cannot occupy the same space for his geographical location ties certain customers to him. This is often called "spatial monopoly." The customer's approach and attitude are essential, for it is noteworthy that buyers take the product differences into account when purchasing.

Behind the acceptance of differentiation are differences in tastes, desires, incomes, locations of buyers, and the uses for the commodities. It may safely be generalized that such differences among buyers have always existed, and it follows that products have differed. Of course, the merchandising tools of advertising and promotion, plus technological advances, have emphasized and widened the scope of product differentiation. This differentiation, which is a reality in the economy, leads Chamberlin and others to point out the necessity of substituting for the concept of a "competitive ideal" an ideal involving both monopoly and competition. In the economist's role, and in the immediate situation of public policy, it would be advantageous to measure and evaluate activities in the economy against an ideal which represents something more readily approaching reality. Pure monopoly, on the one hand, is impossible because of substitutability. Pure competition is not possible because of the presence of heterogeneous products and markets.

Differentiation and monopoly

With heterogeneous products each seller has a "complete monopoly" of his own product. This type of monopolist, however, is not free from outside competition but only partially insulated from it. The monopolist's demand curve is vitally affected by competing substitutes. Control over total supply of all related products is impossible. Recognition and acceptance of Chamberlin's concept that the real world evidences a complex of monopoly and competition, based on product diversity—a natural consequence of the system of demands—leads to several useful analytical concepts. These include market segmentation, local oligopoly, and multilevel competition.

The economics of differential advantage, building on the foundations laid by Chamberlin, holds that no one enters business except in the expectation of some degree of differential advantage in serving his customers, and that competition consists of the constant struggle to develop, maintain, or increase such advantages. In large part, these efforts in any industry or area, of course, offset each other and cancel out; and to the extent that they do, a kind of "equilibrium" results, consisting of the offsetting of various differential advantages. It is possible under certain restricted assumptions to define with precision an equilibrium situation where a general and complete "balance" of such efforts would be achieved. But in real life, conditions are constantly changing, so that at any particular time some firms will be gaining and others falling back. Any concept of competition which does not include its dynamic aspects would have little relevance to reality.

This summary of the economics of differential advantage suggests several aspects of the theory which require further explanation. It is necessary to examine the following areas: (1) bases on which a differential advantage may be obtained; (2) risk and uncertainty involved in the expectation and exploitation of a differential advantage; (3) entry and exit of firms; (4) industry structure, "balance," and equilibrium; and (5) problem solving by firms and by public administration.

Differential advantage and the "product"

From the broad definition of "product" it is possible to determine these general bases for differential advantage. Differential advantage today rests on technological as well as on legal or geographical grounds. The legal and geographical grounds account for differential advantages due to trademarks, patents, and to location (spatial monopoly). The technological basis for obtaining a differential advantage receives increased emphasis in the American economy, in which there has been a shift in relative importance away from geographical advantage to technological advantage. The various aspects of technological advantage are in general related to use requirements, production processes, and marketing methods. An advantage may be obtained by styling a product to meet a particular consumer taste or desire, such as the production of golf clubs for left-handed players. Advantages based on production processes may be exploited by use of unique assembly-line methods, new equipment, or application of results from a time and motion study. Marketing methods offer an ever-widening basis for exploiting an advantage. A differential advantage may be obtained by a new and different distribution system, or by a revised warehousing or inventory control system.

In this kind of competitive process the innovator may enjoy monopolistic profits for a time. When he introduces his new product or his new method of production or marketing, he is a monopolist at least in the formal sense that he is the only seller of the product or process.

Business expectation as to differential advantage is subject to uncertainty. In attempting to exploit any anticipated advantage, the firm risks resources and effort on the possibility that its expectations may be justified. Even if successful, the duration of an advantage is highly uncertain with the present pace of technological change. The chances are good that some other firm will soon find a way of competing away any excess profits by introducing another innovation along the same or some other dimension of differential advantage. It is not necessary for dozens of firms just like the innovating firm to enter the field in order to deprive it of excess profits. There are several dimensions of differential advantage, actual or potential, in any field. All are vulnerable to immediate attack with the exception of those backed up by the power of the state—as, for example, patents. Geographic advantage may, it is true, place an effective barrier around a trade territory for some commodities. But over a period of time it is constantly shifting and being transformed through improved transportation and communication, through technological developments, and through changes in the distribution of natural resources and of markets. In brief, the existence of opportunity creates an almost irresistible attraction to profit-seeking resources.

Differential advantage and competition

Competition among problem solvers is inherently dynamic. If a seller is at a competitive disadvantage under present conditions, he is likely to direct much of his organization's skill and resources to redressing the balance. He is in no way compelled to play the competitive game as it stands but is constantly exploring new dimensions of advantage. Sellers' competition is not merely a matter of tactics as in the case of two military forces in fixed positions gradually wearing each other down. Competition is a war of movement in which each of the participants is searching for strategies which will improve his relative position.

Further insights into the concept of differential advantage have been provided in a recent essay by Professor J. M. Clark. Clark points out that active competition consists of a combination of (1) initiatory actions by a business unit and (2) a complex of responses by those with whom it deals and by its rivals. The more aggressive firm will give the buyers more inducement (lower prices, better quality, a differentiated product to suit the buyers' tastes, greater selling efforts). The resulting advantage to the initiator consists of increased sales, wholly or partly at the expense of rivals. A rival's response seeks to neutralize or offset the initiator's advantage by offering the buyers something more effective, establishing a positive sales-increasing advantage for himself. In poker-playing terms, he may "see" the initial move or "raise" it.

Differentiation and the neutralizing process

Inasmuch as the initiator's and rival's inducements are confined to price, the neutralizing process—the meeting of price reductions—is conceived as being complete and instantaneous. But with respect to quality (or other variables of "product"), formal theory had previously emphasized the initiating action (establishing of a quality differential) and minimizes the neutralizing process, treating the initiating process as establishing a limited monopoly. The outcome of initiating and responding actions hinges on the relative speeds, or expected speeds, of the initiator's gain and of the neutralizing process whereby rivals destroy or offset his differential advantage, the initiator's actions becoming standard practice.

The initiation and neutralization generally take a substantial time in the case of new productive methods or products (technological advantage along the dimension of consumer uses, production processes). Incentive to innovate or differentiate would vanish if the initiator expected neutralization to be complete before he had recovered the costs of innovation. Thus the elements of risk and uncertainty enter. Fortunately, the pessimistic viewpoint of immediate neutralization is not common. Most innovators expect some enduring residue of advantage. If neutralization were permanently blocked with no further exploitation of a differential advantage possible or permitted, the initiator would have a limited monopoly, in the sense of a permanent differential advantage. To the extent that patent rights, secret processes, or strictly locational advantages exist, such a condition may be approximated.

Instantaneous neutralization occurs only in the case of price reductions on homogeneous or very closely competitive products, with few sellers. But even here, the initiator can shade list prices, vary his discount policies, make forward contracts, or benefit from other market "imperfections," so that competitive action seldom stalls completely unless marketing processes are strongly standardized. As the opportunity to differentiate marketing practices is widely available and attractive, even this qualification nearly disappears.

Clark maintains that the desirable case "lies somewhere between too prompt and too slow neutralization." He does not call this an "optimum" for the reason that the term suggests a precision that no actual system could obtain. "Neutralization needs to take time enough to leave the innovator incentive that is adequate, but not more, and then diffuse the gains as promptly as is consistent with there being ample gains to diffuse." Such neutralization in our terms is the offsetting or destroying of rivals' differential advantages. It may take away the sales gains the innovator has made, or it may merely stop further gains. It may stop further gains quickly and encroach more gradually on gains already made, so that a residue of these gains may last a fairly long time. "If such a residue is expected, it is the innovator's chief incentive, since small but long-lasting gains outweigh large temporary ones."

QUESTIONS

1. What does the phrase "competition for differential advantage" mean?
2. Alderson talks about "heterogeneous markets." What does he mean and how are they relevant to public policy?
3. What alternative methods does Alderson suggest are possible to differentiate a market offering?
4. Is seeking differential advantage desirable from a macro view? Explain.
*5. Are Alderson's ideas relevant in the broader context discussed by Kotler and Levy (Reading 4)?

Foote explains how the concept of competition for a differential advantage can be put into practice through market segmentation. In addition, he demonstrates that market segmentation often works best when a firm seeks an innovative strategy rather than imitating its competitors.

---

6. MARKET SEGMENTATION AS A COMPETITIVE STRATEGY*

Nelson N. Foote

LET US ASSUME we have made the discovery that consumers of ice cream differ significantly in their preferences for chocolate, straw-

---

* Reprinted by permission of the Rand McNally College Publishing Company from Leo Bogart, ed., *Current Controversies in Marketing Research* (Chicago: Markham Publishing Company, 1969), pp. 129–39. At the time of writing, Dr. Foote was with the General Electric Company.

berry, and vanilla. And let us assume that these flavor preferences are not distributed randomly among all kinds of people, but are differentially associated with some other characteristic of customers for ice cream, such as hair color, and that these associations are substantial in degree and practical to ascertain. For example, let us say that brunettes tend strongly to like chocolate, redheads to favor strawberry, and blondes, vanilla. Finally, let us imagine that this pattern is just that simple and orderly—product differences nicely match customer differences.

Then what?

What is the businessman who wants to sell ice cream in this market to do about our findings? Is he to conclude that he should offer all three flavors, the same as the rest of the industry, lest he forego any important sources of sales? Or should he try to serve only blondes and brunettes, since there are not enough redheads to make serving them profitable? Or should he seek to establish a reputation as the producer of the finest Dutch chocolate ice cream, so that he captures nearly all that segment of the market? Or should he go after the great mass of vanilla fans, by upgrading this lowly flavor with a French accent? Or should he take account of his newness or smallness in the industry and challenge the incumbent giants of the trade by introducing pistachio or frozen custard? Or should he offer the normal product line of his industry, but allow some major chain of retail outlets to apply its store brand to his product? Should he go after the door-to-door trade with a very short line—like Neapolitan only—or open his own chain of soda fountains with 28 flavors? Or should he be creative and try to think up some utterly new way to exploit his knowledge of differing customer preferences, since all these strategies—and more besides—are already in use today in the ice cream business?

Plainly, even if one knew far more than is known already about patterns of correlation between product and customer differences in any particular market, it takes a lot of thinking and doing before this knowledge can be turned into a calculated competitive strategy. Meanwhile we find examples of marketing managers who have very successfully employed a strategy of market segmentation, quite without the resources of detailed information that as professional marketers we like to think are indispensable to decision-making in matters of such complexity and risk.

It seems important throughout discussion of market segmentation to recognize that the main source of interest in the concept is its potential value as a competitive strategy. There may be quite a number of people whose interest is in promoting the sale or purchase of data regarding the "stratigraphics" of consumer choice. But unless these data can be put to practical use in improving or defending the market position or profits of their user, only the data seller will benefit, and he not for long. So my self-chosen assignment here is to bear down on the task of thinking out the use of such data in actual marketing management. Although I make my living as a marketing researcher, I think that we need more thinking on this matter as much as we need more research.

Immediately, however, the question arises of who is going to discuss competitive strategy in public—especially in the presence of competitors of his own firm—save in empty generalities. A salesman of research data, or representatives of advertising agencies or media, might set forth some hypothetical tactics of market segmentation as a means of soliciting business. But other than personal vanity or the desire to solicit another job, what would induce someone connected with a manufacturer or a retailer to disclose his thinking about competitive strategy? The incentives of professional exchange of technique or the teaching of younger members of the fraternity are not sufficient justification. Many kinds of professional know-how are properly kept proprietary by the firm which paid for their development. If market segmentation is to be analyzed publicly and candidly from the standpoint of an actual competitor in a market, it has to be justified by some benefit that it will bring to this competitor. If it were not my conviction that in fact it is to the benefit of every competing firm that market segmentation be discussed publicly in terms of its implications for competitive strategy, you would not be listening to these words at this moment.

Moreover, we can go one step further and declare that market segmentation as a competitive strategy is also in the interests of customers. If it were not—if it did not offer customers a firmer base for choice among competing offerings and a wider array of genuine choices—it would not work as a competitive strategy. Like any deal, market segmentation is good business only when both parties to the transaction benefit. Market segmentation is thus in effect a logical extension of the basic principles of marketing.

The process of market segmentation, however, when approached as a task of formulating and executing a marketing strategy, involves matching not merely customer characteristics and product characteristics, but a tripartite matching of customers and offerings *and* the array of competitors in the market, as seen from the standpoint of any one competitor within this constellation. If we think of offerings by competitors as expressions of their differing *capabilities,* it will not only be easy to remember the three Cs—*customers, competitors,* and *capabilities*—but the full task of developing a strategy is more clearly pushed into view.

Let me illustrate concretely by referring to one of our most respected competitors in the Chicago area, the Zenith Radio Corporation. Zenith won a preeminent position in the television receiver market some ten years ago by becoming established in the minds of consumers as the leading exemplar of product reliability. Its policy of manufacturing products of good workmanship goes back many years, but during the middle fifties many consumers became quite concerned to identify the set that would, they hoped, give them the least trouble from breakdown. That was when Zenith's market share soared, until it surpassed the erstwhile industry leader. Servicemen and the radio-TV specialty stores with which they are associated lent vigorous aid. Zenith's management and its advertising agency pressed the opportunity that had widened for them. But Zenith had not adopted product reliability as a self-consciously opportunistic, short-term tactic. As far as known, Zenith's strategy was not derived through marketing research, although marketing research by competitors soon verified its efficacy. After some delay, other competitors raised their quality control standards, but none has been able, coming in later on a me-too basis, to emulate Zenith's success. One could quibble about some details of Zenith's reputation—whether hand-writing is in fact more or less reliable than printed circuits, whether reliability has not been confused to some extent with repairability, whether Zenith sets any longer enjoy the lowest breakdown rate—but from the marketing standpoint, Zenith remains king about that segment of the set market which emphasizes reliability above other virtues when buying sets. The quality standards of the whole industry were forced up by Zenith's success, an outcome of obvious benefit to the consumer, but of at least equal benefit to all the other competitors in the industry, whose personnel devote their whole lives to their industry and much prefer feeling proud of their occupation to feeling ashamed of it.

The meaning of the Zenith example would be very incomplete, however, if we paid attention only to the success story and failed to note that there are many other virtues in television sets which consumers prize besides reliability. If there were not, it would be hard to explain why the Zenith brand share at its zenith rose barely above a fifth of the market. To be sure, Zenith may have preferred its profitability to the greater volume it may have deliberately foregone by upholding a price premium. On the other hand, maybe not; a price premium is just about the loudest advertisement for quality there is.

Meanwhile Zenith's major rival did not simply decide it had to emulate Zenith, but staunchly pursued its strategy of industry statesmanship through the introduction of color, achieving handsome victory and reward from matching its offering with the rising wants of all those customers who were reaching for color in magazines, movies, photography, and other visual media. Alongside these two industry leaders were certain other manufacturers, one of whom has done well by stressing portability and personalization, another by treating the television set as a major piece of furniture, and so on. What is important here is that several competitors held their own or improved their position, even during the period of greatest success by Zenith and RCA, not by seeking to manufacture some hypothetically optimum television set, but by addressing themselves to some substantial segment of the market which *they saw themselves as peculiarly fitted to serve.* The firms which got shaken out during the past dozen years—among which some were big for a time—or which severely lost position can best be described as undistinguishable in their capabilities and offerings, hence undistinguished by consumers.

Now what has been added to the understanding of market segmentation by the example of television receivers? What has been added that is indispensable is the element of competitive capability—a virtue that one particular competitor preeminently possesses—which matches a substantial or rising consumer want. In colloquial terms, what have I got that the other guy hasn't, and which the customer wants badly enough to walk a mile for it?

A few years back, we looked at some commonplace demographic characteristics of television customers arrayed by the brands they tended to favor. When we looked at these demographic characteristics simultaneously, certain results were far more revealing in combination than singly. Only a limited example—because here we are indeed verging on the disclosure of competitive intelligence: we found that one highly meaningful segment of the market—meaningful in terms of sensitivity of discrimination among brands—consisted of households below the median in years of schooling but above the median in income. For convenient reference we called them merely the new-rich, obviously an inexact term. One particular brand seemed to be designed and advertised and priced—properly overpriced, as it were—specifically for this segment, and in fact it enjoyed at that time an inordinate share of their set-buying. Now that company has not noticeably changed its offerings during recent years; they still seem pointed toward the new-rich segment; but its brand share has dwindled substantially. It appears that people with more money than schooling nonetheless are able to learn from experience and do upgrade their taste, given a little time.

The moral of this example is that market segmentation has to be viewed as a continuous process, and marketing strategy has to keep in step with the changing structure of the market. While this implication is probably obvious, perhaps less obvious is the corollary that, just as consumers learn, it is necessary for competitors to learn to exercise differing capabilities from those which may have won them success in the past. And here we come to a matter which lies beyond not only research but also ordinary logic and in the realm of managerial will. Who is to tell a manufacturer that he is capable of doing something he has not done before, and of doing it better than any of his other competitors? By definition, the ordinary kinds of evidence are lacking because there is no past experience to be projected forward.

In the course of interpersonal relations among individuals, a teacher or a parent may tell a child that he posseses talents he did not previously recognize; the child may then adopt this observation as a conviction about himself which empowers him to demonstrate that it is true. All of us are familiar enough with instances of this outcome not to need to debate whether they occur. The faith of a coach in an athlete, of a critic in a writer, of an employer in an employee, of a wife in a husband, is often the ingredient which brings out a latent capability. Because so little is understood about the process, we cannot make it happen on demand. We are fortunate to recognize it when it does happen, even more so when we spy the opportunity beforehand and do not waste it, for ourselves or for others. Even further beyond present understanding is the possibility of specifying here a reliable formula whereby the management of a company can truly discern those latent talents in its own organization which can be mobilized more effectively by itself than by any of its competitors to satisfy some important emerging customer want.

I do know this, however: recognition of such a talent feeds on itself; it is a cumulative process, a benevolent spiral. I am positive that when the management of Zenith found itself being recognized by consumers for its virtues of good workmanship, it was immensely stimulated to push further in that direction. Thus one of the most valuable functions of marketing research in implementing a strategy of market segmentation is to listen to what is being said about a company by its customers in terms of recognizing its special talents. Developing something that is already there—watering a plant that is already growing, to mix a metaphor—is surely much easier and more likely to succeed than trying to create new capabilities out of whole cloth or, for that matter, borrowing the garments of others, in the sense of imitating or acquiring another company and offering that as an expression of one's own capability.

Part of the growing sophistication of consumers is their increasing interest in the character of the organization they are dealing with. At General Electric we are acutely conscious that certain of our competitors, whose products are no better and sometimes not as good as ours by any measure of product quality, nonetheless enjoy the preference of certain customers. This problem repeatedly confronts the manufacturer who finds himself in competition with retailers who handle only store brands. The whole fascinating issue of what is going to emerge as private branding widens its sway is too vast to open up here. Yet it deserves mention here as constituting market segmentation on an utterly different axis from market segmentation on the axis of product features and brand images.

Segmentation varies in degree as well as in kind. The famous case of the ordinary salt which "rains when it pours" illustrates a valued product feature which has maintained for a particular brand a large and stable market share for many years, while conferring on consumers a valued satisfaction for which they are quite willing to pay a price premium and a rewarding degree of brand loyalty. Many such product features are easily imitated, however, and the reputation for distinctiveness originally achieved may dissolve in the minds of consumers despite advertising. The impermanence of minor product features as a source of competitive distinctiveness and effective market segmentation is a conspicuous failing of the current picture in package goods competition. Like rock-and-roll music, there is too little difference between the new ones and the old ones to make much difference. The proliferation of trivial product differences which appeal to trivial differences among consumers and represent trivial differences among the capabilities of their makers is in effect a mockery of the theory of market segmentation. This proliferation of trivial differences provokes denunciation by producers, retailers, and consumers alike as market fragmentation rather than segmentation and makes an industry vulnerable to the outsider who commences to segment on a different axis. The effective response to the trivialization of market segmentation, however, is not to abandon it as a strategy. To do that would be to abdicate all initiative to competitors. The way out of the expensive waste of trivial segmentation is to engage in serious segmentation, which means segmentation on a larger scale or even on another axis.

Serious, large-scale innovation seems often to come from outside an industry rather than inside. Examples like General Motors in locomotives, Volkswagen in autos, IBM in typewriters, Corning in housewares, Lestoil in detergents, come to mind. Rivalry within a going constellation of competitors seems often to lead to implicit imitation, even when everyone involved is convinced that he is trying to be different from everyone else. How this result occurs is not hard to discern. Close rivals tend very easily to magnify the importance of small differences, whether initiated by themselves or others. If created by another, a close competitor often feels he must come up with a rival innovation but only of corresponding scale.

One detects nothing very distinctive about Silvertone television sets, to mention another respected Chicago competitor. Viewed as manufactured products, they are close to the industry's average line. But where Zenith stresses the reliability built into the product, Sears stresses the services offered by the stores in which Silvertone sets are bought—the promptness of repair service, the easy credit, the ample parking, the special sales well advertised in local newspapers or by direct mail. That is, Sears segments the market on another axis than Zenith. But thus far, Silvertone has encroached far less upon Zenith's clientele than upon the portions of the market occupied by companies whose offerings are less distinctive.

We shall come back to this intriguing question of how far the competition of store brands with manufacturer brands may go before some equilibrium is reached. Some companies as yet have a less urgent private-brand problem anyway, like the auto and gasoline firms and the sellers of services—insurance, banking, air travel, lodging, dry cleaning—which distribute through their own exclusive retail outlets. So for some moments longer, let us stay within the sphere of competition among manufactured products and nationally advertised brands.

Assuming this sphere, we can now state our main hypothesis in further detail: Market segmentation works best as a competitive strategy, i.e., contributes most to the success of competitors and the satisfaction of customers, when product and brand and maker are closely identified in the minds of all concerned.

If we were to assume that one by one more competitors in a market choose to attract particular segments of customers on the basis of correct appraisal of their own special capabilities to satisfy these segments, then the competitors who do not make such deliberate choices will find themselves increasingly confined to the miscellaneous and dwindling residue. As alluded to in our first example, such a development is to some extent a description of what has already happened in some markets, so we may be prophesying simply an intensification of current tendencies rather than anything new under the sun. In other words, self-conscious segmentation may become not only a means of success but the price of survival in a market.

Beyond the ordinary criteria of survival or success as measured in profitability and market share, however, are some other benefits of segmentation to an industry and the various competitors in it. We have mentioned the feeling of pride in their occupation and the quality of its products which most people desire in their life work. Some other benefits of belonging to an industry which steadily adds to the values it offers its customers also deserve explicit recognition. They include the fact that being bested by a competitor whom one respects is easier to accept than being bested by a competitor whom one does not respect. There is a good deal of satisfaction to the producer as well as the consumer in seeing an industry progress over time through advanced applications of science and technology. In an industry plagued with cut-throat price competition instead of value competition, imitation is almost inevitable, because no one can afford the research and development required for innovation. In the vicious downward spiral which obtains in such an industry, jobs are insecure because companies are insecure; and morale and morality seem to decline together. Enough examples spring to mind. An industry trapped in such a spiral, worst of all, has rarely been able to reverse it without outside help, as from major suppliers. DuPont, for example, has struggled quite nobly to raise the plastics molding industry from its swamp. Customers themselves, especially in recent years, have sometimes under these conditions willingly paid substantial premiums for quality and reliability, and this has brought a turnabout, but not before the damage became painful to all concerned.

Both competitors and customers share the benefit of stabilized markets wherein strong degrees of mutual loyalty exist between particular companies and particular segments of customers. Distribution and advertising costs are significantly lower under conditions in which repeat sales make up a high proportion of total sales. The model line of any competitor can be shorter, yet his volume nowadays may be higher, than when he tries to carry everything everyone else in the industry offers. All phases of marketing are much more intelligently, effectively, and efficiently conducted when companies and customers, having chosen each other with care and sophistication, can rely on each other's growing discrimination and sympathetically anticipate the orderly developing and unfolding and matching of their future wants and capabilities. Some marketing researchers even envision a paradise in which companies will spend as much money in listening as in talking and will make more money doing so.

Let us commence to summarize while injecting a few additional elements into this consideration of market segmentation as a competitive strategy. Our first proposition was that any approach to market segmentation which dealt only with matching customer characteristics with product features was seriously incomplete. The very incentive for exploring market segmentation is to gain advantage—to seek some basis for customer preference—against the array of other competitors and their offerings in a particular market. If one plays only with customer characteristics and product features, he may arrive at the notion of some optimum product for an average customer, in effect, a recipe for reducing his product to commodity status, hence the very opposite of market segmentation, which implies product differentiation. But if he goes to the opposite extreme and tries to equal or surpass the total array of differing products offered by all competitors to all segments of his market, he courts the usual fate of me-too-ism, while suffering impossibly mounting marketing costs. Hence he must seek to identify those offerings which most appeal to some desirable segment of the total market and simultaneously express those capabilities in which he is strongest. The problem of choice here is analogous with that of the boy who must seek distinction from a brother who excels him athletically and another, who excels him academically: what talent can he develop which, though different, will seem equivalent in the eyes of those whose approval he seeks? To be all things to all people, to excel in every virtue, is impossible; to be average in all means indistinguishability. Achieving only trivial distinctiveness is a barely veiled form of imitation, although it can immensely add to promotional expense in an industry. Hence the evolution of a criterion for selecting which customer segments and matching product distinctions to pursue must come from and be disciplined by correct identification of the real strengths and weaknesses of the company itself, as compared with other competitors in its market.

Companies, like individuals, sometimes involuntarily suffer crises of identity, as when merged with other companies. A company embarking upon market segmentation as a competitive strategy is deliberately precipitating a crisis of identity. In place of identity, however, which seems to apply only to the maker of a product rather than to a triple set of interrelations, I believe the concept of theme is more applicable and explanatory of the common element which has to be discovered or invented to match customer characteristic with product feature with company capability. The so-called total marketing approach in its sophisticated form seems finally to come forth with such recognizable themes. The theme of *ease of use* of essentially highly technical equipment has served Kodak for generations and recurs in numerous notable expressions—from the Brownie to the Instamatic, from the ubiquitous yellow box to the universally recognizable name itself. It illustrates how versatile in its manifestations a theme can be.

But just as product innovation can be trivialized through pointless small variations which make no real contribution to anyone, the concept of theme can be trivialized also, and in fact is, whenever some advertising agency tries to adorn an advertiser with a superficial image that has no real structural relationship to customer segments, competitive constellation, or company capabilities.

The concept of theme is useful in teaching marketing and market segmentation to managers whose experience has been in more exact fields. It helps to avoid the mental blocks that arise when segmentation is grasped as a series of pigeonholes in which various kinds of customers are filed for separate treatment, whereas the manager is eager for all the sales he can get from any source whatever, and finds it hard enough to devise one marketing strategy without having to devise many. To return to our main example, the television receiver market, the theme of reliability can be applied by one manufacturer to all the models in his line and throughout all the functions of marketing in his total marketing program. But the same manufacturer could hardly pursue simultaneously with equal thoroughness and equal success such contrasting themes as modern and traditional cabinetry, portability, technical innovation, and retail convenience, although he may keep pace with the industry average in these respects. Market segmentation does not deal with water-tight compartments, but with emphases sufficiently simple and distinctive to win notice and preference among customers to whom they are important, without alienating customers by being deficient in the other virtues which they more or less take for granted.

In terms of demographic and other statistical dimensions by which customers and products may be differentiated, the possibilities for market segmentation are troublesomely infinite. But when the problem of choosing a theme to emphasize is disciplined by attempting to match customers, competitors, and capabilities, these troubles are usually reduced to very few choices that are actually open to a particular firm—though hopefully at least one. The real difficulties of choice are not statistical but spiritual—the anguish of facing up to the fact that if a company is going to move in one direction, it must forego moving in all the others. Such a decision comes especially hard in diversified companies, yet some diversified companies have achieved real synergy through this discipline.

Once this clarifying commitment has been made, its effect on everyone in the organization is to release spontaneous ingenuity in its implementation. A good theme stimulates numberless applications and suggestions, furnishes a guide in numberless subordinate decisions, and eases numberless chores of communication, both inside and outside.

Not only does a positive theme help to mobilize an organization in pursuit of its marketing objectives and heighten their satisfaction, but it wins respect from competitors, even while strengthening and securing its position against them. Spirit is harder to imitate than matter; hardware is easy to copy, but the spirit of a whole organization is not. The competitor who wishes to emulate the success of a competitor's dominant theme must, instead of echoing it, come up with an equivalent theme that uniquely fits himself to his situation, that matches his own three Cs. . . .

QUESTIONS

1. Discuss why competing for a differential advantage leads to market segmentation.

2. Compare and contrast Foote's main hypothesis with the major points of the marketing concept.

3. Why does Foote place so much emphasis on competitors, and even include them in his "3 Cs"?

4. What does Foote mean by "theme"? Illustrate.

°5. Does Foote seem to agree with Alderson's treatment (Reading 5) of "differential advantage"?

This article traces the evolution of the marketing mix concept and explains why Borden feels it is so important. Further, his two outlines, "Marketing Mix of Manufacturers" and "Market Forces Bearing on the Marketing Mix," succinctly summarize much of what marketing management involves. But the most important point in the article is that the market offering of a firm is a blend of product, distribution, promotion, and price rather than any one of these factors individually.

---

7. THE CONCEPT OF THE MARKETING MIX*

Neil H. Borden

I HAVE ALWAYS found it interesting to observe how an apt or colorful term may catch on, gain wide usage, and help to further understanding of a concept that has already been expressed in less appealing and communicative terms. Such has been true of the phrase "marketing mix," which I began to use in my teaching and writing some 15 years ago. In a relatively short time it has come to have wide usage. This note tells of the evolution of the marketing mix concept.

The phrase was suggested to me by a paragraph in a research bulletin on the management of marketing costs, written by my associate, Professor James Culliton.[1] In this study of manufacturers' marketing costs he described the business executive as a

"decider," an "artist"—a "mixer of ingredients," who sometimes follows a recipe as he goes along, sometimes adapts a recipe to the ingredients immediately available, and sometimes experiments with or invents ingredients no one else has tried.

I liked his idea of calling a marketing executive a "mixer of ingredients," one who is constantly engaged in fashioning creatively a mix of marketing procedures and policies in his efforts to produce a profitable enterprise.

For many years previous to Culliton's cost study the wide variations in the procedures and policies employed by managements of manufacturing firms in their marketing programs and the correspondingly wide variation in the costs of these marketing functions, which Culliton aptly ascribed to the varied "mixing of ingredients," had become increasingly evident as we had gathered marketing cases at the Harvard Business School. The marked differences in the patterns or formulae of the marketing programs not only were evident through facts disclosed in case histories, but also were reflected clearly in the figures of a cost study of food manufacturers made by the Harvard Bureau of Business Research in 1929. The primary objective of this study was to determine common figures of expenses for various marketing functions among food manufacturing companies, similar to the common cost figures which

---

* Reprinted from the *Journal of Advertising Research*, © Advertising Research Foundation, Inc. (1964), pp. 2–7. At the time of writing, Neil H. Borden was a faculty member at the Harvard Business School.

[1] James W. Culliton, *The Management of Marketing Costs* (Boston: Division of Research, Graduate School of Business Administration, Harvard University, 1948).

had been determined in previous years for various kinds of retail and wholesale businesses. In this manufacturer's study we were unable, however, with the data gathered to determine common expense figures that had much significance as standards by which to guide management, such as had been possible in the studies of retail and wholesale trades, where the methods of operation tended toward uniformity. Instead, among food manufacturers the ratios of sales devoted to the various functions of marketing such as advertising, personal selling, packaging, and so on, were found to be widely divergent, no matter how we grouped our respondents. Each respondent gave data that tended to uniqueness.

Culliton's study of marketing costs in 1947–48 was a second effort to find out, among other objectives, whether a bigger sample and a more careful classification of companies would produce evidence of operating uniformities that would give helpful common expense figures. But the result was the same as in our early study: there was wide diversity in cost ratios among any classifications of firms which were set up, and no common figures were found that had much value. This was true whether companies were grouped according to similarity in product lines, amount of sales, territorial extent of operations, or other bases of classification.

Relatively early in my study of advertising, it had become evident that understanding of advertising usage by manufacturers in any case had to come from an analysis of advertising's place as one element in the total marketing program of the firm. I came to realize that it is essential always to ask: what overall marketing strategy has been or might be employed to bring about a profitable operation in light of the circumstances faced by the management? What combination of marketing procedures and policies has been or might be adopted to bring about desired behavior of trade and consumers at costs that will permit a profit? Specifically, how can advertising, personal selling, pricing, packaging, channels, warehousing, and the other elements of a marketing program be manipulated and fitted together in a way that will give a profitable operation? In short, I saw that every advertising management case called for a consideration of the strategy to be adopted for the total marketing program, with advertising recognized as only one element whose form and extent depended on its careful adjustment to the other parts of the program.

The soundness of this viewpoint was supported by case histories throughout my volume, *The Economic Effects of Advertising.*[2] In the chapters devoted to the utilization of advertising by business, I had pointed out the innumerable combinations of marketing methods and policies that might be adopted by a manager in arriving at a marketing

[2] Neil H. Borden, *The Economic Effects of Advertising* (Homewood, Illinois: Richard D. Irwin, 1942).

plan. For instance, in the area of branding, he might elect to adopt an individualized brand or a family brand. Or he might decide to sell his product unbranded or under private label. Any decision in the area of brand policy in turn has immediate implications that bear on his selection of channels of distribution, sales force methods, packaging, promotional procedure, and advertising. Throughout the volume the case materials cited show that the way in which any marketing function is designed and the burden placed upon the function are determined largely by the overall marketing strategy adopted by managements to meet the market conditions under which they operate. The forces met by different firms vary widely. Accordingly, the programs fashioned differ widely.

Regarding advertising, which was the function under focus in the economic effects volume, I said at one point:

In all the above illustrative situations it should be recognized that advertising is not an operating method to be considered as something apart, as something whose profit value is to be judged alone. An able management does not ask, "Shall we use or not use advertising," without consideration of the product and of other management procedures to be employed. Rather the question is always one of finding a management formula giving advertising its due place in the combination of manufacturing methods, product form, pricing, promotion and selling methods, and distribution methods. As previously pointed out different formulae, i.e., different combinations of methods, may be profitably employed by competing manufacturers.

From the above it can be seen why Culliton's description of a marketing manager as a "mixer of ingredients" immediately appealed to me as an apt and easily understandable phrase, far better than my previous references to the marketing man as an empiricist seeking in any situation to devise a profitable "pattern" or "formula" of marketing operations from among the many procedures and policies that were open to him. If he was a "mixer of ingredients," what he designed was a "marketing mix."

It was logical to proceed from a realization of the existence of a variety of "marketing mixes" to the development of a concept that would comprehend not only this variety, but also the market forces that cause managements to produce a variety of mixes. It is the problems raised by these forces that lead marketing managers to exercise their wits in devising mixes or programs which they hope will give a profitable business operation.

To portray this broadened concept in a visual presentation requires merely:

1. A list of the important elements or ingredients that make up marketing programs.

2. A list of the forces that bear on the marketing operation of a firm and to which the marketing manager must adjust in his search for a mix or program that can be successful.

The list of elements of the marketing mix in such a visual presentation can be long or short, depending on how far one wishes to go in his classification and sub-classification of the marketing procedures and policies with which marketing managements deal when devising marketing programs. The list of elements which I have employed in my teaching and consulting work covers the principal areas of marketing activities which call for management decisions as revealed by case histories. I realize others might build a different list. Mine is as follows:

Elements of the marketing mix of manufacturers

1. *Product Planning*—policies and procedures relating to:
   a. Product lines to be offered—qualities, design, etc.
   b. Markets to sell—whom, where, when, and in what quantity.
   c. New product policy—research and development program.
2. *Pricing*—policies and procedures relating to:
   a. Price level to adopt.
   b. Specific prices to adopt—odd-even, etc.
   c. Price policy—one-price or varying price, price maintenance, use of list prices, etc.
   d. Margins to adopt—for company, for the trade.
3. *Branding*—policies and procedures relating to:
   a. Selection of trade marks.
   b. Brand policy—individualized or family brand.
   c. Sale under private label or unbranded.
4. *Channels of Distribution*—policies and procedures relating to:
   a. Channels to use between plant and consumer.
   b. Degree of selectivity among wholesalers and retailers.
   c. Efforts to gain cooperation of the trade.
5. *Personal Selling*—policies and procedures relating to:
   a. Burden to be placed on personal selling and the methods to be employed in:
      1. Manufacturer's organization.
      2. Wholesale segment of the trade.
      3. Retail segment of the trade.
6. *Advertising*—policies and procedures relating to:
   a. Amount to spend—i.e., the burden to be placed on advertising.
   b. Copy platform to adopt:
      1. Product image desired.
      2. Corporate image desired.
   c. Mix of advertising—to the trade, through the trade, to consumers.

7. *Promotions*—policies and procedures relating to:
   a. Burden to place on special selling plans or devices directed at or through the trade.
   b. Form of these devices for consumer promotions, for trade promotions.
8. *Packaging*—policies and procedures relating to:
   a. Formulation of package and label.
9. *Display*—policies and procedures relating to:
   a. Burden to be put on display to help effect sale.
   b. Methods to adopt to secure display.
10. *Servicing*—policies and procedures relating to:
    a. Providing service needed.
11. *Physical Handling*—policies and procedures relating to:
    a. Warehousing.
    b. Transportation.
    c. Inventories.
12. *Fact Finding and Analysis*—policies and procedures relating to:
    a. Securing, analysis, and use of facts in marketing operations.

Also, if one were to make a list of all the forces which managements weigh at one time or another when formulating their marketing mixes, it would be very long indeed, for the behavior of individuals and groups in all spheres of life has a bearing, first, on what goods and services are produced and consumed, and, second, on the procedures that may be employed in bringing about exchange of these goods and services. However, the important forces which bear on marketers, all arising from the behavior of individuals or groups, may readily be listed under four heads, namely, the behavior of consumers, the trade, competitors, and government.

The next outline contains these four behavioral forces with notations of some of the important behavioral determinants within each force. These must be studied and understood by the marketer, if his marketing mix is to be successful. The great quest of marketing management is to understand the behavior of humans in response to the stimuli to which they are subjected. The skillful marketer is one who is a perceptive and practical psychologist and sociologist, who has keen insight into individual and group behavior, who can foresee changes in behavior that develop in a dynamic world, who has creative ability for building well-knit programs because he has the capacity to visualize the probable response of consumers, trade, and competitors to his moves. His skill in forecasting response to his marketing moves should well be supplemented by a further skill in devising and using tests and measurements to check consumer or trade response to his program or parts thereof, for no marketer has so much prescience that he can proceed without empirical check.

Here, then, is the suggested outline of forces which govern the mixing of marketing elements. This list and that of the elements taken together provide a visual presentation of the concept of the marketing mix.

Market forces bearing on the marketing mix

1. *Consumers' Buying Behavior*—as determined by their:
   a. Motivation in purchasing.
   b. Buying habits.
   c. Living habits.
   d. Environment (present and future, as revealed by trends, for environment influences consumers' attitudes toward products and their use of them).
   e. Buying power.
   f. Number (i.e., how many).
2. *The Trade's Behavior*—wholesalers' and retailers' behavior, as influenced by:
   a. Their motivations.
   b. Their structure, practices, and attitudes.
   c. Trends in structure and procedures that portend change.
3. *Competitors' Position and Behavior*—as influenced by:
   a. Industry structure and the firm's relation thereto.
      1. Size and strength of competitors.
      2. Number of competitors and degree of industry concentration.
      3. Indirect competition—i.e., from other products.
   b. Relation of supply to demand—oversupply or undersupply.
   c. Product choices offered consumers by the industry—i.e., quality, price, service.
   d. Degree to which competitors compete on price vs. nonprice bases.
   e. Competitors' motivations and attitudes—their likely response to the actions of other firms.
   f. Trends technological and social, portending change in supply and demand.
4. *Government Behavior*—controls over marketing:
   a. Regulations over products.
   b. Regulations over pricing.
   c. Regulations over competitive practices.
   d. Regulations over advertising and promotion.

When building a marketing program to fit the needs of his firm, the marketing manager has to weigh the behavioral forces and then juggle marketing elements in his mix with a keen eye on the resources with which he has to work. His firm is but one small organism in a large universe of complex forces. His firm is only a part of an industry that is competing with many other industries. What does the firm have in terms of money, product line, organization, and reputation with which to work? The manager must devise a mix of procedures that fit these resources. If his firm is small, he must judge the response of consumers, trade, and competition in light of his position and resources and the influence that he can exert in the market. He must look for special opportunities in product or method of operation. The small firm cannot employ the procedures of the big firm. Though he may sell the same kind of product as the big firm, his marketing strategy is likely to be widely different in many respects. Innumerable instances of this fact might be cited. For example, in the industrial goods field, small firms often seek to build sales on a limited and highly specialized line, whereas industry leaders seek patronage for full lines. Small firms often elect to go in for regional sales rather than attempt the national distribution practiced by larger companies. Again, the company of limited resources often elects to limit its production and sales to products whose potential is too small to attract the big fellows. Still again, companies with small resources in the cosmetic field not infrequently have set up introductory marketing programs employing aggressive personal selling and a "push" strategy with distribution limited to leading department stores. Their initially small advertising funds have been directed through these selected retail outlets, with the offering of the products and their story told over the signatures of the stores. The strategy has been to borrow kudos for their products from the leading stores' reputations and to gain a gradual radiation of distribution to smaller stores in all types of channels, such as often comes from the trade's follow-the-leader behavior. Only after resources have grown from mounting sales has a dense retail distribution been aggressively sought and a shift made to place the selling burden more and more on company-signed advertising.

The above strategy was employed for Toni products and Stoppette deodorant in their early marketing stages when the resources of their producers were limited (cf. case of Jules Montenier, Inc. in *Borden and Marshall*).[3] In contrast, cosmetic manufacturers with large resources have generally followed a "pull" strategy for the introduction of new products, relying on heavy campaigns of advertising in a rapid succession of area introductions to induce a hoped-for, complete retail coverage from the start (cf. case of Bristol-Meyers Company in *Borden and Marshall*).[4] These introductory campaigns have been undertaken only after careful programs of product development and test marketing have given assurance that product and selling plans had high promise of success.

Many additional instances of the varying strategy employed by small versus large enterprises might be cited. But those given serve to illustrate

---

[3] Neil H. Borden and M. V. Marshall, *Advertising Management: Text and Cases* (Homewood, Illinois: Richard D. Irwin, 1959), pp. 498–518.

[4] Ibid., pp. 518–33.

the point that managements must fashion their mixes to fit their resources. Their objectives must be realistic.

LONG VS. SHORT TERM ASPECTS OF MARKETING MIX

The marketing mix of a firm in a large part is the product of the
evolution that comes from day-to-day marketing. At any time the mix
represents the program that a management has evolved to meet the
problems with which it is constantly faced in an ever-changing, ever-
challenging market. There are continuous tactical maneuvers: a new
product, aggressive promotion, or price change initiated by a competitor
must be considered and met; the failure of the trade to provide adequate
market coverage or display must be remedied; a faltering sales force
must be reorganized and stimulated; a decline in sales share must be
diagnosed and remedied; an advertising approach that has lost effectiveness must be replaced; a general business decline must be countered.
All such problems call for a management's maintaining effective channels
of information relative to its own operations and to the day-to-day behavior of consumers, competitors, and the trade. Thus, we may observe
that short-range forces play a large part in the fashioning of the mix
to be used at any time and in determining the allocation of expenditures
among the various functional accounts of the operating statement.

But the overall strategy employed in a marketing mix is the product
of longer-range plans and procedures dictated in part by past empiricism
and in part, if the management is a good one, by management foresight
as to what needs to be done to keep the firm successful in a changing
world. As the world has become more and more dynamic, blessed is
that corporation which has managers who have foresight, who can study
trends of all kinds—natural, economic, social, and technological—and,
guided by these, devise long-range plans that give promise of keeping
their corporations afloat and successful in the turbulent sea of market
change. Accordingly, when we think of the marketing mix, we need
to give particular heed today to devising a mix based on long-range
planning that promises to fit the world of five or ten or more years
hence. Provision for effective long-range planning in corporate organization and procedure has become more and more recognized as the ear-
mark of good management in a world that has become increasingly
subject to rapid change.

To cite an instance among American marketing organizations which
have shown foresight in adjusting the marketing mix to meet social
and economic change, I look upon Sears Roebuck and Company as
an outstanding example. After building an unusually successfully mail
order business to met the needs of a rural America, Sears management
foresaw the need to depart from its marketing pattern as a mail order
company catering primarily to farmers. The trend from a rural to an

urban United States was going on apace. The automobile and good roads promised to make town and city stores increasingly available to those who continued to be farmers. Relatively early, Sears launched a chain of stores across the land, each easily accessible by highway to both farmer and city resident, and with adequate parking space for customers. In time there followed the remarkable telephone and mail order plan directed at urban residents to make buying easy for Americans when congested city streets and highways made shopping increasingly distasteful. Similarly, in the areas of planning products which would meet the desires of consumers in a fast-changing world, of shaping its servicing to meet the needs of a wide variety of mechanical products, of pricing procedures to meet the challenging competition that came with the advent of discount retailers, the Sears organization has shown a foresight, adaptability, and creative ability worthy of emulation. The amazing growth and profitability of the company attest to the foresight and skill of its management. Its history shows the wisdom of careful attention to market forces and their impending change in devising marketing mixes that may assure growth.

USE OF THE MARKETING MIX CONCEPT

Like many concepts, the marketing mix concept seems relatively simple, once it has been expressed. I know that before they were ever tagged with the nomenclature of "concept," the ideas involved were widely understood among marketers as a result of the growing knowledge about marketing and marketing procedures that came during the preceding half century. But I have found for myself that once the ideas were reduced to a formal statement with an accompanying visual presentation, the concept of the mix has proved a helpful device in teaching, in business problem solving, and, generally, as an aid to thinking about marketing. First of all, it is helpful in giving an answer to the question often raised as to "what is marketing?" A chart which shows the elements of the mix and the forces that bear on the mix helps to bring understanding of what marketing is. It helps to explain why in our dynamic world the thinking of management in all its functional areas must be oriented to the market.

In recent years I have kept an abbreviated chart showing the elements and the forces of the marketing mix in front of my classes at all times. In case discussion it has proved a handy device by which to raise queries as to whether the student has recognized the implications of any recommendation he might have made in the areas of the several elements of the mix. Or, referring to the forces, we can question whether all the pertinent market forces have been given due consideration. Continual reference to the mix chart leads me to feel that the students' understanding of "what marketing is" is strengthened. The constant presence and use of the chart leaves a deeper understanding that marketing is the devising of programs that successfully meet the forces of the market.

In problem solving the marketing mix chart is a constant reminder of:

1. The fact that a problem seemingly lying in one segment of the mix must be deliberated with constant thought regarding the effect of any change in that sector on the other areas of marketing operations. The necessity of integration in marketing thinking is ever present.
2. The need of careful study of the market forces as they might bear on problems in hand.

In short, the mix chart provides an ever-ready checklist as to areas into which to guide thinking when considering marketing questions or dealing with marketing problems.

MARKETING: SCIENCE OR ART?

The quest for a "science of marketing" is hard upon us. If science is in part a systematic formulation and arrangement of facts in a way to help understanding, then the concept of the marketing mix may possibly be considered a small contribution in the search for a science of marketing. If we think of a marketing science as involving the observation and classification of facts and the establishment of verifiable laws that can be used by the marketer as a guide to action with assurance that predicted results will ensue, then we cannot be said to have gotten far toward establishing a science. The concept of the mix lays out the areas in which facts should be assembled, these to serve as a guide to management judgment in building marketing mixes. In the last few decades American marketers have made substantial progress in adopting the scientific method in assembling facts. They have sharpened the tools of fact finding—both those arising within the business and those external to it. Aided by these facts and by the skills developed through careful observation and experience, marketers are better fitted to practice the art of designing marketing mixes than would be the case had not the techniques of gathering facts been advanced as they have been in recent decades. Moreover, marketers have made progress in the use of the scientific method in designing tests whereby the results from mixes or parts of mixes can be measured. Thereby marketers have been learning how to subject the hypotheses of their mix artists to empirical check.

With continued improvement in the search for and the recording of facts pertinent to marketing, with further application of the controlled experiment, and with an extension and careful recording of case histories, we may hope for a gradual formulation of clearly defined and helpful marketing laws. Until then, and even then, marketing and the building of marketing mixes will largely lie in the realm of art.

QUESTIONS

1. According to Borden, which of the several marketing mix variables is most important? Why?
2. Borden suggests that marketing management is an art. What would be needed to call it a science?
*3. Is Borden's "marketing mix" concept related to market segmentation as discussed by Foote (Reading 6)? Explain.

Energy and raw material shortages will have an impact on the marketing strategies of firms for many years. For some firms, shortages will mean opportunities while for others they will mean problems. Professor Cravens postulates four market condition–production capability possibilities. He then discusses the strategy and action implications of each of the combinations.

---

8. MARKETING MANAGEMENT IN AN ERA OF SHORTAGES*

David W. Cravens

THE NATION's accelerating energy crisis combined with rapidly increasing consumption throughout the world is causing substantial shifts in many industries. The scramble for sales has become a scramble for products and services to meet customer needs. These same shortages threaten to severely limit market opportunities for other industries. The widespread impact of an emerging era of scarcity raises important questions and issues regarding the appropriate role of marketing management. Consider, for example, these problems:

The frustrations of the sales force employed by a large book printer who has been informed that plants are operating at full capacity and new business will have to be severely limited.

° Reprinted with permission from *Business Horizons*, February 1974, pp. 79–85. At the time of writing, Dr. Cravens was a member of the business administration faculty of the University of Tennessee.

The challenge faced by management of a large motel chain in seeking to develop a profitable strategy during a period when occupancy rates will be significantly lowered by reduced pleasure travel in automobiles.

The task of determining an appropriate advertising budget and message design by a large oil company.

The dilemma confronting the vice-president of sales of a small chemical distributor who can sell all the chemicals that suppliers will allocate over the next twelve months with one-half to two-thirds of his current sales force.

These are but a few of the many situations that marketing management will face during future periods of shortages. For some businesses, the energy shortage will present new opportunities; for many others it will create excess capacity or an inability to meet growing customer needs with existing production or distribution systems. It is clear that past consumption patterns must be altered in the decade ahead in response to energy shortages. The growing world appetite for all types of energy in combination with increasing resource limitations promise to significantly alter business strategies for many firms.

The role of marketing in the enterprise is to identify those customer needs and wants the firm is best equipped to serve; to design an integrated marketing strategy to make available the firm's offering to customers in the marketplace; and, through this process, to achieve marketing objectives (for example, contribution to profits and increase in market share). Our purpose is to examine the nature and scope of the marketing management challenge in a time of scarcity and to outline strategy guidelines for firms with too much business as well as those confronted with limited short-term growth opportunities and possible declines. Although the magnitude and scope of the impact of shortages in various industries may be difficult to estimate at the present time, it is essential that all firms develop and maintain a strong market-oriented posture in the decade ahead.

THE MANAGEMENT CHALLENGE

The shutoff of Arab oil to the United States in late 1973 promises to accentuate the energy shortage, but the embargo is only one of the major trends that has caused world-wide shortages of several resources. Rapidly expanding demand throughout the world has quickly absorbed scarce supplies of a variety of basic commodities such as grain, lumber, fertilizer, cotton, and wool. Thus, unlike the problems precipitated by an economic recession, in many sectors there is inadequate capacity to meet needs. Shortages of basic resources such as oil have set off a series of chain reactions in industries dependent on oil and petroleum products. It seems clear that at least a few years will pass before the various imbalances in supply and demand will reach more stable levels.

Moreover, some estimates suggest that a decade or more will elapse before needed adjustments can be made.

Alternative strategy situations

The marketing management challenge during this era is essentially a "problem of regulating the level, timing, and character of demand for one or more products of an organization."[1] Beyond variations in the demand for products and services are the effects of shortages in resources and/or productive capacity. These two influences together create the four broad types of market strategy situations shown in Figure 1. Increasing marketing demand in combination with the product or

FIGURE 1
Alternative marketing strategy situations

Market demand	Resources and productive capacity	
	Adequate	Inadequate
Increasing	A. Growth strategy	B. Market retention strategy
Declining	C. Market building and/or diversification	D. Balancing and realignment strategies

service capability to meet market needs is a growth situation as shown in position A. It is clearly the most desirable strategic position of the four. A life insurance firm might appropriately fit into this strategic category.

Unfortunately, many firms that have pursued growth strategies for the past decade will, as a result of the energy crisis, be forced into one of the other three positions. Of course, none of these is as desirable as being able to effectively serve increasing market demand.

A firm that is unable (due to lack of resources and/or productive capacity) to adequately meet rising demand needs to adopt a market retention strategy. The energy crisis promises to push many firms into this strategic situation. Examples of industries that are likely to be unable to meet existing demand include those producing and marketing synthetic fibers, clothing, steel, and plastics. All gasoline retailers will no doubt face this situation as long as fuel shortages and price controls remain.

Demand is declining in both positions C and D. The important question is whether the situation is relatively permanent or is caused by temporary environmental influences. For example, shortages of fuel could significantly reduce sales of recreational vehicles for several years. Alter-

---

[1] Philip Kotler, "The Major Tasks of Marketing Management," *Journal of Marketing*, vol. 37 (October 1973), p. 42.

natively, preferences for recreation may be so strong that consumers will seek ways (for example, using car pools and mass transit) to conserve enough fuel to make shorter trips in their campers. Thus, the strategic challenge for a firm like Winnebago Industries is assessment of the duration and severity of a decline in demand. Their strategic position is a market building situation as shown in cell C. A projected permanent decline in consumer demand would suggest diversification through product development or by other means.

A firm facing declining demand with inadequate resources and/or productive capacity is confronted with a need for both balancing and realignment strategies if the demand decline is considered permanent. Resource constraints would probably enable such a firm to achieve favorable cost-revenue relationships over the short term. Yet a permanent decline in demand would create the need for a realignment strategy aimed at development of new markets. Even before the energy crisis, Greyhound Corporation experienced a leveling off and probable long-term decline in bus ridership. For several years, Greyhound has pursued a diversification strategy to broaden its market and product-service base. Now, however, fuel shortages may revive declining markets for such services as bus travel, mass transit, and railroad passenger travel; Greyhound's bus service may shift into the growth strategy situation of position A.

Marketing management tasks

Recognizing the alternative strategy situations that can confront a given enterprise, what are the appropriate marketing management tasks to be performed? Marketing management consists of performing the management function in three major decision-making areas: analysis of the marketing environment in order to identify opportunities and constraints confronting the organization; market opportunity analysis leading to identification of specific targets; and development of an integrated marketing strategy (combination of product or service, price, advertising, sales force, and distribution channel) for successfully reaching target customers. Thus, marketing management is

. . . the analysis and planning leading to selection of one or more market targets—the design of an integrated marketing strategy to reach selected market targets—and implementation and control of planned strategy to achieve corporate marketing objectives.

Firms confronted with one or more of the four types of marketing strategies shown in the figure will find variations in both the importance of various marketing tasks as well as appropriate action guidelines. Thus, marketing management must match its efforts to the strategy position occupied by the firm. Within a general framework of sound marketing management practice, action guidelines should be developed for focusing decision making in essential areas.

ACTION GUIDELINES

The marketing management actions needed in the various market-resource situations clearly differ in degree rather than in kind. Yet, depending upon the opportunities and constraints confronting a given firm, the types and extent of executive and technical skills needed are likely to vary. Thus, it is important to develop an appropriate decision-making perspective toward a particular market-resource position.

Growth strategy

An environment calling for a growth strategy is certainly the most favorable situation to be experienced by an enterprise. Yet the marketing manager should be alert for possible environmental changes that could influence existing opportunities or impose new constraints. Effective ways should be developed to identify possible social, technological, economic, and governmental changes that may reduce market growth. Moreover, the rapid pace of environmental change that promises to occur in the next decade emphasizes the importance of managerial analysis of the marketing environment by all firms, regardless of their market-resource position. In support of this, one management authority has observed:

Social expectations and changing environment are altering and will continue to alter top management practice and structures. Increased emphasis on strategic planning and identification of opportunities and threats in the environment will put a company in a better position to exploit the opportunities and avoid the threats.[2]

Since environmental analysis is a capability that is not as well developed in many firms as are market analysis and marketing strategy design, the challenge seems clear.

Market opportunity analysis in a growth strategy situation should be directed toward identification and assessment of the various parts or segments that comprise an aggregate market. Market segmentation offers an effective strategy to a firm for strengthening market position and developing a competitive advantage. Segments offering the most promising economic and strategic advantages should be selected as primary market targets. For example, a small manufacturer of press-formed powder metal parts identified four user industries as prime targets for its products and concentrated company efforts on meeting the needs of these customer groups.

---

[2] George A. Steiner, "Changing Managerial Philosophies," *Business Horizons*, vol. 14 (June 1971), p. 10.

The one or more market targets selected by the enterprise provide the focus for design of integrated marketing strategies to serve customers comprising each target. A growth strategy situation should enable a firm to work toward the design of more effective strategies to serve target markets. Attention should be given to experimentation with alternative strategies. Various strategy questions should be raised and assessed: Should an industrial manufacturer shift from manufacturer representatives to a company sales force? Where should new product development efforts be concentrated? What role should advertising play in marketing strategy? Should a wholesale grocery firm expand into retail supermarkets? These are illustrative of the many strategy questions which confront marketing management in a growth strategy situation.

Market retention strategy

A firm in this strategic position is first concerned with forecasting the rate and nature of environmental changes that promise to ease resource and production constraints. Depending upon the extent and duration of shortages, buyers' preferences and purchasing behavior may shift so that difficulties will be encountered in attracting them back when resource limitations are eased. For example, food shortages lasting for long periods are likely to cause consumers to develop new preferences and eating habits, thus influencing market opportunities for manufacturers and distributors of food products.

Inability to serve all market needs accentuates the importance of identifying the various segments within a given market which a firm is best equipped to serve. A large printing firm is currently evaluating its customers to determine which groups offer the most promising long-term market commitments in terms of company capabilities and growth potential. Market segmentation shifts from a desirable strategy in a growth situation to a necessary approach for a market retention strategy.

Market opportunity analysis should result in the establishment of priority targets for focusing marketing strategy. Realignments of marketing resources (product, price, channels of distribution, advertising, and sales force) should be made to more effectively serve high priority targets. Emphasis should be placed on strengthening all aspects of marketing strategy. For example, realignment of targets is likely to require changes in sales force goals and deployment. Salesman training and development efforts can be used to facilitate shifts in market emphasis.

Management must guard against arbitrary cutbacks in marketing resources during a market retention situation simply because all available products can be sold relatively easily. This should be a period of strengthening marketing capabilities rather than eliminating them. Of course, relatively ineffective marketing efforts should not be continued.

Market building strategy

A firm confronted with a situation calling for a market building strategy faces a more difficult challenge than a firm facing either of the two situations previously described. A key question is whether the decline is likely to be temporary or long-term. Environmental analysis should be focused upon this question. For example, the large automobile manufacturers are no doubt carefully assessing probable trends in public versus private transportation. The energy crisis raises important issues about possible environmental trends and possible forced preference shifts in an automobile-oriented society. Environmental analysis is probably the most critical marketing management task in a market building strategy situation. In addition to assessing the nature and scope of a decline in existing markets, attention should also be given to environmental changes which could be favorable to new market development.

Segmentation strategy becomes vital in a market building situation. Firms with adequate capabilities to serve a declining market should be carefully assessing sectors of the market not now being served. An aggressive search should be made for new opportunities, perhaps in international markets. Emphasis should be upon broadening market coverage rather than restricting efforts to a few top priority market targets, as market retention strategy does. Yet such an approach should be designed to avoid seeking unprofitable market opportunities.

The task of marketing strategy design is concerned with achieving efficient use of marketing resources. Consideration should be given to possible elimination of actions which do not contribute to retaining present profitable business or to new market development. Expenditures should be reduced in noncritical areas. Correct assessment of market trends and opportunities provides an essential guide to determining the appropriate scale and allocation of marketing resources during a period when company capabilities exceed market opportunities. Depending upon the severity of market decline, cutbacks may be essential to achieving short- to intermediate-range company performance goals.

Balancing and realignment strategy

Although few firms are confronted with this strategy situation, those facing a market retention environment could be forced into a balancing situation in cases where supply and demand are allowed to achieve a balance through price increases. For example, severe price increases can substantially reduce customer purchases of various food products. Declining market demand in combination with product or service shortages may enable a firm to balance revenues and costs at a profitable level over the short run.

Nevertheless, estimates of the extent and duration of market decline are critical to longer-range corporate marketing strategy. It is probable that this situation will occur only on a short-term basis. In view of this, it is crucial for management to attempt to forecast which of the other three strategy positions the firm is likely to move into. Moreover, identification and assessment of environmental changes may indicate that diversification is appropriate.

Market opportunity analysis should be made of the various segments comprising a firm's total market. Targets should be selected where long-term opportunities are the most promising. Assessment should also be made of new product-market opportunities for firms where either markets are expected to decline for a long period and/or resource constraints are likely to continue indefinitely.

Marketing strategy design in a balancing situation should be concerned with the allocation of limited resources to the most promising long-term targets. Since the situation is likely to change over the short term, marketing management should assess existing strengths (and weaknesses) to provide a basis for responding to a possible new market-resource combination.

Summary of action guidelines

The major guidelines discussed for the four marketing strategy situations are summarized in Figure 2. This discussion should be viewed as illustrative of how marketing management can effectively contribute to various strategic positions. The purpose is to suggest the nature and types of marketing tasks appropriate under different market-product conditions and to outline a reasoning process for developing a perspective toward the management job. Also, the four strategy situations are not exhaustive in that various stages can exist between market growth and decline.

Various factors other than market situation and product (or service) availability are relevant in strategy formulation for a given firm. For example, whether a product is new to the marketplace or is in a mature stage of market development is an important element in marketing strategy design. Acknowledging this, the purpose here has been to examine the interaction of two primary dimensions related to corporate strategy which are influenced by a shortage of resources.

THE FUTURE

Marketing management can and should play a vital role in corporate strategy regardless of the market-product situation. Because of the increasing importance of environmental assessment and market opportunity analysis, marketing can contribute significantly to overall organiza-

FIGURE 2
Alternative marketing strategies, management tasks, and action guidelines

Strategy situation	Analysis of the marketing environment	Market opportunity analysis	Marketing strategy design
A. Growth strategy	Monitoring for possible changes that could reduce market growth (for example, social, technological, governmental, and economic changes).	Analysis of aggregate market to identify most promising targets (market segmentation); selection of segments with most promising economic and strategic advantages.	Development of most effective combinations of marketing resources for each selected market target. Experimentation with alternative marketing strategies.
B. Market retention strategy	Forecasting rate and nature of environmental changes that will ease resource and production constraints.	Assessment of existing market targets to determine most promising long-term market commitments. Establishment of priorities for focusing marketing strategy.	Realignment of marketing strategy to focus on high priority market targets; emphasis on strengthening all aspects of marketing strategy (for example, deployment and development of sales force).
C. Market building strategy	Forecasting of environmental trends to determine if market decline is likely to be temporary or long term. Identification of changes favorable for new market development.	Identification of most promising segments of market with regard to future growth. Search for new market opportunities (for example, possible international markets).	Emphasis on efficient use of marketing resources. Possible elimination of marketing actions which do not contribute to market development. Reduction of expenditures in noncritical areas.
D. Balancing and realignment strategies	Estimating extent and duration of market decline. Identification and assessment of environmental changes suggesting likely realignment direction.	Detailed assessment of various segments comprising total market. Focus on targets where long-term opportunities most promising. Assessment of new product-market opportunities.	Allocation of limited resources to most promising market targets. Assessment of company strengths for possible realignment to a different strategy situation.

tional strategy analysis and design. The marketing manager and his staff provide an important base of knowledge, experience, and information concerning the firm's external environment. Successful firms in the next decade will find it essential to give increased attention to the societal environment and to specific markets in order to identify strategy opportunities and constraints and to guide marketing efforts.

Current shortages and their impact upon market opportunities serve only to emphasize what successful business executives have recognized for many years: markets are rarely stable—change is an inherent characteristic in the marketplace. A more subtle implication of a continuing era of shortages is that marketing management must be more than selling. The important tasks of environmental assessment and market opportunity analysis can provide important information and direction to over-all corporate strategy development as well as to marketing strategy design. For example, shortages will force shifts in consumer preferences. Estimating the degree to which these preferences will remain after shortages are eased presents marketing management with a significant challenge. Effective information feedback from the marketplace will be essential in monitoring and predicting changes.

Those firms currently unable to meet customer demand with available products must guard against neglecting their marketing capabilities. Marketing management should be encouraged to develop strengths so that the firm maintains a differential advantage in the marketplace. As has been clearly demonstrated by the energy shortage, consumerism, pollution, and other societal influences, changing environmental conditions can rapidly turn an opportunity into a threat. Economic, social, technological, and governmental processes promise to increasingly force business to modify its marketing strategies in the decade ahead. A strong marketing management team will be essential to over-all corporate success.

QUESTIONS

1. Professor Cravens identified several industries that will face improved opportunities and several that will have problems as a result of shortages. Identify another industry in each of the two categories and explain what strategy a firm in each of the industries should follow.

2. Identify a firm or industry which should follow each of Cravens' four strategies (select new examples, i.e. ones not used by Cravens) and explain why.

3. Would you expect consumerism to increase or decrease in the near future as a result of shortages?

*4. Are the "marketing concept" (Reading 3) and "competition for differential advantage" (Reading 5) still relevant concepts in an era of shortages? Explain and illustrate.

2

Selecting target markets

MARKETING STRATEGY planning consists of two steps: (1) selection of a target market, and (2) development of an appropriate marketing mix for that target market. The readings in this section are concerned with the first step—selecting a target market. The next section focuses on the second step.

There are two important aspects in selecting a target market. One is what technique(s) to use to identify possible target markets, and the other is what dimensions should be included when segmenting a market. In other words, one aspect deals with methodology and the other deals with the variables which are involved. The articles in this section examine both of these aspects.

When selecting a target market, the firm must also evaluate the potential of each of the several possible markets with respect to its own resources and objectives. Most firms face more market opportunities than they can possibly serve. Thus, they must look at each possible target market and make estimates of the potential of each. The final readings in this section discuss approaches for estimating market potential.

Markets are people. But what kind of people? Traditional demographic methods of classifying people into markets have lost much of their ability to discriminate prospects from non-prospects, or poor prospects from good prospects. This article brings many of the traditional as well as newer methods of market definitions together into a conceptual whole.

9. WHAT IS A MARKET?*

Jack Z. Sissors

WHAT IS A market? Almost all marketing and advertising executives could answer the question, and yet many would give different answers to the same question.

Their answers might differ because their particular jobs require only the use of limited definitions of a market. For example, a media planner in an advertising agency might define a market either in terms of geographical places where purchasers live or with respect to number of demographic characteristics of purchasers.

On the other hand, a marketing manager might think of a market in more comprehensive terms. He might include geographical places, demographic characteristics, and also social-psychological descriptions of purchasers; identification of heavy-user groups; total number of units sold per year; or his brand's share of total sales of a given product class.

But it makes sense for all users of the term "market" to have a fairly comprehensive understanding of its meaning if they are going to communicate with each other on the same semantic levels. To the extent that there is consistency of meaning by various users of the term, there also is some possibility for effective communication.

The purpose of this article is to examine some of the ways markets may be defined, and then to present an overall view which may aid executives in making better decisions about markets.

---

* Reprinted with permission from the *Journal of Marketing*, published by the American Marketing Association, vol. 30, July 1966, pp. 17–21. At the time of writing, Dr. Sissors was a faculty member at the Medill School of Journalism of Northwestern University.

Traditional ways of looking at markets

A market usually is identified with a generic class of products. One hears of the beer market, the cakemix market, or the cigarette market. These are *product markets,* referring to individuals who in the past have purchased a given class of products.

For the sake of convenience, these individuals are classified into groups, all of whom have similar characteristics. The use of a product identification of a market carries with it an assumption that may or may not be valid. The assumption usually is made that those persons who *will* buy a product in the future will be very much like those who have purchased it in the past. This assumption is usually valid, because purchasers are likely to repurchase the same product in the future if their wants or needs have been satisfied.

But occasionally new purchasers are found to have different characteristics than past users. Sometimes through special promotional efforts an advertiser may attract new users to his brand. The new users, then, may be quite different from past users. So it might be better to use the term *"prospects"* rather than "market."

A more precise definition of a market however, would not be limited to a generic class of products, but to a specific subclass of that product. For that reason, the cigarette market often is identified by the particular kind of cigarettes under consideration. One hears of the menthol-cigarette market, or the filter-tip market, or some other subclassification. The more precisely that subclass product users are identified, the better is the possibility for understanding markets.

Finally, a subclass may be identified further by *brand name.* At this point the user of the term "market" has moved in his thinking from a general to a specific group of potential purchasers. There are times, of course, where any one of the product definitions may be more appropriate than any other one; but in general it is sensible to identify as precisely as possible which product market is under consideration.

Once the market has been identified by *generic product class, subclass,* or *brand,* purchasers may be described by a number of means: (1) size of the market; (2) geographical locations of purchasers; (3) demographic descriptions of purchasers; (4) social-psychological characteristics; (5) reasons why products are purchased; (6) who makes the actual purchases, and who influences the purchaser; (7) when purchases are made; (8) how purchasing is done. Even more descriptive classifications could be added, such as methods of distribution, effects of pricing changes, or results of sales promotion. But those numbered above are the most common.

1. Size of the market. One way to understand a market is to appreciate its size, that is, the number of purchasers. Size may be discussed in terms of the number of units sold, or in total dollar sales. Sometimes size of market may be discussed in terms of total number of purchasers or purchasing units, such as households. One of the most frequently discussed aspects of a product market deals not so much with its total size but with each brand's share (or proportion) of the total market.

2. Geographic locations of purchasers. Where do purchasers live? Many years ago the answer to this question might have been: "everywhere." The implication was that there were purchasers in every community in the country.

Today most marketers believe that a truly national market is a myth. Products are not sold in every community in the country, but in areas where sales potentials are good. So the locational description becomes important. The distribution of sales for a given product is identified by region, county, and city.

Furthermore, not only are the geographic areas identified by name but by population size. County-size and city-size identifications help market planners to know where to promote their products.

3. Demographic descriptions of purchasers. Who is the purchaser of a product or a brand? Here one finds groups of purchasers classified by age, sex, income, occupation, education, marital status, number of persons in the family, race, and religion. At times some special classification is necessary to describe product users because the above-mentioned data do not differentiate the purchasers from nonpurchasers.

4. Social-psychological characteristics. If a market consists of purchasers, then it should be possible to show how purchasers differ from nonpurchasers through one or more demographic variables.

Occasionally, however, demographic data do not reveal such differences. Then it becomes necessary to look for other ways of differentiating the market. Social-psychological classifications have been used at times for such purposes. Purchasers may be classified on the basis of social class, human values, degrees of introversion-extroversion, degrees of submissiveness-aggressiveness, degrees of venturesomeness-cautiousness, or other ways beyond the normal demographic classifications.

Social class, for example, is often used, because it can be shown that some products have status appeal which purchasers feel they will "inherit" if they own the product. This is not true for all products, nor for all persons. Also, the need for status varies a great deal from person to person, even within the same social class. Automobiles probably have high status value for some persons, and so a brand market may be defined in terms of the social class in which they belong. But not all persons buy automobiles as status symbols; some buy them principally as means of transportation, and social-psychological classifications of such purchasers would not be very meaningful.

No matter which classifications are used, social-psychological differentiation of purchasers may be important to the marketer for decision-making purposes. It may be especially important in advertising communication, where special copy appeals may have more meaning for one social-psychological class than for another.[1]

Furthermore, such classifications may be used in matching markets with media. If a clearer definition of purchasers is the result of social-psychological classification, then the selection process will require that marketers use media that reach the largest number of such classes at reasonable costs.

Then, too, social-psychological differentiation of markets may be helpful in learning how the needs and wants of purchasers differ from non-purchasers. It may help to explain why they buy one product or brand rather than another. Such differentiation may have two important consequences: (1) the manufacturer may improve his product or even produce a new product in order better to serve consumer wants; (2) the manufacturer may emphasize in his advertising those attributes of products about which consumers are most concerned, and eliminate those which have little or no influence in purchase decisions.

5. *Reasons why products are purchased.* Why people buy a generic product class or a special brand is of great interest. Involved in such an analysis might be a simple investigation of the major and minor uses of a product. Purchasers might be asked to provide reasons why they buy. Both direct and indirect questioning techniques are used to find answers to the question. Then it may be possible to describe the market on the basis of such reasons.

6. *Who makes the actual purchases, and who influences the purchaser.* One of the most important market descriptions concerns who buys the products, and who influences buying. This becomes important in devising advertising creative and media strategy. Should major emphasis be placed on communication to buyers, to influencers, or both?

7. *When purchases are made.* Often it is important to know at what times of the week, month, or year that the largest number of purchases are made. Such data help the market planner to direct his promotional activities to the best times of the year.

8. *How purchasing is done.* A description of the market also covers a number of important aspects: (a) whether buying is by impulse or by requests for specific brands; (b) most frequently purchased package size; (c) number of units purchased at one time; (d) frequency of purchase.

Other possibilities

There are occasions when it is convenient to identify markets on some other basis than the preceding classifications. Sometimes markets

---

[1] Wilbur Schramm, "How Communication Works," in *The Process and Effects of Mass Communication* (Urbana: University of Illinois Press, 1954), p. 13.

are identified by a single demographic variable such as age—the youth or teenage market, for example. At other times markets are identified by consumers' environments, such as farm or college markets.

However, these definitions are so general that they usually require additional explanations to make them meaningful. The fact that teen-agers or farmers can be singled out as the "targets" for the sale of products usually is too general to be of much value. It is more meaning-ful to discuss generally defined markets in terms of a specific product class, such as the teenage market for face soaps, or the farm market for work clothes.

Sometimes markets are defined in terms of geographical places. One hears of the Chicago market or the St. Louis market or the suburban market. Such terms are useful to media decision-makers, since media usually are disseminated from a central city surrounding a buying area. Then it is usually more appropriate to speak of advertising in the Chi-cago market than in the city of Chicago; the former term implies a broad buying area that extends far beyond the city limits.

A newer concept of market definition is that markets be identified by consumer needs rather than by product classes. Theodore Levitt argues that a market is composed of persons who have various needs and wants.[2] Ideally, when such needs or wants are recognized by the manufacturer, a special product is produced and sold to fulfill them. But manufacturers may be misled into thinking that their competition consists only of manufacturers of their class of product, when in reality their market is composed of all manufacturers who meet a special con-sumer need.

Levitt encourages the marketing executive to obtain a new perspective about his business by looking at his company as a "customer-satisfying process," rather than as a "goods-producing process."[3] This changed point of view enhances his company's chances for success; and it helps to identify competitors more clearly than through traditional methods. As an example, the competitors of railroad companies are not just other railway companies, but all companies that produce transportation means.

SOME QUALITATIVE DIMENSIONS

But the question still exists—what is the *quality* of the market? Once the market has been described by traditional means, it is possible to have a limited idea of its quality. Quality is defined here as *a measure of good sales potential*.

But traditional methods of market description tend to be rather crude

---

[2] Theodore Levitt, "Marketing Myopia," in *Harvard Business Review*, vol. 38 (July–August 1960), p. 55. (See Reading 2.)

[3] Same reference as footnote 2, at p. 45.

when it comes to identifying and separating the best prospects from the total market. Theoretically everyone in the market may be considered a prospect, although obviously some prospects are better than others.

The crudeness of traditional descriptive methods may be due to the techniques of grouping or classifying prospective purchasers. Each individual in a classification cannot be considered as good a prospect as any other individual; but grouping tends to obscure such differences. So, for every descriptive classification mentioned previously it might be possible to subdivide the market on a continuum from poor to good prospects.

Market segmentation

Which members of a market are the best prospects? The answer is: those segments in which most sales have been concentrated. The following demographic data for a cold cereal show that some segments are better than others:

Age group	Percent of total sales
Under 35	35.0
35 to 44	23.2
45 and over	41.8

The best prospects are located in the 45-and-over age group. Another good group of prospects would be in the under-35 classification. Obviously the 35-to-44 age group has the least potential.

But segmentation would not be made on only one descriptive category. Any classification which shows differences in purchasing volume could be segmented until new dimensions of the market appear. These new dimensions focus attention on the best prospects.

Segmentation may be used in another way also, that is, to divide the reasons for buying a given product or brand into subgroups. In other words, the best prospects may buy a product, but for different reasons.

One group may buy for the utility which they get out of the product. Another group buys because of the symbolic status value they see in the product. A third group may use the product in an unusual way. Finally, there may be other groups composed of those who buy for a combination of reasons.

Segmentation becomes important in identifying each group, and perhaps treating each group in a different marketing way both as to copy strategy and media strategy.

Concentration on the best potential market segments is a reasonable first consideration in decision-making. After a substantial basic market or core market has been established, the manufacturer then may turn his attention to market segments which have less potential. This decision may depend mostly on the degree to which the core market has been exploited. Strategy planners usually specify to what extent such segments should be tapped. The risk of failure is great when market energy is dissipated over too many poor prospect segments instead of concentrating on high sales-potential market segments.

Segmentation of the market may also be important from a production and inventory standpoint. Some models, sizes, and colors of a brand sell much better than others to various segments of the market. It is important to concentrate on the best segments with the most desirable kind of product.

Heavy user versus light user

Another method of looking at the market qualitatively is to consider the differences between heavy and light users. These differences can be plotted on a continuum from one extreme to the other. Thus, it has been demonstrated that users of a product may be divided into heavy-user and light-user halves.[4] For 18 product categories the heavy-half users bought much more of a product than did the light-half users; and in some cases the heavy-half users accounted for 91% of all sales made.

Quantity of products purchased might simply be studied on a continuum, however, showing percentages of purchases, and the largest segments noted. It may not be the top 50% but the top 25% that represent the best prospects. In fact, the best prospects might turn out to vary, through this analysis, for different kinds of products. A recent study shows that for some categories—like car rentals by men, liquid dietary products, and automatic-dishwasher detergents—less than 10% of all users made over 85% of all purchases.[5]

Frequency of purchase

Although frequency of purchase is a traditional descriptive measure, it was not related to heavy usage. It might be valuable, however, to study such a relationship. The study of heavy users indicates that the heavy-using households buy more often than the light users.[6]

If data on the relationships between purchase frequency were related to data on heavy-user market segments, then it might be possible to

---

[4] Dik Warren Twedt, "How Important to Market Strategy Is the 'Heavy User'?" *Journal of Marketing*, vol. 28 (January 1964), pp. 71–72.

[5] Norton Garfinkle, "The Marketing Value of Media Audiences—How to Pinpoint Your Prime Prospects," speech to the Association of National Advertisers, January 19, 1965. Published in mimeograph form in Information Service for Association of National Advertisers members, 16 pages plus 13-page Appendix.

[6] Same reference as footnote 4, at p. 71.

obtain newer insights into the total market. From such a market evaluation the best prospects might be identified more readily, and special promotional effort directed to only those who represent the "best prospects."

Brand loyalty

To what extent is there brand-switching or brand loyalty?

There are indications that heavy-half users buy more different brands and have less brand loyalty than the lighter half.[7] This may be worthwhile exploring in greater detail.

But since heavy-half users also have been found to buy more frequently, the relationship between all three dimensions should be studied simultaneously. In such a study it would be necessary to learn whether brand loyalty is related to frequency of purchase and/or heavy volume of purchases. Through a study of such relationships it may be possible to identify and separate the best prospects from the total market. In other words, brand loyalty is a qualitative market-dimension which may or may not be important in locating best prospects in the market.

Readiness to buy

Still another qualitative dimension of the market is the degree to which individuals or groups are ready to buy a product. In the case of a necessity such as food or low-priced impulse items, this dimension is less important than in the case of hard goods, which represent relatively large expenditures of money.

But it is obvious that those who intend to buy relatively soon are better prospects now than those who are not sure, or those who are not likely to buy. This dimension has been described as "a psychological continuum which runs from a firm intention to buy the item in the immediate future, to a firm intention not to buy the item, ever"; and it is important "to pay attention to how far from buying the unready consumer is."[8]

Readiness to buy helps the marketer to get another idea of the quality of the market, and this is but another dimension of "what is a market."

Other qualitative dimensions

The identification of favorable versus unfavorable attitudes toward a class of products or a brand, if plotted on a continuum, might show

[7] Dik Warren Twedt, "How to Select Media with Heavy Product Users," *Media/scope,* vol. 8 (November 1964), pp. 95–100, at p. 95.

[8] William D. Wells, "Measuring Readiness to Buy," *Harvard Business Review,* vol. 39 (July–August 1961), pp. 81–87, at p. 81.

qualitative dimensions of a market. The effect of price on various segments of the market could also be used. No matter what technique is employed, though, there is certainly a need to go beyond the traditional methods of market description in order to learn "what is a market."

SO WHAT?

So, what is a market? It is many things related to selling products which meet consumers' needs and wants. Most important, however, a market is a group of potential purchasers of a given product and brand.

In order to understand and make decisions about a market, it is necessary to be able to differentiate prospects from nonprospects. It is possible to make some differentiations on the basis of physical and psychological characteristics; but there is a need for better differentiation. In a dynamic society such as ours, differences between prospects and nonprospects have become "blurred" when studied on the basis of traditional marketing definitions.

Differences based on objective distinctions may have lost their significance to such an extent that newer means are necessary to understand a market.[9] For that reason the marketer needs to consider the *qualitative* dimensions of purchaser groups. As time goes on, newer methods of differentiation will be discovered which may provide even more understanding.

It follows, therefore, that better understanding may lead to better decision-making about markets. Probably the most important key to understanding the market lies in the *willingness to study a market as a conceptual whole* rather than as a collection of fragmentary parts.

A GRAPHIC PRESENTATION OF A MARKET

Finally, in order to bring the many dimensions of a market together into sharper focus, consider Figure 1.

It shows the market with two main dimensions: physical and behavioral. Each of these two main groups has been subdivided into the categories discussed previously.

A magnifying glass is shown as a means of examining the market, so as to focus attention on the best prospects. All of the criteria for determining best prospects are located in the magnifying glass.

Figure 1 points up the need for considering all of the many ramifications of the term "market." To consider any one only, to the exclusion of others, limits the full perspective of "what is a market," and can be expensive.

---

[9] Darrell Blaine Lucas, and Steuart Henderson Britt, *Measuring Advertising Effectiveness* (New York: McGraw-Hill Book Company, 1963), p. 302.

FIGURE 1
A graphic picture of a market

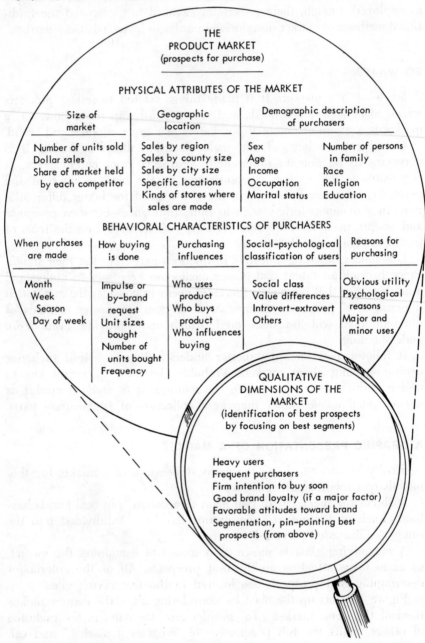

THE
PRODUCT MARKET
(prospects for purchase)

PHYSICAL ATTRIBUTES OF THE MARKET

Size of market	Geographic location	Demographic description of purchasers	
Number of units sold	Sales by region	Sex	Number of persons
Dollar sales	Sales by county size	Age	in family
Share of market held	Sales by city size	Income	Race
by each competitor	Specific locations	Occupation	Religion
	Kinds of stores where	Marital status	Education
	sales are made		

BEHAVIORAL CHARACTERISTICS OF PURCHASERS

When purchases are made	How buying is done	Purchasing influences	Social-psychological classification of users	Reasons for purchasing
Month	Impulse or	Who uses	Social class	Obvious utility
Week	by-brand	product	Value differences	Psychological
Season	request	Who buys	Introvert-extrovert	reasons
Day of week	Unit sizes	product	Others	Major and
	bought	Who influences		minor uses
	Number of	buying		
	units bought			
	Frequency			

QUALITATIVE
DIMENSIONS OF THE
MARKET
(identification of best prospects
by focusing on best segments)

Heavy users
Frequent purchasers
Firm intention to buy soon
Good brand loyalty (if a major factor)
Favorable attitudes toward brand
Segmentation, pin-pointing best
prospects (from above)

QUESTIONS

1. What is a market?
2. Why is it necessary to use so many different dimensions to describe a market?
3. If it is not possible to use more than 3 or 4 dimensions to segment a market, how would you decide which ones to use? Illustrate for a big purchase, such as a new car.
4. Pick a specific cereal product you have bought or selected recently. Then, using Sissors' categories, pick out the dimensions you feel are most relevant for explaining your decision. Then list any other dimensions about you which could be helpful in marketing mix planning to sell you this product. Explain the implications for marketing mix planning.
°5. Would the same kinds of dimensions be relevant for the non-business organizations discussed by Kotler and Levy (Reading 4)?

There are different ways to segment a market. While most of the approaches can be valuable, few get at the basic reason a person spends money to buy a product or service—that is, the benefits a person expects to receive from the purchase. Haley, in the following article, discusses an approach called benefit segmentation which focuses specifically on this factor.

---

10. BENEFIT SEGMENTATION: A DECISION-ORIENTED RESEARCH TOOL*

Russell I. Haley

MARKET SEGMENTATION has been steadily moving toward center stage as a topic of discussion in marketing and research circles. Hardly a conference passes without at least one session devoted to it. Moreover, in March the American Management Association held a three-day conference entirely concerned with various aspects of the segmentation problem.

---

* Reprinted with permission from the *Journal of Marketing*, published by the American Marketing Association, vol. 32, July 1968, pp. 30–35. At the time of writing, Mr. Haley was Vice President and Corporate Research Director of D'Arcy Advertising in New York City.

According to Wendell Smith, "Segmentation is based upon developments on the demand side of the market and represents a rational and more precise adjustment of product and marketing effort to consumer or user requirements."[1] The idea that all markets can be profitably segmented has now received almost as widespread acceptance as the marketing concept itself. However, problems remain. In the extreme, a marketer can divide up his market in as many ways as he can describe his prospects. If he wishes, he can define a left-handed segment, or a blue-eyed segment, or a German-speaking segment. Consequently, current discussion revolves largely around which of the virtually limitless alternatives is likely to be most productive.

Segmentation methods

Several varieties of market segmentation have been popular in the recent past. At least three kinds have achieved some degree of prominence. Historically, perhaps the first type to exist was geographic segmentation. Small manufacturers who wished to limit their investments, or whose distribution channels were not large enough to cover the entire country, segmented the U.S. market, in effect, by selling their products only in certain areas.

However, as more and more brands became national, the second major system of segmentation—demographic segmentation—became popular. Under this philosophy targets were defined as younger people, men, or families with children. Unfortunately, a number of recent studies have shown that demographic variables such as age, sex, income, occupation and race are, in general, poor predictors of behavior and, consequently, less than optimum bases for segmentation strategies.[2]

More recently, a third type of segmentation has come into increasing favor—volume segmentation. The so-called "heavy half" theory, popularized by Dik Twedt of the Oscar Mayer Company,[3] points out that in most product categories one-half of the consumers account for around 80% of the consumption. If this is true, the argument goes, shouldn't knowledgeable marketers concentrate their efforts on these high-volume consumers? Certainly they are the most *valuable* consumers.

---

[1] Wendell R. Smith, "Product Differentiation and Market Segmentation as Alternative Product Strategies," *Journal of Marketing*, vol. 21 (July 1956), pp. 3–8.

[2] Ronald E. Frank, "Correlates of Buying Behavior for Grocery Products," *Journal of Marketing*, vol. 31 (October 1967), pp. 48–53; Ronald E. Frank, William Massy, and Harper W. Boyd, Jr., "Correlates of Grocery Product Consumption Rates," *Journal of Marketing Research*, vol. 4 (May 1967), pp. 184–90; and Clark Wilson, "Homemaker Living Patterns and Marketplace Behavior—A Psychometric Approach," in John S. Wright and Jac L. Goldstucker, eds., *New Ideas for Successful Marketing*, Proceedings of 1966 World Congress (Chicago: American Marketing Association, June, 1966), pp. 305–31.

[3] Dik Warren Twedt, "Some Practical Applications of the 'Heavy Half' Theory" (New York: Advertising Research Foundation 10th Annual Conference, October 6, 1964).

The trouble with this line of reasoning is that not all heavy consumers are usually available to the same brand—because they are not all seeking the same kinds of benefits from a product. For example, heavy coffee drinkers consist of two types of consumers—those who drink chain store brands and those who drink premium brands. The chain store customers feel that all coffees are basically alike and, because they drink so much coffee, they feel it is sensible to buy a relatively inexpensive brand. The premium brand buyers, on the other hand, feel that the few added pennies which coffees like Yuban, Martinson's, Chock Full O'Nuts, and Savarin cost are more than justified by their fuller taste. Obviously, these two groups of people, although they are both members of the "heavy half" segment, are not equally good prospects for any one brand, nor can they be expected to respond to the same advertising claims.

These three systems of segmentation have been used because they provide helpful guidance in the use of certain marketing tools. For example, geographic segmentation, because it describes the market in a discrete way, provides definite direction in media purchases. Spot TV, spot radio, and newspapers can be bought for the geographical segment selected for concentrated effort. Similarly, demographic segmentation allows media to be bought more efficiently since demographic data on readers, viewers, and listeners are readily available for most media vehicles. Also, in some product categories demographic variables are extremely helpful in differentiating users from non-users, although they are typically less helpful in distinguishing between the users of various brands. The heavy-half philosophy is especially effective in directing dollars toward the most important parts of the market.

However, each of these three systems of segmentation is handicapped by an underlying disadvantage inherent in its nature. All are based on an ex-post facto analysis of the kinds of people who make up various segments of a market. They rely on *descriptive* factors rather than *causal* factors. For this reason they are not efficient predictors of future buying behavior, and it is future buying behavior that is of central interest to marketers.

BENEFIT SEGMENTATION

An approach to market segmentation whereby it is possible to identify market segments by causal factors rather than descriptive factors, might be called "benefit segmentation." The belief underlying this segmentation strategy is that the benefits which people are seeking in consuming a given product are the basic reasons for the existence of true market segments. Experience with this approach has shown that benefits sought by consumers determine their behavior much more accurately than do demographic characteristics or volume of consumption.

This does not mean that the kinds of data gathered in more traditional types of segmentation are not useful. Once people have been classified into segments in accordance with the benefits they are seeking, each segment is contrasted with all of the other segments in terms of its demography, its volume of consumption, its brand perceptions, its media habits, its personality and life-style, and so forth. In this way, a reasonably deep understanding of the people who make up each segment can be obtained. And by capitalizing on this understanding, it is possible to reach them, to talk to them in their own terms, and to present a product in the most favorable light possible.

The benefit segmentation approach is not new. It has been employed by a number of America's largest corporations since it was introduced in 1961.[4] However, case histories have been notably absent from the literature because most studies have been contracted for privately, and have been treated confidentially.

The benefit segmentation approach is based upon being able to measure consumer value systems in detail, together with what the consumer thinks about various brands in the product category of interest. While this concept seems simple enough, operationally it is very complex. There is no simple straightforward way of handling the volumes of data that have to be generated. Computers and sophisticated multivariate attitude measurement techniques are a necessity.

Several alternative statistical approaches can be employed, among them the so-called "Q" technique of factor analysis, multi-dimensional scaling, and other distance measures.[5] All of these methods relate the ratings of each respondent to those of every other respondent and then seek clusters of individuals with similar rating patterns. If the items rated are potential consumer benefits, the clusters that emerge will be groups of people who attach similar degrees of importance to the various benefits. Whatever the statistical approach selected, the end result of the analysis is likely to be between three and seven consumer segments, each representing a potentially productive focal point for marketing efforts.

Each segment is identified by the benefits it is seeking. However, it is the *total configuration* of the benefits sought which differentiates one segment from another, rather than the fact that one segment is seeking one particular benefit and another a quite different benefit. Individual benefits are likely to have appeal for several segments. In fact, the research that has been done thus far suggests that most people would like as many benefits as possible. However, the *relative* importance they attach to individual benefits can differ importantly and, accordingly, can be used as an effective lever in segmenting markets.

---

[4] Russell I. Haley, "Experimental Research on Attitudes toward Shampoos," an unpublished paper (February 1961).

[5] Ronald E. Frank and Paul E. Green, "Numerical Taxonomy in Marketing Analysis: A Review Article," *Journal of Marketing Research*, vol. 5 (February 1968), pp. 83–98.

Of course, it is possible to determine benefit segments intuitively as well as with computers and sophisticated research methods. The kinds of brilliant insights which produced the Mustang and the first 100-millimeter cigarette have a good chance of succeeding whenever marketers are able to tap an existing benefit segment.

However, intuition can be very expensive when it is mistaken. Marketing history is replete with examples of products which someone felt could not miss. Over the longer term, systematic benefit segmentation research is likely to have a higher proportion of successes.

But is benefit segmentation practical? And is it truly operational? The answer to both of these questions is "yes." In effect, the crux of the problem of choosing the best segmentation system is to determine which has the greatest number of practical marketing implications. An example should show that benefit segmentation has a much wider range of implications than alternative forms of segmentation.

An example of benefit segmentation

While the material presented here is purely illustrative to protect the competitive edge of companies who have invested in studies of this kind, it is based on actual segmentation studies. Consequently, it is quite typical of the kinds of things which are normally learned in the course of a benefit segmentation study.

The toothpaste market has been chosen as an example because it is one with which everyone is familiar. Let us assume that a benefit segmentation study has been done and four major segments have been identified—one particularly concerned with decay prevention, one with brightness of teeth, one with the flavor and appearance of the product, and one with price. A relatively large amount of supplementary information has also been gathered (Table 1) about the people in each of these segments.

The decay prevention segment, it has been found, contains a disproportionately large number of families with children. They are seriously concerned about the possibility of cavities and show a definite preference for fluoride toothpaste. This is reinforced by their personalities. They tend to be a little hypochondriacal and, in their life-styles, they are less socially-oriented than some of the other groups. This segment has been named The Worriers.

The second segment, comprised of people who show concern for the brightness of their teeth, is quite different. It includes a relatively large group of young marrieds. They smoke more than average. This is where the swingers are. They are strongly social and their life-style patterns are very active. This is probably the group to which toothpastes such as Macleans or Plus White or Ultra Brite would appeal. This segment has been named The Sociables.

In the third segment, the one which is particularly concerned with

TABLE 1
Toothpaste market segment description

Segment name	The sensory segment	The sociables	The worriers	The independent segment
Principal benefit sought . . .	Flavor, product appearance	Brightness of teeth	Decay prevention	Price
Demographic strengths	Children	Teens, young people	Large families	Men
Special behavioral characteristics	Users of spearmint flavored tooth-paste	Smokers	Heavy users	Heavy users
Brands disproportionately flavored	Colgate, Stripe	Macleans, Plus White, Ultra Brite	Crest	Brands on sale
Personality characteristics . .	High self-involvement	High sociability	High hypochondriasis	High autonomy
Life-style characteristics . . .	Hedonistic	Active	Conservative	Value-oriented

the flavor and appearance of the product, a large portion of the brand deciders are children. Their use of spearmint toothpaste is well above average. Stripe has done relatively well in this segment. They are more ego-centered than other segments, and their life-style is outgoing but not to the extent of the swingers. They will be called The Sensory Segment.

The fourth segment, the price-oriented segment, shows a predominance of men. It tends to be above average in terms of toothpaste usage. People in this segment see very few meaningful differences between brands. They switch more frequently than people in other segments and tend to buy a brand on sale. In terms of personality, they are cognitive and they are independent. They like to think for themselves and make brand choices on the basis of their judgment. They will be called The Independent Segment.

MARKETING IMPLICATIONS OF BENEFIT
SEGMENTATION STUDIES

Both copy directions and media choices will show sharp differences depending upon which of these segments is chosen as the target—The Worriers, The Sociables, The Sensory Segment, or The Independent Segment. For example, the tonality of the copy will be light if The Sociable Segment or The Sensory Segment is to be addressed. It will be more serious if the copy is aimed at The Worriers. And if The Independent Segment is selected, it will probably be desirable to use rational, two-sided arguments. Of course, to talk to this group at all it will be necessary to have either a price edge or some kind of demonstrable product superiority.

The depth-of-sell reflected by the copy will also vary, depending upon the segment which is of interest. It will be fairly intensive for The Worrier Segment and for The Independent Segment, but much more superficial and mood-oriented for The Sociable and Sensory Segments.

Likewise, the setting will vary. It will focus on the product for The Sensory Group, on socially-oriented situations for The Sociable Group, and perhaps on demonstration or on competitive comparisons for The Independent Group.

Media environments will also be tailored to the segments chosen as targets. Those with serious environments will be used for The Worrier and Independent Segments, and those with youthful, modern and active environments for The Sociable and the Sensory Groups. For example, it might be logical to use a larger proportion of television for The Sociable and Sensory Groups, while The Worriers and Independents might have heavier print schedules.

The depth-of-sell needed will also be reflected in the media choices. For The Worrier and Rational Segments longer commercials—perhaps 60-second commercials—would be indicated, while for the other two groups shorter commercials and higher frequency would be desirable.

Of course, in media selection the facts that have been gathered about the demographic characteristics of the segment chosen as the target would also be taken into consideration.

The information in Table 1 also has packaging implications. For example, it might be appropriate to have colorful packages for The Sensory Segment, perhaps aqua (to indicate fluoride) for The Worrier Group, and gleaming white for The Sociable Segment because of their interest in bright white teeth.

It should be readily apparent that the kinds of information normally obtained in the course of a benefit segmentation study have a wide range of marketing implications. Sometimes they are useful in suggesting physical changes in a product. For example, one manufacturer discovered that his product was well suited to the needs of his chosen target with a single exception in the area of flavor. He was able to make a relatively inexpensive modification in his product and thereby strengthen his market position.

The new product implications of benefit segmentation studies are equally apparent. Once a marketer understands the kinds of segments that exist in his market, he is often able to see new product opportunities or particularly effective ways of positioning the products emerging from his research and development operation.

Similarly, benefit segmentation information has been found helpful in providing direction in the choice of compatible point-of-purchase materials and in the selection of the kinds of sales promotions which are most likely to be effective for any given market target.

GENERALIZATIONS FROM BENEFIT SEGMENTATION STUDIES

A number of generalizations are possible on the basis of the major benefit segmentation studies which have been conducted thus far. For example, the following general rules of thumb have become apparent:

It is easier to take advantage of market segments that already exist than to attempt to create new ones. Some time ago the strategy of product differentiation was heavily emphasized in marketing textbooks. Under this philosophy it was believed that a manufacturer was more or less able to create new market segments at will by making his product somewhat different from those of his competitors. Now it is generally recognized that fewer costly errors will be made if money is first invested in consumer research aimed at determining the present contours of the market. Once this knowledge is available, it is usually most efficient to tailor marketing strategies to existing consumer-need patterns.

No brand can expect to appeal to all consumers. The very act of attracting one segment may automatically alienate others. A corollary to this principle is that any marketer who wishes to cover a market fully must offer consumers more than a single brand. The flood of new brands which have recently appeared on the market is concrete recognition of this principle.

A company's brands can sometimes cannibalize each other but need not necessarily do so. It depends on whether or not they are positioned against the same segment of the market. Ivory Snow sharply reduced Ivory Flakes' share of market, and the Ford Falcon cut deeply into the sales of the standard size Ford because, in each case, the products were competing in the same segments. Later on, for the same companies, the Mustang was successfully introduced with comparatively little damage to Ford; and the success of Crest did not have a disproportionately adverse effect on Gleem's market position because, in these cases, the segments to which the products appealed were different.

New and old products alike should be designed to fit *exactly* the needs of some segment of the market. In other words, they should be aimed at people seeking a specific combination of benefits. It is a marketing truism that you sell people one at a time—that you have to get *someone* to buy your product before you get *anyone* to buy it. A substantial group of people must be interested in your specific set of benefits before you can make progress in a market. Yet, many products attempt to aim at two or more segments simultaneously. As a result, they are not able to maximize their appeal to any segment of the market, and they run the risk of ending up with a dangerously fuzzy brand image.

Marketers who adopt a benefit segmentation strategy have a distinct competitive edge. If a benefit segment can be located which is seeking exactly the kinds of satisfactions that one marketer's brand can offer better than any other brand, the marketer can almost certainly dominate the purchases of that segment. Furthermore, if his competitors are looking at the market in terms of traditional types of segments, they may not even be aware of the existence of the benefit segment which he has chosen as his market target. If they are ignorant in this sense, they will be at a loss to explain the success of his brand. And it naturally follows that if they do not understand the reasons for his success, the kinds of people buying his brand, and the benefits they are obtaining from it, his competitors will find it very difficult to successfully attack the marketer's position.

An *understanding* of the benefit segments which exist within a market can be used to advantage when competitors introduce new products. Once the way in which consumers are positioning the new product has been determined, the likelihood that it will make major inroads into segments of interest can be assessed, and a decision can be made on whether or not counteractions of any kind are required. If the new product appears to be assuming an ambiguous position, no money need be invested in defensive measures. However, if it appears that the new product is ideally suited to the needs of an important segment of the market, the manufacturer in question can introduce a new competitive product of his own, modify the physical properties of existing brands, change his advertising strategy, or take whatever steps appear appropriate.

Types of segments uncovered through benefit segmentation studies

It is difficult to generalize about the types of segments which are apt to be discovered in the course of a benefit segmentation study. To a large extent, the segments which have been found have been unique to the product categories being analyzed. However, a few types of segments have appeared in two or more private studies. Among them are the following:

The Status Seeker.	A group which is very much concerned with the prestige of the brands purchased.
The Swinger	A group which tries to be modern and up to date in all of its activities. Brand choices reflect this orientation.
The Conservative	A group which prefers to stick to large successful companies and popular brands.
The Rational Man.	A group which looks for benefits such as economy, value, durability, etc.
The Inner-directed Man	A group which is especially concerned with self-concept. Members consider themselves to have a sense of humor, to be independent and/or honest.
The Hedonist	A group which is concerned primarily with sensory benefits.

Some of these segments appear among the customers of almost all products and services. However, there is no guarantee that a majority of them or, for that matter, any of them exist in any given product category. Finding out whether they do and, if so, what should be done about them is the purpose of benefit segmentation research.

CONCLUSION

The benefit segmentation approach is of particular interest because it never fails to provide fresh insight into markets. As was indicated in the toothpaste example cited earlier, the marketing implications of this analytical research tool are limited only by the imagination of the person using the information a segmentation study provides. In effect, when segmentation studies are conducted, a number of smaller markets emerge instead of one large one. Moreover, each of these smaller markets can be subjected to the same kinds of thorough analyses to which total markets have been subjected in the past. The only difference—a crucial one—is that the total market was a heterogeneous conglomeration of sub-groups. The so-called average consumer existed only in the minds of some marketing people. When benefit segmentation is used, a number of relatively homogeneous segments are uncovered. And, because they are homogeneous, descriptions of them in terms of averages are much more appropriate and meaningful as marketing guides.

QUESTIONS

1. What is the difference between a descriptive dimension and a causal dimension? Which should prove a better tie to future purchases? If so, should we ever use the other type for segmenting markets?

2. Take a particular consumer goods market, the ice cream market for example, and develop a table like Table 1 for this market. (Use your own judgment—do not conduct a survey, etc.).

3. For each of the segments you listed in question 2, suggest what a good marketing mix might look like.

*4. Does "benefit segmentation" have any relevance for Kotler and Levy's non-business organizations (Reading 4)? If so, illustrate. If not, explain why.

*5. Will "benefit segmentation" thinking be as relevant in a shortage economy (See Reading 8)? Explain.

Life-style or psychographic characteristics, which go beyond demographics, can be valuable bases of market segmentation. Use of these characteristics is relatively new and somewhat controversial. This edited reading provides several good examples of the output of such work and how it can help advertisers select media.

11. ARE MEDIA DECIDERS THINKING LIFE-STYLE?*

WHAT'S HAPPENED to psychographics?

The correlation of individual self-image with brand and media preferences was being talked up a few years ago as the ultimate method for matching media to market objectives.

In its dazzling promise psychographics appeared likely to surpass demographics and other head counts in producing positive and predictable marketing results. But like atomic energy and its potential for unlimited power, psychographics still remains just over the horizon for most advertisers as a practical means for answering the problems of the media market place, where research often offers questionable guidance.

Views of the usefulness of psychographics vary depending on the ability of marketing and media people to devise specific applications. The Bureau of Advertising, for example, finds the utility of psychographics is limited in assessing daily newspaper audiences. But Dr. Leo Bogart, of the Bureau, says psychographics can be useful in formulating copy appeals for population segments for specific products. The Bureau points out that all segments of the population, regardless of how they are defined in terms of life style, read newspapers. And in Los Angeles, the *Times* is applying its own psychographic study to that sprawling market as an aid to copywriters.

Dewey Yeager, ad manager at Nestle, told Media Decisions that psychographics played a major role in determining target markets for instant coffee and tea brands. On the other hand, Henry Hayes, media director at Pepsi Cola, characterized psychographics as "a long run for a short slide."

The difference between companies that find psychographics helpful and those that don't seems to be that the ones who find it helpful are looking for broad directives on which they can build reasoned judgments whereas those that don't are looking for specific audience-matching tools.

Henry Arnsdorf, ad director for Prudential Insurance Co. commented recently, "We know too much about how many, and too little about who."

And Don Osell, ad manager for Green Giant, told a meeting of media representatives, "We want to know more about the reader of your magazine, who he is."

---

* Reprinted with permission from *Media Decisions*, February 1974, pp. 62–65, 96–99.

Media exposure of four housewife types

	Happy go lucky, not price conscious	Ex-career woman, housewife	Abject follower	Happy, home oriented, price conscious
Watch TV five or more hours per day	16%	22%	40%	43%
Magazines Read				
Time	18	32	13	13
Newsweek	15	22	12	7
TV Guide	46	59	54	71
Reader's Digest	24	44	33	39
Life	32	53	44	35
Ladies Home Journal	44	39	37	37
Better Homes & Gardens	20	30	28	39
Vogue	12	9	7	7
True Story	1	1	14	15
Redbook	20	38	25	26

Source: Data from questionnaire prepared by Motivational Programmers, Inc. for one of its manufacturer clients. The four categories of housewives were decided upon from their life-styles after results were tabulated. Note that heavy TV viewing does not affect quantity of magazine reading.

Index of characteristics of TV show viewers

		Index
Affectionate	Love American Style	132
Creative	Sixth Sense	164
Awkward	Odd Couple	225
Dominating	American Sportsmen	159
Self-Assured	Mod Squad	135
Reserved	Doris Day Show	147
Stubborn	Jimmy Stewart Show	157
Sociable	Dean Martin Show	119
Trustworthy	O'Hara, U.S. Treasury	115
Funny	Courtship of Eddie's Father	159
Efficient	Rowan & Martin	132
	New Dick Van Dyke Show	132
Frank	Face the Nation	138
	Meet the Press	137
	Issues and Answers	181

Index 100-average viewer of show.
Source: Axiom Market Research Bureau.

Arnsdorf, Osell, and others want to know more about the life style and the psychological set of specific media audiences. But two questions have haunted the possible users of psychographics to whom broad answers are not enough:

1. Can a market be segmented accurately by psychographics?
2. Can a media mix be postulated on a psychographic profile?

A third question is sometimes asked, but this is more a matter of semantics than anything else: Just what is a psychographic element? Some think of it as an observable matter of life style (like going to the theatre a lot, being excessively active in hometown charity work, traveling a lot for pleasure). Others define psychographic elements as purely psychological traits (like being an extrovert or an introvert, or being either a hypochondriac or a hair-shirt). And some mediamen tend to equate the two, thinking of life-style and psychography as synonymous. Obviously the two have their relationships, but the current trend among researchers is to treat them separately.

No replacement for demos

In talking to media people at agencies and brand managers in client organizations, Media Decisions frequently found the belief that psychographics and/or life style information is of value as additional insight. But most mediamen do not believe that this additional knowledge will supplant the demographic data or become the primary input for media decision-making.

Dr. Timothy Joyce of Axiom Market Research Bureau (AMRB) did considerable work with psychographic research in England before moving into the spotlight as an audience demographic expert and creator of TGI, the Target Group Index, here in the U.S.

"There is more hope of getting at least an approximate measure of advertising effectiveness," he says, "if the determinants of choice in both demographic and psychographic terms are accounted for.

"Previous research in Britain, where TGI has been in operation since 1968, has shown two things:

"1. Links between brand choice and media choice are strong and persistent over time.

"2. On average, only some 30% or 40% of the variances in these links can be accounted for by demographic characteristics which the brand franchise and the media audience have in common.

"It seems likely, on the basis of inspection of very many detailed relationships, that self-expressive choice on the part of consumers is to some extent responsible for these links (i.e. the propensity of consumers to choose brands they *feel* best match their personalities as they see them)."

Joyce authored a major work on the subject, "Personality Classification of Consumers," while he was still in England.

In it he wrote: "Links with viewing certain TV programs are often very clear cut. In many cases one has the impression that the self-concept of the viewer is indeed the image of the program itself. This would support the hypothesis that consumer choice does involve matching of self-image with the image of the chosen object."

Psychographics of a headache

Psychographic profilers have defined many life-style segments. Now they can even describe the psychographics of a headache.

This unique profile was produced for the Newspaper Advertising Bureau. It shows who is most likely to get a headache, and accordingly, who is a ready target for a headache remedy.

Women, it showed, suffer more headaches than men. The report shows 76% of women reported using a headache remedy in a four week period, as compared with 63% of men.

Among women, The Indulger is the most frequent user of headache remedies. The study says, "this kind of woman usually finds housework boring. She escapes from daily pressures by acquiring material things." Nearly 82% of The Indulgers, who make up one-sixth of the adult female population, took headache remedies 6.7 times in a four week span.

Among men, The Sophisticated Man got headaches most often, but the less frequent headaches of The Quiet Family Man were more violent.

The Sophisticated Man (10% of the adult male population) is intellectual, concerned about social issues, and admires men with artistic and intellectual achievements. He reaches for a headache remedy 7.2 times in a four week period.

The Quiet Family Man, a self sufficient individual who wants to be left alone and is basically shy, resorts to headache remedies 3.8 times in a four week period. This type represents 8% of the adult male population.

Among Sophisticated Men, 67% took headache remedies in a four week period as compared with 53% for Quiet Family Men.

These psychographic findings were based on a study of 4,000 men and women in 2,500 households.

The study was carried out for the Bureau of Advertising and can be obtained from the bureau in full detail.

Joyce goes on to conclude that "the links between media exposure and brand choice can arise in a number of ways. Partly they are accidental. Partly they presumably reflect demographic and psychographic links which operate as independent causal variables. Partly they may reflect advertising effectiveness itself, which (where it exists) will bring about a relationship between exposure to media carrying the advertising and use of the brand advertised."

One researcher, John Henderson, developed a report on the "Life Style of the Top 100 Markets," that was published in Media Decisions in October 1971. The research was sponsored by RTVR (RKO Television Representatives, Inc.) when Tom Judge was vp-general manager there. John based his description of market life styles on the demographics reported in the 1970 U.S. Census and the change in demos since the 1960 Census. In his analysis he characterized the markets as *experimental, transitional,* or *traditional*—and also demonstrated the differences in some markets between families living in the suburbs and the city centers.

Henderson based his reasoned analysis of life-style on nine indicators: Age, family size, income, education, homes, neighborhoods, mobility, family background, and courtroom encounters—all factors on which hard data was supplied by the Census. "It's important to note," John told us, "that the classification in each market is based on an analysis of all indicators. Any single indicator by itself can be grossly misleading."

One of the noteworthy things that John Henderson did in this study was to relate family demographics to family life-style in geographic segments. The result was a practical life-style tool for marketing and media planners.

How brand managers apply psychographics

Although agencies and even research people are uncertain of the value of psychographic or life style data, there are those on the brand manager side who have seen its potential and put it to use. Among them are Alka Seltzer, American Motors and Sara Lee. And a big name among them is that of Dr. Emanuel Demby, the godfather of psychographics and board chairman at Motivational Programmers Inc., in Princeton, N.J.

Cal Hadock, director of research at Miles Laboratories, Elkhart, Ind., is impressed by the ability of Dr. Demby and his firm to draw marketing inferences from the numbers through psychographics.

"For our purposes, psychographics is an extraordinary new tool though still in its infancy. We have found it useful in marketing Alka-Seltzer. It has enabled us to find people with a predisposition to buy our product. It has given us new insights into our over-all marketing strategy with Alka-Seltzer. We use it for both copywriting approaches and for the determining of media considerations."

Bill McKenna, group marketing manager for the Kitchens of Sara Lee, in Chicago, had this to say:

"Sure, we believe in psychographics.

"We had Dr. Demby do a market definition study for us and we achieved some very worthwhile results. It was eye-opening to see how two demographically matched groups could differ so in their life style, outlook and buying attitudes.

"The study caused some major changes in our marketing procedures for Sara Lee. First of all, there was a change in our copy theme. Formerly we depended solely on appetite appeal. Now we are introducing other elements. And we are considering alternative media. We are taking another look at magazines and daytime TV."

Dr. Demby also had a hand in American Motors presentation of the strong car warranty, the Buyer Protection Plan. As Dr. Demby explained it to us, American Motors was looking for a thrust in media that would call attention to the Buyer Protection Plan and its automotive products in 1972.

"When American Motors sponsored TV coverage of President Nixon's trip to Moscow, they weren't looking for income or age levels. They were looking for alertness. They equated an alert inquisitive audience with potential interest in a new car.

"You see, people in the same socioeconomic groups do not all react the same. It's not enough to know whether a person can afford a product, or even if he needs, or likes it. How does it fit his life style? How does it relate to his self concept?"

The point of view of another researcher who is high on psychographics was covered at some length in *Media Decisions* of May 1973 (See "The New Six," page 62 in that issue). As explained there Arthur Boudin of Commercial Analysts contends that this kind of information is important input for anyone who wants to link media to market segment.

Says Boudin, in part: "We have converted personality testing into an instrument with which to describe segments of the population. . . . Two other dimensions which explain why people behave as they do can now be measured objectively. Social role identification and social aspirations. . . . Until you can identify people's wants and needs, you can't begin to explain why they behave as they do, nor can you put together a strategy to appeal to them. Demographics explains only a very little in terms of market behavior. . . . We can't explain why a decision is made in a market where there are numerous choices without psychographics. With it you can optimize a product's acceptance by tailoring a product to a specific market."

A few ad agencies have made considerable use of psychographic research. In the vanguard is Leo Burnett Co. in Chicago, which has been applying it to decision-making since 1967.

The Burnett agency has worked closely with Drs. William Wells and Richard Jackson of the University of Chicago and their firm, Market Facts Inc. The data is gathered from a consumer panel that is questioned on attitudes and self image, brand use, and media preferences.

In the Burnett view, "life style segments provide more depth and vitality than previous segmentation concepts based only on demographics, social class, or product behavior. It is this breadth and depth of understanding about consumers that makes life style useful for marketing planning. It is our belief that this approach—life style segmentation— will provide a meaningful, helpful actionable base for future planning."

But can you pick media on the basis of psychographic profiles? Dr. Seymour Banks, Burnett vp of media and program analysis thinks you can make better selections with it than without it.

The Burnett agency is using several life style profiles in conjunction with an instant coffee account. The target segments are labeled "the old-fashioned homebody," "the housewife role hater," and "the proper matron."

The homebody is described as a person "with old-fashioned ideas, values and habits. Her life centers around the kitchen and she has a narrow view of the world. She is coping with her economic status."

The role hater "is dissatisfied with her family's achievements, lacks self-confidence, has no outside interests, and dislikes her principal home-maker role."

The proper matron "is an older upscale woman who has simplified her life. She has very proper attitudes about conduct, appearance and the family role."

Matching TV viewing preferences for these life style targets are identified as medical shows, family shows, Westerns, cops, and variety shows. "The old fashioned homebody also has above average preference for daytime soap operas and game shows; the housewife role hater and proper matron are about average in preference for daytime soap operas."

The question persists, what do you do with psychographic or life style data when you get it?

Joseph T. Plummer, the life style specialist at Leo Burnett in Chicago, makes this observation: "The experience at Burnett has emphasized two crucial elements in the process of applying life style research to advertising. The first crucial element is the importance of the time and analytic effort applied to the interpretation of the data and its relation-ship to what is currently known about the market and product.

"The second crucial factor is communicating the results and implications to the creative and marketing people. Very early in our experience at Burnett we found that written reports or straightforward chart presentations were not working.

"What we found to be an exciting, successful approach was to have a modified bull session with the creative and account people. This session is guided by the researchers who have done some real hard thinking about the data and what they mean.

"In these sessions each person—creative, account, media and research people—has the relevant data in front of him so that everyone can contribute and share points of view. At the end of the session everyone emerges with a vivid picture of the target consumer, some thoughts about direction and often the core of some creative expression."

In addition to instant coffee and tea, Burnett has applied life style data to beer, gasoline, a heavy-duty hand soap, and take-out fried chicken accounts. In a campaign for an unidentified beer (but readily recognizable as Schlitz) Plummer described how life style data was used to develop a new campaign.

"The problem arose when both client and agency developed a generalized feeling that the most recent commercials in a campaign that had been running for four years were not as powerful as earlier ones had been.

"The major life style patterns that emerged indicated that the heavy beer drinker was a risk-taker and a pleasure-seeker, or at least that was how he fancied himself. This pattern was reflected in the heavy beer drinker's greater agreement than the non-user with statements like 'I like to take chances,' 'If I had my way I would own a convertible,' 'I smoke too much,' '*Playboy* is one of my favorite magazines.'

"More than the non-user, the heavy user tended to have a preference for a physical male oriented existence. And finally, that life style data showed an enjoyment of drinking, especially beer, which was seen as a real man's drink.

"The resulting campaign was built around the imagery of the sea to dramatize the adventure of one of the last frontiers. The focus of the new campaign was on the *life style* of the men of the sea—men who live their lives with gusto and enjoy a 'gusto brew.'

"It was felt that the target consumer, regardless of his everyday role, could identify with these men, their life style and the beer. All of the evidence gathered from sales, awareness studies, and copy research indicates that the campaign is an effective one." The Schlitz market share tends to verify that evaluation.

So where does life style analysis fit in with media selection at Burnett? Dr. Banks told Media Decisions that life style data is "helping to describe fundamental strategies to give media personnel the flavor of audience we are trying to reach rather than serving as a simple arithmetic measuring device.

"We use it whenever we can to help get a better feel for media. We haven't had any real surprises from it, like finding that all the readers of a shelter magazine are swingers, but it has confirmed our previous judgments and enriched them greatly."

Dr. Banks says media preferences are themselves a factor in determining life style: "Media comes in as a measure of helping to define statements, and so can be useful in determining broad media strategies."

While life style information is limited, it cannot be gathered on all programs viewed, and for all magazines. Dr. Banks characterized life style data as a "useful adjunct to Nielson data. From life style data we do factoring on Simmons, look at the way they cluster on overall patterns, and select representative samples from each cluster."

As to how life style data influences media decision making, Dr. Banks described a campaign for an unidentified product for which a substantial TV campaign was planned. The target audience contained a significant component of business executives. The plan was challenged by the marketing director who argued that executives are not TV watchers.

"We were able to show through life style surveys that executives from that sample watched TV an average of 20 hours a week," Dr. Banks said. "In surveys they characterize themselves as light TV watchers or do not consider it their medium as they do magazines. They do not identify with specific content of shows, specific programs, but think of themselves as heavy magazine readers."

Another instance where life style plays a role in media selection is the Dewar's Scotch campaign. Two series of magazine ads were created, one stressing the authenticity of the liquor and its part in Scottish history, the other, a series of profiles of modern, successful young, Dewar's scotch drinkers, containing the logo of the Scotsman from the other ad.

The ads stressing authenticity are placed in magazines such as *Time*, *U.S. News & World Report*, and *New Yorker*, while the profiles campaign, appealing to a different life style segment, run in *Playboy, Harpers, Esquire, New York* and *MS*, among others. Life style data played a role in media placement in the Dewar's campaign, Banks indicated.

Again, Dr. Banks stressed that while life style data was largely a tool for the creative department, it is an important part of the background data used in media selection at Burnett.

The negative view

We also talked to Harold Israel, the expert on psychographics at W. R. Simmons Research Associates. The 1971 survey had included 14 additional questions to determine how respondents think of themselves. Self image options included categories such as self-confident, domineering, etc.

While the information was published as a bonus report to the subscribers, very few people made use of it, Israel told us. The Simmons people believe life-style indicators may be somewhat useful to copywriters but not of much use to media decision makers.

"It's tenuous as far as media segments are concerned, with samples our size," Israel said. "You can't really type media from the data. Our subscribers are the media people, and unfortunately our data seldom filters to the creative people."

Hans Carstensen, senior vp and media director at N. W. Ayer & Son, made this evaluation recently: "For the foreseeable future, we suspect psychographics' major applications will be in the creative area providing new techniques and improving advertising's ability to communicate and persuade.

"Demographics, on the other hand, will probably continue to be the major segmenting technique for media purposes. This is not to say, however, that work in psychographics relating to media should not, or will not be pursued. In fact the search for practical applications of psychographics to media selection is already a subject of major interest in many quarters of the marketing community."

Ed Papazian, vp and director of media at BBDO, said in his Mediology column in Media Decisions for October 1973: "The media research firms can ask their already burdened respondents all the questions they like, but even if one assumes that adults who have sat through three hour interviews or filled out 50-page questionnaires, can answer questions about their psychological make-up meaningfully, the relationship between their replies and ad or commercial 'impact' is hardly established. If anything, most of the attempts to delve into this area suggest *no relationship.*"

A summation has been offered by Dr. Paul Erdos, president of the Erdos and Morgan Research Service. He says: "Psychographics represents a valuable addition to the tools used for media research. As have been the case with many other worthwhile innovations in the field, the enthusiasm of the innovators and the bandwagon spirit of some of the imitators tended for a while to make it into a fad and cure-all.

"It isn't, but when the noise abates, the new technique will still be around and used when needed."

✿   ✿   ✿

At present psychographics is much more than a gleam in the creator's eye, but less than a universal yardstick by which to achieve fool-proof merchandising and media selecting techniques. And like truth, its usefulness lies in the eye of the beholder. Still, some creative and media people find it an immensely exciting and useful tool.

QUESTIONS

1. Define "psychographics" and "life-style."
2. Evaluate the concept of life-style as a basis for market segmentation. How does it differ from and/or support other approaches to segmentation?
3. Beyond use in selecting appropriate media, how might life-style concepts aid the marketing manager?

*4. Do "life cycle" and "psychographics" have any relevance for Kotler and Levy's non-business organizations (Reading 4)? If so, illustrate. If not, explain why.

*5. Will "psychographic" thinking be as relevant in a shortage economy? Explain. (See Reading 8.)

In the industrial market, customers' purchases may be large and their needs quite varied. Here, the marketing manager may seek to simultaneously segment the market and identify the specific prospects to be contacted. The following article illustrates several approaches, all based on using S.I.C. codes which are widely used in industrial markets.

---

12. PINPOINTING PROSPECTS FOR INDUSTRIAL SALES*

Francis E. Hummel

FINDING NEW prospects and new accounts is the "lifeblood" of any expanding industrial concern. Yet many companies approach this problem in a relatively haphazard manner.

Sources of information as to prospective new accounts are commonly found by one or more of the following methods: (1) from requests received directly from industrial prospects; (2) from advertising, trade shows, and other promotion efforts; (3) from "leads" supplied by associates and friends; and (4) from salesmen "cold-turkey" calls on industrial plants in their territory.

Many times these activities result in many wasted sales calls, particularly when salesmen merely follow "smoke-stacks" in an effort to obtain new potential accounts. And often many good prospects are overlooked. Marketing analysis can aid in the search for new prospects by predetermining those industrial firms who afford the greatest probability of using a given industrial product and becoming a new account. This can be accomplished by first determining the industries having use for the product and the relative purchasing requirements of each industrial segment. These data can be used in conjunction with industrial directories, sur-

---

* Reprinted with permission from the *Journal of Marketing*, published by the American Marketing Association, July 1960, pp. 26–31. At the time of writing, Mr. Hummel was a marketing manager with Stanley Hardware.

veys, trade show attendance lists, advertising, and promotional inquiries to determine the probable best sources for sales calls.

The first step is to classify the firm's industrial market. This serves as a basis for the preliminary research needed to determine potential accounts.

The classification system most widely used is the Standard Industrial Classification System. The S.I.C. is a numerical system set up by the federal government to classify the many different segments of industry. For manufacturing industries the S.I.C. System combines and classifies all manufacturing into twenty major industry groups (designated by a 2-digit code—example: #20, Food and Kindred Products).

Each group then is subdivided into about 150 industry groups (designated by a 3-digit code—example: #202, Dairy Products).

A further breakdown reveals approximately 450 individual industries (designated by a 4-digit code—example: #2021, Creamery Butter). Thus, each industry has a classification number—the more digits, the finer the classification.

This classification is based on the *product produced* or *operation performed*. A few industries have other classification fundamentals, such as materials or processes used. However, in general, establishments involved in similar production operations are grouped together and the product is the major determining factor of classification.

INDUSTRIAL BUYING MOTIVES

The S.I.C. classification system can be viewed in the light of the buying motives of industrial purchasing agents. Purchasing agents buy things that help their concern to solve production, distribution, control, or development problems. For example, the machine-tool firm buys ball bearings to make a better product; the box shop buys automatic gluers to increase production.

The industrial market is made up of manufacturing plants whose problems can be solved through the use of particular products or services, and who buy them as the best solution to *their problems.* If the problems of all industrial plants could be categorized into those that can or cannot be solved through the use of certain products, it could be determined what plants are in a certain market and the exact problems each one faces.

The industrial purchasers' problems stem from the product manufactured or the operations performed. The S.I.C. System is based on these factors. Therefore, if you know the S.I.C. number of a manufacturing plant, you have a good clue to the problems it faces. If you know the size of the plant, you have a good idea of the extent of the problem.

Since plants in the same S.I.C. make essentially the same kind of products and have the same or similar production problems, the first determining factor must be the listing of those industries making up the market for the product. Second, the relative importance of each S.I.C. industry must be determined in relation to each other along with the approximate need of each S.I.C. for your product. Thus, an estimate of the consumption of the product can be made by industries, areas, and specific firms from published S.I.C. data on production.

The various industries (usually 4-digit S.I.C.) can be determined, along with their relative importance for a particular market, by three complementary methods: (1) sales analysis, (2) judgment analysis, and (3) marketing surveys.

1. Sales analysis. For established products, the first step is to analyze past sales records and assign appropriate 4-digit S.I.C. numbers to the plant of each customer. At the same time other valuable statistical data can be collected regarding dollar sales, models, attachments, etc. from the sales records. Punch-card analysis is essential for large studies.

This analysis yields valuable information *only* about *past* accomplishments by industries; it tells *nothing* of *potential* industries not sold.

2. Judgment analysis. One or more persons thoroughly familiar with the market for the product can go through the S.I.C. manual and check off the 4-digit classifications which they believe fall into the market. Naturally, accuracy depends upon the experience, ability, and judgment of the persons selected.

3. Marketing surveys. Inquiries can be solicited through news releases, advertising, and by a widespread sample mail survey. The inquiry returns are tabulated by S.I.C., indicating those companies and industries having use for the product.

This method is particularly applicable to a new product or to any established product about which there is some doubt as to whether or not present customers encompass all the S.I.C.'s in the potential market. The value of this method depends upon receiving an adequate cross-section of the market and reliable respondent information.

Basic factors

By taking the above steps, preliminary data will be available to determine with a reasonable degree of accuracy the composition of the industrial market for the products under consideration. Three basic factors will be evident:

The industries having use for the product (called S.I.C. Effective Industries).

The proportion of plants within *each* industry that have use for the product (called S.I.C. Percentage).

The relative value of each S.I.C. as a proportion of the total market (called S.I.C. Weight).

For example, the above steps were taken by a manufacturer in analyzing the market for an inspection gauge. Marketing analysis showed that S.I.C. 3423 (hand-and-edge tool industry) was one of the Effective Industries. And 80 percent of the plants in S.I.C. 3423 had inspection problems best solved through the use of its product. However, this 80 percent of the hand-tool industry plants (S.I.C. %) represented only 2.2 percent of the total market for the product (S.I.C. Weight).

Another Effective Industry, S.I.C. 3722, Aircraft engines and engine parts, was found to be a major user. And 100 percent of all the plants in S.I.C. 3722 (S.I.C. %) had inspection problems best solved through the use of its products, representing 30 percent of the total market for the product (S.I.C. Weight).

These data can then be used as the basis for determining prospects. But the S.I.C., even on a 4-digit basis, is not a fine enough classification to assume that all plants in the same S.I.C. have identically the same problems. Therefore, the fact that a sale has been made to *one* plant in any particular S.I.C. does not necessarily mean that *all* the plants in the S.I.C. are potential customers. For example, the S.I.C. does not distinguish between plants that manufacture their own component parts and those that assemble parts made elsewhere.

PINPOINTING PROSPECTS

Once the composition of the industrial market is determined—that is, the industries having use for the product, the number of plants in each industry, and the relative market values of each industry—marketing research can utilize this information to pinpoint those industrial concerns that have a use for the product or that afford the greatest probability of becoming a new account. These prospects must be defined by names and addresses of companies—not merely percentage or dollar figure by areas—so that field salesmen can call for specific follow-up.

There are four major areas where marketing research can determine industrial concerns that have a high probability of becoming new industrial prospects—by use of (1) industrial directories, (2) surveys, (3) trade-show attendance lists, and (4) advertising and promotional inquiries.

Industrial directories

A number of state and regional industrial directories published are by various organizations such as Chambers of Commerce and State Development Commissions that list the industrial plants within their areas.[1] These directories give names and addresses of industrial plants and products produced. Some provide additional data, such as employment and names of executives. Unfortunately they vary in completeness of data given and the method of classifying firms. There are only eighteen

---

[1] For an annotated bibliography of state industrial directories, see: M. J. Reutter and N. R. Kidder, "State Industrial Directories," *Sales Management*, vol. 81, (July 10, 1958), pp. 72–78.

directories classifying firms on a 4-digit S.I.C. basis. To utilize the remaining directories most effectively, the listings must be classified into the S.I.C.

Such industrial directories provide an excellent source for finding new prospects. For each 4-digit S.I.C. making up the market for a product, each firm listed can be checked in relation to the sales and prospect files of the concern. Such an analysis gives a listing of plants by industries that probably are prospects. If the S.I.C. percentages and weights have been predetermined, the probability of any given firm becoming a good prospect is evident.

For example, one machine-tool manufacturer carefully analyzed each industrial directory in the United States. Preliminary research revealed that five S.I.C.'s made up over 75 percent of the market for its specialized equipment. Only these industries were studied in detail. For each sales territory a master sales-analysis list was developed. The five S.I.C. industries were listed along with the names and addresses of each concern. Employment figures were noted where available. S.I.C. percentages and weights were shown for each industry under study. For each concern it was determined whether it had been sold or contacted previously. If no record of either, it was added to the new-prospect list for contact by a field salesman. In this manner a number of firms were discovered that had use for the equipment and were potential future customers.

Another metal working concern utilized a similar approach. Personal sales calls were made on firms listed in the directories for four major 4-digit S.I.C. groups which accounted for 60 percent of the market. The next eight S.I.C. groups, having lower S.I.C. percentages and weights, accounted for only 22 percent of the market. Therefore, these "new prospects" were first contacted by telephone to determine whether they had a use for the product under study. Personal sales calls were then made on those firms reporting in the affirmative. This procedure resulted in a 25 percent saving in sales time and expenses.

Surveys

A second way of determining new industrial prospects is through the use of market-research surveys. Such surveys made for a given product can provide information whether specific plants are in the market for that product, and the extent to which they are in it.

For example, a New England manufacturing firm had an established product which was sold for years primarily to ball bearing manufacturers. Management felt that the product should have more widespread use in the broad metal-working field. A mail questionnaire was developed to send to many 4-digit S.I.C.'s in the metal-working industry. The questionnaire asked whether the plant used product "X" (product "X" being a type of product made by several firms—not a brand name), the number of production workers in the plant, how product "X" was used, from whom the plant purchased it, the approximate annual dollar value of purchases, the names and titles of the officials responsible for specifying and purchasing this material, and their comments.

TABLE 1
Sales-planning-blueprints,* survey of metal-working plants for product "X," Dayton-Cincinnati area.

S.I.C. no. workers	Plant surveyed	Plant uses product "X" for:	Products in which "X" used	From whom purchased	Approx- imate value	Comments
3545	Cutting Tools, Gages, M.T. Attachments					
215	National Tool Co. 123 Fourth Ave. Dayton, Ohio R. L. Henchman, Plant Manager	Seal out dust	Spindles	A.B.C. Co.	$5,000	A.B.C. delivery poor
3621	Motors, Generators, Generator Sets					
25	G. Biggs, Inc. 456 Seventh Ave. Dayton, Ohio A. J. Israel, Mgr. Manufacturing	Keep lub- rication in	Fractional horsepower motors	General National Co.	$ 185	Good price, service Quality high
3729	Aircraft Parts and Sub-Assemblies					
50	E. J. Walsh Co. Prospect Street Cincinnati, Ohio E. J. Walsh Gen. Mgr. etc.	Seal out light cushion- ing	Precision assemblies	Connecticut Superior Co.	$8,500	Good price Need special size for precision parts. Estimated value $5,000 annual. Conn. Superior research facili- ties poor for engineering design.

* All names and addresses are fictitious, but the information in the Blueprint is drawn from an actual case. The mark Sales-Planning-Blueprint is a service mark owned by Kidder and Company. Un- authorized use of the mark is prohibited. Copyright, Kidder and Company, Cambridge 38, Massachu- setts, 1957.

Table 1 is a sample of results obtained. The following important information became available from this study:

1. The names and addresses of good prospective accounts were learned, and a knowledge of use of product and the competition and annual volume purchased. For example, the National Tool Company, a man- ufacturer of cutting tools, purchased $5,000 a year of competitor A.B.C. Company's product for use as a component in sealing out dust. Better deliveries were desired.

2. New uses for the product were determined. For example, pressure sealing was the prime discovery.
3. A list of the major disadvantages of Product "X" was compiled. Unfavorable comments regarding Product "X's" performance under cold temperatures resulted in redesign of the brand.
4. Data were obtained which could be further analyzed for use in advertising. For example, a number of concerns reported that they did not use the product because their requirements called for special sizes. The past advertising and sales-promotion brochures of the firm stressed standard lines. Future promotion was then designed to include mention of available engineering services to "tailor-make" the product for special requirements.

Trade-show attendance lists

Registration lists of major trade shows can also be helpful in determining new accounts.

Classified registration lists are more frequently being supplied by progressive show managements. The lists are simply compilations of information taken from registration cards filled out by show visitors. The information includes the visitor's name and job title, company name and address, number of production employees, and major products produced by the plant. Such information permits each visitor to be classified by company size, location, and S.I.C. type of product.

These lists provide excellent data for marketing analysis, and obvious sales-promotion advantages. For example, a manufacturer of specialized machinery used the 1955 Machine Tool Show listings as an aid in determining market coverage and building a prospect list, particularly for some of its weaker sales areas. The registration lists were analyzed as follows: (1) The data from all registrants in the areas under study were assembled separately. (2) Only plants within certain 4-digit S.I.C.'s making a market for the machinery were studied; plants were further subdivided by S.I.C. weights and potentials along with plant size. (3) These plants were then compared with present prospect lists, and sales lists to determine specific coverage and possible new accounts. In addition, the company compiled its own list of show visitors to its *booth*. Such concerns not previously contacted were considered prime prospects because their representatives took the time to visit the manufacturer and obviously had an interest in the product.

Another firm used the 1956 Material Handling Institute Exposition data which classified its registration list by twenty-two job titles and forty-five industry classifications. The firm analyzed only industries that were original-equipment users, and carefully compared this list to past sales records. A number of new prospects were discovered by this analysis, and each was contacted subsequently by the field sales force.

One limitation of using trade-show attendance lists is that trade shows pull registrants most heavily from the local surrounding trading area of 200 to 300 miles. This means that distant areas under study must be evaluated accordingly because many plants may not have sent representatives to the show.

Advertising and promotional inquiries

Finally, a thorough analysis of advertising and promotional inquiries can be made. This method is particularly useful in determining markets for new industrial products. It makes use of the S.I.C. in order to "spot" those industries giving a genuine interest in the product.

For example, one manufacturer developed a high-frequency electric spindle for use on its precision machinery. These high-speed rotational units offered other industrial possibilities among many different industries. Therefore, an analysis of the broad industrial U.S. market was needed to determine specifically what other applications of the product were possible. It was decided that the most economical and efficient approach would be to solicit inquiries from the manufacturing community and to determine from those inquiries received, the industries having a potential use for the product. They would serve as a basis for conducting further research.

A small advertising campaign was conducted in the *Saturday Evening Post* designed to reach a broad section of manufacturing industry. In addition, publicity releases were prepared for twenty selected business publications to cover the broad design and metal-working field.

As inquiries were received as a result of the publicity, the sales department immediately answered them. The appropriate 4-digit S.I.C. number was then assigned to each inquiry, based on the major product produced by the plant. This showed that many plants within the same S.I.C. industry were interested in the product. These industries were then segregated and studied in detail by further surveys—both mail and personal interview. This resulted in a number of new applications and customers.

The use of inquiries derived from advertising and publicity offers many advantages for determining the market for both new and existing products. This approach is particularly applicable where people in the industry are not aware of the new industrial product, and for an industrial product which may have broad industrial usage.

QUESTIONS

1. How are the firms within an S.I.C. code category similar?
2. Should S.I.C. code categories always be thought of as homogenous market segments? Explain.

3. Which of the four approaches to pinpointing markets would you try first? Why? Then, how would you move on to the others?

°4. What type of information about final consumers might be used to develop a coding system for them similar to the S.I.C. codes for industrial firms? (See Readings 9–11.)

A basic problem facing marketing managers is how to use available data to make effective decisions. This article discusses the use of Survey of Buying Power data for planning. Several real examples illustrate the possibilities.

---

13. SALES MANAGEMENT'S SURVEY OF BUYING POWER—INFORMATION FOUNDATION FOR PIVOTAL DECISIONS*

Thayer C. Taylor

PLANNING—'WHERE DO WE WANT TO GO?'

GENERAL ELECTRIC's major appliance group massages *Survey of Buying Power* data in a mathematical model to get a better fix on those markets where aggressive marketing action will bring the handsomest returns. Stanley Home Products checks the *Survey* data to find out which branch offices are chalking up "real" sales growth and which are making only fictitious gains. Jane Colby, Inc., matches *Survey* data against sales orders to spotlight markets where competitors are doing a better job. Swift & Co., as part of a program to make field sales managers more marketing-minded, gives them territorial profiles constructed from *Survey* data.

These firms, and hundreds like them, strive to upgrade the information foundation that sales managers rely upon when making important decisions. As consultant Roger M. Peterson of A. T. Kearney & Co. observes, "The whole secret today is to work smarter, not just harder." The sales manager who wants to "work smarter" needs all the factual information

---

* Reprinted by permission from Thayer C. Taylor, "Sales Management's Survey of Buying Power—Information Foundation for Pivotal Decisions," © 1972, *Sales Management's Survey of Buying Power;* further reproduction is forbidden. At the time of writing, Mr. Taylor was Senior Editor for Management Sciences of *Sales Management* magazine.

that can be put at his disposal because of the increased competitive pressures in the marketplace, the rising cost of wrong decisions which rivals are quick to exploit, and the greater emphasis placed on scientific decision-making.

The *Survey of Buying Power,* with its many-splendored facts on people, their buying power, and their spending patterns, dovetails nicely with three of the most critical phases of the sales manager's job—planning, organizing, reviewing. In his planning phase, he sets the goals for his sales force. In his organizing phase, he marshalls his resources so that they will be utilized most effectively. In his reviewing phase, he measures his level of achievement and maps corrective action if it's called for.

The first step the sales manager takes in his planning phase is to size up the structure of the territory because that is his arena of responsibility. Of course, internal shipment records tell him who his customers and prospects are and their relative importance. But this is, at best, a very narrow perspective of the marketplace in which he competes.

Because no company operates in a vacuum, the sales manager must have a good grasp of the market's environmental characteristics, asking himself: "What are the most important factors that affect my business? What relationships do they have to one another and to my own sales? What opportunities and or threats do they pose for me?"

The *Survey* gives him the most authoritative, up-to-date reading on the three most critical environmental factors: population, buying power, and spending patterns in retail stores. Furthermore, the quantitative totals are made even more useful by qualitative breakdowns. Population is delineated by race, sex, size of family, and age of household head. Income is fleshed out with six income groups for cities and counties, eight for metropolitan areas. Retail sales are broken down for five store categories in cities and counties, 12 in metro areas.

It is this kind of multi-level detail that makes Ralph I. Tober, sales research manager, Swift & Co., Chicago, stress: "The more data the sales manager has on his market, the better he can serve that market, plan for growth, and have a better chance of reaching his objectives." One company that agrees with this thinking is Metropolitan Life Insurance Co., New York, which provides field sales managers with a detailed profile of their territories by rearranging the *Survey's* city and county data, showing population, households, distribution of households by income range, per household Effective Buying Income (EBI), and total disposable income.

A key element of the current marketing revamp at Swift & Co., aimed at making field sales managers more marketing-minded, is a factbook drawn from *Survey* data that shows each sales manager his market's population, households, EBI, retail sales, and sales of food stores, supermarkets, and eat-and-drink places (equivalent to restaurant sales). The statistics are presented at the county level so that, as sales research boss Tober notes, "the managers will get a good idea of where to place their emphasis." The purpose of the factbook (first of its kind at the meat packer) Tober adds is to: "help the sales manager do a better job in his market planning, routing of salesmen, and picking sales goals."

Where it all starts

The big reason why Metropolitan Life, Swift, and others want their sales managers to be more knowledgeable about their local selling environments is that the sales manager's whole planning cycle begins with accurate knowledge of the market's potential business volume. He cannot know what his sales and profit contributions to the company will be, how many salesmen he will require, how much advertising and sales promotion support he will need until he has developed concrete ideas on the amount of business that is out there and the share of it that he can win.

So pertinent is the selection of *Survey* data, and so complete its breadth of detail, that many smaller- and middle-sized companies rely upon it almost exclusively as their market research department or marketing intelligence system. These firms use the *Survey* data as ready-made benchmarks for creating sales potentials. Stanley Home Products, Westfield, Mass., does just that when preparing sales goals for its 300 branches. Sales administrator Francis Della Luna first looks at the *Survey's* state retail sales totals, then matches them with his company's sales to calculate the degree of penetration. Then he studies the population and household totals for the sales territories and compares them with the previous year or a base period. This clues him as to whether a branch is just keeping pace with population growth, trailing it, or moving ahead of it. This indicates how "real" the branch's sales growth is. That is, if population growth is par, the sales growth must be at a faster rate to be real growth. All of this is then worked into general guidelines for the company's dealers for the upcoming year.

Most companies, of course, focus on the *Survey* data that come closest to meeting the needs of their product line. Macklanburg-Duncan Co., Oklahoma City, Okla., maker of building speciality products, uses the sales totals of lumber-building materials-hardware stores as a rough benchmark of future business. Sales vice president Laurence H. Koster takes $\frac{1}{10}$ of 1% of the category's sales for a geographical unit as the minimum goal to shoot for, then modifies it according to the salesman's travel time.

Often, the *Survey* provides the only reliable benchmarks available for sales executives who are in data-poor industries. Larry A. Donlin, sales manager of Telectron, Inc., Fort Lauderdale, Fla., which markets radio controls for electric garage door-openers, uses EBI figures as guideposts for sales potential simply "because there are no other valid criteria available." He uses the EBI on the county level as a common denominator, dividing it by the number of units sold to get a penetration level, which is then used as a guideline for the upcoming year's business potential.

The uses to which the *Survey* data can be put are limited only

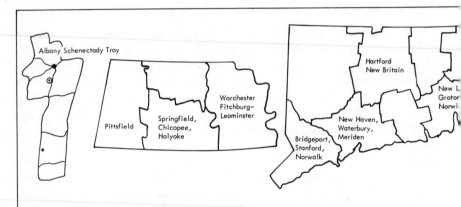

HOW THE SURVEY ALLOCATES MARKET POTENTIAL BY TYPE OF PRODUCT

Although the Buying Power Index (BPI) applies mostly to Average-Priced Products, it is easily customized to suit the needs of any type of product. All the user need do is change the weights and/or the components that make up the index. Here is how the BPI provides three different perspectives of the same market, which in this case consists of Connecticut, five counties in western Massachusetts, and seven counties in eastern New York. In the left hand column, the sales manager uses the BPIs as they appear in the *Survey*, totals them up for his regional market, and then apportions the potential among the different counties. Here, the BPI formula has a weight of five for the county's share of EBI, three for the share of retail sales, and two for the share of population.

In the middle column, the marketer of a Low-Priced Food Product, sold primarily in supermarkets, substitutes food store sales for retail sales. Because he considers product distribution the most important factor, he gives it a weight of five; EBI a weight of three, population a weight of two. You will note that New Haven, Worcester, and Dutchess Counties are now relatively more important than previously.

In the right hand column, a seller of High-Priced Durable Products is primarily interested in households with incomes over $10,000, and gives this factor a weight of six. Because his product is bought by the executive's imagination. APECO Corp., Evanston, Ill., employs the Buying Power Index (BPI)—which weighs a geographical unit's share of total population, EBI, and retail sales—to improve the profit accountability of its 35 branches. Stuart Musick, administrative sales manager, reports that previously such outlays as national advertising, home office administration, and so on, were charged against the branches

on a family, rather than per capita basis, he uses households instead of population, giving them a weight of one. The product is sold mostly through department stores, so he uses the general merchandise category and gives it a weight of three.

Such customized uses of the BPI often turn up hidden relationships. For example, one would assume that Fairfield County's high-income households make it the leading prospect for a High-Priced item. But you will note that Hartford County has the biggest share-of-market among all the counties. This indicates that Hartford's retail outlets are the critical element and that the marketer's distribution strategy must pay special attention to retailers in that county.

Market potential by county

	Average-priced products	Low-priced food product	High-priced durable product
Connecticut			
Fairfield	17.10	16.43	16.97
Hartford	15.27	14.67	17.15
Litchfield	2.48	2.52	2.07
Middlesex	1.96	2.02	1.85
New Haven	13.29	13.41	13.42
New London	3.86	3.76	3.64
Tolland	1.65	1.60	1.33
Windham	1.35	1.51	1.30
Western Mass.			
Berkshire	2.60	2.79	2.36
Franklin	0.88	0.89	7.55
Hampden	7.30	7.45	4.64
Hampshire	1.88	1.97	1.45
Worcester	10.29	10.74	9.19
Eastern, N.Y.			
Albany	6.05	5.74	7.55
Columbia	0.82	0.85	0.72
Dutchess	3.75	4.28	3.59
Putnam	0.93	1.01	0.81
Rensselaer	2.64	2.53	2.62
Saratoga	2.17	2.27	2.08
Schenectady	3.62	3.54	3.80

Numbers may not add to 100 due to rounding.
Source: Sales Management's 1972/1973 Survey of Buying Power©
SM.

according to their share of company sales. However, he points out, this penalized those branches that did a better job of topping their potential. Thus if New York City's potential was 9.5% of total sales and it actually brought in 12.5%, it was in effect being penalized 3%. Musick had the accounting system changed so that budgeted cost items were charged according to the branch's BPI. The change, he observes, "helped spot and plug profit drains, developed a deeper mutual respect between marketing and accounting personnel, and provided branch sales managers more clearly defined profit goals."

Of course, most companies marry the *Survey* data with information from other sources, such as their own factory and warehouse shipments or industry and government reports, to give the *Survey* statistics added dimensions. Several of the leading petroleum marketers, in building a fix on territory potential, starts with Bureau of Public Roads data on gasoline consumption by states and modify these totals with Department of Transportation reports on truck registrations to determine how much gasoline was sold to passenger cars in each state. The *Survey's* gas station sales totals are then used to apportion the state consumption totals among the different counties and cities, which are then aggregated into the sales territories.

Ionics, Inc., Bridgeville, Pa., maker of water softening equipment, is guided by EBI per household and family size. Household income is an important indicator, says Walter J. Polens, vice president-sales, "because our product is a high-ticket item" and family size is watched carefully "because the more people there are in the family, the bigger the type of equipment that can be sold to them. This gives us an idea of the amount of business we can expect in a territory. We further refine this with information about water hardness in the area inasmuch as, obviously, people in a hard water area are much more likely to listen to our sell."

Something for industrials, too

One of the more widespread fallacies surrounding the *Survey* is that it can be used only by consumer goods marketers. True, its statistics— population, income, retail sales—are more oriented to products consumed by households. However, because of the close interdependence between the different sectors of the economy, consumer and industrial markets do not operate in separate worlds, so to speak, and, in fact, do have many common areas where they overlap. Industry roughly follows population movement and EBI levels often highlight the differences between an industrialized market and a nonindustrialized one. Thus the more enterprising industrial marketers are able to adopt the *Survey* data to their own purposes.

Such a marketer is James B. Novello, marketing analyst of Victor

Comptometer Corp., Chicago. He finds total retail sales to be an effective gauge of cash register potential, the obvious implication being that the more retail activity there is in a city or county, the greater the demand for cash registers in the retail outlet.

He combines *Survey* data with information from three sources to build a customized index of business potential. First, using the annual County Business Patterns reports or the quinquennial Census of Business, he will give each county a percent of U.S. retail and service establishments. Next, he distributes his own sales among the counties in similar fashion, and then does the same with industry data on total cash register shipments. Finally, using the *Survey*, he gives each county its BPI and share of U.S. retail sales. Then he adds the five percentage shares and divides by five to calculate a potential business index which, he says, "tell us how much we should expect from each of our 75 branches."

Victor Comptometer also relies on some 750 franchise dealers who report to its branch offices. Novello checks the *Survey's* city data in awarding territories to dealers. "We try to assign whole counties to a dealer, but in areas around big cities you may have to deal with split counties." For example, in Cook County, one dealer might be given Chicago, a second dealer the balance of the county. Here, Chicago's share of Cook County's BPI and retail sales is used as a means of assigning quotas to the two dealers.

Another industrial marketer using the *Survey* is marketing manager William A. Risberg, of Thomas & Betts Co., Elizabeth, N.J., maker of electrical and electronic connectors. Making the assumption that his products are used pretty evenly throughout the country, he uses a county's share of population and EBI as "instant potentials" of business volume. He says that past comparisons have shown that a territory's share of company sales jibes pretty closely with its combined population and EBI shares. "This gives us a good fix on the sales volume we can expect from a territory," he says, "and is the basis of discussions with our distributors on how much business they should do next year."

Robert Grimaldi, midwest sales manager of Sweda International, Chicago, finds that a territory's retail sales and BPI seem to follow the curve of his company's sales pretty closely, "We have established norms so that, for example, if a territory has a BPI of 1.4040 and retail sales of $5-billion, it should produce around $5 million of business for that branch office. We use these norms to select the top markets where we want to concentrate our money and men."

Of course, the numbers produced by these applications of *Survey* data are rarely considered as ends in themselves. They must be tempered by human judgment sensitive to factors quantitative measures can't consider. For example, Thomas & Betts' William A. Risberg looks at the suggested potential from the perspective of the territory's industrial makeup. "If a distributor is located in Southern California, and we have products tailored for the aerospace industry, obviously his potential is much bigger than that suggested by an index. You must factor in what might be called educated seat-of-the-pants judgment."

Industry composition is not the only difference that must be weighed. Andy B. Harvey, general sales manager, Maico Electronics, Minneapolis, modifies index-derived potentials when inexperienced dealers are involved. A new dealer is given a first year task of 75% of his territorial potential; for his second year, potential plus two times his first year's sales divided by three; for his third year, potential plus the previous two years' sales divided by three.

MARKET DISTINCTIONS MEAN MARKET OPPORTUNITIES

Is San Diego the pill-popping hub of the U.S.? Does Dallas lack good restaurants? Although the upward rise in consumer affluence is pretty general throughout the U.S., the ways in which consumers use their income gains differ sharply from market to market. The allocation of retail sales among the different store types provides valuable insights into these market-by-market distinctions. In San Diego, for example, almost 10% of the retail dollar is spent in drug stores, while a few hundred miles north in Portland, Ore., consumers plunk down only 2% of the retail dollar in similar outlets. When it comes to dining out, Dallas consumers allocate only 6% of their retail spending to eating and drinking places, while in New York the ratio is almost twice as high (helped along, of course, by expense accounts).

Sales executives among local media use these percentage break-outs to see if the composition of advertising revenues matches the relative importance of the various retail categories in their local bailiwicks. If food stores in New Orleans, for example, contribute only 20% of local media revenues while siphoning off 26% of local consumer spending, it suggests that these outlets are under-represented when it comes to advertising.

Consumer goods marketers too rely on these percentages because they reflect the relative importance of retail categories in local markets. Hence they have a bearing on decisions pertaining to selection of distribution channels, placement of point-of-purchase materials, and use of cooperative advertising. Retailers, themselves, use the break-outs to compare the pattern of consumer spending with national or state averages. Striking differences between local and national allocations would suggest changes in product offerings or merchandising emphasis.

Spending variations among selected major metro markets

Metro area	Total retail sales (mil $)	Percent by type of store								
		Food	Eat and drink	General merchandise	Apparel	Furniture furnishing appliances	Automotive	Gas station	Lumber building hardware	Drug
New York, N.Y.	$22,652	24.2	11.0	20.8	8.5	4.8	10.3	4.2	2.5	2.6
Chicago, Ill.	15,245	20.3	8.8	23.7	7.0	4.4	17.0	5.4	3.3	4.2
Los Angeles-Long Beach, Cal.	14,984	21.3	9.5	19.4	5.1	4.4	18.7	6.7	2.3	3.9
Boston, Mass.	6,802	22.4	8.9	22.0	6.1	4.8	14.2	5.3	3.3	3.1
San Francisco-Oakland, Cal.	6,743	22.7	10.3	18.1	5.8	4.4	17.3	6.2	2.4	4.0
Washington, D.C.	6,491	20.4	7.7	20.0	5.3	4.3	18.4	6.0	2.6	5.0
Pittsburgh, Pa.	4,187	24.5	7.4	22.6	5.0	4.4	16.9	6.5	3.2	3.3
Houston, Texas	3,860	22.2	6.7	21.0	4.9	3.9	18.0	6.6	2.8	4.0
Minneapolis-St. Paul, Minn.	3,574	18.5	7.8	26.5	4.3	4.5	16.7	7.0	4.5	3.4
Dallas, Texas	3,236	20.2	6.4	21.1	4.5	3.9	22.8	6.6	3.4	3.6
Atlanta, Ga.	3,165	19.3	6.6	23.7	4.3	3.5	19.7	6.7	4.0	3.3
Paterson-Clifton-Passaic, N.J.	2,983	24.5	7.3	22.8	5.8	4.4	17.2	6.3	3.8	3.6
Seattle-Everett, Wash.	2,867	20.8	8.7	21.0	3.7	3.5	17.4	6.6	4.0	3.5
Miami, Fla.	2,819	21.5	9.7	18.6	6.5	4.7	18.8	5.6	2.3	4.1
Kansas City, Mo.	2,783	20.7	7.3	22.7	4.9	3.4	18.7	7.7	3.9	4.6
San Diego, Cal.	2,782	21.6	8.7	19.4	4.9	4.6	18.9	7.2	5.8	9.7
Milwaukee, Wis.	2,552	22.2	9.9	20.6	5.3	4.8	16.8	6.2	6.0	4.7
Riverside-San Bernadino-Ontario, Cal.	2,306	23.0	8.6	15.3	3.9	4.3	18.0	10.0	3.7	3.4
Phoenix, Ariz.	2,176	22.5	7.5	17.3	3.6	3.9	22.8	7.2	3.6	4.8
Portland, Ore.	2,166	21.0	8.0	23.7	4.0	4.0	18.9	6.5	3.1	2.2
Indianapolis, Ind.	2,151	19.8	7.6	22.3	3.2	4.0	19.8	7.1	5.3	4.5
New Orleans, La.	1,979	26.2	8.6	23.9	6.0	4.3	13.6	5.1	2.6	3.9

Source: Sales Management's 1972/1973 Survey of Buying Power© SM.

Grist for computers

While the territorial potential indicates where selling emphasis should be placed in the upcoming year, many companies use the *Survey* data as inputs for mathematical models that are designed to highlight opportunity areas. The Louisville, Ky., major appliance operation of General Electric Co. recently ran selected data from the *Survey* through a standard correlation model to see if there was any significant relationship between sales growth and specific *Survey* data. The 15 top appliance markets were used along with population, population growth rate, EBI per household, households with an EBI over $15,000, sales of the furniture-appliance and general merchandise store groups, and population over 50 years of age. According to Frank W. Archer, manager-market development, "We found a very positive correlation between population change and our own business; that is, we seem to do better in the markets with a fast population growth. On the other hand, the general merchandise store totals seemed to have a negative correlation, which may be due to the strong private label activity of the major retailers."

Using this as a starting point, Archer's group will next look at all of GE's markets in light of what the model revealed. Markets where GE's sales have not kept pace with population growth will be spotlighted as candidates for special emphasis, such as putting more salesmen into the field or getting new distributors. Other uses can be made of the model's results. "If we have a choice of making a stronger effort in Market A or Market B," Archer notes, "this indicates we may be better off in the one with faster population growth. On the other hand, we can take a look at markets where we haven't kept up and look for the explanatory factors."

The important thing about running *Survey* data through mathematical models is that the models often reveal relationships between the numbers and company sales that are not readily apparent. For example, as Archer points out, "It can identify markets where special opportunities exist that you are not aware of." Application programs for running such correlation models are widely available from computer vendors, software houses, or service bureaus.

The big favorite

Probably the most widely used single data bit in the *Survey* is the BPI, often called the Buying Power Quota. The reason, Sweda's Robert Grimaldi says, is that "it has the three most important elements: population, income, spending. If you had an index with just population, it could be that most of the people were on welfare. Or if the index just had EBI, it could be that the area was completely residential with no retail activity. You need an index with all three factors so you will know whether the market is growing, whether the income rests on a strong basis, and what people are buying."

The BPI, like all the other *Survey* data, can be used either as a ready-made index or tailored to fit a particular product or line of products. Although it is oriented to what could be called average-type products enjoying broad distribution and widespread usage, its assigned weights can be reshuffled to meet specific circumstances. Thus while the BPI gives a weight of 5 to a market's percent of U.S. EBI, a weight of 3 to its percent of retail sales, and a weight of 2 to its percent of population, a seller of a low-priced food item gives a weight of 4 to population, 4 to food store sales, and only 2 to income on the grounds that frequency and volume of food store shopping have more of an impact on the sales of his product than does income. A shoe company, noting that retail footwear sales lagged behind the rush of upper-income households to the suburbs, changes the weights to 3 for population, 3 for income, and 4 for retail sales.

The BPI can be customized even further by replacing the population-EBI-retail sales triad with any of the particular breakdowns that the user feels explain sales of his products. For example, a major appliance firm uses households instead of population, high-income groups rather than EBI, and department and furniture-appliance store sales in place of total retail sales. A firm selling color film and cameras uses families with children under six, households with an EBI over $7,000, and drug and department store sales.

Rather than reshuffle the weights, some firms use parts of the *Survey* in conjunction with other information to create their own indexes. Toro Manufacturing Co., Minneapolis, Minn., makers of power mowers and snow throwers, uses the number of owner-occupied dwellings, households with more than $2,500 in EBI, and a weather factor (such as average annual inches of snowfall). This index is then applied against known industry sales to determine industry sales on the county level.

Other companies that feel the BPI may be too general for their type of product can construct their own index by tapping published profiles of spending patterns. For example, the annual *Survey of Consumer Finances*, published by the Survey Research Center, University of Michigan, Ann Arbor, Mich., includes demographic breakdowns of purchases of new and used cars, housing, household durables, recreation items, stocks, and mutual funds by income group and age of household head. By studying these findings, the marketer can determine the relative importance of each group to his own product. He could then match this with *Survey* data that show the distribution of these groups in his sales territories, and multiply the number of pertinent households by the assigned relative weights.

For example, the *Survey of Consumer Finances*, usually published in the spring, shows that purchase frequency of recreation items rises with income. Also, that younger households in the 25-34 and 35-44 age groups are the most likely purchasers, followed by households under 25. The marketer could give these groups the heaviest weights and apply them against the numbers of such groups as recorded in the *Survey of Buying Power*.

A second widespread fallacy surrounding the BPI is that it can be used only by national-scale marketers. As a matter of fact, there are few companies that sell in all 3,078 counties. Most companies, indeed, sell in local or regional markets, but the smallest of these can use the *Survey* as fruitfully as do their biggest competitors.

Remember that when a customized BPI is constructed, total retail sales, or one of the store categories, should always be included. That's because the retail sales volume indicates the degree of product availability or the extent of its distribution—always an important factor in estimating the eventual sales volume of the company's product.

The marketer who sells in only a limited number of counties can adapt the *Survey* to fashion his own BPI in one of two ways. On the one hand, he can add up the BPIs of the counties he sells in and have this grand total represent 100%. He would then divide the BPI of each county into 100 to arrive at the county's appropriate percent of over-all potential. On the other hand, he could divide the total BPI for his counties into 100 and apply the resulting number as a multiplier of each county's BPI.

In neither case is the value of the individual county BPI distorted by the adjustment process. The relative positions of the different counties remain the same as they are reported in the *Survey*. Thus if County A's BPI is twice as important as County B's in the *Survey*, it will remain so even after the seller's national market has been compressed into smaller local or regional markets.

EDITORS' NOTE: *The original article now goes on to present additional examples of the use of* Survey *data for organizing and controlling marketing effort. Basically, the approaches are similar. In fact, if the planning effort has been done well, then there is a logical flow into these next two management activities. But management must want to do this kind of analysis to get good results. The original article concluded on this theme as follows:*

"There is virtually no limit to the riches represented by the Survey's *mother lode of vital marketing information. If the sales manager has the will to be a more sophisticated market planner, market organizer, and market analyst, he will find a way to massage the data so that it will help him carry out his determination."*

QUESTIONS

1. Discuss briefly how *Survey of Buying Power* data could be used to segment a market.

2. Review the illustrative applications of *Survey* data and criticize the one you feel is the most questionable. Explain why (your assumptions will be very important here, so state them carefully).

3. Illustrate how *Survey* data could help plan a firm's marketing mix.

° 4. Can "psychographic" and/or "benefit segmentation" data be derived from *Sales Management* data? Explain. (See Readings 10 and 11.)

3

Development of the
marketing mix

THE SECOND STEP in marketing strategy planning is the development of an appropriate marketing mix for each target market. A marketing mix is a combination of the variables which are under the control of the marketing manager and include (1) product, (2) place, (3) promotion, and (4) price—the four *P*s. Because each market segment can be different from others in the same market grid, it is usually necessary to develop a separate marketing mix for each target market.

Most of the fourteen readings in this section are concerned with (or examples of) making decisions about the four *P*s so as to gain a differential advantage in one or more market segments. While a few of the readings are concerned with constraints on marketing mix planning, such as shortages, inflation, and actual or potential legislation, the primary focus is still on the four *P*s.

There are several articles on each of the *P*s, but it is important to keep in perspective that, eventually, all four *P*s must be blended into one marketing mix. Most of the authors in this section would agree with this, but their own special interest or experience causes them to focus on only one *P*. Sometimes, however, although they may seem to be considering only one *P*, actually they are "thinking" all four but with their special *P* as the dominant or all important one. Watch out for this kind of "myopia."

The uncontrollable variables which surround a firm, in this case product shortages and price controls which caused more shortages, have a strong impact on the strategies of a firm. Some of the resulting changes are discussed in the following article. Note, in particular, the impact and likely future impact on production-oriented firms and executives.

14. THE SQUEEZE ON PRODUCT MIX*

"IT'S NOT NICE to fool Mother Nature," warns the TV commercial for Chiffon margarine and, with that, the imperious lady aims a lightning bolt at the non-butter spread in the little plastic tub. Any day now Anderson, Clayton & Co., which makes Chiffon, expects to be hit by real-life lightning: the plastic shortage. If and when that happens, an already thunderous set of cost, supply, and profit pressures will multiply, forcing the company either to switch to an alternate package or temporarily to drop Chiffon from its product line.

"Every day brings a new set of conditions," grumbles a harassed Richard V. Kuska, vice-president for grocery products marketing. "It's a whole new way of life for us."

It's a new way of life for everyone. Because of worsening raw-material scarcities, price controls, and the fear of an energy crunch, companies of every size, shape, and business are reexamining their product lines and shifting the whole thrust of their product mix and marketing strategy. Their object is to maximize profit and to make the most efficient use of the materials and energy that are in short supply. Lower-margin products are being dropped or deemphasized in favor of those that offer higher margins. Often this means cutting back on commodity products to concentrate on higher-margin specialty items, or deferring big investments in products of limited potential while stressing longer-range products.

Along the way, the new pressures on the product mix are forcing companies to do something they should have done long ago: dump the obvious losers in their lines and pay closer attention to the 20% or 30% of their products that often account for 70% or more of profits. Companies are also being forced to look harder at the way they process raw materials. Industry experts claim that up to 10% of all petroleum, for instance, is either wasted or inefficiently used.

* Reprinted with permission from *Business Week* (January 5, 1974), pp. 50–55, © McGraw-Hill, Inc., 1974.

Already the product toll is staggering. In its pursuit of higher profits, General Electric Co. has dropped blenders, fans, heaters, humidifiers, and vacuum cleaners. Shell Chemical Co. is ending production of styrene butadiene rubber, isoprene rubber, and fertilizer (ammonia, urea, and ammonium sulfate). Philco-Ford Corp. has eliminated 50% of its color-TV screen sizes and 40% of its refrigerator models. Crown Zellerbach Corp. and other papermakers have cut their lines by as much as 60%. As if the fuel shortage was not bad enough, longer-range profit pressures have forced auto makers to cut their product line from an all-time peak of 375 models in 1970 to 300 this year. . . .

As a top chemical executive sums it up: "More and more companies have simply stopped trying to be all things to all people."

A shift from volume to profits

American business has moved a long way from the marketing philosophy of the 1950s and 1960s, dominated by the so-called full-line product concept. In those days, many companies, caught up in the growth fever that hit its peak in the mid-1960s, acquired new product lines or entire companies and put their emphasis on sales rather than profits. "By emphasizing sales," says John Howard, marketing professor at Columbia University's Graduate School of Business, "they could justify special products for almost every market segment as long as they added to total volume." With today's emphasis on profits, plus the added element of price controls and shortages that eat into profits, many of these same companies finally are measuring the high cost of overhead involved in going after some of those product segments. "One by one," says Howard, "they are chopping out marginally profitable products and redirecting their efforts."

The implications are vast, not only for the product mix itself but also for broader corporate marketing strategies and the total buyer/seller relationship:

Products will become more functional and sport fewer frills, reflecting the narrowing of product lines and substitutions, compromises, and other efforts to conserve dwindling resources of raw materials. "Annual reports and brochures do not really need to be so fat, glossy, and expensive," says one paper executive. "And cartons for liquor and perfume don't have to cost 50¢ each. Nor do match packs or even Christmas cards have to be coated with tinfoil and other flashy laminations. We have overengineered our products, and our clients have grown accustomed to 90 GE brightness [a General Electric numerical scale] when 80 GE brightness is perfectly adequate."

Product strategies will become more flexible and marketing timetables will be speeded up, as raw-material logistics gain equal importance with how well a company reads its markets. "How can you commit yourself now for 18 months in advance?" asks William G. Salatich, president of Gillette North America. "The entire supply situation could change in that time. If you switch from polystyrene to polypropylene, because of shortages, you can bet everyone else is changing, too. So you have a new shortage where none existed before."

New-product development will suffer. Raw material uncertainties, rising costs, and the deemphasis or elimination of smaller market segments will make management far more critical of new product ideas. E. Patrick McGuire, senior research specialist for the Conference Board and author of a major new study on product development, cites a general law that covers the situation. "It says in effect that the more you spend on a girl, the harder it is to kiss her goodbye," he notes. "In other words, the more you invest to bring a product to market, the tougher it is to kill it off. Yet we're already seeing a lot of companies do just that."

"All this really leaves marketing in a state of flux," says Richard W. Hansen, marketing professor at Southern Methodist University's School of Business. "For years, everything we worked on was aimed at expanding markets and increasing volume. Now we are seeing the marketing role become that of managing demand"—in other words, either stimulating or discouraging demand, depending on cost and supply problems.

"What you end up with," adds Jerry Wasserman, senior consultant with Arthur D. Little, Inc., "is a whole new function and dynamic in your product mix. And while material shortages and government controls may be only temporary, all this is bound to have a lasting effect on the way industry sells its goods and services."

New measures of performance

In winnowing their product mix, most companies measure product performance against the same criteria they have always used: sales, profits, market potential, pricing environment, and raw material availability. The change has come in the nature of the equation. Suddenly it is bewilderingly fluid and complex, shifting almost day by day.

Benzene, for instance, can go into a slew of products of varying profitability, ranging from nylons and phenolics to styrenes. "Say a guy has some flour and a dozen eggs," one chemical executive notes. "He can make library paste, or he can go all the way and make a soufflé." The problem is that even if rising costs and raw ingredient shortages fail to puncture his soufflé, price controls may. The result is some of the severest profit pressure in years.

J. M. Smucker Co., the jam, jelly, and preserve maker, has dropped several private-label products. "Our profit was below 5%," explains a Smucker executive. "When soybean oil increased from 9¢ to 30¢ per lb. and we couldn't pass on the increase, we had to sell at a loss. So we got out. When we were making 7% to 8% net profits, we could live with low-profit items. But today even the best items are returning less than 5%."

After a 200% jump in the cost of soya and linseed oils in the last nine months, the Foundry Products Div. of International Minerals & Chemical Corp. faced a different problem with alkydisocyanate, an industrial binder. In that instance, the Cost of Living Council gave the company permission to pass along the cost increases. By doing so, IMC knew it was running a risk that the added costs would price its product out of the market. But the company wanted to keep its high profit margin on alkydisocyanate—it runs 40% higher than that on the company's lower-priced furan-type resins. As a result, alkydisocyanate now costs about 55¢ per lb., up from 25¢ just before Christmas. While furan-type resins are also climbing in price, they still sell for only 27.5¢ per lb.

Now IMC is pondering a heavier push for its furan-type resins and possibly giving the ax to alkydisocyanate—except where customers will pay the price for the higher-quality product. "If we can get an order for even one batch [30,000 lb.] of alkydisocyanate, we'd go ahead and make it," says Jerry Young, manager of administration.

Lowering quality standards

To beat the shortages, product planners are developing a whole arsenal of alternatives. One of their major weapons is product "modification" or downgrading. Oilmen point out that accepting a 5% lower viscosity rate might increase the supply of a given oil product by 10%. Oil customers are also starting to accept a 10-degree "pour point," rather than zero. "How often do you need zero pour point anyway?" one oilman asks. "For us, it means so many more barrels per day of production. You might argue that we're producing a poorer quality of oil. But we're producing more oil. That can't be all bad."

At Scovill Mfg. Co., zinc supply and cost headaches are forcing the same kind of approach. "Right now," says Forrest W. Price, group vice-president for housewares, "the flag is up on our stand mixer because of its heavy zinc content. We've had zinc price increases of 300% in 12 months. We use 5½ lbs. of zinc in our stand mixer, and most of our motor mounts inside our appliances have varying amounts of zinc. So we say, 'Let's get away from zinc.' We have had an alternative product in development for the last couple of years. Now we are shifting our development and engineering time toward getting that speeded up."

To boost profitability on its existing mixers, Scovill may strip down its top-of-the-line chromium mixer. "For instance," says Price, "we may remove the timer. We certainly are not going out of the stand mixer business. But we have already decided what models to drop or modify."

Why have 5-ft. of cord on an appliance when you probably need only 3-ft., Price asks. "So we're shortening cords," he says. "During World War II, appliances were even shipped without cords, and single detachable cords were used for several appliances."

Such economies can work wonders with an unprofitable product line. When Scovill acquired the Westinghouse housewares division last year, the division had lost money for the previous 17 years. "We turned it into a profitmaker in 60 days," says Price. Scovill scrapped electric blanket production, chopped the number of electric-fan models by 50%, and modified several other products to make them more profitable.

Scovill did the same thing with its Dominion line, acquired in 1969. "Dominion had an excellent toaster that was being built in an uneconomic facility," says Price. "It was well engineered but difficult to manufacture and still meet competition." After a thorough study aimed at redesigning the toaster with fewer parts, Scovill ended up scrapping the line after nine months.

"Our industrial processes were developed in a period of affluence," notes Paul Gallagher, materials manager for Hewlett-Packard Co. "Now the goal is to use enough materials to make a good product, but not to overuse any."

Previously, Gallagher's own industry—electronics—used electronic-grade chemicals for almost all its products. Now it is switching to lower-grade chemicals. For instance, trichloroethylene, a degreasing solvent, is scarce in electronic grades, which come in 1-gal. containers, but plentiful in commercial grades, packaged in 55-gal. drums. The switchover is not a matter of cost savings alone, Gallagher stresses. "This is a seller's market," he says. "We look for availability rather than traditional cost savings."

Fewer products, less waste

The polyethylene shortage is forcing paper companies to do the same thing—for instance, conserving material by going to thinner grades. "Opacity is a luxury that we may have to give up," warns William G. Gray, vice-president of Potlatch Corp.'s paper group. Gray claims that cutting paper opacity to "reasonable levels" would conserve 20% of pulp and chemical additives—as well as increase Potlatch's profits. By cutting tissue-paper quality the same way, costs could be whittled another 30%. "Such standards are already accepted in Europe," he says, "and they may have to be accepted in the U.S., unless housewives want to go back to laundering handkerchiefs and dinner napkins. Even then, would the cotton industry be ready for us?"

Perhaps the highest toll taken by product proliferation—and one of the biggest targets of product pruners—is what one observer calls "product-mix productivity." In other words, an increase in the product line also increases total loss of manufacturing time for changeover from one product to another, cutting into both manufacturing productivity and profits.

Last summer, Automated Building Components, Inc., a Miami manufacturer of gang-nail plates that tie roof trusses together, cut the number of plate sizes that it stocks for builders by one-third, while maintaining the same size of total inventory. Instead of making 300,000 plates in 300 sizes, the company now makes 300,000 in 200 sizes. This saves on production switchover time. ABC has also cut back on packaging. Rather than neatly packing its intermediate sizes, the company has started "tumbling" them into boxes, in the same way that it packages small sizes. "Being so precise," says Chairman and President J. Calvin Juriet, "cost us valuable time and labor, and we are particularly short on labor."

Executives at Sun Oil Co.'s Lubrication & Metalworking Materials Div. concede that their own product proliferation got totally out of hand through the 1960s and drove the division into the red. Beginning in late 1970, Sun whittled its number of metalworking oils from 1,150 grades to 92, its lubes from 1,000 grades to 200, and its greases from 225 grades to 29.

"Most of those products were specific formulations for a single customer," says William H. Naylor, division manager. "The gradations were minute, but each required downtime in the refinery or mixing plant. We were not quite aware of what we were doing to ourselves." Pruning the product line not only cut refinery downtime for minor product changes but also reduced kettle-cleaning time in the mixing plant. Naylor estimates that fully 20% of a 30% boost in total production since the program began came from greater productivity. While the division is back into the black, Naylor concedes that product-by-product accounting of costs and profits is still not as precise as he wants it.

Persuading the customer

Pruning products is one thing. Selling a more limited line to customers can be another. "We have cut products—for instance, low-end tablet paper—and merchants screamed," says one paper executive. "They want you to carry a full line. If we sold just facial tissues and left out toilet and kitchen tissues, our customers wouldn't want us. And they don't have to raise hell on the phone. You just don't hear anything from them."

But he is hopeful. Six months ago, his company ran into the same attitude among industrial and commercial customers. "They rejected any talk of cutting product specs," he says. "Now they are willing to discuss it as long as volume continues at the same levels. Their attitude is not surliness, just acceptance. We have to rethink our product lines. But at the same time, we have to be sympathetic to the needs of customers."

W. A. Franke, executive vice-president of Southwest Forest Industries, Inc., adds, "If you've got good salesmen, they can convince your customers that you're trying to make your resources go further." In its own case, Southwest has dropped 10 of its 500 grades, is consolidating others, and is lowering the weight of its high-grade newsprint from 32 lb. to 30 lb. This conserves energy, as well as raw materials, since it takes less time to dry the paper. "We'll get longer runs on our machines, instead of switching between grades, and newspapers will presumably get more mileage out of a ton of fiber," Franke adds.

Consolidated Papers, Inc., is throwing in another bonus: a price break on higher-quality alternatives. Because of rising costs for raw pulp and starch and the general unavailability of protein, Consolidated dropped a key quality product—No. 5 web-offset coated paper—and put heavier emphasis on its higher-grade No. 4 paper. While No. 4 costs about $27 per ton more to produce than No. 5, its profit margins were higher. So in an effort to persuade customers to trade up, Consolidated was able to cut the price of No. 4—pegging it roughly midway between the old price for No. 5 and No. 4—and still preserve a comfortable profit.

Because of the price cut and a continued rise in costs, however, No. 4 paper is now pushing the cost limits. Pulp prices, which jumped from $175 to $230 per ton in a single year, are expected to rise another $35 per ton in the next few months. "And if prices keep climbing," says Marketing Vice-President Lawrence H. Boling, "our profit picture will change again. Right now, we're rejecting the suggestion of dropping No. 4. But it is still being considered."

'These are drastic times'

The reigning concern is the big customer—the one who keeps coming back for more. "If a guy shows up in Vegas with a dollar," says M. H. P. Morand, marketing vice-president for Dow Chemical U.S.A, "you take him to the birdcage, or chuck-a-luck, where the house margin is 30%. But if the guy looks like a repeat customer, you steer him to roulette or craps, where his odds are better. Our business thrives on marriages rather than shackups. Sometimes you've got to pass up the quick thrills."

To spread the word to its big buyers in the auto, rubber, and basic metals industries, Sun Oil's Lubrication & Metalworking Materials Div. sent its top executives on the road, beginning in late 1972. They told customers that the product-line squeeze was coming and that the product mix had to be rationalized to increase output and restore profit. "We made it clear," says division manager Naylor, "that if the company could not pull a better profit out of the business and had to abandon it, as so many other oil companies already had, industry would be in trouble. We tried to explain to Ford, for instance, that its competition for oil products was not General Motors—it was all of industry—and that Firestone and Du Pont need oil as badly as GM does."

The customer response, says Naylor, often was, "You're taking a long time to tell me I'm going to have to pay more." Says he: "Our answer was, 'O.K., but your style of buying is helping force the price up. You write a spec, and it reflects only your precise needs, or maybe the emotional needs of the guy who wrote the spec. He wants it perfect and unique. You may be asking too much.'"

The ultimate answer, of course, would simply be to produce to order. While many industrial-goods companies operate this way, most consumer companies that deal in huge product quantities find it impractical. A few, however, are reconsidering. One of them is Scovill.

"I don't know if we could get away with it or not," concedes Scovill's Price. "It's a little drastic, a little unorthodox." But then again, he notes, these are drastic times. "We know how many blenders are sold in the marketplace," Price says. "We know how many we shipped last year and to whom. And we can pretty well forecast how many we'll need this coming year. But it takes 30 to 60 days to stock the distributor, and it takes him 30 days to get into retail distribution." This time lag complicates Scovill's reading of the market and its product-mix decisions.

"So we may change our whole marketing strategy," says Price. "We may ask the customer, 'What do you want? Let me know over a longer period of time. I'll build what you want rather than me trying to outguess you.'" Price has already discussed the idea with customers. "They love it," he says. "But they'd have to give me a firm commitment before I'd give them a commitment. That's what my vendor is doing to me. We used to be able to buy from him every 60 days without any problems and get shipment 15 days later." No more.

A major new discipline

If raw material and energy shortages continue, some marketing men claim that business will have to go much further in shaking up its product mix. Some even foresee a major shift away from products and into services, since service industries consume far less energy and raw materials.

"Instead of producing autos designed for planned obsolescence every five or six years," says Southern Methodist University's Hansen, "perhaps we should design them for the long run and promote a large service industry that would restyle and refurbish cars. Auto makers might end up with one-tenth their current employment and one-tenth their product line. But taking up the slack would be thousands and thousands of service shops."

Far more of a certainty than such fundamental changes in the auto business will be the emergence of product management as a major discipline that goes far beyond pruning product lines and keeping tabs on product costs and profitability. More and more, product management will become an important part of total corporate management and a key tool for increasing corporate profitability and productivity. This will involve product planners communicating far more with corporate production, engineering, and financial types, as well as with suppliers who may need help in some of their own planning and logistics.

"This is just beginning to come," says one marketer, "as we start to computerize product cost-accounting and get a better handle on the interrelationship of products within a line and the interrelationship of that line to total corporate performance. Up to now, product management has always been a little like religion. Almost everyone recognizes it in one form or another, but few go to church on Sunday." In the months ahead, a growing number of companies will be moving into the front pew.

QUESTIONS

1. What impact will the squeeze on product lines have on the ability of firms to serve segmented markets? Is market segmentation an obsolete concept in a shortage economy?
2. Is it "right" for a firm to drop product lines which some customers are presently buying—finding them the best products available (*for them*)? What about the macro responsibility of serving consumers' needs?
°3. What effect do you think the thinning of product lines will have on the nature of the search for and the ability of a firm to achieve a differential advantage? (See Readings 5 and 6.)
°4. Explain one of the examples in this article in terms of Cravens' alternative actions in a shortage economy (Reading 8).

As a product progresses from its introduction through maturity to decline, different strategies are required. In this article, Levitt discusses the several life cycle stages and suggests that most firms should lengthen the maturity stage. He offers four possible extension strategies.

---

15. EXPLOIT THE PRODUCT LIFE CYCLE*

Theodore Levitt

MOST ALERT and thoughtful senior marketing executives are by now familiar with the concept of the product life cycle. Even a handful of uniquely cosmopolitan and up-to-date corporate presidents have familiarized themselves with this tantalizing concept. Yet a recent survey I took of such executives found none who used the concept in any strategic way whatever and pitifully few who used it in any kind of tactical way. It has remained—as have so many fascinating theories in economics, physics, and sex—a remarkably durable but almost totally unemployed and seemingly unemployable piece of professional baggage whose presence in the rhetoric of professional discussions adds a much coveted but apparently unattainable legitimacy to the idea that marketing management is somehow a profession. There is, furthermore, a persistent feeling that the life cycle concept adds luster and believability to the insistent claim in certain circles that marketing is close to being some sort of science.[1]

The concept of the product life cycle is today at about the stage that the Copernican view of the universe was 300 years ago: a lot of people knew about it, but hardly anybody seemed to use it in any effective or productive way.

Now that so many people know and in some fashion understand the product life cycle, it seems time to put it to work. The object of this article is to suggest some ways of using the concept effectively and of turning the knowledge of its existence into a managerial instrument of competitive power.

Since the concept has been presented somewhat differently by different authors and for different audiences, it is useful to review it briefly here so that every reader has the same background for the discussion which follows later in this article.

° Reprinted with permission from the *Harvard Business Review*, vol. 43, November–December 1965, pp. 81–94, © 1965 by the President and Fellows of Harvard College; All Rights Reserved. At the time of writing, Professor Levitt was on the faculty of the Graduate School of Business Administration of Harvard University.

[1] For discussions of the scientific claims or potentials of marketing, see George Schwartz, *Development of Marketing Theory* (Cincinnati, Ohio, South-Western Publishing Co., 1963); and Reavis Cox, Wroe Alderson, and Stanley J. Shapiro, ed., *Theory in Marketing* (Homewood, Illinois, Richard D. Irwin, Inc., Second Series, 1964).

HISTORICAL PATTERN

The life story of most successful products is a history of their passing through certain recognizable stages. These are shown in Exhibit I and occur in the following order:

Stage 1. Market Development—This is when a new product is first brought to market, before there is a proved demand for it, and often before it has been fully proved out technically in all respects. Sales are low and creep along slowly.

EXHIBIT I
Product life cycle–entire industry

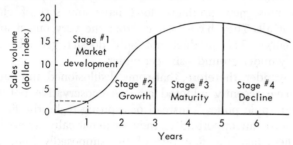

Stage 2. Market Growth—Demand begins to accelerate and the size of the total market expands rapidly. It might also be called the "Takeoff Stage."

Stage 3. Market Maturity—Demand levels off and grows, for the most part, only at the replacement and new family-formation rate.

Stage 4. Market Decline—The product begins to lose consumer appeal and sales drift downward, such as when buggy whips lost out with the advent of automobiles and when silk lost out to nylon.

Three operating questions will quickly occur to the alert executive:

Given a proposed new product or service, how and to what extent can the shape and duration of each stage be predicted?

Given an existing product, how can one determine what stage it is in?

Given all this knowledge, how can it be effectively used?

A brief further elaboration of each stage will be useful before dealing with these questions in detail.

DEVELOPMENT STAGE

Bringing a new product to market is fraught with unknowns, uncertainties, and frequently unknowable risks. Generally, demand has to be "created" during the product's initial *market development stage.* How long this takes depends on the product's complexity, its degree of newness, its fit into consumer needs, and the presence of competitive substitutes of one form or another. A proved cancer cure would require virtually no market development; it would get immediate massive support. An alleged superior substitute for the lost-wax process of sculpture casting would take lots longer.

While it has been demonstrated time after time that properly customer-oriented new product development is one of the primary conditions of sales and profit growth, what have been demonstrated even more conclusively are the ravaging costs and frequent fatalities associated with launching new products. Nothing seems to take more time, cost more money, involve more pitfalls, cause more anguish, or break more careers than do sincere and well-conceived new product programs. The fact is, most new products don't have any sort of classical life cycle curve at all. They have instead from the very outset an infinitely descending curve. The product not only doesn't get off the ground; it goes quickly under ground—six feet under.

It is little wonder, therefore, that some disillusioned and badly burned companies have recently adopted a more conservative policy—what I call the "used apple policy." Instead of aspiring to be the first company to see and seize an opportunity, they systematically avoid being first. They let others take the first bite of the supposedly juicy apple that tantalizes them. They let others do the pioneering. If the idea works, they quickly follow suit. They say, in effect, "The trouble with being a pioneer is that the pioneers get killed by the Indians." Hence, they say (thoroughly mixing their metaphors), "We don't have to get the first bite of the apple. The second one is good enough." They are willing to eat off a used apple, but they try to be alert enough to make sure it is only slightly used—that they at least get the second big bite, not the tenth skimpy one.

GROWTH STAGE

The usual characteristic of a successful new product is a gradual rise in its sales curve during the market development stage. At some point in this rise a marked increase in consumer demand occurs and sales take off. The boom is on. This is the beginning of Stage 2—the *market growth stage*. At this point potential competitors who have been watching developments during Stage 1 jump into the fray. The first ones to get in are generally those with an exceptionally effective "used apple policy." Some enter the market with carbon-copies of the originator's product. Others make functional and design improvements. And at this point product and brand differentiation begin to develop.

The ensuing fight for the consumer's patronage poses to the originating producer an entirely new set of problems. Instead of seeking ways of getting consumers to *try the product*, the originator now faces the more compelling problem of getting them to *prefer his brand.* This generally requires important changes in marketing strategies and methods. But the policies and tactics now adopted will be neither freely the sole choice of the originating producer nor as experimental as they might have been during Stage 1. The presence of competitors both dictates and limits what can easily be tried—such as, for example, testing what is the best price level or the best channel of distribution.

As the rate of consumer acceptance accelerates, it generally becomes increasingly easy to open new distribution channels and retail outlets. The consequent filling of distribution pipelines generally causes the entire industry's factory sales to rise more rapidly than store sales. This creates an exaggerated impression of profit opportunity which, in turn, attracts more competitors. Some of these will begin to charge lower prices because of later advances in technology, production shortcuts, the need to take lower margins in order to get distribution, and the like. All this in time inescapably moves the industry to the threshold of a new stage of competition.

MATURITY STAGE

This new stage is the *market maturity stage.* The first sign of its advent is evidence of market saturation. This means that most consumer companies or households that are sales prospects will be owning or using the product. Sales now grow about on a par with population. No more distribution pipelines need be filled. Price competition now becomes intense. Competitive attempts to achieve and hold brand preference now involve making finer and finer differentiations in the product, in customer services, and in the promotional practices and claims made for the product.

Typically, the market maturity stage forces the producer to concentrate on holding his distribution outlets, retaining his shelf space, and, in the end, trying to secure even more intensive distribution. Whereas during the market development stage the originator depended heavily on the positive efforts of his retailers and distributors to help sell his product, retailers and distributors will now frequently have been reduced largely to being merchandise-displayers and order-takers. In the case of branded products in particular, the originator must now, more than ever, communicate directly with the consumer.

The market maturity stage typically calls for a new kind of emphasis on competing more effectively. The originator is increasingly forced to appeal to the consumer on the basis of price, marginal product differences, or both. Depending on the product, services and deals offered in connection with it are often the clearest and most effective forms of differentiation. Beyond these, there will be attempts to create and promote fine product distinctions through packaging and advertising, and to appeal to special market segments. The market maturity stage can be passed through rapidly, as in the case of most women's fashion fads, or it can persist for generations with per capita consumption neither rising nor falling, as in the case of such staples as men's shoes and industrial fasteners. Or maturity can persist, but in a state of gradual but steady per capita decline, as in the case of beer and steel.

DECLINE STAGE

When market maturity tapers off and consequently comes to an end, the product enters Stage 4—*market decline*. In all cases of maturity and decline the industry is transformed. Few companies are able to weather the competitive storm. As demand declines, the overcapacity that was already apparent during the period of maturity now becomes endemic. Some producers see the handwriting implacably on the wall but feel that with proper management and cunning they will be one of the survivors after the industry-wide deluge they so clearly foresee. To hasten their competitors' eclipse directly, or to frighten them into early voluntary withdrawal from the industry, they initiate a variety of aggressively depressive tactics, propose mergers or buy-outs, and generally engage in activities that make life thanklessly burdensome for all firms, and make death the inevitable consequence for most of them. A few companies do indeed weather the storm, sustaining life through the constant descent that now clearly characterizes the industry. Production gets concentrated into fewer hands. Prices and margins get depressed. Consumers get bored. The only cases where there is any relief from this boredom and gradual euthanasis are where styling and fashion play some constantly revivifying role.

PREPLANNING IMPORTANCE

Knowing that the lives of successful products and services are generally characterized by something like the pattern illustrated in Exhibit I can become the basis for important life-giving policies and practices. One of the greatest values of the life cycle concept is for managers about to launch a new product. The first step for them is to try to foresee the profile of the proposed product's cycle.

As with so many things in business, and perhaps uniquely in marketing, it is almost impossible to make universally useful suggestions regarding how to manage one's affairs. It is certainly particularly difficult to provide widely useful advice on how to foresee or predict the slope and duration of a product's life. Indeed, it is precisely because so little specific day-to-day guidance is possible in anything, and because no checklist has ever by itself been very useful to anybody for very long, that business management will probably never be a science—always an art—and will pay exceptional rewards to managers with rare talent, enormous energy, iron nerve, great capacity for assuming responsibility and bearing accountability.

But this does not mean that useful efforts cannot or should not be made to try to foresee the slope and duration of a new product's life. Time spent in attempting this kind of foresight not only helps assure that a more rational approach is brought to product planning and merchandising; also, as will be shown later, it can help create valuable lead time for important strategic and tactical moves after the product is brought to market. Specifically, it can be a great help in developing an orderly series of competitive moves, in expanding or stretching out the life of a product, in maintaining a clean product line, and in purposely phasing out dying and costly old products.[2]

❋   ❋   ❋

STAGE RECOGNITION

The various characteristics of the stages described above will help one to recognize the stage a particular product occupies at any given time. But hindsight will always be more accurate than current sight. Perhaps the best way of seeing one's current stage is to try to foresee the next stage and work backwards. This approach has several virtues:

It forces one to look ahead, constantly to try to reforesee his future and competitive environment. This will have its own rewards. As Charles F. Kettering, perhaps the last of Detroit's primitive inventors and probably the greatest of all its inventors, was fond of saying, "We should all be concerned about the future because that's where we'll have to spend the rest of our lives." By looking at the future one can better assess the state of the present.

Looking ahead gives more perspective to the present than looking at the present alone. Most people know more about the present than is good for them. It is neither healthy nor helpful to know the present too well, for our perception of the present is too often too heavily distorted by the urgent pressures of day-to-day events. To know where the present is in the continuum of competitive time and events, it often makes more sense to try to know what the future will bring, and when it will bring it, than to try to know what the present itself actually contains.

Finally, the value of knowing what stage a product occupies at any given time resides only in the way that fact is used. But its use is always in the future. Hence a prediction of the future environment in which the information will be used is often more functional for the effective capitalization on knowledge about the present than knowledge about the present itself.

SEQUENTIAL ACTIONS

The life cycle concept can be effectively employed in the strategy of both existing and new products. For purposes of continuity and clar-

---

[2] See Philip Kotler, "Phasing Out Weak Products," *HBR*, March–April 1965, p. 107.

ity, the remainder of this article will describe some of the uses of the concept from the early stages of new product planning through the later stages of keeping the product profitably alive. The chief discussion will focus on what I call a policy of "life extension" or "market stretching."[3]

When a company develops a new product or service, it should try to plan at the very outset a series of actions to be employed at various subsequent stages in the product's existence so that its sales and profit curves are constantly sustained rather than following their usual declining slope.

In other words, advance planning should be directed at extending, or stretching out, the life of the product. It is this idea of *planning in advance* of the actual launching of a new product to take specific actions later in its life cycle—actions designed to sustain its growth and profitability—which appears to have great potential as an instrument of long-term product strategy.

NYLON'S LIFE

How this might work for a product can be illustrated by looking at the history of nylon. The way in which nylon's booming sales life has been repeatedly and systematically extended and stretched can serve as a model for other products. What has happened in nylon may not have been purposely planned that way at the outset, but the results are quite as if they had been planned.

The first nylon end-uses were primarily military—parachutes, thread, rope. This was followed by nylon's entry into the circular knit market and its consequent domination of the women's hosiery business. Here it developed the kind of steadily rising growth and profit curves that every executive dreams about. After some years these curves began to flatten out. But before they flattened very noticeably, Du Pont had already developed measures designed to revitalize sales and profits. It did several things, each of which is demonstrated graphically in Exhibit II. This exhibit and the explanation which follows take some liberties with the actual facts of the nylon situation in order to highlight the points I wish to make. But they take no liberties with the essential requisites of product strategy.

Point A of Exhibit II shows the hypothetical point at which the nylon curve (dominated at this point by hosiery) flattened out. If nothing further had been done, the sales curve would have continued along the flattened pace indicated by the dotted line at Point A. This is also the hypothetical point at which the first systematic effort was made

---

[3] For related ideas on discerning opportunities for product revivification, see Lee Adler, "A New Orientation for Plotting a Marketing Strategy," *Business Horizons*, Winter 1964, p. 37.

EXHIBIT II
Hypothetical life cycle–nylon

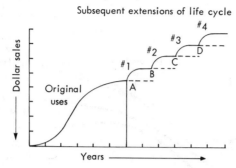

Subsequent extensions of life cycle

to extend the product's life. Du Pont, in effect, took certain "actions" which pushed hosiery sales upward rather than continuing the path implied by the dotted line extension of the curve at Point A. At Point A action #1 pushed an otherwise flat curve upward.

At points B, C, and D still other new sales and profit expansion "actions" (#2, #3, #4, and so forth) were taken. What were these actions? Or, more usefully, what was their strategic content? What did they try to do? They involved strategies that tried to expand sales via four different routes:

1. Promoting more frequent usage of the product among current users.
2. Developing more varied usage of the product among current users.
3. Creating new users for the product by expanding the market.
4. Finding new uses for the basic material.

        ✿   ✿   ✿

Had it not been for the addition of new uses for the same basic material—such as warp knits in 1945, tire cord in 1948, textured yarns in 1955, carpet yarns in 1959, and so forth—nylon would not have had the spectacularly rising consumption curve it has so clearly had. At various stages it would have exhausted its existing markets or been forced into decline by competing materials. The systematic search for new uses for the basic (and improved) material extended and stretched the product's life.

        ✿   ✿   ✿

EXTENSION STRATEGIES

The existence of the kinds of product life cycles illustrated in Exhibits II and III suggest that there may be considerable value for people involved in new product work to begin planning for the extension of

EXHIBIT III
Innovation of new products postpones the time of total maturity–nylon industry

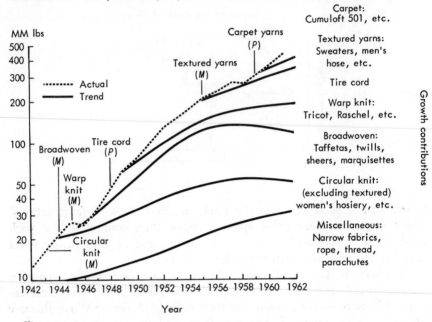

Key:
M = Material influences
P = Product influences
Source: *Modern Textile Magazine*, February 1964, p. 33. © 1962 by Jordan P. Yale.

the lives of their products even before these products are formally launched. To plan for new life-extending infusions of effort (as in Exhibit II) at this pre-introduction stage can be extremely useful in three profoundly important ways.

1. *It generates an active rather than a reactive product policy.* It systematically structures a company's long-term marketing and product development efforts in advance, rather than each effort or activity being merely a stop-gap response to the urgent pressures of repeated competitive thrusts and declining profits. The life-extension view of product policy enforces thinking and planning ahead—thinking in some systematic way about the moves likely to be made by potential competitors, about possible changes in consumer reactions to the product, and the required selling activities which best take advantage of these conditional events.

2. *It lays out a long-term plan designed to infuse new life into the product at the right time, with the right degree of care, and with the right amount of effort.* Many activities designed to raise the sales and profits of existing products or materials are often undertaken without regard to their relationship to each other or to timing—the optimum

point of consumer readiness for such activities or the point of optimum competitive effectiveness. Careful advance planning, long before the need for such activity arises, can help assure that the timing, the care, and the efforts are appropriate to the situation.

For example, it appears extremely doubtful that the boom in women's hair coloring and hair tinting products would have been as spectacular if vigorous efforts to sell these products had preceded the boom in hair sprays and chemical hair fixers. The latter helped create a powerful consumer consciousness of hair fashions because they made it relatively easy to create and wear fashionable hair styles. Once it became easy for women to have fashionable hair styles, the resulting fashion consciousness helped open the door for hair colors and tints. It could not have happened the other way around, with colors and tints first creating fashion consciousness and thus raising the sales of sprays and fixers. Because understanding the reason for this precise order of events is essential for appreciating the importance of early pre-introduction life-extension planning, it is useful to go into a bit of detail. Consider:

For women, setting their hair has been a perennial problem for centuries. First, the length and treatment of their hair is one of the most obvious ways in which they distinguish themselves from men. Hence to be attractive in that distinction becomes crucial. Second, hair frames and highlights the face, much like an attractive wooden border frames and highlights a beautiful painting. Thus hair styling is an important element in accentuating the appearance of a woman's facial features. Third, since the hair is long and soft, it is hard to hold in an attractive arrangement. It gets mussed in sleep, wind, damp weather, sporting activities, and so forth.

Therefore, the effective *arrangement* of a woman's hair is understandably her first priority in hair care. An unkempt brunette would gain nothing from making herself into a blond. Indeed, in a country where blonds are in the minority, the switch from being an unkempt brunette to being an unkempt blond would simply draw attention to her sloppiness. But once the problem of arrangement became easily "solved" by sprays and fixers, colors and tints could become big business, especially among women whose hair was beginning to turn gray.

The same order of priorities applies in industrial products. For example, it seems quite inconceivable that many manufacturing plants would easily have accepted the replacement of the old single-spindle, constantly man-tended screw machine by a computerized tape-tended, multiple-spindle machine. The mechanical tending of the multiple-spindle machine was a necessary intermediate step, if for no other reason than that it required a lesser work-flow change, and certainly a lesser conceptual leap for the companies and the machine-tending workers involved.

For Jell-O, it is unlikely that vegetable flavors would have been very successful before the idea of gelatin as a salad base had been pretty well accepted. Similarly, the promotion of colored and patterned Scotch tape as a gift and decorative seal might not have been as successful if department stores had not, as the result of their drive to compete more effectively with mass merchandisers by offering more customer services, previously demonstrated to the consumer what could be done to wrap and decorate gifts.

3. *Perhaps the most important benefit of engaging in advance, pre-introduction planning for sales-extending, market-stretching activities later in the product's life is that this practice forces a company to adopt a wider view of the nature of the product it is dealing with.* Indeed, it may even force the adoption of a wider view of the company's business. Take the case of Jell-O. What is its product? Over the years Jell-O has become the brand umbrella for a wide range of dessert products, including cornstarch-base puddings, pie fillings, and the new "Whip'n Chill," a light dessert product similar to a Bavarian Creme or French Mousse. On the basis of these products, it might be said that the Jell-O Division of General Foods is in the "dessert technology" business.

In the case of tape, perhaps 3M has gone even further in this technological approach to its business. It has a particular expertise (technology) on which it has built a constantly expanding business. This expertise can be said to be that of bonding things (adhesives in the case of Scotch tape) to other things, particularly to thin materials. Hence we see 3M developing scores of profitable items, including electronic recording tape (bonding electron-sensitive materials to tape) and "Thermo-Fax" duplicating equipment and supplies (bonding heat-reactive materials to paper).

CONCLUSION

For companies interested in continued growth and profits, successful new product strategy should be viewed as a planned totality that looks ahead over some years. For its own good, new product strategy should try to predict in some measure the likelihood, character, and timing of competitive and market events. While prediction is always hazardous and seldom very accurate, it is undoubtedly far better than not trying to predict at all. In fact, every product strategy and every business decision inescapably involves making a prediction about the future, about the market, and about competitors. To be more systematically aware of the predictions one is making so that one acts on them in an offensive rather than a defensive or reactive fashion—this is the real virtue of preplanning for market stretching and product life extension. The result will be a product strategy that includes some sort of *plan for a timed sequence of conditional moves.*

Even before entering the market development stage, the originator should make a judgment regarding the probable length of the product's normal life, taking into account the possibilities of expanding its uses and users. This judgment will also help determine many things—for example, whether to price the product on a skimming or a penetration basis, or what kind of relationship the company should develop with its resellers.

These considerations are important because at each stage in a product's life cycle each management decision must consider the competitive requirements of the next stage. Thus a decision to establish a strong branding policy during the market growth stage might help to insulate the brand against strong price competition later; a decision to establish a policy of "protected" dealers in the market development stage might facilitate point-of-sale promotions during the market growth stage, and so on. In short, having a clear idea of future product development possibilities and market development opportunities should reduce the likelihood of becoming locked into forms of merchandising that might possibly prove undesirable.

This kind of advance thinking about new product strategy helps management avoid other pitfalls. For instance, advertising campaigns that look successful from a short-term view may hurt in the next stage of the life cycle. Thus at the outset Metrecal advertising used a strong medical theme. Sales boomed until imitative competitors successfully emphasized fashionable slimness. Metrecal had projected itself as the dietary for the overweight consumer, an image that proved far less appealing than that of being the dietary for people who were fashion-smart. But Metrecal's original appeal had been so strong and so well made that it was a formidable task later on to change people's impressions about the product. Obviously, with more careful long-range planning at the outset, a product's image can be more carefully positioned and advertising can have more clearly defined objectives.

Recognizing the importance of an orderly series of steps in the introduction of sales-building "actions" for new products should be a central ingredient of long-term product planning. A carefully preplanned program for market expansion, even before a new product is introduced, can have powerful virtues. The establishment of a rational plan for the future can also help to guide the direction and pace of the on-going technical research in support of the product. Although departures from such a plan will surely have to be made to accommodate unexpected events and revised judgments, the plan puts the company in a better position to *make* things happen rather than constantly having to react to things that *are* happening.

It is important that the originator does *not* delay this long-term planning until after the product's introduction. How the product should be introduced and the many uses for which it might be promoted at the outset should be a function of a careful consideration of the optimum sequence of suggested product appeals and product uses. Consideration must focus not just on optimum things to do, but as importantly on their optimum *sequence*—for instance, what the order of use of various appeals should be and what the order of suggested product uses should be. If Jell-O's first suggested use had been as a diet food, its chances of later making a big and easy impact in the gelatin dessert market undoubtedly would have been greatly diminished. Similarly, if nylon hosiery had been promoted at the outset as a functional daytime-wear hosiery, its ability to replace silk as the acceptable high-fashion hosiery would have been greatly diminished.

To illustrate the virtue of pre-introduction planning for a product's later life, suppose a company has developed a nonpatentable new product—say, an ordinary kitchen salt shaker. Suppose that nobody now has any kind of shaker. One might say, before launching it, that (1) it has a potential market of "x" million household, institutional, and commercial consumers, (2) in two years market maturity will set in, and (3) in one year profit margins will fall because of the entry of competition. Hence one might lay out the following plan:

I.   *End of first year: expand market among current users*
     Ideas—new designs, such as sterling shaker for formal use, "masculine" shaker for barbecue use, antique shaker for "Early American" households, miniature shaker for each table place setting, moisture-proof design for beach picnics.

II. *End of second year: expand market to new users*
     Ideas—designs for children, quaffer design for beer drinkers in bars, design for sadists to rub salt into open wounds.

III. *End of third year: find new uses*
     Ideas—make identical product for use as a pepper shaker, as decorative garlic salt shaker, shaker for household scouring powder, shaker to sprinkle silicon dust on parts being machined in machine shops, and so forth.
     This effort to prethink methods of reactivating a flattening sales curve far in advance of its becoming flat enables product planners to assign priorities to each task, and to plan future production expansion and capital and marketing requirements in a systematic fashion. It prevents one's trying to do too many things at once, results in priorities being determined rationally instead of as accidental consequences of the timing of new ideas, and disciplines both the product development effort that is launched in support of a product's growth and the marketing effort that is required for its continued success.

QUESTIONS

1.   How does a product's stage in the life cycle affect marketing mix planning? Illustrate with a specific product, say a new dessert concept.

2. Illustrate what could be done for a specific industrial product, say a new hand-held wood cutting tool, to move it through Levitt's four approaches for extending the product life cycle.

3. Is Levitt really talking about extending product life cycles or starting new ones?

*4. Energy and raw materials shortages (see Readings 8 and 14) are causing many firms to thin their product lines and delay or eliminate the introduction of new products. How will this affect product life cycles and the strategic importance of the life-cycle concept?

*5. Would Levitt's ideas be relevant for Kotler and Levy's nonbusiness organizations (Reading 4)? Explain, with an illustration.

This article reports on some potentially very powerful federal legislation concerning consumer product safety. Then, the authors examine the implications of this legislation for manufacturers, wholesalers, retailers, and consumers.

---

16. THE CONSUMER PRODUCT SAFETY ACT: A SPECIAL CASE IN CONSUMERISM*

Walter Jensen, Jr., Edward M. Mazze, and Duke N. Stern

A NEW ERA in marketing legislation began when, on October 28, 1972, President Nixon signed the Consumer Product Safety Act.[1] This act, which went into effect on December 26, 1972, created an independent Consumer Product Safety Commission. The commission has powers to prescribe mandatory safety standards for virtually all *consumer* products except those for which specific safety legislation already exists. The act specifically excludes the following articles: tobacco and

---

* Reprinted with permission from the *Journal of Marketing*, published by the American Marketing Association, October 1973, pp. 68–71. At the time of publication, Walter Jensen, Jr., was associate professor of business law, Edward M. Mazze was professor of business administration, and Duke N. Stern was assistant professor of business administration, all at the Virginia Polytechnic Institute and State University.

[1] Consumer Product Safety Act of 1972 (CPS Act), Pub. L. no. 92 (October 28, 1972), 41 U.S.L.W. 57 (October 31, 1972).

tobacco products; motor vehicles and motor vehicle equipment;[2] economic poisons;[3] aircraft and aircraft parts;[4] boats subject to safety regulation under the Federal Boat Safety Act of 1971;[5] and drugs, devices, cosmetics, and foods.[6] If the act is implemented in accordance with the expressed will of Congress, it might prove to be the most far-reaching consumer-oriented law regulating marketing practice since the Federal Trade Commission Act of 1914.[7]

This article has two principal purposes: (1) to examine the implications of this legislation for consumerism, and (2) to review the historical development of this legislation. As a result of the act, it is expected that manufacturers will be confronted with new pressures for more stringent labeling requirements, tighter product recall procedures, and more rigid bookkeeping systems.[8] Consumers will gain by having more accurate and complete information concerning the safety of products.

In view of recent changes in consumer attitudes, the need for legislation which concentrates upon the marketability of a product rather than upon a manufacturer's compliance with vague and ill-defined safety standards became apparent. Self-regulation of product safety standards by trade associations, independent testing laboratories, and consumer groups had proven ineffective. Prior to the enactment of the Consumer Product Safety Act, safety legislation on a national basis consisted of a series of isolated statutes which purported to remedy specific hazards among a narrow range of product categories. Moreover, authority was divided among many federal agencies.

A National Commission on Product Safety was created in 1967. It was empowered to study all aspects of product safety and to make recommendations for legislation which would apply to all states on a uniform basis. The commission contended that existing federal legislation was characterized by unnecessary administrative requirements, inadequate sanctions, distorted priorities, and misdirected technical expertise.[9] This inadequacy of existing legislation, both nationally and locally, and the ineffective controls on product hazards prompted the federal government to investigate new methods to protect the consumer. A new type of product safety legislation was required.

---

[2] Traffic and Motor Vehicle Act of 1966, 15 U.S.C. §1391 (3)-(4) (1970).

[3] Federal Insecticide, Fungicide and Rodenticide Act of 1947, 7 U.S.C. §135 (1970).

[4] Federal Aviation Act of 1958, 49 U.S.C. §1301 (1970).

[5] 46 U.S.C. §1451 et seq.

[6] Federal Food, Drug, and Cosmetic Act of 1938, 21 U.S.C. §321 (f)-(i) (1970); Poultry Products Inspection Act of 1957, 21 U.S.C. §453 (e)-(f) (1970); Federal Meat Inspection of 1967, 21 U.S.C. §601 (j) (1970); and Egg Products Inspection Act of 1971, 21 U.S.C. §1033 (1970).

[7] 15 U.S.C. §44 et seq. (1914).

[8] Traffic and Motor Vehicle Act of 1966, 15 U.S.C. §1381 et seq. (1970).

[9] Final Report of The National Commission on Product Safety 2 (1970).

THE ACT

The Consumer Product Safety Act presents several challenges to marketing practice and some opportunities for the consumer. The act is a result of congressional findings that unsafe consumer products are distributed in unacceptable numbers; hence, consumers are frequently unable to anticipate and guard against the risks of unsafe products. More than 20 million Americans are injured in their homes each year as a result of accidents which are associated with unsafe consumer products. Of this total, 110,000 persons are permanently disabled and 30,000 others have lost their lives. The annual cost of product-related injuries exceeds $5.5 billion.[10] It has been estimated that 20% of these injuries could have been prevented if manufacturers had produced safe, well-designed products.

The Consumer Product Safety Act was intended to protect consumers from the risks of injury which result from unsafe consumer products. The act requires the formulation of uniform safety standards which are designed to minimize conflicting state and local regulations.[11] The act also creates a five-member Consumer Product Safety Commission, which functions as an independent regulatory agency. A major function of the commission is the gathering and dissemination of information which relates injuries to specific products. In addition, the commission is empowered to create an advisory council of fifteen experts in consumer safety. Five of these experts will be from consumer product industries, five from consumer organizations, and five others from governmental agencies at the local, state, and federal levels. Although the council possesses only advisory functions, its powers may prove to be substantial.

Since the act is broad in scope, it affects those consumer products which are not already regulated by the federal government. When added to the current list of consumer protection laws, the act clearly reflects the national government's widening interest in consumer protection. This list includes, among others, the National Traffic and Motor Vehicles Safety Act of 1966; the Flammable Fabrics Act Amendments of 1967; the Food, Drug and Cosmetic Act of 1906; the Radiation Control for Health and Safety Act of 1968; and the Poison Prevention Packaging Act of 1970. When compared with existing consumer-oriented legislation, the Consumer Product Safety Act not only possesses more effective legal and administrative sanctions but also represents a broader spectrum for the application of safety standards.

Although the act's regulatory machinery is still in the formative stage, it is apparent that certain sections will have an immediate impact on

---

[10] *Hearings on National Commission on Product Safety before the Senate Comm. on Commerce,* 91st Cong., 2d Sess., at p. 37 (1970).

[11] Same reference as footnote 1.

consumerism: (1) product certification; (2) notification and repair, replacement or refund; and (3) inspection and recordkeeping. The act might make it necessary for firms to institute special product design groups composed of members from all departments of the company involved in the product development process. It is also expected that consumer organizations will advise their members to monitor products in terms of the new safety standards.

Product certification

Section 14 of the act[12] requires manufacturers to conduct a "reasonable testing program" to make sure their products conform to established safety standards. After the products are tested, a manufacturer must provide distributors or retailers with a certificate which states that all applicable consumer protection safety standards have been met. Moreover, no product may be imported into the United States unless it complies with these certification and labeling requirements.

Section 14 holds the manufacturer accountable for knowledge of all safety criteria applicable to the product and requires that safety standards must be described in detail. The manufacturer is also required to maintain technical data relating to the performance and safety of the product. This information may have to be given to the consumer when purchasing the product. It is anticipated that, as the commission begins its operations, the basis for the first group of government standards will be formed from (1) voluntary and consensus product standards already adopted by industry groups; and (2) guidelines from other governmental bodies, such as the Bureau of Consumer Safety under the Food and Drug Administration.

The commission can require the use of specific labels which set forth the results of product testing. If this procedure is followed, companies will be compelled to revise and reissue new product labels. This requirement will have its most significant impact in the production process, where the design of numerous products must conform to new federal standards. Since safety standards will be formulated at various governmental and independent testing stations, a manufacturer may find that his finished product no longer meets federal standards.[13] Product lines may have to be altered drastically. Moreover, cost considerations and lead time for redesign of a product might place a manufacturer in an unfavorable market position. To prevent this situation from happening, manufacturers may be required to give notice to the commission prior to the introduction of new products into the market. Procedures for predistribution notification will probably be established in 1975.

---

[12] Same reference as footnote 1.
[13] Same reference as footnote 1.

The act does limit the commission's jurisdiction to consumer products which present definite risks of death, personal injury, or product-related accidents. The breadth of coverage for the act is so large that one can safely predict that a significant number of products will most likely be banned from the market. It is assumed that consumer groups will attempt to have as many products as possible included in the safety standards provision.

A potential benefit of this section of the act to the manufacturer and the consumer will be the uniformity of safety standards for products sold in the United States. This will prohibit states from establishing safety standards which are not identical to those established at the federal level. This requirement will prove to be of considerable advantage to manufacturers who have been faced with a wide range of state and local regulations in the past. Manufacturers will now be compelled to conform principally to national standards, and their efforts in product design will be simplified to some degree.

Notification and repair, replacement, or refund

Section 15 requires a manufacturer to take corrective steps if he becomes aware that one of his products either fails to comply with an applicable consumer product safety rule or contains a defect which could create a substantial product hazard.[14] If a manufacturer, distributor, or retailer knows that a product is defective or not in compliance with the safety rules, he is obligated to inform the Consumer Product Safety Commission. If, after investigation, the commission determines that a product hazard exists, the manufacturer, distributor, or retailer may be required to publicize the information to consumers.

The commission can also issue orders compelling the manufacturer:

1. To bring such product into conformity with the requirements of the applicable consumer product safety rule or to repair the defect in the product
2. To replace the product with a like or equivalent product which complies with the applicable consumer product safety rule
3. To refund the purchase price of the product less a reasonable allowance for use[15]

The consumer cannot be charged for electing any of the three remedies. This section of the act assumes the manufacturer, distributor, or retailer is in a position where he should "reasonably" know that existing information about his product could perhaps support a conclusion that it is defective or presents a substantial hazard to the public.

---

[14] Same reference as footnote 1.
[15] Same reference as footnote 1.

Inspection and bookkeeping

The commission is given powers which include the right to inspect facilities where consumer goods are manufactured, stored, or transported. Section 16 requires that inspections be conducted at "reasonable times and in a reasonable manner."[16] The commission can require all manufacturers, private labelers, and distributors to establish and maintain books and records and to make available additional information as it deems necessary.

While the act's record-keeping requirements are not clearly defined, this legislation will undoubtedly result in increased costs of doing business as new requirements are imposed on manufacturers, distributors, and retailers. The commission can require businessmen to keep extensive records showing compliance with the act. Manufacturers and distributors may have to maintain lists of purchasers or a list of returned warranty cards. The latter alternative may not be a viable one since consumers often do not fill in and return warranty cards to the manufacturer. It will now become essential for the manufacturer to educate the consumer on the importance of the product warranty.

PRODUCT SAFETY AND THE COMMON LAW

The origins of this legislation are in the common law, where "product liability" refers to the liability of a manufacturer or seller for injuries to a buyer or other individual caused by a defective or hazardous product. The common law imposed liability on a broad group of persons involved in the marketing process, including manufacturers, suppliers, manufacturers of component parts, wholesalers, assemblers, and retailers. Testing laboratories and similar agencies which issue seals of approval as to the quality of a product have also come under judicial scrutiny even though their inspection and certification is based on a small number of samples.[17] Other potentially liable groups are advertising agencies and persons who knowingly promote a defective product.

Product liability cases are based on the landmark case of *MacPherson* v. *Buick Motor Company*,[18] which held that a manufacturer of an automobile with a defective wheel is liable in negligence to a buyer who purchased from a dealer even though the customer had no direct contact with the manufacturer. Liability is assumed for injuries to the consumer when the results of such injury are reasonably foreseeable regardless of whether the product is itself dangerous or harmful. A consumer need not prove that a manufacturer was guilty of negligence.[19] The manufac-

---

[16] Same reference as footnote 1.

[17] *Hanberry* v. *Hearst Corporation*, 81 Cal. Rep. 519, 1Cal. App. 1969.

[18] 217 N.Y. 382, 111 N.E. 1050 (1916).

[19] *Greenman* v. *Yuba Prods.*, 59 Cal. 2d 57, 377 P. 2d 897, 27 Cal. Rptr. 697 (1962).

turer, rather than the injured consumer, is forced to bear the costs of marketing defective products. Nonetheless, a manufacturer can escape liability by proving that his product is not defective or dangerous.

As an aid in product testing, many private organizations such as the American Standards Institute and Underwriters' Laboratories have published safety and quality standards. Violation of such standards when incorporated into statutes is often regarded by the courts as a basis for negligence. Moreover, the law requires manufacturers to design their products so that they will not create an unreasonable risk of injury to those consumers who buy or use the product.

In spite of its flexibility and adaptability to changing circumstances and social needs, the common law does not adequately protect the consumer from unsafe products. In its final report, the National Commission on Product Safety emphasized that the common law has traditionally concentrated its efforts upon providing an injured consumer with legal remedies with which to obtain redress *after* he has been injured. Although many common law remedies are available to aid a consumer's recovery of damages for injuries which result from the use of hazardous or poorly designed products, the common law has clearly been unable to prevent such injuries from occurring in the first place.

The Consumer Product Safety Act has a protective effect designed to reduce the risk of unreasonable hazards currently associated with consumer products and is intended to supplement or replace existing common law remedies. Nonetheless, the act provides that manufacturers and private labelers are not to be exempted from common law liability merely because they have complied with consumer product safety rules. Moreover, a failure by the Consumer Product Safety Commission to prevent the use of a consumer product because it is allegedly unsafe cannot be admitted in evidence or used as a defense to a suit brought under the common law.[20]

CONCLUSION

It is difficult to assess the substantive aspects of the Consumer Product Safety Act before its enforcement machinery is put into operation. The language of the act is very broad, and the methods of enforcement have not been tested. The commission's responsibilities remain unclear. For example, the commission may test its powers by calling for product formulas and ordering companies found guilty of marketing unsafe products to pay damages. The requirements of this act along with the provisions of the "truth-in-packaging" statutes will give the consumer more accurate and thorough information about the product, information which is not often part of a company's sales presentation or advertising.

There are still many unanswered questions of a technical nature.

---

[20] Same reference as footnote 1.

Nonetheless, if the stated goals of the act are achieved, consumers will benefit from safer products. Marketing practitioners generally feel that the impact of governmental policies and programs on the product area are already enormous. This new legislation will revolutionize the demands on industry and the expectations of consumers.

QUESTIONS

1. List and discuss the major points contained in the Consumer Product Safety Act.
2. Why must wholesalers and retailers be concerned about the Act if manufacturers make the products? Is this fair? Will it work?
3. Are there any benefits for manufacturers in the Act? If so, explain how they will benefit.
4. Why was such an act deemed necessary; couldn't common law and the courts take care of any problems?
5. Do you feel that enough consumers really are concerned about product safety to warrant passing such legislation? Shouldn't consumers be "trusted" to make good (safe?) choices in the marketplace, or should "experts" decide on what products should be offered? Why? What will be the impact on consumer satisfaction? Discuss the government's role in our macro marketing system.

Most farmers produce undifferentiated "commodities" and suffer the ups and downs of pure competition. To increase their chances of survival, however, some commodity producers have attempted to develop brand names for their products. The following article discusses Frank Perdue's success with branding chicken.

---

17. PERDUE CHICKEN SPREADS ITS WINGS*

HE LOOKS A little like a banty rooster and comes on just as plucky. "It takes a tough man," says 52-year-old Frank Perdue, "to make a tender chicken."

Perdue should know. As president and chief executive of Perdue, Inc., of Salisbury, Md., he heads an $80-million agri-conglomerate that

---

° Reprinted with permission from *Business Week* (September 16, 1972), pp. 113, 116. © 1972, McGraw–Hill, Inc.

has taken only four years to double its sales and become the country's biggest producer of branded "broilers" or processed chickens. By creating a brand identity for a commodity product, Perdue this year will be able to sell more than 60-million broilers for as much as 10¢ per lb. above the average market price. In short, Perdue is trying to do for chickens what Chiquita did for bananas. Both his whole chickens and packages of legs, thighs, and other parts come with distinctive red and yellow "Perdue" tags that promise "quality guaranteed or money back."

Sales campaign

Undaunted by the fact that General Mills, Quaker Oats, Ralston Purina, and Textron have all been driven out of the highly volatile $4-billion broiler business, Perdue and his New York ad agency—Scali, McCabe, Sloves, Inc.—have saturated New York City with subway, radio, television, and newspaper ads. Today, when Perdue walks the streets of Manhattan, many New Yorkers instantly recognize him as the utterly convincing, thin-lipped, metallic-voiced martinet who stars in his own commercials, telling customers "my chickens eat better than you do," and "I wouldn't put my name on a bad chicken."

According to the company's latest surveys, local brand awareness is up to 51%. In one month alone, some 10,000 New Yorkers contacted Perdue for a list of stores selling his chickens, while 22,000 customers who have written him to praise, criticize, or satisfy their curiosity about his business have received his free 59-page cookbook.

After his initial success in New York, Perdue is now beginning to spread his wings and take his message to chicken buyers in Philadelphia, Buffalo, Hartford (Conn.), Trenton (N.J.), and Baltimore. Eventually, he may expand nationwide. "People will go out of their way to buy a superior product," as Perdue claims in one of his trade ads. "And you can charge them a toll for the trip."

Though Perdue's market surge is new, his company is not. Since 1920, when Frank Perdue was born, his family has raised poultry on the Delaware-Maryland-Virginia shore. Until 1940, however, Perdue's father supplied only table eggs. Then the family-owned company followed the poultry market into the production of broilers for resale to Swift & Co., Armour Co., and other processors. In 1952, when Perdue took over as president, the company was selling 2.6-million broilers a year and bringing in $6-million from sales of live chickens. Over the next 15 years, Perdue proceeded to build a network of associated businesses that has come to include one of the East Coast's largest grain storage and poultry feed milling operations, soybean processing, mulch plants, a hatchery, and 600 farmers who raise broilers under contract to Perdue.

By 1967 sales were running more than $35-million a year, mainly from selling live birds. Then the chicken business took a sharp new turn, as processors began lining up more and more contract growers of their own and cutting out Perdue and other middlemen. "The situation was good for processors," says Perdue. "In commodities, profit depends on small markup and high volume, and a processor's normal profit on chickens runs $\frac{1}{4}\cent$ to $\frac{1}{2}\cent$ per lb." As they signed more of their own contract farmers, processors were able to expand their margins and drive a harder bargain with their outside suppliers. In the buyer's market of 1967, says Perdue, "processors were paying us 10¢ per lb. for what cost us 14¢ to produce. Suddenly, processors were making as much as 7¢ per lb."

More baskets

Rather than get out of the business, Perdue decided to integrate and build an organization that coordinates egg hatching, chick delivery and feeding, broiler processing, and overnight delivery to market.

At the same time, Perdue also decided to establish a quality, brand-name chicken and aim for premium prices. According to the National Broiler Council, four other companies—all regional—have made this transition, but Perdue enjoys one big advantage over them: His operation is only a few hours away from such major urban markets as Washington, D.C., Baltimore, Philadelphia, and New York. Meantime, Pittsburgh, Hartford, Syracuse, Buffalo, and Boston lay only an overnight truck ride away. Perdue picked New York as his first target because of its above-average incomes, concentration of both people and specialty butcher shops, and, as agency president Marvin Sloves puts it, "the New York consumer is tough, and we knew if we could crack this market, we could crack almost any market."

Care and feeding

To boost the quality of his flocks, Perdue hired two professors from North Carolina State University and set up a computer program that specifies the exact feeding formulas for each stage of a broiler's growth, aiming for optimum conversion of feed into meat and the healthy yellow skin coloring so important to consumers. "I just feel that quality always wins," Perdue says. "And I tried to make very sure that we had a good product when we started advertising."

In his television advertising, Perdue talks with all the fervor and sincerity of a Southern preacher. "When people ask me about my chickens," he says in one typical 60-second spot, "two questions invariably come up. The first is, 'Perdue, your chickens have such a great golden-yellow color it's almost unnatural. Do you dye them?' Honestly, there's absolutely nothing artificial about the color of my chickens. If you had a chicken and fed it good yellow corn, alfalfa, corn gluten, and marigold petals, it would just naturally be yellow. You can't go around dyeing chickens. They wouldn't stand for it." The other question, as he poses it, goes: " 'Perdue, your chickens are so plump and juicy, do you give them hormone injections?' This one really gets my hackles up. I do nothing of the kind. When chickens eat and live as well as mine do, you don't have to resort to artificial techniques . . ."

With his campaign, Perdue estimates that he has moved into more than half of the butcher shops and other small retail food outlets in the New York market, along with a dozen or so supermarket chains. While he refuses to discuss markups or profits ("you have to assume that it paid off"), his competitors claim that his added costs, including trade and consumer advertising, run at least 2¢ to 4¢ per lb.

Perdue would seem to make it back handily. At a Hill's supermarket on Long Island this week, Perdue broilers are priced at 37¢ per lb., compared with 29¢ per lb. for broilers at nearby Pathmark and Shop-Rite stores. In one of his ads, Perdue even claims that a New York chain marked his chicken up 10¢ per lb. above its normal price. "You know what happened?" he asks. "They sold just as many as ever."

Competition

Perdue may run up against stiffer competition in the future. "We have been watching Perdue very closely for the past year and a half," says H. M. Parker, national marketing manager for Holly Farms of Wilkesboro, N.C., one of the country's two largest (156-million broilers a year) chicken processors. "We think Perdue is highly vulnerable to competition."

Though nearly all of its chickens are now sold under Safeway and other supermarket private brand names, Holly Farms has just begun a year-long prototype brand-name promotion in Chicago. "We believe this has got to be the way to go," says Parker. Many other processors feel the same way.

Perdue, meantime, is not about to stand still. Besides broadening his marketing area for branded chickens, he is now considering branded turkeys, following the example of Swift's famous Butterballs. In typical Perdue fashion, he has put the question to the public—in the form of a new television commercial. "It's not a bad idea," he concedes on the air. "A turkey as good as a Perdue chicken. It would require a lot of work. And I'm not going to waste my time if you're happy with the turkeys you're getting now. Lemme know what you think."

QUESTIONS

1. What factors account for Perdue's success in branding chicken?
2. Based on the Perdue Chicken example, can all products be successfully marketed as branded products? Why or why not? What conditions seem to be necessary for successful branding?
3. Branded commodities, such as Perdue chicken and Chiquita bananas, are priced higher than unbranded products. Given the higher price, is the consumer better off with the branded products? If so, why? If not, why do the products sell?
°4. Which of the concepts explained in Readings 9–11 seem to be most relevant in explaining Perdue's success?

Traditional channels of distribution are typically used "because that's the way it has always been done." Distribution can be used as a strategic tool, however. Davidson presents several examples of successful strategic breakthroughs originated by various channel members. The examples illustrate the opportunities available to innovative marketers who are able to see better ways of distributing goods. Some ideas for finding breakthroughs are presented at the end of the article.

---

18. INNOVATION IN DISTRIBUTION*

William R. Davidson

Innovation in distribution

Marketing management is often viewed as the task of optimizing the relationship between controllable variables in a firm's marketing mix and the noncontrollable or environmental variables. Among the noncontrollable items commonly accepted as given for a particular planning period are the nature of competition, industry demand, role of government, and the available structure of distributive outlets. In a manufacturing company, the marketing effort is likely to be focused strongly upon

° Reprinted by permission from M. S. Moyer and R. E. Vosburgh, eds., *Marketing for Tomorrow . . . Today* (Chicago: The American Marketing Association, 1967), pp. 33–36. At the time of writing, the author was Professor of Marketing at The Ohio State University.

product, price, advertising, and personal selling, these being the major marketing mix ingredients that can be most readily adjusted to the state of the environment.

Frequently overlooked is the opportunity to make a breakthrough by innovating in distribution channels. While marketing channels are commonly regarded as a variable aspect of marketing mix of the manufacturer, they often receive less attention than consideration of product, price and promotion, simply because much of the channel, in the typical case, is "out there" where it is difficult to do much of anything about it, especially in the short run.

Upon reflection, almost any knowledgeable person would agree that the spatial and temporal availability of a product offering has a great deal to do with the profitable exploitation of opportunity. This is essentially the role of the distribution channel, and one too often neglected as higher priority is accorded to more highly variable matters.

Channel decisions are commonly analyzed from the standpoint of a manufacturer, with conventional discussions providing lists of pros and cons of common alternative arrangements. The conventionalism is likely to thwart a visionary approach. It will be apparent in the following discussion that real breakthroughs in distribution are likely to originate with any level of the channel, i.e., they may be the innovation of a retailer, a wholesaler, an agent or broker as well as a manufacturer.

Since this is an area of much conceptual and semantic confusion, some clarification is in order.

CHANNEL CONCEPTS

The term "channel of distribution" is part of the working vocabulary of every business executive, yet many would be hard pressed to define it. This is not surprising because a wide variety of interpretations are available in the literature on the subject. The marketing manager should be well aware of the great diversity, for it emphasizes the great need for being very explicit about exactly what is meant in conversations, even with one's close associates.[1]

This variety of viewpoints leads to lack of clarity on several points. Does the channel have to do primarily with the change of ownership of goods or with the physical movement of product? Is the nature of a given channel determined by the manufacturer, acting as a seller, or by middlemen and consumers, carrying out their role as buyers? Is the

---

[1] Portions of the following discussion have been adapted from material previously published by the author and his associates, especially William R. Davidson, "Channels of Distribution—One Aspect of Marketing Strategy," *Business Horizons*, Special Issue, February 1961, pp. 84 ff; William R. Davidson and Alton F. Doody, *Retailing Management*, New York, Ronald Press Company, 1966, Chapter 2; and Theodore N. Beckman and William R. Davidson, *Marketing*, New York, Ronald Press Company, 8th ed, 1967, Chapter 9.

channel made up only of middlemen or intervening intermediaries, or does it include the manufacturer at one end and the consumer at the other?

The channel for exchange

Given some product to be marketed, several jobs must be done. First, there is the question of arrangements for bringing about changes in ownership by performance of the functions of exchange, buying, and selling. Second, there is logistical tasks of adjusting the physical supply of a product to the spatial and temporal aspects of demand. This involves the functions of transportation and storage, and related activities such as physical handling and control of inventories. Third, there is the necessity of various facilitating or auxiliary functions, such as the collection and dissemination of marketing information, management of market risks, financing of marketing activities, and standardization and grading.

Generally speaking, the functions of exchange may be considered as paramount because planning for physical supply and performance of facilitating functions do not become relevant in the typical marketing organization unless there is profitable opportunity for transfers of ownership.

It appears, therefore, most realistic to define the channel of distribution as consisting of "the course taken in the transfer of title to a commodity."[2] It is the route taken in transferring the title of a product from its first owner (usually a manufacturer) to its last owner, the business user or ultimate consumer. Such a route necessarily includes both the origin and the destination; hence it should be viewed as including the manufacturer and the ultimate consumer, as well as any intervening middlemen, inasmuch as all three are originators and performers of much marketing activity.

The channel of logistics

The general tendency is for the physical flow of merchandise to accompany the route of exchange. This is not, however, universally the case, and there are indications that separate structural arrangements for logistics or physical distribution are increasingly important.

There has been a growing tendency to streamline physical distribution by setting it apart from the complex of channel links used for obtaining sales. In some companies, a department of logistics or physical distribution combines a number of previously scattered activities, including finished goods inventory control, transportation and traffic warehousing,

---

[2] Theodore N. Beckman and William R. Davidson, *Marketing*, New York, The Ronald Press Company, 8th ed, 1967, p. 230.

order processing, container design, and sometimes even manufacturing scheduling.[3]

While the flow of exchange activity and the flow of physical distribution still tend to coincide in many cases, it is increasingly recognized that this coincidence may be only one of a large number of theoretical possibilities. The concept of separability of exchange and supply activities, in instances of traditional coincidence, may comprise the vision for new breakthroughs.

The exchange channel is primarily concerned with those activities that increase demand and which bring about changes of ownership, such as selling, advertising, display, product information, trade and consumer credit, etc.

The flow of logistical services includes those activities having to do with the location, movement, and size of the physical supply of a product, and the adjustment of it to demand.

Structure of distribution

It is important to distinguish the concept of distribution channel from that of distribution structure. A *single* channel of distribution is brought into being when a particular set of exchange relationships is established linking a manufacturer with an ultimate consumer. For example, a single channel would be established when an insecticide manufacturer begins selling to a given hardware wholesaler, thereby establishing consumer contact through the retail stores served by the wholesaler. From the wholesaler's point of view, a single channel is formed by the establishment of trading relationships with any given store. Thus, any one manufacturer may actually be utilizing a large number of specific or single channels, even in one marketing area. This is true in the sense that there are many traceable or separable flows of exchange or ownership.

As indicated above, if the physical flow of product does not accompany the route taken in the transfer of title, there may be many additional specific logistical channels.

The structure of distribution for a product type is composed of all of the networks in use at a given time to connect all of the manufacturers of that product type with all of the ultimate consumers or industrial users, of that product class. It includes all of the exchange flows and all of the logistical flows when these are separate.

In marketing management, it is often said that the structure of distribution is a given environmental factor. The individual firm may make choices among the various routes or channels that are in the structure. The structure itself, however, is taken as a noncontrollable variable.

---

[3] John F. Magee, "The Logistics of Distribution," *Harvard Business Review*, vol. 38, July–August 1960, pp. 89 ff.; Edward W. Smykay, Donald J. Bowersox and Frank H. Mossman, *Physical Distribution Management*, New York, The Macmillan Company, 1961.

While this may be a good assumption to make for various short term practical purposes, it may make one blind to great opportunities that a more visionary approach would unfold. A real breakthrough in some cases is the successful discovery of a route not previously used by any firm in a given industry. Then the new channel arrangement would be new to the entire structure of distribution as well as to the first user of it. Such an innovation, as will be shown by later examples, may originate from visionary approaches taken at any level or plane of distribution, by manufacturers, wholesalers, or retailers.

HISTORIC BREAKTHROUGHS

The manner in which marketing vision has led to major distribution breakthroughs may be illustrated with several classic examples. From the many historic cases that might well be chosen, three have been selected because of their varying nature and because of the manner in which their longstanding effects are still apparent. It is observable in each instance how an innovative mind conceived the opportunity to achieve a differential advantage by viewing the process of distribution in a new way.

A & P's cash-and-carry stores

The Great Atlantic & Pacific Tea Co., founded in 1859, developed originally as a service retailer, characteristic of its times. It had trading stamps, delivery service, charge accounts, and premiums for promotions. In 1912, John Hartford, a founder's son with marketing vision, observed an unusual New Jersey store that did a large volume of business on the basis of limited service and low prices. Sensing a possible distribution breakthrough, he got approval of an experiment at A. & P. This involved a small unit that could be operated in many cases by one man. Services were cut to the bone by eliminating stamps, streamlining the inventory, and operating on a cash-and-carry basis. Traditional grocery store gross margins at the time were about 25%. With its new stores, A. & P. had a differential of about 10 to 15% of sales, thus giving it a cost-protected price advantage over service competitors. So successful was this breakthrough that the company opened 7,500 stores of the new type within three years—about seven per day.[4]

The dealer structure of General Motors

Prior to 1920, automobile distribution was largely from manufacturer to "distributor-wholesaler" who resold to dealers within their respective territories. It became apparent to Alfred P. Sloan, Jr., then chief executive officer, that the economic position of dealers in the mid-1920's was deteriorating and that dealer franchises were less in demand. There

---

[4] "Pinching 500,000,000,000 Pennies," *Fortune*, vol. 67, March 1963.

were increasing problems of achieving market penetration, liquidating inventories at the end of model runs (then the financial responsibility solely of the dealer), of maintaining communication between manufacturers and dealers, and of preserving dealer financial solvency.[5]

Sloan and his General Motors associates decided that something drastic had to be done not only for the sake of dealers but for the soundness of the enterprise as a whole. The decision was to involve the corporation, to an extent wholly unprecedented in the industry, in the retail distribution of its products, while still retaining independent franchised dealers.

Sloan attributed much of the success and stability of General Motors in the years that followed to these early changes in relationships in the distributive organization.

Distributive breakthroughs at Sears

Few indeed are the business organizations that would vie with Sears, Roebuck & Company with regard to outstanding visionary developments in distribution.[6]

The failure of country general stores and small town merchants in the post-Civil War period to respond to rising income levels paved the way for mail order pioneers. Sears won the confidence of customers by truthful descriptions of goods illustrated in catalogs and in a firm "money-back" guarantee. Merchandise was bought in large quantities and priced to appeal to a rural target market.

Success continued with the firm's outstanding response to changing environmental conditions. The company took maximum advantage of the early availability of a most efficient delivery system, rural free delivery and parcel post. Later, as people began to desire personal selection of goods, Sears opened their retail stores, 324 establishments between the years 1925 and 1929. General Robert E. Wood, then the principal Sears executive, was the only major department executive with the vision to anticipate the future *influence of the automobile and suburban living*. While other merchants concentrated upon downtown locations that were oriented to public transit facilities, Sears expanded rapidly in newer outlying areas. At the time the company was often criticized or ridiculed by competitors for building stores upon "farm land." Once established, however, these stores often had a spatial monopoly that went largely unchallenged until the post-World War II era.

CONTEMPORARY ILLUSTRATIONS

Distribution breakthroughs need not bring into being new types or methods in the sense that they were previously unknown. The break-

---

[5] Adapted from Alfred P. Sloan, Jr., *My Years with General Motors*, Garden City, New York, Doubleday & Company, Inc., Chapter 16, "Distribution and the Dealers."

[6] "Sears Makes It Look Easy," *Fortune*, vol. 69, May 1964, pp. 120 ff.

through may involve a new approach to working with a given type of situation, of utilizing a type of capability with reference to other products, or of applying concepts that have been perfected in some other field. Some contemporary cases are illustrated in the following paragraphs.

Coca-Cola as a distribution network

Depth of marketing vision has been explained as the successful seeking of the understanding of the essential being of a company, its distinctiveness or differential advantage with respect to ability to exploit profitable opportunities.

The Coca-Cola Company is normally described as a manufacturer of popular soft drinks, but one factor in addition to popularity is also of importance in analyzing the success of the company.

But if we define Coca-Cola as a remarkable distribution network, we may be closer to its essential being. The company's great leader of the 1920's, Robert Woodruff, said it another way when he laid down the policy of putting Coca-Cola everywhere "within an arm's length of desire." Today, Coca-Cola is distributed in some 1,600,000 outlets, more than any other product in the world. . . . It is put in all these outlets by over 1,000 local franchised bottlers in the United States. Because these bottlers, guided by the parent company, have created this extraordinary distribution, the marketing of newer brands is facilitated. So, with increasing competition on all sides, the heart of their success is the means of achieving widespread availability.[7]

Programmed merchandising at Scott's

The O. M. Scott & Sons Company of Marysville, Ohio is the leading manufacturer and marketer of lawn products. In the mid-1960's while Scott's had significant distribution among department stores, the sales achieved in most such outlets were usually quite disappointing. Top management of most department stores was oriented to fashion apparel or home furnishing, or both, often with minimal interest in lawn products.

The solution was for Scott's to become much more highly involved in department store merchandising activities. Special programs were worked out in detail for each major department store account that could be interested in substantially expanding its volume of lawn products sales. Plans for monthly sales by product were developed by Scott account executives. These were projected to dollar totals and incorporated into the store's departmental plan well ahead of each six-month merchan-

---
[7] Lee Adler, "A New Orientation for Plotting Marketing Strategy," *Business Horizons*, vol. 7, Winter 1964.

dising season, thereby automatically generating sufficient "open-to-buy" to cover planned sales. Promotional activities for each month (each week for the peak season) were detailed in advance, with responsibility clearly defined for each store location. All operating requirements were oriented to the conditions at the individual store. Some of these programs involved 40 or more pages of plans developed for an individual account. They were sufficiently complete that the department manager rarely had to make a personal judgment that was not covered. Very large year-to-year sales increases were a common experience.

Total supplier distribution at Cotter

The retail hardware trade has long been dominated by the small independent merchant. In 1958 the typical independent was finding it difficult to compete effectively with the pricing and often superior merchandising of branches of department stores in suburban centers, discount outlets, upgrading of units of variety store chains, general merchandise diversification in some supermarket companies and drug chains, and catalog retailing.

In the late 1940's and 1950's, distribution in the hardware trade was originally quite complex, with many contacts between retailers and the various agencies that supplied them. Much of the effort at the wholesale level was devoted to competitive activities, as one wholesaler vied with another, attempting to get a larger share of the dealer's business. This also meant that vast quantities of the retailer's time was taken up in contacts with order-taking salesmen of many suppliers.

Perceiving the inefficiencies and competitive limitations of such a distribution pattern, a small group of hardware retailers had earlier banded together in Chicago. Under the guidance of John Cotter, a recognized leader in the hardware trade, they established a retailer-owned cooperative to serve as a complete supplier to members. It was named Cotter & Company. This program adapted various merchandising approaches and operating methods that had been developed earlier by chain stores and by voluntary chains in other lines.

The efficiencies of this operation are claimed by Cotter to amount to direct savings in the range of 6% to 8% of sales at the wholesale level, as compared with traditional methods of hardware wholesaling. By utilizing some ideas and working with proven principles of closer integration of efforts between channel levels, Cotter achieved fabulous growth in the fairly stable hardware trade.

EVALUATION OF CHANNEL DISTRIBUTION RELATIONSHIPS

The general discussion in the early parts as well as the more specific historic and contemporary examples just presented provide ample evidence that a channel of distribution is something more than a marketing choice that is made by a manufacturing company. It shows, moreover, why many manufacturers have had to modify their thinking about factors that influence channel choices. In any company that follows a program of modern, consumer-oriented marketing management, considerations relating to consumer requirements are elevated to paramount status, and factors relating to company situation are subordinated, at least in the sense that the latter must be adjusted to the former. This means that the manufacturer must look beyond his own circumstances and beyond the situation of intermediaries in the channel, so that he is attuned to the wants and interests of the consumer in the market segment he is trying to reach.

Charting the channel

Too often channel relationships do not receive due attention since they involve matters that are "outside" the company and, hence, are more easily taken for granted than other activities such as marketing research, advertising, or personal selling. These "internal" functions come up for more frequent review or appraisal since responsibility for them tends to be fixed on the organizational chart or in job descriptions, and the cost of them is conspicuously identified on accounting statements.

In manufacturing companies, opportunities for more frequent and more realistic appraisal of channel problems and relationships might be provided by new approaches to charting the organization of marketing activities. An organization chart might well show not only the various departments within the marketing division of the company, but also all of the vertical links in the channel users to effect transfers of title to eventual users, and, moreover, the different types of outlets on each horizontal plane or state of distribution.

Another recommendation is to prepare operating statements that reveal sales performance and cost situations through the channels used. At the top of such a statement would be sales, stated in terms of prices paid by the ultimate user, and showing as expenses the costs of marketing through the various channels of use.

In any event, manufacturers will have made progress in solving channel of distribution problems when they recognize two considerations. First, channel activities must be thought of as only one aspect of the total marketing mix and one that must be coordinated with other ingredients, as these contribute to the objective of reaching a defined market; second, in the long run, the nature of channels is determined from "the bottom up" rather than from "the top down."

Finally, it may be concluded that the ability to achieve a differential advantage in distribution through marketing vision is related to ability to perceive the ways either in which wants are satisfied or in which satisfaction is being thwarted. By focusing attention upon values created through distribution, or upon values desired but remaining unfulfilled, some firms will look beyond the more readily controllable factors of product, price, and promotion, and achieve real breakthroughs by innovation in the flow of ownership transfer and product movement through distribution channels.

QUESTIONS

1. Do you think the possibilities of breakthroughs in distribution will increase or decrease in the future? What factors affect such opportunities? (Be specific, referring to Davidson's examples.)
2. Who should be responsible for channel development? Why is it so commonly neglected?
3. How could one go about looking for a distribution breakthrough?
°4. Explain one of Davidson's breakthrough examples in terms of Alderson's "search for differential advantage" (Reading 5).

The classical consumer goods classification system (convenience, shopping, specialty goods) can be of great value in planning strategy. Bucklin's review of this classification system is omitted in this edited version of his article, which focuses more on his extension of these concepts to retail store types. These ideas are relevant to both retailers and channel members who must select retailers. Bucklin provides a good example of how a small retailer could improve its strategic planning with these store-goods classes.

---

19. RETAIL STRATEGY AND THE CLASSIFICATION OF CONSUMER GOODS*

Louis P. Bucklin

WHEN Melvin T. Copeland published his famous discussion of the classification of consumer goods, shopping, convenience, and speci-

* Reprinted with permission from the *Journal of Marketing*, published by the American Marketing Association, January 1963, pp. 51–56. At the time of writing, Dr. Bucklin was Assistant Professor of Marketing at the University of California in Berkeley.

alty goods, his intent was clearly to create a guide for the development of marketing strategies by manufacturers.[1] Although his discussion involved retailers and retailing, his purpose was to show how consumer buying habits affected the type of channel of distribution and promotional strategy that a manufacturer should adopt. Despite the controversy which still surrounds his classification, his success in creating such a guide may be judged by the fact that through the years few marketing texts have failed to make use of his ideas.

The purpose of this article is to attempt to clarify some of the issues that exist with respect to the classification, and to extend the concept to include the retailer and the study of retail strategy.

* * *

The new classification

The classification of consumer goods that results from the analysis is as follows:

Convenience Goods: Those goods for which the consumer, before his need arises, possesses a preference map that indicates a willingness to purchase any of a number of known substitutes rather than to make the additional effort required to buy a particular item.

Shopping Goods: Those goods for which the consumer has not developed a complete preference map before the need arises, requiring him to undertake search to construct such a map before purchase.

Specialty Goods: Those goods for which the consumer, before his need arises, possesses a preference map that indicates a willingness to expend the additional effort required to purchase the most preferred item rather than to buy a more readily accessible substitute.

EXTENSION TO RETAILING

The classification of the goods concept developed above may now be extended to retailing. As the concept now stands, it is derived from consumer attitudes or motives toward a *product*. These attitudes, or product motives, are based upon the consumer's interpretation of a product's styling, special features, quality, and social status of its brand name, if any. Occasionally the price may also be closely associated with the product by the consumer.

Classification of patronage motives

The extension of the concept to retailing may be made through the notion of patronage motives, a term long used in marketing. Patronage

---

[1] Melvin T. Copeland, "Relation of Consumers' Buying Habits of Marketing Methods," *Harvard Business Review*, vol. 1 (April 1923), pp. 282–289.

motives are derived from consumer attitudes concerning the retail establishment. They are related to factors which the consumer is likely to regard as controlled by the retailer. These will include assortment, credit, service, guarantee, shopping ease and enjoyment, and usually price. Patronage motives, however, have never been systematically categorized. It is proposed that the procedure developed above to discriminate among product motives be used to classify consumer buying motives with respect to retail stores as well.

This will provide the basis for the consideration of retail marketing strategy and will aid in clearing up certain ambiguities that would otherwise exist if consumer buying motives were solely classified by product factors. These ambiguities appear, for example, when the consumer has a strong affinity for some particular brand of a product, but little interest in where he buys it. The manufacturer of the product, as a result, would be correct in defining the product as a specialty item if the consumer's preferences were so strong as to cause him to eschew more readily available substitutes. The retailer may regard it as a convenience good, however, since the consumer will make no special effort to purchase the good from any particular store. This problem is clearly avoided by separately classifying product and patronage motives.

The categorization of patronage motives by the above procedure results in the following three definitions. These are:

Convenience Stores: Those stores for which the consumer, before his need for some product arises, posssesses a preference map that indicates a willingness to buy from the most accessible store.

Shopping Stores: Those stores for which the consumer has not developed a complete preference map relative to the product he wishes to buy, requiring him to undertake a search to construct such a map before purchase.

Specialty Stores: Those stores for which the consumer, before his need for some product arises, possesses a preference map that indicates a willingness to buy the item from a particular establishment even though it may not be the most accessible.

The product-patronage matrix

Although this basis will now afford the retailer a means to consider alternative strategies, a finer classification system may be obtained by relating consumer product motives to consumer patronage motives. By cross-classifying each product motive with each patronage motive, one creates a three by three matrix, representing nine possible types of consumer buying behavior. Each of the nine cells in the matrix may be described as follows:

1. *Convenience Store—Convenience Good:*   The consumer, represented by this category, prefers to buy the most readily available brand of product at the most accessible store.
2. *Convenience Store—Shopping Good:*   The consumer selects his purchase from among the assortment carried by the most accessible store.
3. *Convenience Store—Specialty Good:*   The consumer purchases his favored brand from the most accessible store which has the item in stock.
4. *Shopping Store—Convenience Good:*   The consumer is indifferent to the brand of product he buys, but shops among different stores in order to secure better retail service and/or lower retail price.
5. *Shopping Store—Shopping Good:*   The consumer makes comparisons among both retail controlled factors and factors associated with the product (brand).
6. *Shopping Store—Specialty Good:*   The consumer has a strong preference with respect to the brand of the product, but shops among a number of stores in order to secure the best retail service and/or price for this brand.
7. *Specialty Store—Convenience Good:*   The consumer prefers to trade at a specific store, but is indifferent to the brand of product purchased.
8. *Specialty Store—Shopping Good:*   The consumer prefers to trade at a certain store, but is uncertain as to which product he wishes to buy and examines the store's assortment for the best purchase.
9. *Specialty Store—Specialty Good:*   The consumer has both a preference for a particular store and a specific brand.

Conceivably, each of these nine types of behavior might characterize the buying patterns of some consumers for a given product. It seems more likely, however, that the behavior of consumers toward a product could be represented by only three or four of the categories. The remaining cells would be empty, indicating that no consumers bought the product by these methods. Different cells, of course, would be empty for different products.

THE FORMATION OF RETAIL STRATEGY

The extended classification system developed above clearly provides additional information important to the manufacturer in the planning of his marketing strategy. Of principal interest here, however, is the means by which the retailer might use the classification system in planning his marketing strategy.

Three basic steps

The procedure involves three steps. The first is the classification of the retailer's potential customers for some product by market segment, using the nine categories in the consumer buying habit matrix to define the principal segments. The second requires the retailer to determine the nature of the marketing strategies necessary to appeal to each market segment. The final step is the retailer's selection of the market segment, and the strategy associated with it, to which he will sell. A simplified, hypothetical example may help to clarify this process.

A former buyer of dresses for a department store decided to open her own dress shop. She rented a small store in the downtown area of a city of 50,000, ten miles distant from a metropolitan center of several hundred thousand population. In contemplating her marketing strategy, she was certain that the different incomes, educational backgrounds, and tastes of the potential customers in her city meant that various groups of these women were using sharply different buying methods for dresses. Her initial problem was to determine, by use of the consumer buying habit matrix, what proportion of her potential market bought dresses in what manner.

By drawing on her own experience, discussions with other retailers in the area, census and other market data, the former buyer estimated that her potential market was divided, according to the matrix, in the following proportions.

TABLE 1
Proportion of potential dress market in each matrix cell

Buying habit	% of market
Convenience store–Convenience good	0
Convenience store–Shopping good	3
Convenience store–Specialty good	20
Shopping store–Convenience good	0
Shopping store–Shopping good	35
Shopping store–Specialty good	2
Specialty store–Convenience good	0
Specialty store–Shopping good	25
Specialty store–Specialty good	15
	100

This analysis revealed four market segments that she believed were worth further consideration. (In an actual situation, each of these four should be further divided into submarket segments according to other possible factors such as age, incomes, dress size required, location of residence, etc.) Her next task was to determine the type of marketing mix which would most effectively appeal to each of these segments. The information for these decisions was derived from the characteristics of consumer behavior associated with each of the defined segments. The following is a brief description of her assessment of how elements of the marketing mix ought to be weighted in order to formulate a strategy for each segment.

A strategy for each segment

To appeal to the convenience store-specialty good segment she felt that the two most important elements in the mix should be a highly accessible location and a selection of widely-accepted brand merchandise. Of somewhat lesser importance, she found, were depth of assortment, personal selling, and price. Minimal emphasis should be given to store promotion and facilities.

She reasoned that the shopping store-shopping good requires a good central location, emphasis on price, and a broad assortment. She ranked store promotion, accepted brand names and personal selling as secondary. Store facilities would, once again, receive minor emphasis.

The specialty store-shopping good market would, she believed, have to be catered to with an exceptionally strong assortment, a high level of personal selling and more elaborate store facilities. Less emphasis would be needed upon prominent brand names, store promotions, and price. Location was of minor importance.

The specialty store-specialty good category, she thought, would require a marketing mix heavily emphasizing personal selling and highly elaborate store facilities and services. She also felt that prominent brand names would be required, but that these would probably have to include the top names in fashion, including labels from Paris. Depth of assortment would be secondary, while least emphasis would be placed upon store promotion, price, and location.

Evaluation of alternatives

The final step in the analysis required the former dress buyer to assess her abilities to implement any one of these strategies, given the degree of competition existing in each segment. Her considerations were as follows. With regard to the specialty store-specialty good market, she was unprepared to make the investment in store facilities and services that she felt would be necessary. She also thought, since a considerable period of time would probably be required for her to build up the necessary reputation, that this strategy involved substantial risk. Lastly, she believed that her experience in buying high fashion was somewhat limited and that trips to European fashion centers would prove burdensome.

She also doubted her ability to cater to the specialty store-shopping good market, principally because she knew that her store would not be large enough to carry the necessary assortment depth. She felt that this same factor would limit her in attempting to sell to the shopping store-shopping good market as well. Despite the presence of the large market in this segment, she believed that she would not be able to create sufficient volume in her proposed quarters to enable her to compete effectively with the local department store and several large department stores in the neighboring city.

The former buyer believed her best opportunity was in selling to the convenience store-specialty good segment. While there were already two other stores in her city which were serving this segment, she believed that a number of important brands were still not represented. Her past contacts with resources led her to believe that she would stand an excellent chance of securing a number of these lines. By stocking these brands, she thought that she could capture a considerable number of local customers who currently were purchasing them in the large city. In this way, she believed, she would avoid the full force of local competition.

Decision

The conclusion of the former buyer to use her store to appeal to the convenience store-specialty good segment represents the culmination to the process of analysis suggested here. It shows how the use of the three-by-three matrix of consumer buying habits may aid the retailer in developing his marketing strategy. It is a device which can isolate the important market segments. It provides further help in enabling the retailer to associate the various types of consumer behavior with those elements of the marketing mix to which they are sensitive. Finally, the analysis forces the retailer to assess the probability of his success in attempting to use the necessary strategy in order to sell each possible market.

QUESTIONS

1. Relate the job of selecting a target market to the store-goods classification matrix discussed by Bucklin.
2. Draw a three-by-three matrix like Bucklin suggests and insert the name of a local retailer in each box of the matrix. If in doubt about how the "market" would classify a particular store, use your own personal view, but in either case explain why you classify each one the way you do.
°3. Explain the following distribution channel innovations: (a) Sears Roebuck locating retail department stores on urban fringes (Reading 18), and (b) Timex distributing watches through drug stores, by using the store-goods classification concept.

Two articles are treated as a unit here because they both deal with the same topic and come out of the same study. They discuss, from a strategic viewpoint, what may be a new distribution breakthrough. The following paragraphs, from the authors' preface to the first article, explain the focus of both articles.

For reasons explained in the report, we believe that the super-store will have a significant impact on food retailing . . . so much so that it will become a primary direction for new investment by food chain companies. Conversely, we believe that supermarkets will become less and less attractive as sources of growth and profits for chain operators.

The main focus of the report is on the concept of the 'super-store,' not its physical dimensions. This emphasis on a concept means that we are dealing with an abstraction—a general approach to mass retailing, not a specific kind of store building or product assortment. The reason for emphasizing a concept is that we believe the shift from supermarkets to super-stores reflects the evolution of a new approach to serving consumer needs. Like supermarkets, super-stores will vary greatly in size, product lines, and other dimensions. But successful super-stores will, we believe, reflect a common basic concept. Food chain executives should, we think, explore this concept carefully and should be equally thorough in analyzing how the concept might apply to their own customers and competitive situations.

---

20. THE SUPER-STORE—STRATEGIC IMPLICATIONS FOR THE SEVENTIES AND IMPLICATIONS OF THE SUPER-STORE FOR MANUFACTURES*

Walter J. Salmon, Robert D. Buzzell, and Stanton G. Cort with Michael R. Pearce

SINCE ITS beginnings in the early 1930's there have been many efforts to define the supermarket—usually in terms of the minimum floor area or sales volume that a store must have to qualify, together

° Reprinted with the permission of Family Circle, Inc., and the Marketing Science Institute. This was a study commissioned by *Family Circle Magazine* and conducted by the Marketing Science Institute. © 1972 by Family Circle, Inc. At the time

with some description of its operating methods (self-service, "mass display," etc.). But no uniform definition has ever been satisfactory, primarily because supermarkets vary so much depending on the nature and size of market served, competitive conditions, and management philosophies of store operators. (As evidence of the difficulties of defining a supermarket in an operational fashion, the Bureau of the Census has never used the term in its periodic surveys of retail trade.)

There is, of course, no scarcity of "working definitions" for the supermarket. And, as the super-store concept has emerged during the late 1960's and 1970's, many efforts have been made to define it. In our review of published reports and commentaries, and in our interviews with executives of leading chains, we saw and heard a wide variety of definitions. Most of them included some reference to size. There is agreement that the super-store is "big"—but there is no consensus about just *how* big a super-store must be. Some observers suggested a minimum of 20,000 square feet of selling area, while other figures ranged up to 50,000 square feet. Likewise, although it seems clear that super-stores will carry a greater variety of non-food merchandise than conventional supermarkets, there are widely varying opinions on the specific types of products that fit.

In fact, the only clear picture that emerges from our review of industry opinion is that super-stores will vary, just as supermarkets do.

This report is built around definitions which describe the supermarket and the super-store as *concepts*, not as stores of a particular size or with particular product lines. The concepts reflect strategic objectives and operating philosophies designed to guide day-to-day operations toward achievement of these objectives. Merchandise assortments, day-to day operating policies, and buildings are simply ways of implementing the concepts under a given set of market conditions. In other words, the supermarket and super-store concepts are defined in terms of a set of consumer needs each type of operation seeks to serve and a basic approach to serving those needs.

The SUPERMARKET CONCEPT is an approach to retail distribution which is designed to serve the *consumer's total needs for food, laundry, and household maintenance products,* by providing a comprehensive assortment of these products in a single store and by utilizing efficient, low-cost methods of distribution.

The SUPER-STORE CONCEPT is one which is aimed at serving

of writing, Walter J. Salmon was a Sebastian S. Kresge Professor of Marketing, Robert D. Buzzell was Professor of Business Administration, both of the Harvard Business School, Stanton G. Cort was Assistant Professor of Marketing at Indiana University, and M. R. Pearce was a Research Assistant and doctoral candidate at Harvard University.

the *consumer's total needs for all types of routine purchases,* including those now served by the supermarket (as defined above) *and* an extensive range of other products and services.

Similarities—and differences

Clearly, the two concepts are similar in many respects. Both involve serving a set of related consumer needs in an integrated and consistent fashion in one location. Both approaches are intended to permit "one-stop shopping" for some *range* of products and services. However, both concepts go beyond simply providing a variety of merchandise lines in one place. Both concepts imply that the lines should be merchandised in an *integrated and consistent way.* In other words, a consistent merchandising philosophy should be used in presenting meats, perishables, groceries, health and beauty aids, etc. If meat merchandising stresses quality, value, attractive display, and depth of assortment, so should grocery and HBA merchandising.

Both the supermarket concept and the super-store concept also require that the merchandise lines handled by a store be ones whose physical handling characteristics, rate of sale, and sales/service requirements fit into an overall system of merchandising, physical supply, display and "transaction processing." To a limited extent, of course, supermarkets do—and super-stores will—carry products that require "special handling." But these are exceptions; the basic premise of both concepts is one of *low-cost, high-volume, limited-service operations.* This premise can readily be undermined if too many "side shows" are added to the basic product lines.

The key *difference* between the supermarket and superstore concepts lies in the breadth of sets of consumer needs to be served. The supermarket concept seeks to serve food and household maintenance needs, while the super-store concept seeks to serve these and *other routine purchasing needs.* On the surface, the difference may appear academic. However, its implications for strategic planning are both fundamental and concrete. Striving to serve all of the consumer's routine shopping needs involves a view of the food chain's role very different from the view involved in striving to serve the consumer's *food* shopping needs, supplemented by limited assortments of routine non-food items.

The concept of the present-day supermarket is based on the premise that the food retailer possesses the expertise and facilities for efficient procurement, handling, and merchandising of food products and services. This kind of logic led to combining in one store meat, produce, and groceries—and, in the 1920's, the so-called "combination store" evolved. Paper, soaps, cleansers, and basic health and beauty aids typically joined the foods. These were non-foods which consumers were likely to need when they needed food and which fit into the food store's operations.

Service bakeries, dry cleaners, self-service laundries, soft goods, and most hard goods typically did *not* join the foods. Some consumers might need some of these kinds of items when they needed food, but the items did not fit into the food store's method of operations or merchandising expertise.

The starting point for defining the consumer's "routine needs" is the recognition that each household has a range of product and service needs that must be satisfied routinely. These involved purchases that:

the consumer makes at *regular intervals;*

involve relatively small amounts of money (per item, that is) in relation to the household's total expenditures;

satisfy relatively *well-defined* needs; the product features and uses, and the brands and varieties available are generally familiar to the consumer;

the consumer wants to make as efficiently as possible—with primary attention to *convenience* and *cost.*

The vast majority of products normally handled by present-day supermarkets obviously fit this definition of "routine purchase," from the viewpoint of the vast majority of American households. The super-store, as we envision it, will go one step further by providing everything that the supermarket does—*plus* a substantial number of other *routinely* purchased products and services.

The "routine buying list"

The key to defining a super-store is, then, the determination of *which* products and services fit into the consumer's routine buying list. For a typical middle-income household, we believe the list will include:

virtually all *food needs* for home preparation, together with virtually all *laundry and home cleaning products;*

prepared *fast foods* for at home and away-from-home consumption;

most *personal care products* ("health and beauty aids") including where permitted, *pharmacies;*

alcoholic beverages and tobacco products;

some *apparel products,* such as hosiery, underwear, and a variety of children's clothing items;

most low-priced *housewares and hardware items;*

a range of *leisure-time products,* including magazines, books, records, and some hobby and craft items;

many consumable *lawn and garden products;*

gasoline—dispensed from an adjacent self-service facility—and some *automotive supplies;*

many *stationery and sewing supply products;*

most *household services,* such as laundry, dry cleaning, and shoe repair, as well as check-cashing and bill-paying.*

These are routine purchases, we suggest, because they are bought at fairly regular intervals—almost on a replenishment basis. For "Middle America," the needs served by these products and services are well-defined and established; each is a part of the routine of day-to-day life. The products themselves—and the range of brands, types, flavors, etc. available—are for the most part well known. The costs of these products and services (in the amounts typically purchased) are perceived as small, in relation to the middle-income household's income of, say, $10,000 to $15,000.

Another way of looking at routine purchases is to identify the characteristics of products and services that do *not* fit the concept. What kinds of purchases are *non*-routine? For most consumers, non-routine products would include:

"big ticket" items, such as major appliances, whose purchase involves extended deliberation, and where the effort required for comparison shopping is seen as potentially worthwhile. (One food chain executive told us he visualizes the super-store as carrying many so-called shopping goods—but only those that "the woman will buy without the big family conference.");

products and services that require skilled sales or service advice, such as musical instruments, many building supplies, wallpaper;

products involving fashion to the degree that the consumer demands a wide and unpredictable variety of styles, colors, etc.;

complex or unfamiliar products, that require investigation and/or substantial assistance from sales personnel.

THE SUPER-STORE'S CAPABILITIES

If we accept the foregoing definition of "routine purchases," can the super-store profitably handle literally *all* of the product lines that fall within the definition? We think it cannot, for several reasons.

First, there is the matter of *differences among households.* The set of products and services that are viewed as "routine" will obviously vary from one household to another. In the discussion above, we have viewed routine purchases in terms of the probable behavior of middle-

---

* From the consumer's viewpoint, checking and savings account deposits and withdrawals also fit into the category of routine needs, and we believe that consumers would welcome the inclusion of facilities for these banking services within the super-store. Where permitted by law, facilities for these services would be operated by local bank branches that specialize in "consumer" banking activities. They would, in effect, be leased departments although they would in all likelihood be identified by the name of the parent bank.

income households—and, implicitly, we based our thinking on some additional assumptions about a household's needs and preferences. For a first-generation Chinese household, certain kinds of foods (star anise, bean sprouts) may be routine necessities. But the percentage of all households buying these items, in a given month or even year, is very small—except in a few neighborhoods. For this reason, very few super-markets carry Chinese food ingredients. Their rate of movement, relative to minimum space and inventory requirements, is simply not great enough. Super-stores, like present-day supermarkets, will have to limit their product lines to *those routinely purchased items whose rate of movement* is above some reasonable minimum in a given market area. (Because purchasing patterns of different consumer groups vary so much, the specific products carried by super-stores will also vary. Even with the most decentralized form of organization, we question whether a chain super-store can cater to such extreme variations in ethnic or other consumer preferences as star anise.)

Second, the products that a super-store can profitably handle will also be limited by the nature of the store's overall "system design"—the facilities and methods used for merchandising, physical supply, storage, display, and for handling customer transactions. Generally speaking, it seems to us that this system is *not* well-suited to efficient handling of:

very bulky and heavy products (bales of peatmoss);
products requiring extension of credit by the store;
products for which pilferage losses would be excessive, without special protection;
products requiring post-purchase services.

Taking all of these factors into account, then, we believe that the guiding principle for determining what products and services a super-store should handle is:

any and all items that are viewed as routine purchases by a sufficient number of consumers in a given trading area, and which can be efficiently handled by the store's facilities, methods, and personnel.

Super-store—or just a bigger supermarket?

Given the foregoing definition of the super-store concept, and the discussion of product lines that it will offer to consumers, some readers may wonder: is it really something different? Don't many supermarkets already handle practically all of the items on a consumer's "routine buying list," however this is defined?

It is probably true that at least *some* supermarkets presently carry every one of the products and services classified above as routine needs.

For example, according to estimates by *Progressive Grocer,* the percentages of supermarkets carrying selected non-food lines in 1971 were:

Housewares	88%
School Supplies	86%
Stationery	76%
Toys	65%
Books	43%
Garden Supplies	37%
Records	32%
Fresh Flowers	20%

If many supermarkets already carry these and other non-food routine needs, what is different about the super-store? We believe that there are two key distinguishing features:

The super-store will offer reasonable assortments in *all* of the consumer's routine purchase categories, not just *some* of them. Although many present-day supermarkets carry stationery, and many carry garden supplies, and many carry records, very few regularly handle *all* of these and other categories that make up the total "package" of routine needs.

The super-store will offer a *planned assortment* of items in each category—whereas many supermarkets simply "handle some items," often selected on an opportunistic basis. From the consumer's viewpoint the difference is crucial. Although many (perhaps most) consumers are accustomed to buying a few fast-moving health and beauty aids at the supermarket, very few think of the supermarket as their primary source for *most* of their needs. The super-store will offer a sufficiently broad assortment to meet *most* of the needs of *most* consumers—not only for health and beauty aids, but also for all of the other categories of routine needs.

The super-store—and some close relatives

In light of the foregoing somewhat abstract discussion of the super-store concept, the reader may wonder how it relates to various new types of stores that have evolved in the United States and Western Europe during the late 1960's and early 1970's. How, for example, does the super-store differ from the "side-by-side" combination store which is so common in the United States or the "hypermarché" that has been developed in France and Germany?

Both the side-by-side combination store and the hypermarché are retail facilities offering full assortments of food store products and extensive assortments of general merchandise in areas ranging from 30,000 to 200,000 or more square feet. They are designed to attract consumers for non-food shopping trips as well as food shopping trips. An aisle, a partial wall, or a full wall may separate the food and non-food sections. There may be one bank of checkouts for both food and non-foods, or separate banks of checkouts. The food and general merchandise areas may or may not be identified as different stores and may or may not be owned by different companies. The key point is that the consumer is offered under one roof a full assortment from which to select food needs and a reasonably complete assortment from which to select a wide range of non-food lines.

An obvious rationale for a side-by-side combination or hypermarché is that full assortments of both food and general merchandise will attract consumers on both food *and* general merchandise shopping trips. Experience demonstrates that this double attraction has helped both food and general merchandise sales in the past.

Past success, however, may reflect the consumer's lack of alternatives as well as the benefits provided by the side-by-side combination. From the consumer's perspective, the combination is less than ideal. Frequently the more fashion-oriented "non-routine" non-foods are of a lower quality and price level than she prefers. The self-service nature of the operation and the relatively rudimentary decor compatible with a self-service environment restricts the sale of better quality fashion merchandise. Furthermore, if she is on a food shopping trip and needs a few non-food items, the consumer must trek through the whole general merchandise assortment to find those few items. If she is on a non-food shopping trip and needs a few food items, she must trek through the whole food assortment. Typically in most American side-by-side combination stores, she must also suffer the inconvenience of paying for her purchases at two separate banks of checkouts. If there is only one bank of checkouts, then the food customer must accept the slower pace of the checkout line as the clerk seeks to find the sometimes obscure price information on the non-routine purchase. Moreover, if the clerk has been instructed to collect on non-routine purchases pertinent merchandising information such as the style number of the item being sold, then there will be a further delay at the front end.

The customer's alternative to the side-by-side combination store is separate visits to two or more stores which may or may not involve more driving and parking activities. Neither alternative is tailored to her "normal" set of routine needs in either a food or a non-food shopping trip, although she wastes less time in the combination store.

The super-store concept offers a third alternative. Under the concept, food stores put together a more systematically designed combination of routine offerings; the consumer no longer has to waste time roaming through aisles of irrelevant merchandise or traveling from store to store.

The foregoing discussion does not argue that the superstore concept will completely obsolete the side-by-side combination store. In the United States, side-by-side combination stores should continue to prosper within larger cities in middle-to-lower-middle-class blue-collar neighborhoods and in smaller cities and towns outside of metropolitan areas.

In these areas consumers are generally more satisfied with the lower price and quality fashion-oriented items which it is feasible to carry in side-by-side combination stores.

Abroad, the hypermarché may have even brighter prospects. There is a shortage of other suburban retail facilities with adequate selections of non-foods. Most existing supermarket operators have failed to combat vigorously the low price image of the hypermarchés. Finally, longer order cycles on fashion merchandise make the collection of merchandise information in addition to price less important than in the United States. Thus, a single battery of checkouts can serve both food and non-food sections without the consumer delays induced in the United States by the collection of addtional information on the sale of non-routine items.

Super-stores will, however, seriously challenge side-by-side combination stores in the sale of routine general merchandise. In higher income areas, where the phrase "routine purchases" encompasses a greater variety of merchandise and where there is more resistance to the fashion offerings of combination stores, this competition may prove particularly formidable. Combined with increasingly intensive "intra-type" competition and the infringement of the catalog showroom on the hard goods offerings of side-by-side combination stores, the super-store promises to add to the woes of the discount department store.

THE EVOLUTION OF THE SUPER-STORE

We believe that the super-store, as defined in the preceding section, is a natural evolutionary development in the market and competitive environment of the 1970's. The super-store concept, we have suggested, is an *extension* of the supermarket concept. This extended version of the supermarket seems to be a logical one in the years ahead, for two reasons:

It appears well-suited to the changing needs of consumers.

It seems to be a natural outcome of the process of competition among food chains and other types of retail outlets.

Our rationale for expecting the super-store to grow rapidly is explained below. . . .

✿   ✿   ✿

Pressure for change

The concept of serving an increasing range of the consumer's routine shopping needs in an integrated and consistent fashion in one location is far from revolutionary. The super-store concept has evolved as food chains and other firms have experimented with a variety of strategic and operating concepts. The experiments were attempts to find ways to cope with pressures for change in food chain operations.

The need for change is obvious. For all food chains, operating profit has declined by 53% in the last 15 years, from 1.97% of sales in 1956 to 0.92% in 1971. Average return on net worth showed more resistance to decline, but fell by 38% from 14.40% in 1956 to 8.88% in 1971.

Food chains' specific reactions to declining profits varied widely. However, three typical kinds of responses developed. Practically all chains have tried to *decrease distribution costs;* most chains also attempted to *differentiate their food offerings;* and many chains tried to *diversify their product lines,* both within supermarket outlets and through other types of operations.

Improving efficiency in distribution involved capitalizing both on chains' increasing size and on technological improvements. As volume increased, more food chains were able to take over the wholesale distribution function. New distribution centers and new larger stores were able to use advances in materials-handling technology. Improved data handling technology enabled the chains to control the complex and finely tuned wholesale-retail distribution system. The result was improved turnover, at least at the warehouse level.

Differentiating food offerings involved a variety of kinds of actions and combinations of them. The most fundamental way to differentiate a store was to locate it where there was no competition. Chains sought understored trade areas, especially in the burgeoning suburbs. Other forms of differentiation included very broad assortments in a larger store, private labels, discount prices, longer hours of operation, and establishing specialty departments within supermarkets such as delicatessens, in-store bakeries, and so on.

Improving distribution efficiency and expanding food offerings—and even continued expansion of "familiar" non-foods, such as health and beauty aids—were tasks for which food chains were relatively well-prepared. Efficient distribution and merchandising are the traditional fundamentals of the food business. Existing techniques had to be updated and sharpened, but a basic understanding of the business pervaded food chain organizations. Finding profitable adjuncts to traditional and closely related product lines, in contrast, required learning from scratch whole new lines of business.

Horizontal diversification into a variety of mass retail distribution operations proved to be very challenging. Management able to operate general merchandise, variety, drug, take-home food, on-premise food, dry cleaning, service bakery, and specialty food operations could be acquired. Many food chains made such acquisitions. But these managers typically were not accustomed to working with food chains. More importantly, the food chains apparently were not completely sure what they wanted to do with the acquisitions. The result was a painful learning process during which some diversified food chains developed profitable non-food retailing operations, some food chains wrote off attempted diversifications as unsuccessful experiments, and almost no food chains achieved real "synergy" of food and diversified operations.

Non-food retailing operations were typically organized as autonomous divisions. In some cases these divisions have been profitable, but they have done little to augment the profitability of the food distribution operations.

In brief, then, the 15-year period up to 1971 has seen tremendous growth in food retailing, but it has also been a period of more and more intensive competition, with each food chain seeking to attain competitive advantage. One outcome of this pattern of competition has been a move toward fewer, larger stores, carrying increasingly diversified product lines. These recent trends have set the stage, we believe, for the emergence of the super-store as a major element of the distribution system.

THE DECADE AHEAD

Developing a five-year plan in the dynamic environment of food distribution is difficult enough. Thinking 10 years ahead, for purposes of strategic planning, obviously requires more speculation. However, strategic planning requires thinking a few years beyond the five-year plan, because such thinking develops the strategic objectives which the plan should be designed to meet. Therefore, it is useful to attempt an outline of the fundamental conditions which can be expected.

The continuing trends

On the consumer front, several familiar trends seem likely to continue through the coming decade:

Population will continue to climb. . . .

A slightly larger proportion of the population will be in the labor force, and a greater proportion will be in age categories during which earning and spending capacity is high.

Educational levels will continue to increase. . . .

Consumer income will continue to increase, but a smaller proportion of it will be spent in food stores. . . .

Within the food distribution industry itself, it seems likely that *recent trends toward higher unit labor costs and higher occupancy costs will continue.* It will continue to be very difficult to offset these cost increases through higher gross margins. Consequently, net profits on food retailing will be as low—or even lower—in the decade ahead as they are in 1972.

The emerging trends

In spite of the continuing trends, the 1970's will not be a complete replay of the last 15 to 20 years. The environment in which the continuing trends will operate will differ substantially from the environment of the 1950's and 1960's.

Perhaps the most fundamental new condition for the food chain bent on growth is that the *successes of the past will make further growth more difficult.* Much of chains' past growth depended on capturing share of market from other types of food retailers. . . . Supermarkets have supplanted smaller grocery stores, and chains have captured an increasing share of supermarket sales. The chains enjoyed the dual advantages of being abreast of the supermarket development and of being organized to realize economies of scale. In short, the new force in the market aimed at the soft underbelly of a relatively unsophisticated small-unit distribution system.

. . . the combined market share of chains, voluntaries, and cooperatives had reached 77% of retail food sales by 1971. In the largest 25 standard metropolitan areas for which estimates are available, chains commanded an average 70% share of grocery store sales by 1970. Consequently, further growth increasingly will involve head-to-head competition with other chains. Easy pickings from unsophisticated mamas and papas will be hard to find.

The industry's past successes in serving new suburban markets has narrowed another prime avenue for growth. The suburbs will continue to grow, but will not be the virgin territory in the next decade that they were in the last two. Patterns of suburban population growth have become more predictable. Much future growth is likely to involve increasing population density in trade areas already served by stores built in the 1950's and 1960's.

Diversification is a third prime avenue for growth which has become more intensely competitive as a result of past successes. Several food chain companies have sought opportunities for volume growth, improved profiits, and a more glamorous Wall Street image, in mass merchandising—and a few have been successful. By the early 1970's, however, rapid expansion of mass merchandising facilities has filled many of the market voids which existed in the 1950's and 1960's. Furthermore, the general merchandise discount retailers themselves have become more sophisticated competitors. In addition, the increasingly restrictive policies of the Federal Trade Commission with respect to mergers and acquisitions will limit the feasibility of consumating synergistic mergers.

At least three recently emerging trends in the food distribution environment promise to intensify further the problems of achieving growth and profits. The first development is the automated front end, coupled with the uniform product code.* The second is the continuation—and probably intensification—of public policies and government regulations that affect food chains' costs. The third development is some leading food chains' recognition that a change in food retailing concepts is desirable.

The automated front end (AFE) and uniform product code are, of course, still in an experimental stage of development. But it seems virtually certain that some version of the AFE will come into widespread use in the industry during the next five years. An obvious and immediate result of this development will be to increase the capital requirements for a store; and this, along with other factors that require more capital investment, will intensify the need for higher sales volume per store. On the other hand, by making available much more detailed merchandising information, the AFE will make it *possible* for chain merchandising managers and store managers to do a more effective job of selecting product lines and monitoring their performance than has previously been possible.

It is useful, however, to recount briefly some managerial implications of the data which the automated front end will make available. Detailed sales data by store and by time period will be an invaluable tool for "demographic marketing," and in merchandising broader food and non-food assortments. Pricing, advertising, and new item tests will be less costly and more rapid. Presumably, then, chains will come closer to being able to serve local market idiosyncracies as well as independents can.

The *consumerism movement* has already shown great interest in food distribution, and can be expected to do so in the future. Food purchases account for a significant part of consumers' after-tax income. Food prices are likely to rise in the next decade. In addition, the food industry is a very *visible* target for politicians and other critics of marketing practices. Even rare cases of impure products, concern over dangerous food additives, defective packages, deceptive pricing and promotion, etc., all make the food industry a good potential target. Therefore, food chains can expect little consumer or government help in alleviating the

---

* Editors' note: The term Automated Front End refers to a mechanical basket unloader and conveyor system which alines items and passes them under an optical scanner. The scanner, which is hooked to a computerized cash register, reads the product code and price. An inventory entry is made at the same time the cash register records the purchase. After the customer's order has all passed under the scanner, the register calculates the total cost, figures any tax necessary, and indicates the amount the customer must pay. Usually, the system would include an automatic bagger. For the system to operate, however, each item must be identified by a unique product code—a six- or eight-digit number. Since, in all likelihood, the product code would have to be afixed at the time of manufacture, they would have to be uniform for all stores and all items would have to have a similar type of code.

problem of slim margins. Moreover, increasingly restrictive land-use and zoning policies within metropolitan areas will almost surely make new store sites increasingly hard to find—and increasingly costly.

The third emerging trend is the recognition by some of the leading food chains that attempts in the 1950's and 1960's to improve food chain profits by simply increasing non-food assortments did not solve the problem. These chains believe that the key to improved profits is integration of a broader, but carefully selected, assortment of non-foods into a consistent food and non-food merchandising plan. Some chains are experimenting with variations on this general theme. These experiments are significant, because some of the chains conducting them are diversified retailing corporations which have tried the route of operating separate divisions, including a food distribution division operating under the supermarket concept. These chains have built a base of general merchandising skills to apply to their new concept of food retailing; and they appear especially well-equipped to manage the "super-stores" that we envision growing out of the current pattern of trial and error.

Perspective for the coming decade

The foregoing discussion is not intended as another in an all-too-long line of prophecies of doom. It is, however, a prophecy of intensified challenge for food chains bent on growth. Moreover, it is a forecast that the supermarket concept of operation will be increasingly vulnerable to the super-store concept as food chains move toward 1982. It is useful to summarize the four major reasons why the super-store concept matches the environmental demands of the next decade before discussing in the next section the strategic implications of the emerging concept.

1. *Consumers want the advantages of the super-store,* for three reasons. First, consumers will want an ever-expanding variety of products and services in food and non-food categories, as their educational and income levels rise. Because of rising incomes and increased opportunities for achieving desirable "life styles," consumers will regard a wider and wider range of products and services as "routine purchases." Second, consumers will want their routine shopping to be increasingly efficient, as they have a growing range of alternative uses for their time. The super-store concept provides the convenience of one-stop shopping. Third, consumers will want their routine shopping decisions to be as simple as possible. The super-store concept offers a consistent merchandising policy for a wide range of routine shopping needs, which allows the consumer to make only one decision regarding where to shop.

2. *Consumers can make use of the super-store,* because rising per capita income will enable them to buy the variety of products and services they want and because increased car ownership and improved highways will enable them to reach the larger stores, which must draw from larger trading areas than conventional supermarkets.

3. *Food chains need the super-store* concept, for four reasons. First, as competition intensifies, chains bent on growth will need a competitive advantage (i.e., some means of differentiation) to penetrate markets. The super-store concept provides a difference. Second, as competitive and political pressures continue to limit gross margins and as expenses climb, chains will need a more profitable merchandise mix in addition to higher volume. The broadened non-food assortment embodied in the super-store concept provides such an assortment. Third, as stores grow in size and assortment complexity, chains will need a concept for organizing and controlling these units in a consistent way. The super-store concept serves this purpose. Finally, as the investment required to open a new unit grows and the pace of change continues to accelerate, chains will need control both over the food operation and over the other kinds of retail operations complementing the food operation. The super-store concept brings together these kinds of operations under the chain's control.

4. *Some leading food chains have made strides toward developing the core of general merchandising skills necessary for successful operation of the super-store.* Just as importantly, the uniform product code and automated front end promise to make available the merchandising data the managers need.

The super-store concept, therefore, is both desirable and feasible. Some food chains already are experimenting successfully with variations on the theme. Consequently, the probability is high that stores operating under the concept will proliferate and will be powerful competitors.

This forecast raises two key strategic questions. What does the super-store concept mean to food chain operations in the next decade? How should a firm prepare to compete successfully under the new industry conditions? . . .

FOOD CHAIN OPERATIONS: AS THE SUPER-STORE CONCEPT MATURES

The super-store concept will not explode on the retail food distribution industry as an "instant revolution," sweeping away all familiar operating concepts in a few short years. The industry simply has too much inertia to experience such abrupt change.

Food chains will need time to develop and thoroughly analyze new strategic concepts. The chains which accept the concept will find their ability to implement the super-store idea limited by their commitments to existing facilities and operating philosophies, by the experience of their personnel, and by uncertainties inherent in experimenting with a new concept. Consequently, the super-store concept will mature over several years and will coexist with vestiges of the conventional supermarket concept.

* * *

Summary

The stores will offer merchandise and service assortments tailored to meet the consumer's routine shopping needs. The non-food assortment will be broader than offered in the familiar supermarket. The non-food assortment, however, will *not* approach the full range of items carried by the general merchandise segment of a side-by-side combination store. The buildings housing the super-store concept will be larger than the familiar supermarket. Selling space will be on the order of 30,000 square feet. Foods and non-foods will be integrated in the building layout. Merchandise and services will be placed where the consumer can find them efficiently in the process of doing her routine shopping.

Super-stores will not be as dependent as supermarkets on shopping center neighbors to attract traffic. Consequently, more often stores will be free-standing and ownership will more often be vested in the super-store operator.

The stores will offer a wide range of products and services, and long hours of operation. However, how many will be open 24 hours is disputable. To operate these larger and more diverse stores successfully will require improvement in both merchandising management and store management.

Disposition of existing supermarkets, as super-stores capture share of market, will be a significant problem. Together with the maturity of both the supermarket and discount department store aspects of self-service distribution, the premature obsolescence of supermarket facilities will inhibit the super-store concept from stimulating any renaissance in the profitability of food chain companies.

IMPLICATIONS OF THE SUPER-STORE FOR MANUFACTURERS

Apart from its meaning to food store operators, the advent of the super-store also has considerable significance for both present and potential suppliers to food stores.

New opportunities for non-food manufacturers

As the super-store encroaches upon traditional supermarkets, new opportunities will arise from manufacturers who market many of the items which we have classified as routine needs but who do not currently sell through food channels. Today, these items are sold in only a limited number of supermarkets. Tomorrow, this merchandise will be sold in a large number of super-stores.

To take advantage of these opportunities, manufacturers who do not currently sell through food channels will have to learn about the requirements of super-store operators. These requirements may be quite different from those of the general merchandise channels through which such manufacturers now sell. For example, super-store operators will probably want to carry only fast sellers in certain merchandise lines. Furthermore, these fast sellers will have to be packaged so that they conform to the logistical requirements of super-store operators. This means that such merchandise should be relatively easy to price-mark and shelve, entirely pre-wrapped, and reasonably resistant to pilferage. Also, vendors who sell through super-stores for the first time will have to help their new distributors achieve a rate of inventory turnover approaching what they are used to in food. Assortments, minimum order quantities, and warehouse and transportation arrangements, therefore, may have to be modified. Successful vendors of "routine need" products to super-stores will have to keep the requirements of their new outlets uppermost in their minds.

Significance to current food store suppliers

The super-store era also has significance for manufacturers who currently sell to the food trade. Such significance relates to product opportunities, modifications in selling strategy, and logistical opportunities.

1. Product opportunities and threats. In the realm of product opportunity, suppliers of grocery items may now want to invade other categories of routine merchandise which will be sold extensively through super-stores. Food manufacturers' familiarity with the requirements of supermarket selling may encourage them to examine diversification into areas formerly regarded as foreign such as the housewares, stationery, and staple apparel businesses.

The advent of the super-store, however, also poses some *threats* to suppliers of food products. Those manufacturers with "me too" brands in particular product categories may find that the super-store provides no relief from the pressures they feel from supermarkets in the struggle to retain distribution for such brands. Although super-stores will carry a greater variety of merchandise than the supermarkets they replace, it is doubtful that this variety will be represented by greater arrays of "me too" brands. Thus the arrival of these stores probably spells more pressure than ever on the distribution of "me too" products currently sold in supermarkets.

Because of their size, super-stores are also likely to have greater consumer acceptance than the supermarkets that they displace. The greater consumer acceptance should enhance the ability of super-stores to substitute private brands for national brands. In one sense, this is a threat to national brands—particularly if they are marginal national brands. In another sense, it is an opportunity for suppliers of grocery items to reexamine their posture concerning private label merchandise. The likelihood is that super-stores will sell a higher percentage of private

label merchandise in the food category than do the supermarkets which they replace. Alert food manufacturers who have previously steered clear of private label packing may want to take advantage of this fact by entering the private label business.

2. *Sales management.* In addition to its implications for products, the super-store also has significant implications for sales management among traditional food store suppliers. If these traditional suppliers expand their lines to include a wider variety of the routine items that super-stores carry, their sales forces may have to spend more time in each individual super-store helping to merchandise their line. These longer visits, however, will be offset by visits to fewer stores, since a single super-store will replace more than a single supermarket.

On balance, the reduction in the number of stores should more than offset the greater number of items in a line, thus allowing manufacturers to reduce the size of their sales forces. As the size of the sales force declines, however, the remaining men will have to be upgraded. Why? Three reasons stand out. First, because super-store managers will be more capable than supermarket managers and will have better information to rely on. To engage in constructive dialogue with these managers, the manufacturer's salesman also will have to be more capable. Furthermore the variety in the routine items carried in super-stores will vary more than does the variety in food items stocked in supermarkets. Consequently, the super-store manager will need the help of manufacturers' salesmen to tailor selections to the needs of a given store's particular trading area.

Finally, because routine items vary more than food items in such dimensions as handling costs, inventory turnover, and potential markdown percentages, super-store managers will most likely use techniques such as direct product profit rather than gross margin to judge the relative emphasis they give to particular merchandise. To carry on discussions based on these more sophisticated merchandising tools, manufacturers, again, will need more capable salesmen.

3. *Logistical implications.* The emergence of the super-store will also have an impact on manufacturers in terms of logistical systems. Traditional logistical arrangements in the grocery industry are likely to be affected at *both ends* of the spectrum. More slow-moving products may go through the warehouse, while a few exceptionally fast movers may flow directly from the manufacturer's facility to individual super-stores.

Currently, supermarkets handle on a rack-jobber basis a number of slow selling items which they cannot afford to stock in full case quantity. Since super-stores will be considerably larger than supermarkets and will handle more volume, many slow sellers could be stocked in full case quantities in super-stores; such products could thus be handled through the super-store's grocery warehouse. As a result, on slow sellers the advent of super-stores should result in reducing the importance of rack jobbers and increasing the importance of selling direct to the super-store operator.

Quite the opposite phenomenon, however, may occur for products that are fast movers, e.g., beverages, detergents, and the like. For such fast-moving products, it may be practical to stock movable gondolas in the manufacturer's own processing plant and to ship those gondolas directly to the super-store, bypassing the super-store operator's warehouse. This possibility obviously pertains to only a limited number of exceptionally fast-moving items.

QUESTIONS

1. What is the basic conceptual difference between the supermarket and the "super-store" that makes the super-store such an innovation?
2. If super-stores do become a significant factor in retailing, how will they affect manufacturers' strategies? For example, what might the impact be on product mixes?
3. Should super-stores be permitted if they are going to make many present facilities and planned shopping areas obsolete? What if more consumer travel time and energy use is required to get to these bigger stores?
°4. Discuss the super-store concept in terms of Bucklin's store-goods classification system (Reading 19).

In this article, Lewis suggests that the primary purpose of physical distribution (PD) is servicing demand. But he also shows that PD is linked to obtaining demand through the service level, which has strategic implications. Then, Lewis describes the many "trade-off" decisions which must be made when developing a good PD system.

---

21. PHYSICAL DISTRIBUTION: MANAGING THE FIRM'S SERVICE LEVEL*

Richard J. Lewis

FROM ITS BEGINNING in the 1950's the discipline of physical distribution has steadily developed into a major area of business adminis-

* An original contribution. At the time of writing, Dr. Lewis was Professor of Marketing and Transportation Administration at Michigan State University.

tration. During its early period of conception the late Professor Paul D. Converse described physical distribution as "the other half of the total costs of marketing."[1] Today it wouldn't be difficult to find those who would argue that physical distribution is not a part of marketing, but rather its co-equal within a firm's organizational structure. Our purpose here is not to settle the argument, but to understand the role of physical distribution within a firm and how it relates to the firm's marketing efforts.

THE NATURE OF DISTRIBUTION MANAGEMENT WITHIN THE FIRM

An interesting way to approach an understanding of distribution management within a firm is to ask why a firm spends money on distribution efforts. That is, what is the purpose(s) of spending money on distribution? Must money be spent on distribution efforts and, if so, why?

The answer to these questions lies in the *inherent purposes* of distribution expenditures and, hence, the purposes of distribution within a firm. Distribution efforts within a firm are directed at accomplishing two inherent purposes: to obtain demand for the firm's goods and services, and to service and supply the demand. Hence, all distribution activities and their respective costs can be identified by their purpose—they are either demand-obtaining or demand-servicing activities. Figure 1 outlines the approach described above and shows the respective activities related to each purpose. Thus, advertising, personal selling, sales promotion, merchandising, and pricing are all distribution activities directed at the same common purpose of obtaining demand for the firm's goods and services. Warehousing, inventory management, transportation, and order processing and handling are all activities directed at servicing demand for the firm's goods and services.

Where the identification of the purposes to which a firm's distribution effort is directed identifies its *ends,* the identification of the activities used to accomplish the purposes identifies the *means* used. The importance of classifying activities by their purpose is that the activities must be controlled in relationship to the purpose they share in common with each other and that, where appropriate, the interdependent nature of activities is recognized.

In looking at Figure 1, there is a natural tendency to want to make it into an organization chart with all the typical types of professional labels and titles. It is precisely because of this natural tendency that the terms used were the most neutral that could be found that were still appropriate to the discussion. At this point some would wish to label the managerial area Marketing Effort, rather than Distribution Effort. Others would argue that it is the managerial purpose now labeled

---

[1] Paul D. Converse "The Other Half of Marketing," Twenty-Sixth Boston Conference on Distribution (Boston: Boston Trade Board, 1954), pp. 22–25.

FIGURE 1

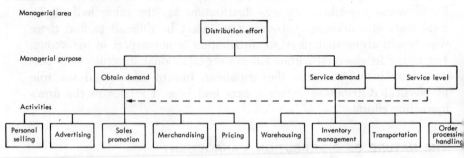

"obtaining demand" that should be called marketing and that "servicing demand" is really the managerial purpose of physical distribution management. However, what is in a name? The understanding we are after is not found in titles, for the titles can be anything so long as there is a clear understanding and classification of the underlying purposes and how the activities relate to these purposes. Professor Donald Bowersox's statement in this connection is appropriate: "It is not the organization, but rather the philosophy of operation, which is of critical importance."[2]

THE NATURE OF PHYSICAL DISTRIBUTION MANAGEMENT

Whether one desires to organizationally place marketing management above physical distribution management or on a level with it, there is no argument with identifying servicing demand as the purpose of physical distribution management. The National Council of Physical Distribution Management defines physical distribution as: "A term employed in manufacturing and commerce to describe the broad range of activities concerned with efficient movement of finished products from the end of the production line to the consumer. . . ."

This focus on the "broad range of activities" concerned with the movement of finished goods distinguishes the physical distribution concept from previous practices and has led to what has been called the "total cost approach." The total cost approach views the costs of the various activities of servicing demand as a *system* of costs resulting in a total cost of performing the supply function.

Prior to the concept of physical distribution management and the total cost approach, the practice was to consider each supply activity separately. Attempts to minimize the costs of each activity were made independently with little or no attention given to the impact this had on the other elements of supply. At least one author suggested that

---

[2] Donald J. Bowersox "Physical Distribution in Semi-maturity," *Air Transportation*, (January 1966), p. 8.

this approach leads to "the popular corporate pastime of relocating rather than reducing costs."[3] An example often used to illustrate the idea is the attempt by the traffic department of a firm to minimize its costs. Such attempts normally lead to larger, infrequent shipments by slower, lower cost modes of transportation. Having purchased the lowest cost mode of transportation that was feasible and having moved only large size shipments, the traffic department can sit back, survey the reduction in its costs, and point with pride to the savings it has accomplished for the firm. However, the cost savings realized by the traffic department do not reflect the impact of the actions on the costs of other supply activities. While the traffic department succeeded in reducing *its costs*, it is highly probably that the warehouse manager is extremely unhappy with his rising costs of holding more inventory and providing more space for the larger shipments. If the firm charges an interest cost on the money tied up while products are in transit to a distribution center and not available for sale, then this cost will also rise due to the increased time the goods are in shipment as a result of using a slower mode of transportation.

The interdependent nature of the costs of supply activities is the basis for the total cost approach and the concept of physical distribution management. It can be viewed as the management of trade-offs. *Efficient* management of cost trade-offs requires that cost increases in some supply activity(s) are traded for greater cost decreases in other supply activities. The total cost approach requires centralized cost control over the various supply activities, which may result in cost increases in some activities that will be more than offset by cost reductions in other activities. Similarly, centralized cost control would not permit indiscriminant cost reductions in any one supply activity if the net effect were to raise the cost of other supply activities above the cost savings and, hence, increase the total costs of supply.

The necessity for centralizing control over cost of servicing demand does not preclude the individual management of the various activities. It does, however, require that the activities be integrated and coordinated and that constraints be placed on the various activities, which will allow the firm to minimize its *total costs* of servicing demand.

CONTROL OBJECTIVE AND THE SERVICE LEVEL

The natural division of distribution purposes, activities, and costs into obtaining demand and servicing demand is further justified by the difference in the objectives of controlling costs associated with each purpose. The objective of controlling costs of obtaining demand is to *maximize the effectiveness* per dollar spent on the various activities (i.e.

---
[3] H. G. Miller, "Accounting for Physical Distribution," *Transportation and Distribution Management* (December 1961), p. 11.

maximize the demand obtained per dollar spent). In contrast, the objective of cost control over the activities used to service demand is to *minimize the costs,* consistent with constraints imposed by the desired level of customer service and other constraints imposed outside the firm's control by competitors.

The service level is the connecting link between the two purposes of distribution within a firm. In the final analysis these two purposes are not independent of each other, since the service level a firm provides is a demand-obtaining force itself. The selection of a service level is a major decision within a firm due to two major operational impacts derived from the decision. First, in setting the service level, the firm is either consciously or unconsciously deciding how important a role it wishes to have service play in obtaining demand for its goods and services. One need only reflect on the importance of the service level of suppliers in the construction industry to see how having the right products, in the right quantities, in the right place, at the right time is critical to the contractor in meeting his schedules.

The service elasticity of demand for the firm's products and services must be determined or estimated so that the correct customer service level can be used as a *demand-obtaining force.* Therefore, planning and control of the overall distribution effort requires determining the complimentary relationship (trade-offs) between the activities of obtaining demand and the service level to be provided by physical distribution management. In Figure 1 the dotted line from the service level to Obtain Demand portrays this relationship. Recognition of this relationship could result in a firm's decreasing its advertising and personal selling budgets and using the money to increase its physical distribution budget, if they felt that an increase in the service level would increase demand more than the decrease realized by lessening advertising and personal selling efforts.

The second major operational impact stems from the fact that, as noted earlier, the operating objective of physical distribution management is to minimize the costs of supply activities while achieving the service level desired by the firm. Therefore, cost minimization is *relative* to a service level that must be achieved. It is not cost minimization *per se* that is being sought, but cost minimization while achieving the service level desired.

SERVICE LEVEL DIMENSIONS

Determining the desired service level requires that operating objectives be established for each of the dimensions of the service level. These dimensions are: order cycle time; percent of demand to be satisfied; quality control relative to order processing; and insuring acceptable physical condition of goods upon delivery.

Order cycle time

The order cycle refers to the total time consumed from placing an order to receiving the goods. From the point of view of the firm's customers, the lower the average time of an order cycle and the lower the dispersion around the average time, the better is the service level. From the customers' point of view, the longer the order cycle, the greater the premium on his ability to forecast his demand and the higher the risk of lost sales. For example, assume the supplying firm has an order cycle to a given customer of forty-five days. Assume further that the customer experiences an unusually high demand and runs out of stock five days after placing an order. This means that he will stay out of stock and lose sales for forty days until the order is finally received. Contrasting the previous situation with one in which the order cycle is one day would mean that, at most, the customer would be out of stock for a maximum of one day.

The dispersion around the average order cycle time is of equal and sometimes greater importance to a firm's customers. It is not very useful to tell a customer that his average order cycle time will be five days if, in reality, his deliveries will actually vary from one day to twenty days. While the average may actually be five days, the average is not typical and cannot be counted on by the customer. He can never be sure when he places an order with the firm whether it will be the one day or the twenty day cycle he is facing. The predictability of order cycle time which results from little or no dispersion around the average is of major importance to a firm's customers.

The resulting problem for physical distribution management is that both lower average order cycle times and small dispersions around the average tend to require higher costs in physical distribution activities. To lower the average order cycle time, the firm must institute faster order processing and physical handling procedures. This requires more personnel and/or higher cost–high speed order communications equipment. To maintain a lower level of dispersion around the average delivery time requires quality control procedures similar to those found in manufacturing.

Percent of demand to be satisfied

Like its customers, the firm has the problem of forecasting its demand and establishing production and inventory levels to meet that demand. If the firm maintains stock levels sufficient to fill 100 percent of its demand at any time, it increases its inventory costs. If the firm lowers its inventory cost by keeping a stock level to fill only 80 percent of demand at peak periods, it either increases the time period necessary to fill some orders or loses the sales. The greater the substitutability

FIGURE 2
The relationship between percent of demand
serviced and investment in inventory

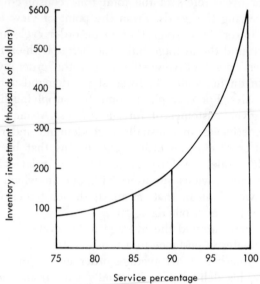

of competitors' products for the firm's, the more sales the firm will lose
and, therefore, the greater its motivation to satisfy a higher percentage
of its demand. Figure 2 shows the general relationship between the percent of demand able to be serviced and its impact on required investment in inventory. While the absolute amount of investment will vary
depending upon the value of the product involved, the relative relationship shown is valid. Note the inventory investment difference needed
by the firm to move from an 80 percent to a 90 percent service level
as opposed to moving from a 90 percent to a 100 percent service level.
It is obvious that the last 10 percent comes at a very high cost in inventory investment.

Order processing quality control

Nothing can be more frustrating to a firm than to have a very fast
order cycle with very little dispersion and a high level of service all
go down the drain because the wrong goods were shipped. The customer
has not been serviced unless the right item, color, size, style, and quantity
has been shipped to the right place. To minimize such mistakes requires
several checks and cross-checks to be sure the order and shipment match
exactly. Therefore, quality control procedures are also needed for filling
orders. While most firms today are very conscientious in designing their
systems for the outflow of their goods, few seem to have spent time
designing a system to return goods when things go wrong. Perhaps

this is the result of giving so much attention to designing and controlling outbound flows that it is hard for the firm to believe things could go wrong. In any case, it is bad enough when a customer receives an incorrect shipment, but the firm can hardly afford to compound the problem by having poorly defined and slow procedures for correcting the situation.

Physical condition upon delivery

Even having the order absolutely correct is not enough if the goods arrive in a damaged, unusable or unsaleable condition. Concern for the physical condition of goods centers around methods of storage used, transportation methods used, and protective packaging of the goods. A real problem for most physical distribution managers concerns trying to determine when and how damage was done. This is especially true where the firm uses a large number of outside firms in designing its service system, such as multiple private transport carriers, public warehouses, and independent middlemen who take physical possession of the goods. The greater the number of independent businesses involved in the physical flow of the product, the greater the opportunity for things to "fall between the chairs" when goods arrive damaged. The author knows of one consumer goods manufacturer who instituted a "get well check" policy. Upon learning of the arrival of damaged goods, the company immediately makes the financial adjustment to the dealer and assumes the responsibility for determining where the damage occurred and who will ultimately be held responsible for any financial loss.

THE ACTIVITIES OF PHYSICAL DISTRIBUTION

To understand how physical distribution management achieves a given service level requires at least a basic understanding of the various physical distribution activities and how they relate to each other and to the service level. Before discussing each activity, it should be noted that a central policy decision which has a major effect on all the activities is the decision concerning the degree to which the firm pursues a centralized versus a decentralized distribution system. The extreme of a centralized policy would be one distribution center from which all orders would be processed and shipped. The degree of decentralization would be determined by the number of distribution centers the firm establishes. The specific impacts of a centralized versus a decentralized policy will be treated within the discussion of each activity.

Warehousing

Warehousing decisions center around determining the size, number, and location of storage facilities needed to service demand. The centralization versus decentralization issue has a direct bearing on warehousing costs. A decision to centralize all activities into one distribution center would result in the warehousing manager having to provide the minimum space for a given level of demand. This is true because centralization of inventory at one point minimizes the total amount of inventory necessary to meet demand at any specified level. The reason for this will be explained in the inventory discussion. It is also true that there will be some economies of scale on the administrative side resulting in a lower total space requirement for administrative personnel. If a firm decides to decentralize, then the warehouse manager must concern himself with determining the total warehousing cost for various *numbers* of warehouses as well as determining the specific *location* of each. A rather substantial body of knowledge has developed on location theories which concerns determining locations which will minimize ton miles shipped, cost-ton miles shipped, and cost-time-ton miles shipped. A typical example of a warehousing decision would be the determination of whether a firm needs a distribution center in the southwestern part of the United States and, if so, precisely where it should be located.

Inventory management

For a manufacturing firm the ability to accurately forecast demand determines its efficiency in inventory management. If the firm knew exactly when the demand would occur and precisely the number of units, it could schedule production accordingly and only hold a small inventory to guard against production failures. Therefore, for the manufacturing firm, the greater the uncertainty of demand, the more difficult the inventory management problem.

For nonmanufacturing middlemen firms such as wholesalers and retailers, there are two sources of uncertainty which cause difficulty in inventory management. Like manufacturing firms, they are faced with some degree of uncertainty in accurately forecasting their demand. In addition, they must be concerned with the degree of uncertainty caused by the variance in order cycle times when dealing with their various suppliers. As noted in the discussion of order cycle time, the dispersion around the average time is of importance to the customer. As seen from the nonmanufacturing firm's point of view, zero dispersion around the average order cycle time would mean the elimination of his second source of uncertainty in managing his inventory.

For the manufacturing firm, a prime consideration is to balance the inventory costs against the manufacturing cost. This dilemma arises due to the conflicting desires to minimize the cost necessary to hold inventories and to maximize the economies of scale realized in large production runs which minimize the per unit production costs. Here again, the "trade-off" concept applies and the firm must determine how much inventory costs and production costs must increase from their independent ideal positions in order for the firm to minimize its total cost of producing and holding finished goods.

A "trade-off" also exists for the nonmanufacturing firm. For middlemen firms the nature of the "trade-off" evolves around minimizing the total of both ordering costs and holding costs. Ordering costs are the expenses incurred in placing a single order times the frequency of orders. Thus, the smaller the quantity ordered, the greater the frequency of orders and the greater the total ordering costs. Holding costs are determined by the average inventory level. The fewer the number of orders, the larger the quantities and the larger the average inventory, which results in higher holding costs. Therefore, when considering the number of orders placed, ordering costs move in the opposite direction of holding costs. A mathematical solution for the "trade-off" between these two costs has been developed to determine the Economic Order Quantity (EOQ).[4]

The EOQ formula is:

$$EOQ = \sqrt{\frac{2as}{i}}$$

where

a = order costs (per order)
s = annual sales rate (in units)
i = interest costs per unit per year

For an example, assume

a = $20
s = 5,200 units
i = $.25 per unit

Therefore:

$$EOQ = \sqrt{\frac{2as}{i}}$$

$$EOQ = \sqrt{\frac{2(20)(5200)}{.25}}$$

$$EOQ = \sqrt{\frac{208,000}{.25}}$$

$$EOQ = \sqrt{832,000}$$

$$EOQ = 912 \text{ units}$$

This EOQ results in approximately five orders per year.

While the EOQ formula provides a guide to efficient inventory management, it is not the final answer. The EOQ is used to determine base stock requirements. Base stock consists of the amount of stock

[4] This illustration follows the one found in Edward H. Bowman and Robert B. Fetter, *Analysis For Production Management* (Homewood Ill.: Richard D. Irwin, Inc., 1961) see pp. 272–276 for the mathematical derivation.

needed to meet the *average* level of demand. Since base stocks cover only the average demand, a firm that provides only base stock inventory would tend to be out of inventory 50 percent of the time. In order to minimize this condition, the firm would need to carry *safety* stocks in addition to base stocks to cover demand above average levels. As shown in Figure 2, as the firm attempts to position its inventory levels to meet a higher and higher percent of demand at any time, the investment in inventory becomes extremely high due to increasing the cost of safety stocks.

In addition to setting higher percentages of demand to be filled, a firm may also increase its safety stock by decentralizing distribution and using several distribution centers. Multiple distribution centers require multiple safety stocks, one at each distribution center, and increase the total uncertainty in forecasting demand. Typically, it is easier to forecast one aggregate demand than to divide up the aggregate and forecast the uncertainty of many smaller segments. Consequently, a decentralized distribution policy causes higher total levels of safety stocks and, hence, higher total inventory costs.

Transportation

The major objectives in managing the firm's transportation requirements center around choosing methods which will minimize transport costs, time in shipment, and loss and damage resulting from shipment. These "trade-offs" within the transportation activity are often in conflict. For example, air freight minimizes the transport time, but at a very high cost. Damage in shipment is often a trade-off between special packaging methods and selection of shipment modes which historically have low damage frequencies.

Beyond the "trade-offs" within the transportation activity are "trade-offs" between it and other activities. In fact, a major objective of the firm in adopting a decentralized distribution policy stems from its desire to minimize the transportation costs. Using many distribution centers accomplishes this by allowing the firm to ship full carload or truckload shipments at the lower C.L. and T.L. rates. It can then reship the small customer orders the short distances from the distribution center to the customer at the higher less-than-carload (L.C.L.) or less-than-truckload (L.T.L.) rates. This minimizes the total transportation costs. Here, however, the firm must concern itself with minimizing the total cost of transporting, warehousing, and inventorying its products. Although the decentralization of warehousing and inventory does lower the total transportation costs, it does, as discussed previously, raise the warehousing and inventory costs. Again we can see the interdependence of the cost of the activities of servicing demand relative to the firm's desire to minimize the total cost of providing a given level of service.

Order processing and handling

The actual order processing and handling deals with the communications necessary to receive, record, and fill an order and with the procedures necessary to physically assemble an order and make it ready for shipment. Management's concern with order processing and handling procedures arises from the amount of time necessary to process and handle an order and the quality control procedures used to insure that the order is filled and shipped correctly.

It does little good for the firm to pay premium prices for transportation speed if the transportation time is considerably less than the order processing and handling time. Slow order processing and handling procedures increase the total order cycle time just as surely as slow transportation times.

To increase the speed of order processing, the firm must turn its attention to high speed data processing techniques to receive, record, process, and check orders. In some cases this is so critical that customers have a direct computer tie-in with their suppliers and are able to know almost instantly what their position is in regard to the number of units on hand of a given product, how many units are on order, how many have been shipped, and when they are expected to arrive.

While procedures used to insure the correctness of order handling tend to increase the total time for order processing and handling, the firm must again determine the "trade-off" between increasing the total order cycle time for these quality control procedures and the costs of shipping the wrong goods.

CONCLUSION

This discussion was not meant to provide a definitive technical treatment of physical distribution management. It is meant to provide the student with some insight into what physical distribution is, what it does, and how it relates to the firm's overall distribution effort. Physical distribution management concerns itself with the management of the firm's demand-servicing activities. They must be coordinated in such a way that their interdependent nature is recognized so that the firm can minimize the total cost of providing its resulting service level.

The service level chosen by the firm can be a demand-obtaining force. Therefore, the firm must consider the cost "trade-offs" between the traditional demand-obtaining activities such as personal selling and advertising, and the service level. In summary, physical distribution management is concerned with the design, implementation, and operation of the firm's demand-servicing system in relationship to how the firm wishes to use the demand-servicing system as a source of obtaining demand for the firm's goods and services.

QUESTIONS

1. Could the concept of service level be used as a means of obtaining a competitive advantage? Explain.
2. How could the concept of elasticity of demand for service aid a manager in selecting and catering to different segments of a market?
3. Many physical distribution managers apparently view their primary task as one of minimizing the total cost of physical distribution. After reading the Lewis article, do you agree or disagree with this view? Why?
°4. Could some kind of change in physical distribution lead to the kind of "distribution breakthrough" discussed by Davidson (Reading 18)? If so, illustrate. If not, explain why.

Promotion is one of the important activities of marketing. Promotion is often fragmented into functional activities like personal selling, advertising and public relations, when it really should be an integrated effort. "Marketing communications" is concerned with such a coordinated whole—basically, communicating information about the firm's product to its target market(s). In this edited version of his article, Ray explains how behavioral and quantitative tools have helped develop the "marketing communications" approach. He presents a sequence of steps for implementing this approach and discusses some of the research findings and tools which are available to help marketers make the necessary decisions.

---

22. A DECISION SEQUENCE ANALYSIS OF DEVELOPMENTS IN MARKETING COMMUNICATION*

Michael L. Ray

MARKETING COMMUNICATION is an area of marketing that provides a unique perspective for looking at the entire field of marketing.

* Reprinted with permission from the *Journal of Marketing*, published by the American Marketing Association, vol. 37, January 1973, pp. 29–38. At the time of writing, Dr. Ray was Associate Professor of Marketing at Stanford University.

This subfield, consisting of a group of functional activities that may be listed under promotion, has existed since modern marketing began. Yet, only within the last decade have serious attempts been made to consolidate personal selling, advertising, packaging, point-of-purchase, direct mail, product sampling, publicity, and public relations under "marketing communication." Marketers have only recently begun to view the area of communication in the sophisticated way possible with today's advanced behavioral and quantitative tools.[1]

These developments have produced the normal amount of failures and false starts typical when new techniques are employed. It now appears, however, that marketing communication is beginning to produce some tangible contributions. The promise of a synergistic effect and more profitable performance in promotional activities due to the application of scientific tools is finally being realized.

This article documents the progress made in the implementation of marketing communication. First, marketing communication is defined in terms of an information gathering and decision sequence which links all elements of the communication mix. Second, the decision sequence and each of its steps is described in terms of the tools now available to decision makers. . . .

A DECISION SEQUENCE

The focal point of the development of marketing communication is the series of decisions that have to be made to carry it out. . . .

[The] general decision process for marketing communication has evolved over the years into the specific and sophisticated sequence illustrated in Figure 1. The decision sequence indicates (1) the relationship between communication functions and other elements of the mix; (2) the links between the various components of the communication mix; (3) the common decisions involved in each of the components of the mix; (4) the common utilization of both communication and sales goals; and (5) the possibilities for adaptation in the decision process based on new information and ongoing decisions.

These five major issues are seldom stated clearly in descriptions of the marketing communication process. Therefore, this lack of attention has greatly retarded the development of marketing communication. The issues are discussed more fully below.

---

[1] For example, Edward L. Brink and William T. Kelley, *The Management of Promotion* (Englewood Cliffs, N.J.: Prentice Hall, 1963); Edgar Crane, *Marketing Communication* (New York: John Wiley and Sons, 1965); James F. Engel, Hugh G. Wales and Martin Warshaw, *Promotional Strategy,* rev. ed. (Homewood, Illinois: Richard D. Irwin, 1971); and Frederick E. Webster, Jr., *Marketing Communication: Modern Promotional Strategy* (New York: The Ronald Press Company, 1971).

The communication mix and other marketing functions

The communication functions in Figure 1 are primarily promotional. They relate to other aspects of the mix through the situation analysis and marketing objectives stages. The situation analysis is explained in communication terms. Although product, price, and channels are not part of the communication mix, they and other parts of the situation are considered because of their communication implications. For example, if products are developed through perceptual mapping procedures,[2] some researchers suggest that the nature of the communication message is predetermined; i.e., all messages should only communicate those product characteristics which are salient to consumers.[3]

How communication functions are linked together

Marketing communication has not worked very efficiently in the past because little apparent commonality existed among the communication functions. How can a manager simultaneously deal with such disparate activities as sales territory assignment, advertising copy writing, and liaison with publications for publicity purposes? The answer is found in Figure 1. The manager allocates financial resources to the functions on the basis of expected response. This tentative budget mix is altered only if decisions and research within each function indicate a need for more or less support. The manager's ability to establish accurate budgets is increased greatly if an information system is used to provide data for evaluation and control. Present and future models for this purpose are discussed in the following sections.

Similar decisions across components

Marketers could not effectively implement marketing communication unless decisions were somewhat similar across communication functions. In fact, communication activities can be efficiently integrated only because they consist of similar, yet different, decisions. As shown in Figure 1, there are essentially five decision areas common to all communication types—communication goals, message strategy, message distribution plan, budget allocation, and implementation. Since these exist for all communication functions, decision making and research information can be applied to all functions. For example, a message strategy designed and tested for advertising may have a clear application in selling, publicity, or direct-mail promotion. For communication goal decisions, com-

---

[2] Edgar A. Pessemier and H. Paul Root, "The Dimensions of New Product Planning," *Journal of Marketing*, vol. 37 (January 1973), pp. 10–18.

[3] Volney Stefflre, "Market Structure Studies: New Products for Old Markets and New Markets (Foreign) for Old Products," in *Application of the Sciences in Marketing Management*, Frank Bass, Edgar A. Pessemier, and Charles King, eds. (New York: John Wiley and Sons, 1968).

parisons across functions are made to determine which function can best accomplish each type of communication goal.

Sales and communication goals reconciled

At one time some marketers viewed these two types of goals as being incompatible. They are reconciled in Figure 1. Sales are the most important goal for the marketing communication program, making sales response the key variable to consider in allocating the tentative budget across elements of the communication mix. Communication goals, such

FIGURE 1
The sequence of marketing communication information gathering and decisions

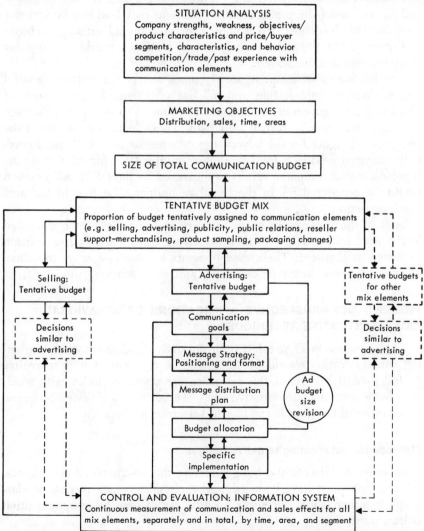

as awareness and attitude change, are still quite important to decision making because they are the focal point for decisions on the use of funds for advertising, selling, and so forth. Thus, both sales and communication goals must be coordinated for the marketing communication decision process to work properly.

Adaptive decisions

A process is "adaptive" if it includes procedures for gathering information and adapting on the basis of that information. The decision sequence shown in Figure 1 is adaptive in that a number of feedback points are used to change the system in accordance with new information and decisions. For instance, the original budget mix is only tentative, and an analysis of the communication elements may lead to a budget-size revision. This feedback loop is shown for only the advertising decisions in Figure 1, but the same reanalysis and feedback would be done for every communication element.

Another series of adaptive loops comes out of the bottom "control and evaluation: information system" box of Figure 1. The results of past campaigns may indicate changes in communications goals, message strategy, and message distribution plan. These loops are shown in the center of the figure for the advertising decision sequence. A final important adaptive feedback loop is shown on the left side of the figure. It indicates that campaign results as measured by the information system would be accounted for in the tentative budget allocation in the next planning period.

Most of the applications of quantitative and behavioral tools discussed in the next section relate to this adaptive characteristic of the decision sequence in Figure 1. These developments involve new ways to collect information, new forms of decisions, and new adaptive models.

PRESENT AND PROSPECTIVE APPLICATIONS OF BEHAVIORAL AND QUANTITATIVE TECHNIQUES

The sequence in Figure 1 is both normative and descriptive. Marketing communication *should be* integrated in this way if it is to realize its full potential. Parts of this sequence *are operative* today with available behavioral and quantitative tools. These tools are reviewed below in the order of the steps in the Figure 1 decision sequence.

Methods for determining tentative budgets

In order to allocate the budget among the communication elements, the manager must have knowledge of their sales responsiveness or elasticity. In other words, he needs an estimate of how his communication dollars work.

Two general methods have been developed to provide these critical estimates. A computer planning model is used to show the manager the implications of his estimates of responsiveness, while the other involves research and analysis to determine what the responsiveness actually is. Computer planning models have been successful devices for dealing with the tentative budget problem.[4] Because the budget is only tentative, any aid the manager can get makes very good use of his knowledge of the market.

These models typically have a data base which indicates past sales, expenditures, and some representation of how the communication and marketing mix elements work together. For each run of the model, the manager supplies a budget allocation and his estimate of the budget change-sales response for each mix element. The model then supplies a profit and loss statement for each time period. The manager continues to make runs of the model, changing budget and response coefficients, until he achieves an acceptable run in terms of reality and profitability.

The marketing communication decision process can then continue. The subsequent goals, message, and distribution decisions for each communication element are attempts to improve the response coefficient estimates. The budget size revision is actually a more sophisticated estimate of response for each element than the original budget estimate.

If the manager wishes to go beyond his own sales response estimates, he can utilize one of several research methods which give empirical estimates of actual market response. Some researchers have developed models which utilize both subjective judgments and empirical response data.[5] From a scientific standpoint, controlled experimentation is the best approach to gathering empirical response data. Test markets are assigned various weights of promotional expenditure, and sales measures are taken. A market group comparison indicates sales responsiveness which then can be used in establishing the budget.

Marketing is one of the few disciplines where services have been set up for field experimentation. In the 1960s, the Milwaukee Advertising Laboratory facilitated field experimentation within that city, and split cable television experimentation facilities are now available.[6] Several

[4] Gerald Eskin, "Concorn Kitchens," unpublished paper, Graduate School of Business, Stanford University, 1970.

[5] Jean-Jacques Lambin, "A Computer On-Line Marketing Model," *Journal of Marketing Research*, vol. 9 (May 1972), pp. 119–126; and John D. C. Little, "BRANDAID: An On-Line Marketing Mix Model," Working Paper 586-72, Sloan School of Management, Massachusetts Institute of Technology, February 1972.

[6] John Adler, "Adtel: A New Product Case History," *Journal of Advertising Research*, vol. 12 (April 1972), inside front cover advertisement; G. Maxwell Ule, "The Milwaukee Advertising Laboratory—Its Second Year," in *Proceedings of the 12th Annual Meeting of the Advertising Research Foundation*, 1966; and Edward Wallerstein, "Measuring Commercials on CATV," *Journal of Advertising Research*, vol. 7 (June 1967), pp. 15–19.

books on experimentation in marketing and communication are available, and success in long-term field experimentation has been reported by Budweiser and others.[7]

On the other hand, experimentation presents certain shortcomings. It is expensive; it cannot be done on a continuous basis; and it is only valid for the particular set of circumstances in which the experiment occurred. The practical alternative to experimentation is continuous campaign monitoring.

With campaign monitoring, measurements of sales and other market response are made on a periodic basis, ideally monthly. This is shown as the evaluation and control information system in Figure 1. These response measures can be related to expenditures during the time periods; therefore, responsiveness can be inferred. The response estimates can then be used to set tentative budgets.

Such information systems are becoming quite common.[8] Several researchers have concentrated on marketing communication effects. Maloney developed a system which made it possible to look at the relationship between media exposure and point-of-purchase deals in affecting purchase.[9] As the data bank of such a system becomes larger and more detailed, it becomes more and more valuable in determining response.

❖   ❖   ❖

Message strategy: Positioning and attitude research

Message strategy consists of two parts: What is said, and how it is said. The "what" part has variously been called the copy platform, the unique selling proposition, the appeal, the brand image, the maker's mark, the message idea, and, most recently, the product positioning.[10] This most recent term is actually quite functional because it implies all the elements necessary at this stage of communication decision. The position consists of product appeals or characteristics to be communicated to target segments. The message can only be constructed with regard to the product's position in the market vis-à-vis buyers, competition, and trade. Each message should reflect this positioning whether

---

[7] Seymour Banks, *Experimentation in Marketing* (New York: McGraw-Hill, 1965); Jack B. Haskins, *How to Evaluate Mass Communication* (New York: Advertising Research Foundation, 1968); and Ambar G. Rao, *Quantitative Theories in Advertising* (New York: John Wiley and Sons, 1970).

[8] Alvin A. Achenbaum, *How Advertising Works: A Study of the Relationship Between Advertising, Consumer Attitudes and Purchase Behavior* (New York: Grey Advertising, 1968); and Henry Assael and George S. Day, "Attitudes and Awareness as Predictors of Market Share," *Journal of Advertising Research*, vol. 8 (December 1968), pp. 3–12.

[9] John C. Maloney, "Attitude Measurement and Formation," paper read at the AMA Test Marketing Workshop, Chicago, 1966, mimeo.

[10] Jack Trout and Al Ries, "The Positioning Era Cometh," *Advertising Age* (April 24, 1972), pp. 35 and 38.

it is transmitted through personal selling, packaging, samples, publicity, or advertising.

The positioning method is supported by recent advances in quantitative techniques. Attitude research has used nonmetric multidimensional scaling to position brands in a multidimensional space based on buyers' perceptions.[11] Managers use the perceptual map to decide how they might influence the position of their product. For instance, they can develop products to fill unsatisfied needs of the market, or they can attempt to change the positioning of their brand through communication. The positioning statement relates to both the dimensions of the map and the target market segment. Ambitious communication programs often attempt to switch dimensions or add completely new ones.

❄   ❄   ❄

Message distribution plan

The message distribution decisions provide the link between the creative message strategy input and the consolidating budget allocation and implementation steps. As such, the distribution decisions have generated new possibilities for the combination of behavioral input and management science models.

In advertising, media-scheduling models have forced managers to consider the interaction between various message strategies and distribution decisions.[12] Some media models allow managers to input different estimates of the response to repetitive exposures, for each media vehicle and market segment.[13] This kind of model puts new demands on behavioral research, thereby necessitating the development of pretesting techniques which will estimate the repetitive effects of various message alternatives. These estimates can then be used in the models to present a sophisticated picture of what the message alternatives might mean in market terms. This behavioral-model approach has already been applied with positive results.[14] Suggestions have been made for using this combination to validate both pretesting techniques and media models.[15]

---

[11] Alvin J. Silk, "The Use of Preference and Perception Measures in New Product Development: An Exposition and Review," *Industrial Management Review*, vol. 11 (Fall 1969), pp. 21–37; and Stefflre, same reference as footnote 3.

[12] Dennis H. Gensch, "Media Factors: A Review Article," *Journal of Marketing Research*, vol. 7 (May 1970), pp. 216–225.

[13] David A. Aaker, "On Methods: A Probabilistic Approach to Industrial Media Selection," *Journal of Advertising Research*, vol. 8 (September 1968), pp. 46–55; and John D. C. Little and Leonard M. Lodish, "A Media Planning Calculus," *Operations Research*, vol. 17 (January–February 1969), pp. 1–35.

[14] M. L. Ray and A. G. Sawyer, "Behavioral Measurement for Marketing Models," *Management Science*, vol. 18, Dec. 1971, pp. 73–89.

[15] Michael L. Ray, "A Behavioral-Laboratory-Model-Field Study of Alternate Message Strategies in Competitive Advertising Situations," Research Paper no. 83, Graduate School of Business, Stanford University, May 1972.

In the personal selling area, models can be used to allocate sales force effort across products, salesmen calls across prospects, and salesmen over geographic areas.[16] As these models are developed, the same type of message strategy-distribution combination seen in advertising may apply to selling. In direct-mail promotion and sampling, computer use of data banks may also lead to this combination. The synergistic promise of marketing communication as originally conceived is finding potential realization in models and behavioral inputs at the message distribution decision point.

Budget allocation

The first sequence of decisions for each communication element ends in a budget allocation for media, time, geography, and segments. This allocation is accomplished after the goals, message, and distribution decisions are made. The total process recycled for each element is the equivalent of what has been called the "objective and task" budgeting approach. In Figure 1, this budgeting approach takes on new significance since it is used as a communication and planning check on the tentative budget. The revised budget for each element is based on much more information and planning than the tentative budget. These revised budgets are a statement of market responsiveness in communication terms rather than in sales terms only. The manager must decide whether to accept any or all of these revised budgets, adjust total budget size, or fall back on original budget statements. This may necessitate a new set of decision making through communication goals, message strategy, message distribution, and allocation. The cycling process for each communication element becomes part of what Little calls an "adaptive control" model. As in Figure 1, models of the communication process are built, they are tested in the market, and then adapted to specific market situations.[17]

The key role of information systems in further advances

Figure 1 represents the advances to date in the application of quantitative and behavioral tools to marketing communication. For further advances, managers must acquire data on communication response. The tentative budget allocation could be made on this information, as well as sales results information. Horizontal lines could be drawn across the "communication goals" boxes for the elements shown in Figure 1. Budgets could be allocated across elements by sales, communication goals, and positioning effects.

---

[16] See "Special Issue on Marketing Management Models," David B. Montgomery, ed., *Management Science*, vol. 18 (December 1971), Part II.

[17] John D. C. Little, "A Model of Adaptive Control of Promotional Spending," *Operations Research*, vol. 14 (November–December 1966), pp. 1075–1097.

The type of control and evaluation system indicated in Figure 1, while often implemented partially, has not become the standard. One can only extrapolate from the few studies mentioned here to help understand the value of such information. If econometric response studies had specific information on which people were exposed to which messages, it would be possible to understand the response elasticities and to develop a very specific marketing communication plan.

❖ ❖ ❖

QUESTIONS

1. Briefly describe Ray's approach to developing marketing communications.
2. Explain how sales and communication goals can and should be reconciled.
3. Does one have to be a behavioral or management science expert to be able to work towards integrating the promotion variables?
*4. Explain how effective market-gridding could facilitate the development of marketing communications (See Readings 6 and 9–13).

In just a few short years, the agency business as we know it today may find its survival threatened. Paul Harper sees major changes in how the advertising agency, if indeed it is still called that, will have to perform in 1980 if it is to survive and prosper.

---

23. THE AGENCY BUSINESS IN 1980*

Paul C. Harper, Jr.

IN 1980, advertising agencies will be doing the same thing they are doing in 1972. They will be trying to influence human behavior in ways favorable to the interests of their clients.

But there the resemblance will stop. Their services, methods, structure and economics will be different. They may not even be called advertising agencies—because that name may no longer fit.

Any service business is a reflection of the aggregate market for its services. By 1980, the market for agency services will have changed as follows:

---
* Reprinted from *Advertising Age* (November 19, 1972). At the time of writing, Mr. Harper was with the Needham, Harper & Steers in New York.

By 1980, few parity products—products that offer no clearly defined advantage—will be advertised extensively.

It is in the parity product area in particular that private brands will take over. As distribution becomes more concentrated, and distributors more powerful, the squeeze on advertised me-too products will become unbearable. As shelf space, floor space and showroom space become more and more costly, more and more parity brands will be thrown out. The distributors' incentive to earn a double profit will become overpowering.

Consumers are accepting fungibility. For years they have suspected that all gasolines were alike. Now they are beginning to believe this about many other frequently purchased categories.

Parity products bow to private label

Furthermore, when they perceive that products are the same, they increasingly tire of being told that they are different. Advertising money spent this way will become less and less productive.

In addition, there are many in the government who think that the advertising of parity products is deceitful and wasteful. They may have their way.

By 1980, for the above reasons, many companies that are now heavy advertisers of parity products will cease to advertise them at all. They will manufacture parity products for private label. And they will not advertise or market a brand of their own—unless it has a meaningful exclusive that can be clearly communicated in advertising.

Thus, large sectors of the current advertising arena will dry up, leaving the field to those advertisers who have something to say.

This will mean that in many product categories the *primary function* of the advertising agency will be strategic planning and conceptual input in the new product area. Because of the central importance of this function, it will require behavioral and business knowledge of a much higher order than is generally present now among agency "strategists."

In the advertising for service businesses, the same forces will work, but to a lesser degree. Advertising of parity services will decrease. The fungible airline hostesses and gas station attendants with their plastic smiles will disappear from advertising. But the major service industries—airlines, automotive service, fast food, insurance, small loans, banking, business machines, car rentals, hotels and travel and others are the most rapidly evolving sectors of the economy—and the new dimensions of service which they will bring forth will require heavy promotion.

Service industry ads shift emphasis

However, funds currently used to advertise mere parity service will be diverted to at least three other kinds of activity:

1. On-premise communications. More use will be made of the captive nature of the customer to both entertain and indoctrinate him as he waits, shops, eats, flies, etc. On-premise promotion will extend into a full range of video, audio, as well as print media.

2. Behavioral training. In an increasingly crowded world, the service industries will spend more communications dollars to train their employes to be polite, clear, prompt, accurate, etc. A dollar spent producing a smile on a real attendant's face will be worth far more in repeat business than an advertised smile that doesn't materialize at point of sale. This will require whole new dimensions in employe recruitment, training and continuing indoctrination.

3. In a society which finally recognizes that commercial success and the social good must be reconciled, there will be more communications which address these common interests. (Auto insurance—safe driving; life insurance—good health; oil industry—pollution reduction; fast food—good nutrition.)

Whether or not there is a net *reduction* in service industry advertising, the strategic emphasis will change, and the use of media will become more segmented and specialized. This will require more strategic guidance from the agency, and it will require the extension of agency service into all forms of communication. Because of this, the highest degree of sophistication will be required of those delivering service to accounts.

Three kinds of market in 1980

By 1980, the "national advertising market" as we know it, where most products and services are advertisable on a national basis, will not exist.

Instead, there will be three kinds of market:

A. The *"fungibles"* market, composed of product and service categories which are fundamentally satisfactory, and not susceptible to, or needful of, further refinement. This market will be:

National and homogeneous.
Dominated by store brands or captive services.
Heavily price promoted.
Virtually unadvertised on a national basis.

B. The *"improvables"* market. This market will be composed of products and services which cater to broad, but not universal, markets, and where continued technological refinement is feasible or where fashion and style are important sales factors. This market also includes major new product and service forms, replacements for existing forms.

Demographically and regionally segmented.
Dominated by manufacturers' brands and independent services—or by the brands of the stronger national distributors.

Heavily advertised in local and regional as well as national media—with presentations varied to meet different demographic tastes and needs.

C. The *"enclave"* market. This market can only be described as a three-dimensional grid—with the axes representing income, geography and life style, and representing, therefore, a wide degree of variation. This will be a diverse, volatile series of smaller markets where the premium is on individuality. Novelty will be a virtue with some, permanence with others, high style with some, homespun style with others. In current terms, it will be composed of a range of tastes and needs represented by *Vogue* on the one hand and the *Whole Earth Catalog* on the other.

Many of these "enclaves" will be viable markets for extensive advertising because of better education, the growing diversity in our society, and the increasing need to express individual identity.

This market will be characterized by:

Products and services designed to serve specialized tastes.

Boutique merchandising (within major distributive centers) and mail order merchandising.

Highly focused advertising in terms of presentation and media. Media usage will take advantage of the new, highly focused forms, such as video cassettes, paperbacks, cable tv. Advertising language will reflect the mode of the submarket being addressed.

Again, because of these new dimensions, the agency of 1980 will be called on for strategic guidance in a complex marketplace, where the "broad strokes" of the past are no longer economical—and where highly focused communications with their efficiencies (and their risks) are required.

By 1980, the western world, as well as large parts of Asia, will be homogeneous as far as marketing techniques, product technology and demographic structure.

This means that not only will these markets be economically interdependent, but they will be technologically and culturally interdependent.

In 1980, the world market for product ideas, merchandising and advertising ideas will indeed be one.

The result of this is that, to survive, the advertising agency of 1980 must be international in its outlook, its input and its physical and human resources.

The government as an advertiser

By 1980, the government will be a major advertiser. As public corporations like the Postal Service and Amtrak prove themselves, others will be spun off. Wherever the government offers a discrete service of economic value to a definable customer group, it should be spun off and charged for. Some will, despite political pressure to the contrary. These services will be advertised.

The new volunteer armed services will require heavy advertising support, and so will recruiting for certain civilian activities.

Eventually, many of the causes now supported by the Advertising Council will become government funded, when the social cost of certain forms of behavior gets too high.

To compete effectively for government business agencies will have to have:

1. A highly developed sense of the difference between the commercial and bureaucratic worlds.
2. Ability to distinguish between the cruder forms of buying behavior and the more complex forms of social behavior which government will be trying to influence.

The government as a regulator

It is not necessary here to review the growing efforts of government to regulate advertising and marketing. Its net effect by 1980 will be:

1. To restrict competitive claims, which will reduce advertising effectiveness, which, in turn, will reduce dollars spent in many categories.
2. To eliminate advertising in some categories and impose ceilings on others.
3. To limit advertising as a percent of content of certain media.
4. By applying increasingly higher clinical and technical standards, to greatly increase the cost and risks of introducing new products in certain fields.

In this climate, it will be essential that the advertising agency be equipped not only to avoid legal pitfalls, but to help develop corporate strategies that work, while still observing legal and regulatory guidelines.

In 1980, therefore, the advertising agency, if that is what it is still called, will be operating in a world where:

Many major current categories of advertising will have dried up, due to (a) inroads of private brands, (b) government action, and (c) public skepticism and indifference.

New major advertised categories will be generated only as real product or service innovations occur. The entire corporate strategy of today's "brand" manufacturers will revolve around meaningful innovation.

Much service industry advertising will be diverted to on-premise promotion or employe training and indoctrination.

Much advertising for certain service industries and for the government will address social issues involving complex facets of human behavior.

The consumer market as a whole will become more complex and segmented.

Dramatic evolution of audio-visual media as well as print media will allow highly focused attack on market segments that would today be inaccessible.

The more highly developed world markets will be truly homogeneous.

In this environment, what kind of an advertising agency will be able to grow and prosper?

Any service business is a reflection of its aggregate market. As the market changes, so must the service business.

Today in 1973, it is already within the capability of many advertisers to perform many of the conventional agency services for themselves. The others they can buy outside piecemeal.

Self-sufficiency is already an option for any advertiser with a medium or large communications budget. By 1980, this option will have been exercised by a large number of today's major advertisers.

Agencies who do not prepare for this day will find themselves scratching for project assignments in the creative and media areas. They will become journeymen and little more. To escape this fate, our industry must redefine its product and structure.

The customer and his future needs

Any agency function that can be performed by others *as well as* the agency is now doing it must be raised to a new level of excellence or scrapped. The *central* function, or product, of the agency (a) must address the basic needs of the marketer of 1980, and (b) must be something he cannot get from any other form of business organization.

Our customers in 1980 will include any type of organization that serves the social good (broadly defined). This will include manufacturers, distributors, service companies, government, other institutions, citizens groups, etc. Each of them will be competing for favorable attention and action in a diverse, complex, noisy and confused arena.

Yet client management then, as now, will continue to have two related problems that can potentially stifle success.

1. Any management must spend much of its time worrying about what goes on in the factory (the hangar, the kitchens, the garage). It must spend part of its time worrying about finance, material resources and logistics. The greater this internal focus becomes, the more apt the management is to make external mistakes.
2. Marketing departments were created to avoid the above problem. But marketing departments must focus on the problems at hand, and they, too, can develop tunnel vision.

They can be, and sometimes are, overwhelmed by the internal orientation of their own top management.

These are dangers now, and they will persist because they are founded in human nature. But in the market of the '80s, where corporate strategy must be fine-tuned to meet even more complex external realities, they will be no longer affordable.

Advertising agencies have always provided "the outside view" of the marketplace. Many times they have served to refocus basic client thinking—and have thus served as ad hoc management consultants. But this function has only been performed intermittently, usually as the result of some particularly close individual relationship—or the presence of some extraordinary creative talent. By and large (and more and more), agencies have performed routinized communications functions, and the bigger the agencies get, the more internally focused their own managements have become.

How agencies can survive in '80s

To survive in the '80s, the advertising agency must rediscover its real exclusive over time; this real exclusive has become encrusted with administrative and structural barnacles. For future survival it must be scraped clean and remarketed.

The agency's exclusive service is precisely the service its customers will need to survive *themselves* in the '80s. This exclusive is strategic communications counsel on the highest level based on the broadest possible experience. Advertising agencies today possess an unparalleled aggregate of knowledge of what works and what doesn't work in the influencing of human behavior—across the entire spectrum of human activity—and in every medium.

Agencies are the *only* kind of business organization that:

Works with clients in every sector of the social and economic structure.

On a continuing basis.

In every medium of communications.

Within a pragmatic framework, where work must show results.

The application of this unique insight in the development of product and communications strategy is our exclusive product. Specifically, the surviving agencies of 1980 will be offering:

1. Continuing predictive counsel on all aspects of the client's marketing arena. (Who is likely to do what, when, for what reasons, and with what impact.) This includes a prediction and analysis of government actions and attitudes. Since the world market is the arena, the counsel will be based on worldwide intelligence and input.

2. Basic product strategy. Continuing counsel in depth on what products and services to offer and to whom.
3. Continuing strategic counsel on every aspect of communications, external, internal and on-premise—including fundamental corporate positioning.
4. Implementation of any aspect of the above counsel (exclusive of manufacturing, finance, direct sales and logistics). (Implementation may even include location of supplementary or even primary research/development facilities, and would certainly include working closely with such facilities.)

The new agency professionalism

The basic product of this new kind of "advertising agency" will *not* be filmed commercials, although we will conceive and produce them; not corporate logos, although we will design them; not sales brochures, although we will write and design them. Our basic product will be *strategic counsel* relating to what values a client offers the public, and how it communicates these values. This new kind of company will comprise an objective strategic adjunct to the management of client organizations. It will offer, on a continuing basis, the authoritative "outside view" that all managements need and will need increasingly in the future.

The agency of the '80s will operate in an environment where:

Most of its present services can be purchased from other sources, or performed by the client himself.

Clients will be operating in an "idea arena" where the currents of change are far more swift, subtle, and fragmented than they are today.

Clients will *not* pay high prices for journeyman media, research, creative and production work.

Clients *will* pay high prices for continuous high level strategic input.

For survival in the '80s, the advertising agency must offer a new dimension of professionalism. And to do so, it must restructure.

To offer this kind of service to a large, diversified client list requires, in operating terms, a *partnership structure*. The management structure of the agency will be expanded horizontally, like that of a law firm, so that all clients will be able to deal with a partner at regular intervals—a partner sufficiently involved to be able to give thoughtful input on a continuing basis.

Steep pyramidal structures will disappear. They do not permit the intensive high level coverage required. They foster the loss of good ideas, because these ideas tend to be handled at too junior a level or at too many levels. They also foster the "bag handler" syndrome, with its deadening build-up of administrative layers.

The management structure of the agency will be simple. It will consist of several more or less horizontally aligned partners. These men and women will be "creative generalists." They will have a thorough grounding in marketing, communications, and business procedures, but they will have an essentially creative turn of mind.

The partners will have working for them, directly, a few highly trained specialists in the analytical disciplines. They will also be assisted by a few junior partners who are creative generalists by nature, and who are in training for full partnership.

Apart from the necessary business management and housekeeping functions this is all that will be left of the "advertising agency" *per se*.

The services of this new "agency" will be paid for by fee. The commission system is clearly irrelevant to this structure and will have largely disappeared.

WHO WILL GET THE ADS OUT?

The account executive

The agency of the future will seek some of its partners from among its account executive staff. But only those who have proven themselves as well-rounded, insightful counselors will be selected. The partnership concept requires a complete redefinition of the "contact" function. The partner is not a "contact man," "an account executive," or a conduit for someone else's thinking. He or she must be capable of generating and implementing whole product strategies, communications strategies. The partner should have enough professional stature and acumen to sit on a client's board of directors.

Creative

In the agency of the '80s the creative department as we now know it will have ceased to exist. Creative people as we now know them will (according to their talents and tastes) have chosen one of three careers:

1. Some, with broad talents, will have become full partners in the new structure.
2. Others will move to boutiques or house agencies.
3. Others will join to form the creative subsidiary of the new advertising agency.

The agency of the '80s will have one or more subsidiaries whose sole function will be the translation of strategy into finished communications material. The creative subsidiary will be a separate profit center whose fees will flow from partnership clients—or from business that it obtains on its own. The agency of the '80s may structure its creative function into more than one subsidiary, in order to avoid problems of conflict—or in order to provide a higher degree of specialization—by media, or by type of communications problem.

In any case, the partner of the "advertising agency" will have an interesting and varied choice of creative resources. This is because the partner will not be required to use the creative subsidiaries of the corporation if he thinks he can get the job done better somewhere else. It may well be that for a specific job of corporate design or an advertising campaign directed toward a specialized market he will go to an outside creative resource. Or, if a partner feels that he can get better continuing work off-premise, he may do so. In any case, the corporation's creative subsidiaries must compete against the field in terms of creative excellence and efficient operation.

Research

Much desk research will be performed by the analysts on the partner's staff. But all field research will be planned and performed by the corporation's research subsidiary—if that subsidiary can compete effectively for the partner's business. Here again the partner will have a choice of all available research houses, and he will pick the one best suited for the job. The corporation's research subsidiary, likewise, will seek and serve business not handled by the partners.

Media

As the marketplace becomes more fragmented and complex, the media function must become more precise, responsive, and fast moving. As more and more advertisers do their media planning and buying outside of the agency framework, it will become harder and harder for the conventional media department to compete.

The media function, too, will be transformed to meet the new conditions. It will become subsidiarized, automated, and centralized. It will compete for the partner's business. It will also seek outside business on its own. Like research, its survival as a function within the corporation's structure will depend on its ability to use all the science and technology available to it, as well as on the judgment and insight of its managers.

Other specialized functions

The corporation will offer other services on a subsidiary basis as those services offer a profit opportunity. This will include sales promotion, design, public relations, government relations, food science, product development and testing, and others further afield.

The partnership and the corporation

Above, the terms "partnership" and "corporation" are used. It is the function of the *partnership* to deliver the unique product of the corporation—counsel in product strategy and communications strategy. It will do this with a minimal staff of its own as described. It will draw on and pay for the services of subsidiaries (or others) as it needs them. It will receive high cost-ratio fees for its counseling work. It will receive cost-plus fees with a nominal mark-up for the implementing services it delivers from the subsidiaries. The subsidiaries are then paid appropriately. The partnership manages client relationships.

The "corporation" is the fiscal and legal entity which ties the partnership and the various subsidiaries together in some kind of business harmony. It will have over-all profit responsibility and will decide on what new ventures should be undertaken and which should be discarded.

When all is said and done the advertising agencies which survive and grow in the '80s will do so because they performed realistically two fundamental business exercises:

1. They have identified what *they do best better than anyone else* against a knowledge of client needs. They will then restructure so that this service is rendered as effectively and profitably as possible.
2. They will have submitted each of their present functions to the profit test. If the function cannot compete profitably against other sources of the same service, it will be dropped. If it can compete it will receive further investment and developments—along with new profit opportunities the agency may identify.

QUESTIONS

1. What forces are causing the forecasted changes in the role and function of advertising agencies?
2. Why might advertising agencies be especially useful in providing "strategic counsel" to clients?
3. Cite an example of a product which you feel will fit into each of Harper's three kinds of markets (i.e. use three products).
4. What does Mr. Harper see as the dual roles of the government vis-a-vis advertising in the future? Comment briefly on the impact on agencies of each of these roles.
*5. Will Harper's "new" agency be any more concerned with "marketing communications" as discussed by Ray? (Reading 22) Explain.

Today's "supersalesman" is far more than a seller of goods and services. In response to keener competition, better purchasing practices, and a growing recognition that you must satisfy a need rather than simply sell a product, a good salesman must relate to all facets of a prospect's business that bear on the product that the salesman is promoting. These might range from equipment amortization and inventory control to distribution. And the salesman must know the answers to a buyer's questions.

24. THE NEW SUPERSALESMAN: WIRED FOR SUCCESS*

IF YOU WANT to rile Herbert D. Eagle, just slide a copy of *Webster's New Collegiate Dictionary* in front of him. "Have you ever read the definition of 'sell'?" fumes Eagle, vice-president of marketing for Transamerica Corp. "Things like 'betray' and 'cheat' are capitalized, and there are phrases such as 'to deliver up or give up in violation of duty, trust, or loyalty.' I've been carrying on a running battle with G. & C. Merriam Co. to change that definition."

If anyone can sell Merriam on a new definition, it is 54-year-old Herb Eagle. As marketing vice-president for giant, fast-growing Transamerica Corp. ($1.6-billion in sales last year), Eagle coordinates the marketing and sales strategies for 42 companies that field more than 6,000 internal salesmen and handle everything from insurance and financial services to car rentals. Eagle also doubles as president of Sales & Marketing Executives International, a professional society of 25,000 members scattered through 49 countries. As the official pick of his peers and thus the closest thing to industry's top salesman, Eagle is a drumbeater in the cause of supersalesmanship and the enormous change that is coming over that fine, old American institution: personal selling.

"A few years back," says Eagle, "it was usually the salesman out there alone, pitting his wits against the resistance of a single corporate purchasing agent. Now, more and more companies are selling on many different levels, interlocking their research, engineering, marketing, and upper management with those of their customers. This way, today's salesman becomes a kind of committee chairman within his company. Some manufacturers call them 'account managers.' Either way, his job is to exploit the resources of his company in serving the customer."

---
* Reprinted with permission of the publisher from *Business Week* (January 6, 1973), © 1973, McGraw-Hill, Inc.

As industries consolidate and larger corporations continue to swallow up the small fry, a growing number of companies are also "preselling" their products through massive promotion, advertising, and improved communications between buyer and seller. The result is that the average salesman's prime responsibility is no longer selling, so much as clinching a sale that has already been set in motion even before he makes his first spiel.

More sales productivity

At the consumer level, this shows up in the cutback of retail sales help and the huge expansion of self-service merchandising. At the industry level, it shows up in a whole new function for the industrial salesman. No longer is he simply a pitchman or prescriber of his company's products. Now he must go beyond that and become a diagnostician.

"If a supplier's job is to service the customer, then the role of the salesman becomes one of problem-identifier first, problem-solver second, and prescriber third," says Charles S. Goodman, professor of marketing at the University of Pennsylvania's Wharton School. "I don't say this is common today. But as the economy becomes more consumer-oriented"—and thus open to greater challenge on product performance—"it's got to go that way."

An even greater goad is today's spiraling cost of selling, which demands that industry get far more out of its sales dollar. Rex Chainbelt, Inc., for instance, spends $5,000 to $20,000 to train a salesman and $30,000 to $35,000 a year to keep him on the road. That averages out to $52.80 per sales call, double the figure of 10 years ago. What is more, as product lines proliferate and product technology gets more complex, manufacturers and wholesalers have gradually boosted their number of internal salesmen to more than 1-million. And some experts claim that the demand for salesmen will grow by another 250,000 jobs a year over the next few years, not including replacements. "Obviously," as Transamerica's Eagle notes, "something has to give."

To cut costs and raise sales efficiency, more and more companies are reexamining the ways that they recruit, train, pay, equip, and manage their salesmen. Many companies are reorganizing their selling structures. Some are experimenting with new compensation and incentive programs. Nearly all are moving away from the old straight commission system to salary-plus-bonus.

"This is primarily the product of looking upon salesmen as account managers," says William E. Cox, professor of marketing at Case Western Reserve University. "You begin asking him to take on a lot of additional duties other than just simply writing an order. He becomes the company's broader marketing representative."

Industry is also drawing on a whole new battery of selling tools, ranging from audio/visual cassettes and special slide projectors to remote portable terminals that can plug the salesman straight into his home-office computer. The computer itself, of course, has become one of selling's biggest tools of all. It can lay out sales territories, budget the salesman's time by customer and product, and keep track of sales costs, time use, itineraries, payables and receivables, expenses, orders, inquiries, and over-all performance.

"Fifteen years ago when I first started selling," says Frederick H. Stephens, Jr., sales vice-president for Gillette Co.'s Safety Razor Div., "we couldn't tell at any point how much volume we did on promotional items, for instance, compared with open stock. Now we have monthly IBM printouts that tell our salesmen how much business he's doing with promotions compared to open stock and total business, how much business is being done in his territory, and how much each customer bought of each item. We used to tell a salesman, 'You're up 4.6% this year, that's pretty good.' Now we can say, 'You're up 4.6% but down 1.6% in discount stores and up only 2.1% over your territory.' And we have the information to get him back in the ballgame."

Identifying customer needs

Unfortunately, most salesmen are still somewhere between the locker room and the playing field. "Selling is very, very inefficient compared to what it could be," says Edward J. Feeney, vice-president of the Systems Performance Div. of Emery Air Freight Corp. "Most salesmen," Feeney claims, "are sitting in lobbies. They're calling on wrong accounts. They're calling on accounts that give them all the business that they can. They're calling on people they think can make the buying decision when, in fact, they do not or cannot make much of it at all. They are efficient in talking about what they do—what their company provides—but not in how it fills the customer's need, because they haven't probed to find out what those needs are."

Those needs usually go far beyond the purchase of any one supplier's equipment or services. Hugh Hoffman, chairman of Opinion Research Corp., cites the experience of one of his company's clients, a major chemical producer. "Its salesmen told us," he says, "that if they're trying to sell plastic film to a packager who has several million dollars' worth of packaging equipment designed to use some other material, they must now know how to unload the present equipment, purchase new equipment, and work out the intricacies of amortization. Without that background, they cannot persuade the customer to accept delivery of a single carload of plastic film."

This is because today's major competitor is no longer one broom salesman against another. It is alternate uses of money. "And the modern salesman," says John R. Robertson, sales manager for the Business Systems Markets Div. of Eastman Kodak Co., "must be able to convince his customer that spending money on the salesman's product is a better investment than spending it elsewhere."

Above all, the supersalesman tries to build more than the old-style buyer-seller relationship. A top marketing executive at International Business Machines Corp., which is one of the companies that has spearheaded the development of superselling, claims that today's salesman must develop a "long-range partnership" with his clients. "The installation of a data-processing system," he emphasizes, "is only the beginning, not the end, of IBM's marketing effort."

To serve their customers better, IBM salesmen not only specialize by product and market. They now specialize by function: installation, equipment protection or maintenance, and upgrading of systems. To sharpen the focus of its salesmen even more, IBM—like most consumer-goods companies—is "segmenting" or targeting its markets. "The costs of developing new accounts by the cold-call approach," says the IBM marketer, "have risen so drastically that we are moving toward far more selective prospecting"—including a special computer experiment for picking only "high-potential prospects."

Among the other special qualities that set off the supersalesman:

Universality. "Ten years ago when I hired a salesman," says James Schlinkert, Pittsburgh-area branch manager for Olivetti Corp. of America, "I was looking for someone who would make a lot of calls and, through sheer effort and exposure, be reasonably successful. Now I want someone more versed in things unrelated to our business. Today's salesman must be able to talk on any and all current subjects—from the economy to world affairs—because these often affect his business." Not too many years ago, adds the marketing vice-president for a major information-systems company, "you'd hire somebody with personality that you thought would wear well, and you'd point him out the door." Now it takes more. "A top manager's time is very precious," he says, "and we have to give him a meaningful message when we meet with him."

Patience. Because product technology has become more complex and salesmen are interrelating more products and moving deeper into systems selling, the time that it takes to close a sale has stretched out. "There are no quick sales today," says Anthony E. Schiavone, an assistant development manager for Rohm & Haas Co. "It may take a year just to get to know a new customer and his problems." Philip Rosell, Western regional sales manager for Singer's Business Machines Group, claims that he was on the verge of quitting Singer two years ago after he had gone his first full year without writing an order. "You have to gear yourself psychologically for a long haul," he says.

Persistence. With growing cost-consciousness, upper management is increasingly involved in major buying decisions. So the supersalesman often tries to go beyond the first level of decision-making. "This is not usually the best-paid or most creative guy around anyway," says one Boston salesman. "It's when you go beyond this level that you can sell the extras. And it's not true that the top guy never sees salesmen. You can often enlist the aid of your own top people and set up a meeting."

More work, less play. Lavish wining and dining of buyers is out. In fact, Don H. Hartmann, president of Crutcher Resources Corp., calls this "probably the biggest thrust of all—the trend away from the massive entertainment of a few years ago." One top Eastern salesman adds, of his relations with his customers: "We're no longer a bunch of drinking buddies. I never have lunch with a man I haven't met before, and I never hesitate to talk business at lunch. After all, our relationship is business and not personal."

Restructuring the territories

Whether he is selling insurance, computers, catalytic crackers, or wholesale cosmetics, today's supersalesman has two big things going for him: improved transportation and communications. This allows him to cover more territory faster and to draw closer to his markets. As the president of a Houston industrial-goods company describes his ideal salesman: "He starts his day flying out nonstop from North Carolina to Chicago, then gets a midafternoon plane to Los Angeles to make two or three calls, and catches a night plane to Dallas. It's a fast-moving situation today. Five years ago, because of aircraft and flight scheduling, we couldn't do this."

Yet how much territory is too much? As far back as 10 years ago, adman and marketing seer E. B. Weiss, a senior vice-president at Doyle Dane Bernbach, was calling for a whole new approach to the organization of sales territories and to the basic corporate selling structure. Then, as now, the problem was to minimize unproductive calls and contacts and to get close to the prospects who had both the need and purchasing authority to buy a given product or service. "The sales organization," Weiss wrote, "must be reorganized so as to be able to open up its channels of communication to those who make buying decisions, rather than to limit itself primarily to buyers who make merely buying motions. This calls for new sales organizational blueprints."

Those changes are finally beginning to come. Today's three basic levels of selling—manufacturing, wholesaling, and consumer and industrial services—are spawning dozens of highly-specialized sub-categories aimed at shortening the lines of communication between buyer and seller. IBM is even experimenting with administrative specialists who help its sales specialists handle order preparation, scheduling, collections, and other paperwork. Along the way, more and more companies are organizing against markets, rather than products. For maximum productivity, a few are even organizing against profits.

"Historically," says Gennaro A. Filice, Jr., vice-president of U.S. marketing for Del Monte Corp., "most food companies have been case-volume-oriented. As long as we could push out a lot of volume, we let the profits take care of themselves. That's no longer true. As products multiply and the competition for shelf space increases, salesmen have to be far more sophisticated in their approach to product management, and the company has to learn to identify those with the most profit potential."

To help pinpoint that potential, Del Monte recently restructured its entire field sales force, expanding from nine regional divisions to 21. "As our emphasis shifted away from case sales," says Filice, "and as the chains got bigger and more dominant, it became more difficult for a salesman to write an order. This restructuring was also designed to get us as close to the customer as possible."

Under Del Monte's new system, the actual selling is handled by an "account representative." He makes the direct calls on retailers and writes up the orders. Then one level below him is the sales representative. He is the junior type who works with store managers on shelf management, restocking, display, and other merchandising chores. Sales representatives are also information-gatherers. Using a new computerized system called "Key Facts," which the company plans to expand nationwide next spring, Del Monte's California salesmen fill out a form during each store visit, listing shelf position, pricing, advertising support, and other basic marketing data. This is fed into the computer and later compared against actual product performance to arrive at maximum profitability.

Women in the sales force

Hunt-Wesson Foods, Gillette, Allied Chemical, and several other companies have found another productivity booster for their field organizations: part-time female workers. Gillette maintains an auxiliary force of 150 middle-aged housewives who operate one rung below the individual store salesmen. The women work 24 hours a week for $3 an hour, plus expenses, and handle retail displays, distribution, and stock replenishment.

"In 1958, when I started selling," says one sales executive at Gillette, "I spent 30% of my time calling on direct customers and 70% calling on local stores to work on display and distribution, and writing up turnover orders"—orders passed on to wholesalers to replenish out-of-stock items. "Today, our salesmen spend 85% of their time on direct accounts and only about 15% of their time at local stores on display and distribution."

Along with tightening the focus of their field forces, more and more companies are also creating broader "account executives," whose job is to crack that tricky, old marketing problem: how to deal with the big chains or a large, diversified company with a variety of product needs. Some suppliers, of course, simply send a battalion of salesmen swarming into such companies at all levels. Now a growing number are creating account executives who oversee all product needs of a single customer, often at the headquarters level. This way, the big customer has one sales contact that can satisfy and interrelate all its needs.

Over the last few years, Dow Chemical Co. has created 14 corporate account managers who operate one notch above the salesman and handle all 1,200 Dow products for a given customer. "There are no firm rules about how big an account must be before a corporate account manager takes over," says M. C. Carpenter, Dow's director of marketing communications. "But they are basically potential multimillion-dollar customers."

At the same time, Dow is trying to crack another problem that comes with the bigness of a customer: the difficulty of getting a territorial fix on where a sale actually occurs. In the past, Dow credited a sale to the office in the territory where the customer was located. Thus, any sale in the Houston area was chalked up to the Houston office, even though the key initiative may have come in New York. Now each sale is credited to the office where the sale originates. "That makes the accounting more complicated and subjective," Carpenter concedes. "But it gives sales managers a better idea of what's really going on in the field. We find out where the key marketing man is."

As sales organizations grow bigger and more complex, the challenge, of course, is to avoid costly duplication of sales effort. Hewlett-Packard Co. ran into this problem. It started out with a highly centralized organization that did most of its selling through outside manufacturers' representatives. By 1963, the company's product line had become so broad and complicated that Hewlett-Packard decided to acquire most of its reps and turn them into a corporate sales staff. "We stayed with reps longer than most companies," says Robert L. Boniface, marketing vice-president. "We felt that it was important to have the sales force represent the customer's viewpoint as much as Hewlett-Packard's. By acquiring them rather than cutting them off, we kept all their experience and momentum."

As Hewlett-Packard moved into medical instruments, calculators, electronic components, and other diverse new markets, the company split its sales staff into eight organizations. "Right away, we developed overlaps," says Alfred P. Oliverio, marketing manager for the Electronic Products Group. "We didn't want two salesmen calling on one customer if the product was not really all that different."

In Hewlett-Packard's most recent shift, the old product-oriented structure gave way to a combined product/market-oriented system. In electronic products, for instance, separate sales groups now concentrate on electrical manufacturing, aerospace, communications, and transportation equipment. Within each group, Hewlett-Packard tries to build a cadre of salesmen, application engineers, and software specialists. "We probably have better than one support person for every salesman," says Oliverio.

Selling the 'dream list'

Hans G. Moser, field director for Northwestern Mutual Life Insurance Co. and a chartered life underwriter, sold $4.5-million worth of life insurance last year. That makes him 29th out of the company's 2,900 agents. Moser's distinctive selling approach is typical of how today's supersalesman tackles his customer.

Like a consumer-goods maker who targets his market, Moser ignores "run-of-the-mill types" and zeroes in on prospects who can either afford heavy insurance now or who are obviously on the way up and will be able to in the future. Moser adopted this tactic when he broke into the insurance business in 1960. "Many of my earlier customers," he says, "are now in a position to set up trust accounts, dabble with stocks, and deal with other sophisticated methods of estate planning. And, of course, I am right in there, making a pitch for life insurance and other securities."

Moser keeps two lists of prospects: one made up of day-to-day business that he expects to close within a month, and the other composed of "dream cases"—each ranging anywhere from $100,000 to $500,000 or more of coverage—that may take three months to a year to close. His goal is to add a new dream case every month and maintain a working inventory of at least 10 or 12 such cases. This way, he closes one every four to six weeks. As part of the same goal, Moser keeps a chart of his best January, February, and so on, and uses it as a composite yearly goal.

In pitching the customer, Singer Business Machines' Philip Rosell has come up with such a winning technique for selling electronic point-of-sale systems to retailers that Singer even asked him to write it up in PERT chart fashion. Salesman Rosell's opening strategy is a letter to the prospect's top operating officer, requesting a meeting. Rosell starts at the top because of the big investment involved in buying his equipment. "We seldom get turned down," Rosell says of his request for that first big meeting. Then Rosell teams up with a local salesman and system engineer, and the three go in together and discuss what the system can do for the prospect. "We don't try to sell him any hardware," Rosell says. "That's what he has a purchasing agent for."

The lessons taught by failure

If the first meeting is encouraging, Rosell follows it up with store surveys and endless conferences and demonstrations for the store's credit, merchandising, data processing, and financial executives. "We infiltrate the whole company," says Rosell. "In every case where we've made a major sale, the company has felt we were part of its team." Rosell recalls only two occasions when he did not follow his usual selling approach. This was at the insistence of the customer, who wanted a consultant to act as go-between. Both times the sale was lost.

What happens when you do blow the big sale? H. Glen Haney, a marketing director for the Univac Div. of Sperry Rand Corp., makes it a point to go back and find out why. "We lost a $4.5-million sale to a large state agency about a year ago," Haney says. "In a four-hour debriefing with the agency head, the state budget bureau people, and all other principals that were involved in the purchase, we found out that the loss of the sale really had nothing to do with the quality of our marketing effort. We lost because we had not clearly enough defined the conversion effort that the customer faced. Though our cost-performance was better than the competition, the agency decided to stay with its current vendor for that reason." Yet the lost sale was not a total loss. "As a result of that session," says Haney, "we have developed a series of conversion tools for our salesmen, aimed at solving that problem."

Owens-Corning Fiberglas Corp. took the same approach when a big customer, a thermoplastic compounder in Detroit, considered switching to an Owens-Corning competitor, which had cut its prices 1½¢ per lb. The competitor had a plant near the compounder, and the compounder decided to pick up its materials there, saving on freight. "It was a legitimate saving," says James MacLean, national sales manager for Owens-Corning's Textile & Industrial Group. "So we put our heads together." The local salesman, along with the group's marketing and packaging experts, finally developed a special package for shipping the material that the compounder could then use to ship his finished product. Savings: 2¢ per lb. for the customer and one industrial account for Owens-Corning.

Sam Jackson, an assistant sales manager for U.S. Steel Corp. in Philadelphia, calls it the difference between moving a product for its own sake and fitting the same product to a customer's system. One of Jackson's customers was bemoaning a 10% hike in the cost of castings. "I suggested that the part could be converted from a casting to welded steel," says Jackson, "and got together with our metallurgical and research people to test the conversion." The customer finally accepted it, saving the 10% boost in cost that he would have paid had he continued to cast the part.

"What makes Jackson stand out is that he knows the different types of metals, the industry that he is selling to, and how to cut costs," says Irwin Rashkover, director of procurement for Gindy Mfg. Corp., a Budd Co. subsidiary. "Jackson knows how to help us save money by working out different tolerances for the steel we buy—for instance, by going to the high side of sheet tolerances. The supersalesman knows this. The ordinary steel salesman doesn't."

Don't take 'no' for an answer

Robert Hawkins, who sells radio communications systems for Motorola, Inc., has the simplest—and oldest—selling technique of all: He refuses to take "no" for an answer. When Hawkins was pitching the field service organization of a national equipment supply house, he insisted that Motorola's one-way paging system could improve service and cut manpower needs. When a purchasing agent shrugged him off, Hawkins went above him to a vice-president and received grudging permission for a one-year study of the company's service coverage and performance in 20 cities. Yet when he completed the study, which showed the need for a paging system, Hawkins still did not receive an order. So he offered to follow that up with an intensive three-month test of the paging system in a single city.

"For the entire three months," says Hawkins, "a day never went by when I didn't spend some time with the prospect." Hawkins even helped the dispatcher to design more efficient routes, while soothing the ruffled nerves of its servicemen. "They were afraid of the dispatcher becoming a Big Brother and controlling their every move," he says. Finally convinced, the company has decided to go nationwide with the paging system.

Sometimes, such indecision can go too far. That is when Olivetti's James Schlinkert calls a halt. "To close a tough sale," he says, "you must establish yourself—not the buyer—as the authoritative person." Schlinkert describes just such a sale that he ran up against a few months ago. A small corporation of five people had a definite need for an accounting system. "We had them all at our office one evening and presented our solution to their problem," says Schlinkert. "They were a hard-nosed lot that had evaluated every other accounting system available. After a couple of hours of haggling over a $15,000 sale, I finally shut off the machine, put the key in my pocket, and virtually threatened to throw them out of my office. Immediately, they became very docile and signed a contract. I shocked my salesman when I did that. But I had to take a calculated risk. The need and solution had been established."

Training today's salesman

Developing such instincts takes years. Some salesmen never develop them, and that puts a heavier burden than ever on today's sales recruiting and training. "In years past," says Transamerica's Herb Eagle, "you figured you could take a new salesman and help him develop the qualities that he needed. With today's higher costs and greater complexity of selling, you have to look for those qualities first off. And if they aren't there, you don't hire."

Five or 10 years ago, for instance, most large technical or engineering companies automatically recruited from engineering schools. Now, many of these same companies are seeking salesmen with a broader outlook and thus are looking for liberal arts, marketing, and other nonengineering backgrounds. "We have even successfully used English, history, and physical education majors," marvels Baxter T. Fullerton, sales vice-president of Warner & Swasey Co.'s Cleveland Turning Machine Div. The trick, of course, is to gain a universal man with broad interests, yet avoid what one Houston educator calls "the round man who is so round that he just rolls and develops no depth or substance."

Other companies are looking less for college graduates and more for seasoned professionals. "We used to steer clear of the retreads," says Peter Warshaw, a division national products manager for Powers Regulator Co. "Today when there's a vacancy, we don't contact colleges at all. We contact employment agencies, professional societies, and use referrals within the industry. We just can't afford to take the guy, make the major investment in him for two or three years, and then have him sell the training that we gave him to someone else." The new man, Warshaw stresses, must also be productive immediately. "The sales quotas are now so large and selling costs so high that we can't afford to have the backup man or bat boy anymore."

At the same time, sales training has broadened out. A growing number of companies offer continuing instruction for all their salesmen—and for good reason. Armour-Dial, Inc., a consumer-goods division of Greyhound Corp., ran a study on salesmen who had attended a recent session at its Aurora (Ill.) sales training center. The result: a boost of 12% in the number of calls per day, 25% in new-product retail placements, 100% in case sales, 62% in displays sold, and 250% in sales to direct-buying or chain accounts.

The big changes coming in sales recruiting and training—and in the salesman's whole approach to his markets—promise to usher in a broad new relationship between him and his company. Robert W. DeMott, Jr., vice-president and general manager of Rex Chainbelt's Industrial Sales Div., notes that about 10 years ago, industry's over-all marketing effort seemed to eclipse selling in importance. "Now, and more so in the future," he claims, "the trend will be to place selling on a par with marketing."

Wharton's Goodman goes one step further, claiming that the supersalesman of the future will even be ahead of company management when it comes to understanding his markets. "This is going to sound heretical," he admits, "but I see emerging a situation in which the salesman's function within a company is recognized as most important, with management performing a largely supportive role."

While he might get an argument on that, no one can dispute his larger point: the supersalesman is here to stay.

QUESTIONS

1. What does "wired for success" mean in the title of this article? Is it an accurate term to use?
2. The new "supersalesman" seems to be a minicompany or at least a mini-marketing manager. Discuss the implications for corporate organization.
3. What factors have contributed to the evolution of a new type of supersalesman? Are these new salesmen better salesmen than the older type? Why?
*4. Are the new "supersalesmen" interested in "marketing communication" as discussed by Ray? (Reading 22)
*5. Are "supersalesmen" needed in an era of shortages? (See Reading 8)

This article discusses and illustrates some of the problems of pricing in an inflationary economy. An electronics industry example shows how prices change over the product life cycle and are dependent on both production costs and competition.

---

25. PRICING STRATEGY IN AN INFLATION ECONOMY*

"LEAD TIME on components we buy used to be 30 days. Now it is a year. Because of component shortages, our inventories have doubled in the last year, while sales are up only 30%. To price a contract under these conditions, we have to double- and triple-check everything. A year or so ago, we budgeted every six months, made cash projections quarterly, and used the computer only for payroll. Now we budget quarterly, make cash projections weekly, and plug virtually every pricing factor into the computer."

---

* Reprinted with permission from *Business Week* (April 6, 1974), pp. 42–49. © 1974, McGraw-Hill, Inc. All Rights Reserved.

Those are the pricing problems in the minicomputer field, as described by Donald W. Fuller, chairman and president of Microdata Corp. of Irvine, Calif. In varying degree, they are also the problems in steel, food processing, petrochemicals, retailing, paper and pulp, and nearly every other business.

In today's inflationary economy, pricing a product or service is like no other pricing in recent history. While nearly all prices are moving higher over the long haul, short-term pricing patterns may be up, down, or every which way.

In the oil and food industries, where demand is high and costs are skyrocketing, prices are up 10% to 50% or more above a year ago. In other industries, notably electronics, cutthroat competition and economies of scale are driving prices through the floor. Three years ago, electronic handheld calculators retailed for $240 each. Now they are down to $19.95. Steel prices verge on the chaotic. After years of tightly competitive, follow-the-leader pricing, shortages and rulings by the Cost of Living Council have all but wrecked the industry's traditional single-tiered pricing structure. This week, for instance, U.S. Steel Corp. is offering hot-rolled carbon bars at anywhere from $178 to $211 per ton, depending upon the area of the country, compared with $188 for Republic, $207 for Armco, and $206 for Youngstown.

As Phase IV controls approach their Apr. 30 cutoff date, there is scant relief in sight. An almost incendiary rate of inflation—easily the country's biggest and most pressing economic problem—is wiping out any relationship between yesterday's price and today's worth of the dollar. As part of the same spiral, costs are surging at a spectacular rate. Raw material shortages are beginning to cripple whole industries. Then, to complicate an already forbidding equation, antitrusters are stepping up their pricing vigilance. "I can't name a major company that hasn't been challenged by the Justice Dept. on its prices," says Fred Kniffen, professor of marketing at the University of Connecticut.

More and more, today's pricing environment demands better, faster, and more frequent pricing decisions than ever before. It is also forcing companies to take a whole new look at pricing and its role in an increasingly complex marketing climate. While the central objective of pricing will always remain the same—to bring in more money than is spent—a growing number of companies are changing many of their basic strategies and tactics for achieving that objective.

Profit vs. volume

For years, most companies used price simply to attract more customers and build more sales. Where they saw the prospect for greater volume, they were often willing to let prices and profit margins slip. Now, corporate policy increasingly stresses profit growth ahead of volume growth, and many companies that previously boosted profits by simply trying to boost volume are focusing more on maintaining profit margins, holding down costs, and pricing for profit, as well as sales.

As one New York metals executive puts it: "All four basic elements of marketing—product, promotion, distribution, and price—contribute toward volume, but only price directly generates profit. The other three represent costs that, if reduced, can generate profit—but then only if the company holds its price."

Fairchild Camera & Instrument Corp., for instance, recently bowed out of a price war with Texas Instruments, Inc. At stake were two control modules for Polaroid Corp.'s SX-70 camera. "We were sorry to walk away from that business," says Wilfred J. Corrigan, Fairchild's executive vice-president. "Our price at the end was very close to Polaroid's requirements. But it wouldn't have provided an adequate margin." A few years ago, Corrigan concedes, Fairchild would probably have held onto that business.

Along the way, Fairchild and other companies are also getting more formal and structured in their pricing. Some companies have pulled pricing responsibility in from the field and are moving it higher in the corporate organization, sometimes all the way up to the chief executive. Others are bringing more specialists into the pricing act: production, marketing, financial, market research, and so on. Many more are making greater use of the computer to sharpen their price and cost analysis. Says one academic: "Before the computer, pricing used to be part of the budget ritual, since it was almost impossible to keep track of the factors going into price. Any good company now has an information flow system that allows prices to be reviewed at least weekly, if not daily."

One of these is the Jewelry Div. of Zale Corp., the big, Dallas-based national retail jewelry chain. Says Marvin Rubin, group vice-president: "We are constantly looking for flags that tell us that costs have gone up and that we had better re-examine our margins." Zale's highest flying flag is a daily computer printout that shows the current relationship between cost and margin on all Zale inventory. This is used by division buyers and management for regular review.

Classic pricing theory

The landmark book on U.S. corporate pricing is *Pricing in Big Business*, published in 1958 by the Brookings Institution and written by A. D. H. Kaplan, Joel B. Dirlam, and Robert F. Lanzillotti. It analyzes the pricing policies and strategies of 20 of the country's largest companies, including Goodyear, U.S. Steel, Sears, Gulf Oil, American Can, Union Carbide, General Electric, and General Foods.

"Undeniably, there are, in many instances, pricing routines that are

THE COMPLEXITIES OF ELECTRONICS PRICING

Pricing strategies among industries, companies, and even divisions within the same company defy generalization. This is especially true of the $35-billion electronics industry, which runs the gamut from TV tubes that have not changed in price for a decade to small handheld calculators that are selling for less than half the price that prevailed a year ago. Yet, like a tiny silicon "chip" that can duplicate the function of a thousand or more transistors, the electronics industry probably comes closest to being a miniature model for all the factors that shape today's complex pricing environment and dictate some of those strategies.

At one end of the industry product spectrum are the "mature" or established products that are either nearing or have surpassed their peak growth period. Among these products, the impact of raw material scarcities, capacity shortages, and high labor costs is clearly visible. Their development has all been amortized, and most possible cost improvements have been made.

'Learning curve.' Prices are firming for these products. For instance, small-signal, "metal can" transistors, ubiquitous little products used in almost every kind of electronic gear, dropped from 37¢ each in 1970 to 33¢ in 1971 to 25¢ in 1972. Last year, the price fell only 2¢. For the semiconductor business, this is virtual stability.

On the other end of the product spectrum, the pricing of new, advanced technology products is different—and growing more so among modern pricing pressures. New semiconductor products tend to be priced closely to the manufacturing cost "learning curve," which correlates a steady increase in production and manufacturing experience with a steady decrease in product rejection rates.

Bernard T. Marren, executive vice-president of American Micro-Systems, Inc., cites as an example a typical new integrated circuit or "chip." The manufacturer's cost per wafer—the basic building block from which finished chips are produced—starts at about $25. Of that, perhaps one-third represents raw material costs, and the rest is labor. "You figure on losing 20% of your wafers in processing, which brings the cost up to $31," says Marren. Then from the surviving wafers, "you sort the good chips from the bad or defective." At a yield of 20 good chips per wafer, the cost for each chip runs $1.55. Assembly and packaging raise the final manufacturing cost to $2.38.

When the manufacturer gets to 80 good chips per wafer, his chip cost falls to 38¢, and his manufacturing cost is about halved. At this stage, changes in raw material and even labor costs make little difference. "A 25% increase in raw material costs would add only about $2 to your wafer cost," Marren notes. "At a yield of 80, the chip cost would be raised only a penny."

Historically, the semiconductor industry prices for market share by anticipating the learning curve effect. "I want to keep my profit margins," says Marren. "But I also want that market share. So I predict future yields based on my experience with similar products in the past, and I price way out on the learning curve." On a product with heavy volume potential, the price may be several months farther along the learning curve than current costs. One example is the 1,024-bit random access memory (RAM) first introduced by Intel Corp. three years ago. This product, which has become the most popular semiconductor memory device for computers and other digital equipment, started out at a price of $28 per unit. It now sells for $3 to $4.

Future costs. One of today's hottest new semiconductor products, the 4,000-bit RAM had to provide a better value than the 1,024-bit RAM. So it could not start out at anything like the $28 level, at which Intel launched the 1,024-bit RAM. It had to sell for less than $15 if it was going to compete on a cost per function basis, even though it offers the bonus of reducing the number of components to be assembled for a given job. In fact, the 4,000-bit RAM is now being quoted at less than $10 in large quantities, despite the fact that it would have to sell for more than $20 if the manufacturers were to cover all their costs.

Over the longer term, other forces and pressures promise to keep industry pricing in total flux. For one thing, says Wilfred J. Corrigan, executive vice-president of Fairchild Camera & Instrument Corp., labor and raw material costs are increasing much faster than ever, "which is affecting the more mature products that already are near the bottom of the learning curve." Offsetting this is an industry trend away from 2-in. silicon wafers toward 3-in. wafers, providing more chips per processing step and thus a lower chip cost. "It's like the pricing in any other industry today," says one Eastern electronics executive. "You simply take it one day at a time."

sometimes expressed as rules," the authors write. "But given the diversity of products that most of the companies sold, it was impossible to equate product policy and company policy in every area. Swift's dog food cannot be priced in the same way or under the same guides as fresh meat. Union Carbide's Prestone antifreeze requires a different type of pricing from the company's oxygen. Thus, there were few companies in a position to say, 'Our policy is to price our products according to a uniform procedure and target.'"

That has not changed today. While most prices reflect the same basic elements—cost, profit, demand, and competition—the weight and priorities assigned to each vary with the nature of the product (commodity or specialty), company (manufacturing, wholesale, or retail), market (consumer or industrial), corporate objectives, management style, and everything else that makes one company different from another. In the chemical industry, Du Pont tends to focus on higher margin specialty products. At first, it prices them high, then gradually lowers the price as the market builds and competition grows. Dow Chemical Co., which stresses lower margin commodity products, takes the opposite tack. It prices low, builds a dominant market share, and holds on for the long pull. As manufacturers, Dow and Du Pont operate in a broad pricing milieu totally unlike that of the two other classes of business: wholesaling and retailing. All three classes use different pricing approaches, since they deal with different markets, different cost structures, and other variables.

* * *

"In the absence of any one ideal pricing formula," says an Eastern textile executive, "most well-managed companies are simply trying to improve the broader mechanism and organization that comes to bear on their particular formula." This means getting more and better pricing information, using it more effectively, and gaining more control. "After all," he adds, "the problem is not setting that initial list price. The problem is that discounts, special services, and other 'price shading' are making the list price almost meaningless. Except where major shortages exist, practically no one pays list anymore unless you're a consumer, and many times not even then. So how can a manufacturer know what his products are selling for?"

Depending upon the industry and company, price shading may knock anywhere from 5% to 20% or more off the price. Some of the most spectacular discounting, of course, comes in the auto business. At the dealer level, the retail "sticker" price on U.S.-made cars is only the top end of a bargaining spread that averages 17% on small cars, 21% on intermediates, 25% on large cars, and 21% to 25% on optional equipment. At the wholesale level, dealer sales bonuses and special allowances do the same thing.

More and more companies, however, are beginning to draw the line. Says J. Fred Weston, professor of economics and finance at UCLA and a long-time pricing authority: "In the past, many companies would publish a list price. Then their salesmen would shade prices all across the board, depending on market conditions, and tell the head office about it later. Now management itself is responding to the market before the salesman makes the sale, rather than afterward."

The effects of shortages

One example is Ducommun, Inc., a $190-million metals and electronics distributor in Los Angeles. "Two years ago," says Executive Vice-President Charles K. Preston, "we decided that since we couldn't raise our prices [because of controls], we'd concentrate on those items that would make us the best profit." So Ducommun boosted its salesmen's commissions 5% to 10% on its higher margin products, such as cutting tools and coated abrasives. "We've also given salesmen the rule," says Preston, "that we want no deviation from book price," unless authorized by management. Within its largest division, Ducommun has even created a price "czar" who consults with salesmen on any price changes. "We monitor the price on every order before the sale closes," says Preston.

❖   ❖   ❖

At Fairchild, semiconductor salesmen have begun operating on price lists established by individual product marketing managers who must approve any special deals. "In the past," says Corrigan, "Fairchild salesmen were able to commit the company to pricing decisions. Today, the selling function no longer even reports to the division general managers who carry profit responsibility."

Like other semiconductor makers, Fairchild is also less willing to write contracts in "step-pricing" terms, a common procedure for passing along cost savings that come with volume production and steadily decreasing product rejection rates. Material shortages, of course, help stiffen the seller's backbone. "Up to a year or so ago, it often took two or three pricing go-arounds with a customer to finally land the contract," says one executive at GTI Corp., a semiconductor industry supplier. "Now, if the manufacturer is meeting his capacity levels, can demonstrate his capability of getting raw materials, and thus better assure on-time delivery, the customer is more willing to pay the suggested selling price, rather than bargain and perhaps lose out on the contract."

To guarantee delivery on ball bearings and other products that have steadily lengthening lead times, many customers are even willing to accept an escalator clause on their orders. This way, they pay the going price at time of shipment, rather than at the time of the order. Sometimes, the customer is not even told beforehand. "You get the stuff," grumbles one maker of logging equipment, "and you find the price is higher than was quoted." Adds a leading gear manufacturer: "Everybody we see is breaking every rule in the book. The price quoted to you when you place the order no longer means a thing. You won't take anybody to court over this. The courts would be jammed for years. So you sit down with your important suppliers and work it out."

As one example, he cites a new deferred pricing system, using standard indices. "You take today's factory price," he says, "and you quote that plus escalation tied to the wholesale price for ferrous and nonferrous metals—if that is what you are dealing in—and the Bureau of Labor Statistics index for machinery. The indices determine changes made at time of delivery." The problem, he adds quickly, "is that the marketing guys have to be retrained to sell this way, and purchasing people have to communicate faster and more fluently with the marketing people."

'Unbundling' services

One of the biggest targets of pricing strategists is the jumble of so-called "free" services that have long inflated costs and distorted prices and profitability. Feeling the pressure of rising labor costs, many retailers, wholesalers, and manufacturers are now starting to "unbundle" these services and charge separately for them.

Grocery wholesalers, for instance, may pass through a straight invoice cost and then charge for delivery, packaging, or other onetime freebies. A growing number of department stores now charge extra for home delivery, gift-wrapping, and shopping bags. "This makes a good deal of sense," says Charles Goodman, marketing professor at the University of Pennsylvania's Wharton School. "People who don't want a service just shouldn't have to pay for it."

Norton Co., the big Worcester (Mass.) abrasives maker, took such thinking one step further. Under its pioneering "Norton Plan," introduced in 1965, the company's Grinding Wheel Div. developed a contract distribution system that uses computers to calculate long-term usage trends and rates among major customers, and writes contracts at set prices. This cuts Norton's selling and handling costs, minimizes some of the peaks and valleys in its production cycle, and reduces inventory requirements both among Norton and its volume customers—allowing Norton to offer lower, long-range prices on larger sales.

A typical abrasive steel conditioning wheel, for instance, is priced regularly at $124.51, based on a bulk rate and subject to a 2% discount for cash prior to 30 days. Under the Norton Plan, the same wheel costs $98.03 or 21.3% less. Today, some 20% to 30% of the division's sales—excluding diamond products, which are not covered—fall within the plan.

"Under regular list pricing structures," says one university pricing expert, "I'm paying more because I don't need the technical services a company is offering. So I think about making the product myself or finding some little guy down the street to make it for me without the selling cost. If I'm Norton Co., I work out a pricing program, and I sell directly or use some other way to protect my market. If you are a price leader and you go to market with a lot of services, you must do this as your product becomes more mature or you'll lose a lot of volume."

Pricing of new products presents different problems, mainly because it is starting to pull in two different directions. One direction is toward "skimming," or charging as much as the traffic will bear. While this generates high initial profits, it also lures competition into the market and quickly drives prices down unless the skimmer has patent or other product protection. "Penetration pricing," on the other hand, relies on low prices to gain instant dominance in a market and to build a stronger long-range position of leadership.

Though opposite in their approach, both pricing strategies share the same basic requirement: an intensive analysis of the market. In the past, many consumer companies and nearly all industrial companies priced new products on the basis of cost, plus some predetermined markup, then adjusted the price to meet or anticipate competition. Now, more and more new product pricing is market- or value-oriented, rather than cost-oriented.

Lesson in skimming

Du Pont is one of the classic skimmers. The assistant director of Du Pont's Film Dept. elaborated on this philosophy in an antitrust case against Du Pont's cellophane in 1953: "The main competitive materials . . . against which cellophane competes are waxed paper, glassine, greaseproof, and vegetable parchment papers, all of which are lower in price than cellophane. We do not meet this price competition. Rather, we compete with these materials on the basis of establishing the value of our own as a factor in better packaging and cheaper distribution costs and classify as our logical markets those fields where the properties of cellophane in relationship to its price can do a better job."

Over the years, as Du Pont builds volume and competition rushes into the market, prices drop rapidly. Du Pont's Dacron, a polyester fiber, has slipped from $2.25 per lb. when it was introduced in 1953 to today's 40¢ range. More recently, the price of Qiana, a five-year-old synthetic fiber with the look and feel of silk, has dipped 35%.

"We were using ingredients we never used before," says a Du Pont spokesman of the Qiana introduction. "And there was no point putting it into men's underwear." Instead, Du Pont launched Qiana in the high-fashion prestige market—with an initial price to match: $5.95 to $8.95 per lb., compared with $8 to $10 per lb. for silk. "You get it into the very highest prestige garments to build a reputation and identity for it," says the Du Pont source. "We got the biggest designers and biggest names [Dior, Cardin, and Givenchy, for instance] to develop this identity." By now, Du Pont claims, the trademark is creating the appetite, so promotion costs and prices continue to drop. "Then to broaden your market," the Du Pont spokesman says, "you go into the next lower price category."

Or you can go the other way, getting customers to trade up to a higher-priced product. One of the shrewdest users of that tactic is the tire industry. In the early 1960s, the bias-ply tire was the industry's dominant product, selling for about $30. Then in 1965, B. F. Goodrich Tire launched the industry's first serious marketing campaign for a U.S.-made radial, selling in the $50 range. Consumers, however, were put off by the big price spread. So in 1968, tiremakers introduced an in-between product: the bias-belted tire, at about $40.

"We knew from experience that the premium-priced tire market is only so big," says Patrick C. Ross, president of Goodrich Tire. "So as the market shifted and the bias-belted tire became the popular tire, the step up to radials was not so great." Last fall, Goodrich moved up one more step, introducing the self-sealing "Golden Lifesaver" steel-belted radial, priced 15% to 20% above regular steel-belted radials.

Goodyear Tire & Rubber Co. is moving in the same direction. This summer, it will launch a national ad campaign for its new Customgard GT radials, priced at $75 to $85 each or about 5% higher than most other steel-belted radials. Instead of steel, Goodyear's new tires use Exten, a specially treated version of Du Pont's new Kevlar tire cord. While Kevlar costs about $2.85 per lb. compared with 80¢ per lb. for steel, it is billed as five times stronger than steel, which means far less belting is needed in each tire.

How high to price?

The big imponderable, of course, is how high to price without pricing yourself right out of the market. The marketing landscape is littered with the mistakes of companies that priced the wrong product too high: Du Pont's Corfam imitation shoe leather, Cartrevision's home video recording system, a new type of sterile slag industrial incinerator from Dravo Corp., to name only a few.

An initial high price also leaves a new product exposed and vulnerable. Wella Corp. introduced its Wella Balsam hair conditioner at a hefty $1.98, compared with $1.19 for standard cream rinses. So Alberto-Culver Co. came in with Alberto-Balsam at $1.49, socked $621,000 into a big advertising sendoff (vs. $62,000 for Wella), and claims it surpassed

Wella in only 10 months. Today, Alberto claims 55% to 60% of the hair conditioner market. "We would have liked the profit margins that Wella had with its higher price," says Randy Irion, Alberto-Balsam's senior brand manager. "But we just couldn't get enough market penetration at $1.98."

Irion and other boosters of "penetration pricing" claim that a low price can unlock markets that may not even have been anticipated. This happened when electronic hand-held calculators broke through the $100 barrier and suddenly began moving from the industrial market into the far larger consumer market. "Nobody had any inkling that consumers would buy these things," marvels one retailer.

The same thing occurred when tiny Southwest Airlines recently came up with a $13 fare between Dallas and San Antonio, Tex. This was half the old fare. Braniff Airways quickly followed suit, and before long, air traffic between the two cities doubled, as businessmen and lower-incomers who previously drove between the two cities began flying. In this case, Southwest and Braniff actually changed some behavior patterns.

"In airlines and certain other industries where you have a heavy fixed cost, you are ahead if you can increase total revenue," stresses Richard W. Hansen, chairman of marketing at Southern Methodist University's School of Business. "Let's say you are operating at 35% of total capacity at a ticket cost of $26. If you can operate at 85% of capacity and charge $13, you are a lot better off." Southwest Airlines certainly is. The new fare helped the three-year-old carrier turn its first profit.

While corporate strategies continue grappling with the problems of modern pricing, they are the first to concede that they will probably never get it totally under control. "This is impossible, since costs are changing on one end of their business, competition and markets are changing on the other, and inflation keeps everything and everyone continually off balance," says Jerry Wasserman, senior consultant with Arthur D. Little, Inc. At the same time, Wasserman adds, "the whole role and function of marketing itself is in even greater flux than usual."

One of the latest shifts, of course, is the trend toward "de-marketing" of products. "For years, we were in a situation where we had a glut of supply relative to demand," says Southern Methodist's Hansen. "That's changing now in a lot of areas, and there is concern about what's going to happen to the marketing role. Rather than trying to increase consumption, some of these industries may take the tack that the oil companies and power utilities are taking: decreasing consumption. And maybe price is what they will use."

Then with a nod toward the idea of de-marketing—and toward the broader changes and ferment within the whole pricing function—Hansen adds with wry amusement: "I think we are in for an interesting period in marketing."

QUESTIONS

1. What forces make pricing more important and difficult in an inflation economy?
2. Are any of the firms discussed in the article using a simple cost-plus approach? If so, which? If not, why not?
3. Explain the pricing approach being used in the electronics industry example.
° 4. What happens to "supersalesmen" (Reading 24) in times of shortages and rapidly rising prices?

Marginal pricing, setting the price so that marginal revenue equals marginal cost, is usually recommended in economic theory. This article shows how the approach was applied in an actual business situation.

---

26. AIRLINE TAKES THE MARGINAL ROUTE*

CONTINENTAL Air Lines, Inc., last year filled only half the available seats on its Boeing 707 jet flights, a record some 15 percentage points worse than the national average.

By eliminating just a few runs—less than 5%—Continental could have raised its average load considerably. Some of its flights frequently carry as few as 30 passengers on the 120-seat plane. But the improved load factor would have meant reduced profits.

For Continental bolsters its corporate profits by deliberately running extra flights that aren't expected to do more than return their out-of-pocket costs—plus a little profit. Such marginal flights are an integral part of the over-all operating philosophy that has brought small, Denver-based Continental—tenth among the 11 trunk carriers—through the bumpy postwar period with only one loss year.

Chief contribution

This philosophy leans heavily on marginal analysis. And the line leans heavily on Chris F. Whelan, vice-president in charge of economic plan-

---

° Reprinted with permission from *Business Week* (April 20, 1963), pp. 111–114. © 1963, McGraw-Hill Inc.

ning, to translate marginalism into hard, dollars-and-cents decisions (see box).

Marginal analysis in a nutshell

Problem: Shall Continental run an extra daily flight from City X to City Y?

The facts: Fully-allocated costs of this flight. $4,500
             Out-of-pocket costs of this flight $2,000
             Flight should gross $3,100

Decision: Run the flight. It will add $1,100 to net profit—because it will add $3,100
             to revenues and only $2,000 to costs. Overhead and other costs, totaling
             $2,500 [$4,500 minus $2,000], would be incurred whether the flight is
             run or not. Therefore, fully-allocated or "average" costs of $4,500 are not
             relevant to this business decision. It's the out-of-pocket or "marginal"
             costs that count.

Getting management to accept and apply the marginal concept probably is the chief contribution any economist can make to his company. Put most simply, marginalists maintain that a company should undertake any activity that adds more to revenues than it does to costs—and not limit itself to those activities whose returns equal average or "fully allocated" costs.

The approach, of course, can be applied to virtually any business, not just to air transportation. It can be used in consumer finance, for instance, where the question may be whether to make more loans—including more bad loans—if this will increase net profit. Similarly, in advertising, the decision may rest on how much extra business a dollar's worth of additional advertising will bring in, rather than pegging the advertising budget to a percentage of sales—and, in insurance, where setting high interest rates to discourage policy loans may actually damage profits by causing policyholders to borrow elsewhere.

Communication

Whelan finds all such cases wholly analogous to his run of problems, where he seeks to keep his company's eye trained on the big objective: net profit.

He is a genially gruff, shirt-sleeves kind of airline veteran, who resembles more a sales-manager type than an economist. This facet of his personality helps him "sell" ideas internally that might otherwise be brushed off as merely theoretical or too abstruse.

Last summer, Whelan politely chewed out a group of operational researchers at an international conference in Rome for being incomprehensible. "You have failed to educate the users of your talents to the potential you offer," he said. "Your studies, analyses, and reports are couched in tables that sales, operations, and maintenance personnel cannot comprehend."

Full-time job. Whelan's work is a concrete example of the truth in a crack by Prof. Sidney Alexander of MIT—formerly economist for Columbia Broadcasting System—that the economist who understands marginal analysis has a "full-time job in undoing the work of the accountant." This is so, Alexander holds, because the practices of accountants—and of most businesses—are permeated with cost allocation directed at average, rather than marginal, costs.

In any complex business, there's likely to be a big difference between the costs of each company activity as it's carried on the accounting books and the marginal or "true" costs that can determine whether or not the activity should be undertaken.

The difficulty comes in applying the simple "textbook" marginal concept to specific decisions. If the economist is unwilling to make some bold simplifications, the job of determining "true" marginal costs may be highly complex, time-wasting, and too expensive. But even a rough application of marginal principles may come closer to the right answer for business decision-makers than an analysis based on precise average-cost data.

Proving that this is so demands economists who can break the crust of corporate habits and show concretely why the typical manager's response—that nobody ever made a profit without meeting all costs—is misleading and can reduce profits. To be sure, the whole business cannot make a profit unless average costs are met; but covering average costs should not determine whether any particular activity should be undertaken. For this would unduly restrict corporate decisions and cause managements to forgo opportunities for extra gains.

Approach

Management overhead at Continental is pared to the bone, so Whelan often is thrown such diverse problems as soothing a ruffled city council or planning the specifications for the plane the line will want to fly in 1970. But the biggest slice of his time goes to schedule planning—and it is here that the marginal concept comes most sharply into focus.

Whelan's approach is this: He considers that the bulk of his scheduled flights have to return at least their fully allocated costs. Overhead, depreciation, insurance are very real expenses and must be covered. The out-of-pocket approach comes into play, says Whelan, only after the line's basic schedule has been set.

"Then you go a step farther," he says, and see if adding more flights will contribute to the corporate net. Similarly, if he's thinking of dropping a flight with a disappointing record, he puts it under the marginal microscope: "If your revenues are going to be more than your out-of-pocket costs, you should keep the flight on."

By "out-of-pocket costs" Whelan means just that: the actual dollars that Continental has to pay out to run a flight. He gets the figure not by applying hypothetical equations but by circulating a proposed schedule to every operating department concerned and finding out just what extra expenses it will entail. If a ground crew already on duty can service the plane, the flight isn't charged a penny of their salary expense. There may even be some costs eliminated in running the flight; they won't need men to roll the plane to a hangar, for instance, if it flies on to another stop.

Most of these extra flights, of course, are run at off-beat hours, mainly late at night. At times, though, Continental discovers that the hours aren't so unpopular after all. A pair of night coach flights on the Houston-San Antonio-El Paso-Phoenix-Los Angeles leg, added on a marginal basis, have turned out to be so successful that they are now more than covering fully allocated costs.

Alternative

Whelan uses an alternative cost analysis closely allied with the marginal concept in drawing up schedules. For instance, on his 11:11 p.m. flight from Colorado Springs to Denver and a 5:20 a.m. flight the other way, Continental uses Viscounts that, though they carry some cargo, often go without a single passenger. But the net cost of these flights is less than would be the rent for overnight hangar space for the Viscount at Colorado Springs.

And there's more than one absolute-loss flight scheduled solely to bring passengers to a connecting Continental long-haul flight; even when the loss on the feeder service is considered a cost on the long-haul service, the line makes a net profit on the trip.

Continental's data handling system produces weekly reports on each flight, with revenues measured against both out-of-pocket and fully allocated costs. Whelan uses these to give each flight a careful analysis at least once a quarter. But those added on a marginal basis get the fine-tooth-comb treatment monthly.

The business on these flights tends to be useful as a leading indicator, Whelan finds, since the off-peak traffic is more than normally sensitive to economic trends and will fall off sooner than that on the popular-hour flights. When he sees the night coach flights turning in consistently poor showings, it's a clue to lower his projections for the rest of the schedule.

Unorthodox

There are times, though, when the decisions dictated by the most expert marginal analysis seem silly at best, and downright costly at worst. For example, Continental will have two planes converging at the same time on Municipal Airport in Kansas City, when the new schedules take effect.

This is expensive because, normally, Continental doesn't have the facilities in K.C. to service two planes at once; the line will have to lease an extra fuel truck and hire three new hands—at a total monthly cost of $1,800.

But, when Whelan started pushing around proposed departure times in other cities to avoid the double landing, it began to look as though passengers switching to competitive flights leaving at choicer hours, would lose Continental $10,000 worth of business each month. The two flights will be on the ground in K.C. at the same time.

❋ ❋ ❋

QUESTIONS

1. A typical complaint of a businessleader who wants to use marginal pricing is inability to define demand and therefore the marginal revenue curve. How does the manager in this article solve this problem?

2. Could the approach used in this example be applied by most firms? Why or why not?

This article treats the controversial and sometimes politically explosive topic of "administered pricing." With a unique blend of economic theory and actual case examples, the author explains why actual prices so often deviate from the "official" company prices, and the prices and price behavior that business critics feel are reality.

---

27. THE MYTHS AND REALITIES OF CORPORATE PRICING*

Gilbert Burck

CORPORATE PROFITS may be recovering briskly this year, but resentment and suspicion of profits are rising briskly too. It is by now an article of faith in some sophisticated circles that the U.S. has become a corporate state, in which giant companies increasingly dominate markets and write their own price tickets regardless of demand

---

* Reprinted with permission from *Fortune Magazine*, April 1972. © 1972, Time, Inc. When this article was written, Mr. Burck was a staff writer for *Fortune Magazine*.

by practicing "administered" and "target return" pricing. Ask ten campus economists whether prices will fall with demand in industries that are concentrated—that is, dominated by a few large firms—and nine of them will tell you that prices won't fall as much as they would if the industry were competitive. And almost everywhere the putative pricing power of big business is equated with the well-known monopoly power that organized labor exercises over wages.

So the pressure is mounting to police pricing practices and other "abuses" in concentrated industries. Senator George McGovern, for example, is denouncing oligopolies as responsible for most of the nation's inflation, and is sponsoring measures to break up big companies. Meanwhile, the notion that price controls should become a permanent American institution is certainly taken seriously by more and more people. The Price Commission itelf, which has adopted the practice of regulating prices by relating them to profit margins of the past three years, seems to be leaning toward a theory of managed prices.

Yet all these passionately cherished attitudes and opinions are based at best on half truths and perhaps on no truth at all. The portentous fact is that the theory of administered prices is totally unproven and is growing less and less plausible as more evidence comes in. Always very controversial, it has lately been subjected to an extended counter-attack of highly critical analysis.

Some of the best work on the subject is being done by the privately funded Research Program in Competition and Business Policy at the University of California (Los Angeles) Graduate School of Management, under Professor J. Fred Weston. For nearly two years now, Weston and his group have been taking a fresh, empirical approach to subjects like industrial concentration, profits, competition, and prices. Their techniques include asking businessmen themselves how they set prices and trying to find out why businessmen's formal statements about their price policies are usually so different from their actual practices.

The program, among other things, hopes to come up with a new theory of corporate profitability. "So far," Weston says, "we find that profit rates are not significantly higher in concentrated than in nonconcentrated industries. What we do find is that there is a relationship between efficiency and profits and nothing else." But a vast amount of work, Weston admits, needs to be done. As happens so often in the dismal science, the more economists find out about a subject, the more they realize (if they are honest) how much they still have to learn.

MR. MEANS SHOWS THE WAY

The argument about administered prices is now nearly forty years old; one philoprogenitive professor who took sides at the start is preparing to instruct his grandson on the subject. Few controversies in all economic history, indeed, have used up so many eminent brain-hours or so much space in learned journals. Much if not most of the argument has been conducted on a macroeconomic level; that is, it has been concerned with analyzing over-all statistics on industrial concentration and comparing them with figures on prices. And that is exactly what was done by the man who started the argument by coining the phrase "administered price" in the first place. He is Gardiner Means, seventy-five, author (with the late Adolph Berle) of the celebrated book *The Modern Corporation and Private Property,* published in 1932.

Like a lot of economists in that day, Means was looking for reasons why the great depression occurred. He noticed that many prices remained stable or at least sticky, even when demand was falling. Thus demand was depressed still further and with it production and employment. Means's figures showed that wholesale prices fluctuated less in highly concentrated industries than in others; so to distinguish these prices from classic free-market prices, which are assumed to fluctuate with demand, he called them "administered" prices, or prices set by fiat and held constant "for a period of time and a series of transactions."

As an explanation for depression, Means's theory got some devastatingly critical attention over the next few years, but it did not fade away. In the middle 1950's it was revived as a major explanation for cost-push inflation, which Means calls administrative inflation; i.e., the supposed power of big business to raise prices arbitrarily. In 1957 the theory was taken up by Senator Estes Kefauver's antitrust and monopoly subcommittee, whose chief economist was John M. Blair, one of the nation's most energetic and passionate foes of industrial concentration. Ere long, dozens of the nation's eminent economists got into the argument, and many confected novel and often persuasive arguments in behalf of the theory of administered prices. Besides Blair, the advocates included the Johnson Administration's "new economists," such as James Duesenberry, Otto Eckstein, Gardner Ackley, and Charles Schultze, with "independent" savants like Adolph Berle and J. K. Galbraith helping out from time to time.

Why did they wait so long?

The burden of proof, of course, is on the advocates of administered-price theory. They must do more than merely nourish a prejudice, particularly if their thesis is to provide a reliable guide for antitrust and other public policy (to say nothing of serving as a base for a new interpretation of the American economy, such as Galbraith vouchsafed to the world in his book, *The New Industrial State*). In other words, they must offer very convincing evidence they are right. That, it is fair to say, they have not done. In 1941 economists Willard Thorp and

Walter Crowder, in a study for the Temporary National Economic Committee, used a sophisticated analysis of price, volume, and concentration to conclude that there was no significant relationship between the level of seller concentration and price behavior and volume. Shortly afterward, Alfred Neal, now president of the Committee for Economic Development, argued that any measure of price inflexibility must consider cost changes, "a matter over which industries have little if any discretion." These and other attacks on Means's theory seemed to dispose of it as a proven cause of depression.

As a major explanation of cost-push inflation, the theory was also subjected to severe criticism. Murray N. Rothbard of the Polytechnic Institute of Brooklyn, for one, simply laughs at the theory of administered prices, and terms it a bogey. "If Big Business is causing inflation by suddenly and wickedly deciding to raise prices," he says, "one wonders why it hadn't done so many years before. Why the wait? If the answer is that now monetary and consumer demand have been increasing, then we find that we are back in a state of affairs determined by demand, and that the law of supply and demand hasn't been repealed after all."

Just two years ago the National Bureau of Economic Research printed a little book calculated to put an end to the argument. It was called *The Behavior of Industrial Prices*, and was written by George J. Stigler, a distinguished economist at the University of Chicago, and James K. Kindahl, of the University of Massachusetts. Stigler and Kindahl correctly observed that, owing to hidden discounts and concessions, a company's quoted prices are often very different from the prices it actually gets. So instead of using official figures compiled by the Bureau of Labor Statistics on sellers' quotations, as Means and others had done, Stigler and Kindahl used prices at which their surveys told them sales were made. These were then matched with figures on industry concentration. The Stigler-Kindahl findings for the period 1957–61 did not differ much from findings made with B.L.S. figures. But the findings for 1961–66 differed considerably, and Stigler and Kindahl at least showed that prices in concentrated industries were not as inflexible as some people thought. What is very important is that Stigler and Kindahl probably understated their case because their surveys did not manage to get at true selling prices. As most business journalists are well aware, companies neither record nor generally talk about all the "under the table" prices and other valuable concessions they make when the market is sluggish.

"NORMAL" PROFIT ISN'T SO NORMAL

While this macroeconomic analysis of price and concentration was going on, a few economists were beginning to take a microeconomic or close-up view of pricing. Why not ask businessmen themselves just how they really price their products? This bright idea, however, proved not so easy to apply as to state. Classic economic theory says business should set prices to balance supply and demand—i.e., "to clear the market." But in 1939 two economists at Oxford University published a survey of thirty-eight British companies that found most of them tended to price their output pretty much on a stodgy cost-plus basis, almost as if they were accountants, or trying to behave like Gardiner Means's oligopolists.

It remained for Professor I. F. Pearce of the University of Nottingham to clear up the paradox. Pearce had been trained as a cost accountant, and understood why prices are not always what they seem. He pointed out that business almost universally bases prices on a cost figure, which in turn is based on both past cost data and future cost estimates; an economist would call this figure the long-term average cost. In most firms, moreover, a recognized profit margin remains stable over periods long enough to be significant, and is therefore considered normal. "What is less generally known, except to those who practice the art of price fixing," Pearce says, "is how often and for what a variety of reasons 'normal' profit is not in fact charged against any particular sale . . . The informal adjustment of margins, since it is both informal and *ad hoc*, tends to be left out of any general discussion of price fixing routine, *and yet the issue really turns upon it.* Margins charged are highly sensitive to the market under normally competitive conditions, and the 'norm' is simply that figure around which they fluctuate."

To demonstrate what he meant, Pearce made an elaborate study of one medium-sized British manufacturing firm. He sent out questionnaires and conducted formal interviews, and made a record of quoted prices

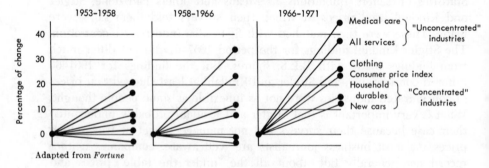

Adapted from *Fortune*

and actual selling prices. He found that a wide variation existed between the margins talked about in interviews and surveys and the margins actually achieved. "Normal" profit margins, in other words, were mere checkpoints in the company's planning process.

Of course, a significant minority of U.S. businesses actually do price on a cost-plus basis—the regulated monopolies like utilities, pipelines, and transportation companies, as well as a lot of military contractors. At first glance, many unregulated companies also seem to price on a cost-plus basis. This is only natural. Since they obviously cannot survive unless they take in more than they spend, the easiest way to think about a price is first to think like an accountant: price equals costs plus overhead plus a fair profit. Cost-plus, furthermore, is a useful ritual, with great public-relations advantages. A smart, prudent businessman would no more publicly brag about charging all the traffic will bear than he would publicly discourse on his wife's intimate charms. Recoiling from branding himself a "profiteer," he admits only to wanting a "fair" return. Ironically, this has made him a sitting duck for economists who accuse him of not striving to maximize his profits because he controls the market, and of changing his prices only when his planned return is threatened.

When it's right to charge all you can get

But no mechanical formula can guarantee a profit. Both cost and profit estimates depend on volume estimates; and volume, among many other things, depends on the right price, whether that price maximizes unit profit right away or not. A company with unused capacity and a growing market may well take the classical course of cutting prices and temporarily earning a smaller return on investment than it considers normal. But it may have equally cogent reasons for not cutting prices. The theorists of administered prices have pointed accusing fingers at business' behavior in the recession of 1957–58, when it raised prices somewhat in the face of falling demand. What happened was that costs were increasing faster than demand was falling. According to the theory of pure competition, they should have raised prices. That they did, both small firms and large.

On the other hand, many companies, particularly those with new products, do charge all the traffic will bear, and so they should. It is not going too far to attribute the innovativeness and technical progress of the Western world to this kind of profit maximizing, and the innovative backwardness of the Soviet Union and East Europe to the absence of it. The hope of realizing extraordinary profits on their innovations, at least temporarily, is what drives capitalist corporations into risking money on research. DuPont's strategy for the best part of fifty years was to develop "proprietary" products and to charge all it could get for them as long as the getting was good. So with the giants in data processing, pharmaceuticals, machine tools, and other high technologies. But these proprietary profits inevitably fire up competition, which invades the market with innovations of its own. Thus the story of Western industrial progress is the story of the progressive liquidation of proprietary positions.

The razor blades were too cheap

This is not to say that all or even most businesses are skillful practitioners of the art of pricing. Daniel Nimer, a vice president of a large Chicago company, has made an avocation of studying pricing and lectures and conducts surveys and seminars on the subject both here and abroad. Nimer believes that business in general is still far too inflexible in its pricing techniques and too prone to take a merely satisfactory return. The most frequent error, Nimer says, is to fail to charge what the traffic will bear, particularly when marketing a novel product. In 1961, Wilkinson Sword Ltd. brought out its new stainless-steel razor blades at 15.8 cents apiece. Overnight Wilkinson accumulated a staggering backlog of orders, the sort of thing that usually results in delivery delays and an expensive crash expansion program. Had Wilkinson started at 20 cents a blade, Nimer believes, it would have been much better able to fortify its position. Among Nimer's pearls of wisdom: (1) A big backlog is a nearly infallible indication of an underpriced product. (2) Always make decisions today that will help you tomorrow, and remember that it is easier to cut prices tomorrow than to raise them. (3) The key to pricing is to build value into the product and price it accordingly. (4) Above all, pricing is both analytical and intuitive, a scientific art.

SETTING A TARGET

The major if not the first case study of U.S. pricing was published in 1958 by the Brookings Institution in its book *Pricing in Big Business*. The authors were A. D. H. Kaplan (who was then a senior staff economist at Brookings and is now retired), Joel B. Dirlam of Rhode Island University, and Robert F. Lanzillotti of the University of Florida. Using questionnaires, interviews, and memos, the trio analyzed the pricing policies of twenty of the largest U.S. companies, including G.E., G.M., Alcoa, A&P, Sears, Roebuck, and U.S. Steel. Although the actual practices of the companies were predictably hard to describe and even harder to generalize about, the authors did manage to narrow the corporations' *goals* to five. The most typical pricing objectives, the authors decided, were to achieve (1) a target return on investment, (2) stable prices and markups over costs, (3) a specified market share, (4) a competitive position. Another objective, not so frequently cited, was to compete by taking advantage of product differences. The study's conclusion, written by Kaplan, was that many big, powerful companies seem not to be overwhelmingly controlled by the market, yet even they do not dominate the market. They do not have things their own way, with steady prices and rates of return, but are constantly forced to examine and change their policies.

Manifestly this study gives scant comfort to the administered-price theorists. Professor Lanzillotti apparently felt it was too easy on big business. Granted money to do further work on the data, he came up with a more critical interpretation of them in an article in the *American Economic Review* of December, 1958. Since Lanzillotti is now a member of the Price Commission and has been described as knowing "more about prices" than anyone else on that body, his thoughts are worth attending to. Lanzillotti devoted much of his thesis to the prevalence of so-called target-return pricing, which at that time was an almost esoteric concept.

When companies use target-return pricing, he explained, they do not try to maximize short-term profits. Instead they start with a rate of return they consider satisfactory, and then set a price that will allow them to earn that return when their plant utilization is at some "standard" rate—say 80 percent. In other words, they determine standard costs at standard volume and add the margin necessary to return the target rate of profit over the long run.

More and more companies, Lanzillotti argued, are adopting target-return pricing, either for specific products or across the board. He also concluded that the companies have the size to give them market power. Partly because of this power and partly because the companies are vulnerable to criticism and potential antitrust action, all tend to behave more and more like public utilities. Target-return pricing, with some exceptions in specific product lines, implies a policy of stable or rigid pricing.

Many of Lanzillotti's conclusions have already proved vulnerable to microeconomic analysis, most particularly at the hands of J. Fred Weston, who launched U.C.L.A.'s Research Program in Competition and Business Policy about two years ago. Prior to that, Weston studied finance and economics at the University of Chicago and wrote the three most popular (and profitable) textbooks on business finance. He got into pricing by a side door, having steeped himself in the literature on corporate resource allocation. He spent a considerable part of three years talking about that subject with executives—at first formally, then informally and postprandially. But he soon began to realize that he was also talking about the way prices were made. So he shifted his emphasis from financial to economic questions, and broadened considerably the scope of his work. Like others before him, he discovered that what businessmen formally say about their pricing and what they do about it are often very different. And their action is more consistent with classical theory than their talk.

In a major paper not yet published, Weston proceeds to apply his investigations to the three "popular" and related theories that were at the heart of the administered-price concept: (1) that large corporations generally try to realize a target markup or target return on investment; (2) that their prices tend to be inflexible, uncompetitive, and unresponsive to changes in demand; (3) that contrary to a fundamental postulate of classic economic theory, large, oligopolistic corporations do not maximize profits, but use their market power to achieve planned or target profit levels.

The constraints of the market

The concept of target pricing, Weston's research showed, was an arrant oversimplification of what actually happens in large companies. "The Brookings study," he explains, "focused on talking to top sales and marketing men, who take a target as given. If you talk to top executives, you find they use the target as a screening device, a reference point." Pricing decisions, he found out, cannot be (and are not) made apart from other business decisions; price lists are based on long-run demand curves. In fact, as the drawing below suggests, all the considerations that go to make investment and other policies also go in pricing, either deliberately or intuitively.

Neither large nor small businesses have price "policies," Weston adds; pricing is too much interwoven with other factors to be formulated independently of them. And most of the people Weston talked to kept emphasizing the constraints of the market. In short, target-return pricing is not what the critics of business think it to be. If anything, it is an interim checkpoint set up by management to specify tentatively the company's potential.

Often, Weston argues, critics of corporate pricing condemn behavior as oligopolistic that does nothing more than follow modern accounting practices. Firms of all sizes use accounting budgets, plans, and controls to formulate performance objectives. Standard volume represents the firms' best judgment of the expected volume of operations, and standard cost is the unit cost at standard volume. And a technique called variance analysis compares management's actual performance with standard performance in order to evaluate and improve the former.

Economic textbooks, says Weston, have failed to keep up with such developments in the art of management, with the result that economists often fail to understand the nature and implications of business planning. In *The New Industrial State*, for example, Galbraith argues that planning by firms, aided by government, is eliminating the market mechanism. Nonsense, says Weston. Planning and control as management uses them do not eliminate the market or its uncertainties. Planning and control are what the market forces you to do. Since they provide a way of judging performance and spotting defects, a device to shorten the reaction time to uncertainty and change, they really increase the market's efficiency.

How Detroit reacts

The administered-price theorists have pointed to the auto industry as the archetype of a disciplined oligopoly whose prices are very rigid.

This characterization is largely based on the industry's practice of setting dealers' recommended prices at the beginning of a model year. Actually, the auto companies change those prices, sometimes frequently and substantially, as the year rolls on and specific models demonstrate their

Pricing decisions cannot be separated from investment decisions

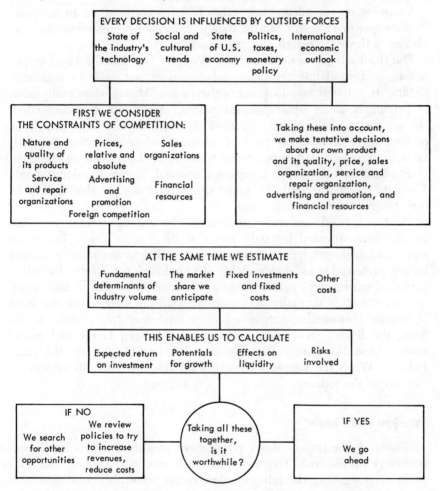

popularity or lack of it. The price changes take a wide variety of forms: bonuses for sales exceeding quotas, bonuses for models not doing well, and so on. As Professor Yale Brozen of the University of Chicago analyzes the industry: "Competition in the auto market actually *makes* the retail price. If the retail price is low relative to wholesale prices, the dealers can't live, and the company must give them better margins; if the retail price is high, the dealers tend to get rich, and the company raises wholesale prices and steps up production."

Now that foreign competition has become so powerful, the auto companies find it harder than ever to price arbitrarily. "Take our Vega," a G.M. man says with some feeling. "If anything is the reverse of target-return pricing, that Vega is. We did not *make* its price. We had to *take* a price that was set by our competitors. Then the only way we could make a profit was to bring our costs down."

Summing up the alleged reluctance of large corporations to compete, Weston quotes Professor Martin Bailey of Brookings, who describes the idea as "a theory in search of a phenomenon."

The third allegation dealt with by Weston—i.e., that the large corporation, in formulating its price policies, does not seek to maximize profits—is a tough one to prove either way. "Management's approach to pricing is based upon planned profits," Lanzillotti has contended. "If we are to speak of 'administered' decisions in the large firm, it is perhaps more accurate to speak of administered *profits* rather than administered *prices*." To support his contention, Lanzillotti re-examined profit data on the twenty companies covered in the Brookings book. The data seemed to verify his belief that large firms are able to achieve their target returns on investment.

Weston noticed two major defects in the argument. One was that targets were specified for only seven of the twenty firms. The other was that Lanzillotti defined return on investment as the ratio of income before preferred-stock dividends to stockholders' net worth, including preferred stock, which makes the return look artificially large. But return on investment is normally and more realistically defined as the ratio of income (before interest payments) to total operating assets. On this basis, the figures show a big discrepancy between target and actual returns. And the Lanzillotti table included results for only the years 1947–55. When the figures were extended through 1967, there was an even larger discrepancy.

"We just don't know"

Moreover, the returns above target were consistent with a lot of contradictory theses—with target pricing, with random behavior, and with profit maximization; the returns below target were also consistent with a number of alternative theses. Weston's final conclusion: Studies by Lanzillotti and by others have established neither that large firms are able to "control" or plan profits, nor that they do not want to maximize or optimize profits. Case not proved: additional evidence and analysis needed.

"The third proposition probably cannot be answered anyway," Weston adds. "How do you know if firms are maximizing their profits? In an early draft I made the mistake of thinking that a company earning more than target was maximizing its profits. This isn't necessarily so.

We just don't know. We are, however, finding out a lot of positive facts about other related things. It has always been assumed, for example, that there will be collusion in an industry with few firms. But the fact is that we are beginning to get solid evidence that competitive efficiency is an important characteristic of such industries." This finding, Weston points out, is consistent with the work of Professor Brozen, who has analyzed in detail the profitability of hundreds of companies. "Concentrated industries are concentrated because that, apparently, is the efficient way to organize those industries," says Brozen. "Unconcentrated industries are unconcentrated because that, apparently, is the efficient way to organize them."

THE BIG COMPANY AS COST LEADER

Standard textbook theory assumes that only "atomistic" industries—i.e., those with many companies and dominated by none—are perfectly competitive in price and highly responsive to changing tastes and technologies. But Weston contends that companies in concentrated industries can and do serve the consumer just as effectively. This view, incidentally, is persuasively set forth in a new book, *In Defense of Industrial Concentration*, by Professor John S. McGee, on leave from the University of Washington. The notion that concentration leads to the end of capitalism, McGee argues, springs from indefensibly narrow definitions of both competition and the aims of the economic system. Economic competition is best understood as an evolutionary process and not as a rigid structure or set of goals. But there is no necessary conflict between concentration and "competitiveness," even when the latter word is used in its narrow sense.

You can't explain the new competition with narrow textbook theory, Weston says. Big companies may be price leaders, but they are also cost leaders. Continually subjected to the efforts of rivals to steal business away, they deal with this uncertainty by reducing costs wherever they can. As Weston sees it, this kind of price leadership does not result in high prices and restricted output, as textbook theory says it should. What it does is to compel companies to try to strike a balance between growing as fast as possible and raising earnings per share as fast as possible.

Are oligopolists more profitable?

Among the other provocative papers financed by the U.C.L.A. program is an unpublished dissertation on the relationship between industrial concentration and prices, by Steven H. Lustgarten, twenty-eight, who now teaches economics at the Baruch College of the City University of New York. His investigations show that during the period 1954–58, prices rose faster in concentrated industries. But the reason seems logical. Firms expanded plant and equipment at an abnormal rate. As production costs increased, prices did too. So Lustgarten could neither confirm nor reject the theory that 1954–58 was a period of profit-push inflation. For the years 1958–63, however, there was no relationship between concentration and price changes. The theory of administered prices, in other words, remained unproven.

A study of concentration and profits was done by Dr. Stanley Ornstein, thirty-three, a consultant to the program. He examined the traditional hypothesis that, as concentration increases, the likelihood of collusion or "weak competitive pressures" also increases and leads to higher profits in concentrated industries than in others. Not so, says Ornstein. Because stock-market prices represent the discounted value of expected future earnings, Ornstein used stock-market values to represent profitability over the long run. To eliminate false correlations, he also examined individual profit rates of the largest corporations in each industry, 131 companies in all, and subjected them to multiple regression analysis, a mathematical technique that is used to determine the relative influences of several variables.

"From 1947 through 1960," Ornstein observes, "the return on equity dropped from around 15 percent to 8 or 9 percent and in a continuous trend. Long-term fluctuations like this shouldn't occur if there is collusion or administered bias." Like Brozen, Ornstein finds no connection between high profits and concentration. On the contrary, he finds there is vigorous competition among so-called oligopolists. His conclusion, made after much analysis, was somewhat more cautious: "This study does not disprove the traditional hypothesis [that oligopoly is characterized by high profitability], any more than previous studies proved it. It does show, however, that prior conclusions have gone far beyond those warranted by economic theory."

Remember the New York Yankees

One of the U.C.L.A. program's most distinguished participants is Professor Harold Demsetz, forty-one, on leave from the University of Chicago, where he taught for eight years. Demsetz' interests at present lie mainly in identifying the true sources of corporate efficiency. He maintains that when there is no real barrier to the entry of new competitors, concentration is not an index of monopoly power. Therefore, if a concentrated industry has a high rate of return, monopoly power is not the cause of it. Concentration results from the operation of normal market forces and from a company's ability to produce a better or cheaper product or both and to market it efficiently. Some companies are downright lucky, and some outperform others, while some are both lucky and superior performers.

Confirming Demsetz' belief, Professor Michael Granfield, twenty-eight, has tentatively concluded that differences in efficiency may account for most differences in profit levels and that high profits do not necessarily imply high prices but often quite the opposite–high volume and low prices. One way he accounts for efficiency is by what he calls Team Theory. "The old saw holds that the team outperforms its individual members; it may be right," says Granfield. "Although other companies are constantly hiring executives away from I.B.M., these companies never seem to do as well as I.B.M."

"Many managerial economies are not always evident," Ornstein adds. "The only way to get them is to get the whole team. The New York Yankees were a winning team for years; the technical skills responsible for their record accounted for only about 10 to 20 percent of the answer. What is really involved is managerial skills, and they can't be duplicated. To some extent a successful management is synergistic. By this I mean that there seem to be managerial economies of scale just as there are multi-plant economies of scale. If so, the argument that you can break up big business and not hurt the consumer is wrong."

It may not be long before the program staff develops a formal theory about what really makes enterprises excel and why the country is better off handling them with a certain amount of care instead of busting them up like freight trains in a classification yard, or subjecting them to permanent price controls.

STORED IN THE MINDS OF MILLIONS

The theory of administered prices, however, is not yet done for. Its new critics will doubtless find the going slow. Before their credo can hope to gain "popular" acceptance, it must first achieve standing in professional economic journals. And it has, for the moment, absolutely no political appeal. Thanks in large part to Ralph Nader, the big corporation is the whipping boy of the day. Indeed, George Stigler glumly predicts that the controversy will continue for another generation or more. "Administered-price theory," he says, "is like the Sacco-Vanzetti case. Whatever the jury's verdict, the defendants' innocence is stored in the minds of millions. So is the 'guilt' of administered prices and the businessmen who practice them."

The administered-price theorists are not resting on their oars, either. Gardiner Means, who started it all nearly forty years ago, now argues that the recent combination of inflation and recession can be explained *only* by his administered-price thesis. In the June, 1972, issue of the *American Economic Review*, he defines his theory and then tears into the Stigler-Kindahl book, which he says misrepresents his position.

What may be more important in its effect on public opinion, John Blair, he of the Kefauver committee, is publishing a monumental 832-

page volume entitled *Economic Concentration—Structure, Behavior and Public Policy.* This opus contains something from almost everybody who has written about concentration and is complete with dozens of charts, as well as an introduction by Means. The fruit of more than thirty years of fighting big business, the work is larded with quotations and chuck-full of footnotes. Blair's mind is made up, and his book is passionately partisan; but that will probably not prevent it from being given glowing reviews in the popular press.

For all this, there seems no doubt that the case against the theory of administered prices will grow stronger. Groups like Weston's are being organized elsewhere. The University of Rochester, for example, has set up the Center for Research in Government Policy and Business in its Graduate School of Management and is looking around for private donations.

No matter what such groups find, it will be salutary. For the controversy about administered prices proves, among other things, how little Americans know about the inner workings of the big corporation, the country's most characteristic institution. And if present trends in research are any indication, the more that can be learned, the stronger will be the case for revising wrong notions about corporate behavior.

QUESTIONS

1. What is "administered pricing"?
2. What factors affect the final price charged the consumer for a product?
3. Does administered pricing benefit or harm the firm's customer? How about the economy?
*4. Is "administered pricing" incompatible with Alderson's view (Reading 5) that firms compete for a "differential advantage"?

4

Marketing management in action

IN ADDITION to making decisions about the four Ps, the marketing manager must also develop a strategic plan for each market and a whole program if several plans are involved. In other words, the strategic decisions on each of the four Ps must be blended together to make a smoothly working whole. The first reading in this section discusses this task.

Good management also requires control of marketing plans and programs. For good control, information systems need to be developed and auditing and cost accounting techniques need to be applied. Three readings discuss these managerial techniques as applied to marketing.

The final article discusses some of the problems and strategies of U.S. auto makers. It illustrates the need for continual planning and *re-planning* in a dynamic, competitive marketplace.

4

Marketing management in action

In an earlier article (no. 15), Levitt discussed the use of the product life cycle for product planning. The following article extends this discussion and illustrates the use of the product life cycle in marketing strategy planning and blending the four Ps into an effective marketing mix.

28. THE PRODUCT LIFE CYCLE: A KEY TO STRATEGIC MARKETING PLANNING*

John E. Smallwood

MODERN MARKETING management today increasingly is being supported by marketing information services of growing sophistication and improving accuracy. Yet the task remains for the marketing manager to translate information into insights, insights into ideas, ideas into plans, and plans into reality and satisfactory programs and profits. Among marketing managers there is a growing realization of the need for concepts, perspectives, and for constructs that are useful in translating information into profits. While information flow can be mechanized and the screening of ideas routinized, no alternative to managerial creativity has yet been found to generate valuable marketing ideas upon which whole marketing programs can be based. The concept of the product life cycle has been extremely useful in focusing this creative process.

The product life cycle concept in many ways may be considered to be the marketing equivalent of the periodic table of the elements concept in the physical sciences; like the periodic table, it provides a framework for grouping products into families for easier predictions of reactions to various stimuli. With chemicals—it is a question of oxidation temperature and melting point; with products—it is marketing channel acceptance and advertising budgets. Just as like chemicals react in similar ways, so do like products. The product life cycle helps to group these products into homogeneous families.

The product life cycle can be the key to successful and profitable product management, from the introduction of new products to profit-

* From *MSU Business Topics*, Winter 1973, pp. 29–35. Reprinted by permission of the publisher, Division of Research, Graduate School of Business Administration, Michigan State University. At the time of writing, Smallwood was Director of Economic and Marketing Research for Whirlpool Corporation.

able disposal of obsolescent products. The fundamental concept of the product life cycle (PLC) is illustrated in Figure 1.

FIGURE 1
Life cycle stages of various products

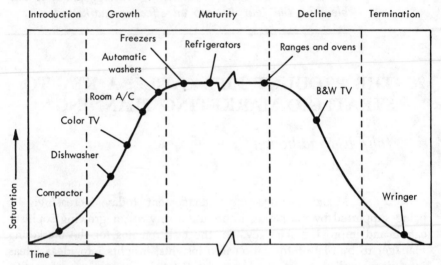

In application, the vertical scale often is measured in saturation of the product (percentage of customer units using), while the horizontal scale is calibrated to represent the passage of time. Months or years are usually the units of time used in calibration, although theoretically, an application along the same concept of much shorter or longer durations (milliseconds in physical sciences, millenia in archaeology) might be found. In Figure 1 the breakdown in the time scale is shown by stages in the maturity of product life. The saturation scale, however, is a guide only and must be used accordingly. When comparing one product with another, it is sometimes best treated by use of qualitative terms, not quantitative units. It is important to the user of the product life cycle concept that this limitation be recognized and conceptual provisions be made to handle it. For example, if the basic marketing unit chosen is "occupied U.S. households," one cannot expect a product such as room air conditioners to attain 100 percent saturation. This is because many households already have been fitted with central air conditioning; thus, the potential saturation attainment falls well short of 100 percent of the marketing measurement chosen.

To overcome this difficulty, marketing managers have two basic options. They can choose a more restrictive, specific marketing unit such as "all occupied U.S. households that do not have forced air heating"; homes without forced air heating are unlikely candidates for central air conditioning. It can be anticipated that room air conditioners will saturate not only *that* market, but portions of other markets as well. On the other hand, on the basis of informed judgment, management can determine the *potential* saturation of total households and convert the PLC growth scale to a measurement representing the degree of attainment of potential saturation in U.S. households. The author has found the latter approach to be the more useful one. By this device, automatic washers are considered to be at 100 percent saturation when they are at their full potential of an arbitrarily chosen 80 percent.

Consider Figure 1, where various products are shown positioned by life cycle stages: the potential saturations permit the grouping of products into like stages of life cycle, even when their actual saturation attainments are dissimilar. One can note that in Figure 1 automatic washers (which are estimated at 58 percent saturation) and room air conditioners (30 percent) are positioned in the same growth stage in Figure 1; freezers (29 percent) and refrigerators (99 percent), on the other hand, are in the maturity stage. This occurs because, *in our judgment,* freezers have a potential of only about one-third of "occupied households" and thus have attained almost 90 percent of that market. Automatic clothes washers, however, have a potential of about four-fifths of the occupied households and at about 70 percent of their potential still show some of the characteristics of the growth stage of the PLC. General characteristics of the products and their markets are summarized in Figure 2.

The product life cycle concept is illustrated as a convenient scheme of product classification. The PLC permits management to assign given products to the appropriate stages of acceptance by a given market: *introduction, growth, maturity, decline,* and *termination.* The actual classification of products by appropriate stages, however, is more art than science. The whole process is quite imprecise; but unsatisfactory as this may be, a useful classification can be achieved with management benefits that are clearly of value. This can be illustrated by examining the contribution of the PLC concept in the following marketing activities: sales forecasting, advertising, pricing, and marketing planning.

Applications of the PLC to sales forecasting

One of the most dramatic uses of the PLC in sales forecasting was its application in explaining the violent decline in sales of color TV during the credit crunch recession of 1969–70. This occurred after the experience of the 1966–67 mini-recession which had almost no effect on color TV sales that could be discerned through the usual "noise" of the available product flow data. A similar apparent insensitivity was demonstrated in 1958, in 1961, and again in 1966–67, with sales of portable dishwashers. However, it too was followed by a noticeable sales

FIGURE 2
Product life cycle

	Introduction	Growth	Maturity	Decline	Termination

MARKETING

Customers	Innovative/ high income	High income/ mass market	Mass market	Laggards/ special	Few
Channels	Few	Many	Many	Few	Few
Approach	Product	Label	Label	Specialized	Availability
Advertising	Awareness	Label superiority	Lowest price	Psychographic	Sparse
Competitors	Few	Many	Many	Few	Few

PRICING

Price	High	Lower	Lowest	Rising	High
Gross margins	High	Lower	Lowest	Low	Rising
Cost reductions	Few	Many	Slower	None	None
Incentives	Channel	Channel/ consumer	Consumer/ channel	Channel	Channel

PRODUCT

Configuration	Basic	Second generation	Segmented/ sophisticated	Basic	Stripped
Quality	Poor	Good	Superior	Spotty	Minimal
Capacity	Over	Under	Optimum	Over	Over

reduction in the 1969–71 period, with annual factory shipments as shown in Figure 3.

In early 1972 sales of both portable dishwashers and color TV sets showed a positive response to an improving economic climate, raising the question as to why both products had become vulnerable to economic contractions after having shown a great degree of independence of the business cycle during previous years. The answer to the question seems to lie in their stage in the product life cycle. In comparing the saturation of color TV and dishwashers, as shown in Figure 3, consider first the case of color TV sales.

We can ascertain that as late as 1966, saturation of color TV was approximately 8 percent. By late in 1969, however, saturation had swiftly increased to nearly 40 percent.

The same observation is true in the case of dishwashers—considered a mass market appliance only since 1965. This is the key to the explanation of both situations. At the early, introductory stages of their life cycles, both appliances were making large sales gains as the result of being adopted by consumers with high incomes. Later, when sales

FIGURE 3
Effect of recession on product sales

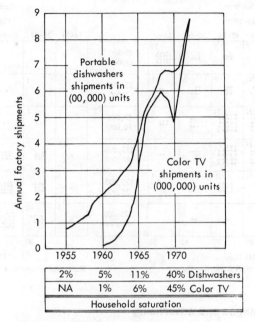

2%	5%	11%	40% Dishwashers
NA	1%	6%	45% Color TV
Household saturation			

Sources: AHAM. EIA. census

growth depended more upon adoption by the less affluent members of the mass market whose spending plans are modified by general economic conditions, the product sales began to correlate markedly to general economic circumstances.

It appears that big ticket consumer durables such as television sets and portable dishwashers tend to saturate as a function of customer income. This fact is illustrated by the data displayed in Figure 4, concerning refrigerators and compactors, where one can note the logical relationship between the two products as to the economic status of their most important customers and as to their position in the product life cycle. The refrigerator is a mature product while the compactor is the newest product in the major appliance family.

The refrigerator once was in the introduction stage and had marketing attributes similar to the compactor. The refrigerator's present marketing characteristics are a good guide to proper expectations for the compactor as it matures from the *introductory* stage through *growth* to *maturity*. One can anticipate that the compactor, the microwave oven, and even nondurables such as good quality wines, will someday be included in the middle income consumption patterns, and we will find their sales to be much more coincident with general economic cycles.

FIGURE 4
Purchase patterns (by age and income of households)

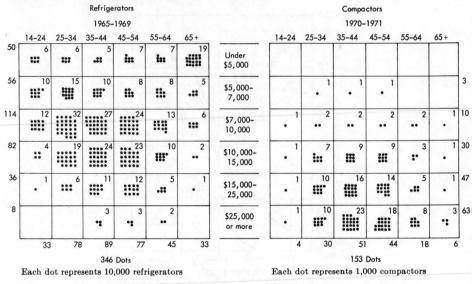

346 Dots
Each dot represents 10,000 refrigerators

153 Dots
Each dot represents 1,000 compactors

Product life stages and advertising

The concept of a new product filtering through income classes, combined with long-respected precepts of advertising, can result in new perspectives for marketing managers. The resulting observations are both strategic and tactical. New advertising objectives and new insights for copy points and media selection may be realized. Consider the advertising tasks by the following phases:

Phase 1

Introduction. The first objective is to make the best customer prospects aware that the new product or service is now available; to tell him what it does, what are the benefits, why claims are to be believed, and what will be the conditions of consumption.

Phase 2

Growth. The next objective is to saturate the mass market with the same selling points as used in Phase 1. In addition, it is to recognize that a particular brand of the product is clearly superior to other "inferior" substitutes while, at the same time, to provide a rationalization that this purchase is not merely a wasteful, luxury indulging activity but that it will make the consumer a better *something,* a better husband, mother, accountant, driver, and so forth.

Phase 3

Maturity. A new rationalization, respectability, is added, besides an intensification of brand superiority ("don't buy substitutes; get the real XYZ original, which incidentally, is *new* and *improved* . . ."). To a great extent, the *product* registration is dropped. Respectability is a strong requisite of the American lower class, which in this phase is the economic stratum containing the most important opportunities for sales gains. Companies do not abandon higher income customers, but they now match advertising to a variety of market segments instead of concentrating on only one theme for the market. Several distinct advertising programs are used. All elements of the marketing mix—product, price, sales promotion, advertising, trading and physical distribution channels—are focused on specific market segments.

Phase 4

Decline. Superior substitutes for a product generally will be adopted first by the people who before were the first to adopt the product in consideration. These people usually are from the upper economic and social classes. Advertising themes reflect this situation when they concentrate on special market segments such as West Coast families or "consumption societies" such as beer drinkers or apartment dwellers.

Product life stages and pricing

As a product progresses through all five stages of the life cycle shown in Figure 1, the price elasticity can be expected to undergo dramatic changes. Generally speaking, price elasticity of a relatively simple product will be low at first. Thus, when customers are drawn from the higher income classes, demand is relatively inelastic. Later, when most customers are in the lower income categories, greater price elasticity will exist.

Of course, increased price elasticity will not automatically lower prices during the growth stage of the PLC. It is in this growth stage, however, that per unit costs *are* most dramatically reduced because of the effect of the learning curve in engineering, production, and marketing. Rising volume and, more important, the *forecasts* of higher volumes, justify increased capital investments and higher fixed costs, which when spread over a larger number of units, thereby reduce unit costs markedly. New competitors surface with great rapidity in this stage as profits tend to increase dramatically.

Pricing in the mature phase of the PLC usually is found to be unsatisfactory, with no one's profit margins as satisfactory as before. Price competition is keener within the distribution channel in spite of the fact that relatively small price differences seldom translate into any change in aggregate consumer activity.

Product planning and the PLC

Curiously enough, the very configuration of the product takes on a classical pattern of evolution as it advances through the PLC. At first, the new device is designed for function alone; the initial design is sometimes crude by standards that will be applied in the future. As the product maturation process continues, performance sophistication increases. Eventually the product develops to the point where competitors are hardpressed to make meaningful differences which are perceptible to consumers.

As the product progresses through the product life cycle these modifications tend to describe a pattern of metamorphosis from "the ugly box" to a number of options. The adjustment cycle includes:

Part of house: the built-in look and function. Light fixtures, cooking stoves, wall safes, and furnaces are examples.

Furniture: a blending of the product into the home decor. This includes television, hi-fi consoles, radios, clocks, musical instruments, game tables, and so forth.

Portability: a provision for increased *presence* of the product through provisions for easier movement (rollers or compactness), or multiple unit ownership (wall clocks, radios, even refrigerators), or miniaturization for portability. Portability and *personalization,* such as the pocket knife and the wristwatch, can occur.

System: a combination of components into one unit with compatible uses and/or common parts for increased convenience, lower cost, or less space. Home entertainment centers including television, radio, hi-fi, refrigerator-freezers, combination clothes washer-dryers, clock radios, pocket knife-can-and-bottle openers are illustrative.

Similar changes can also be observed in the distribution channel. Products often progress from specialty outlets in the introductory stage to mass distribution outlets such as discount houses and contract buyers during the "maturity" and "decline" phases of the PLC. Interestingly enough, the process eventually is reversed. Buggy whips can still be found in some specialty stores and premium prices are paid for replicas of very old products.

CONCLUSION

The product life cycle is a useful concept. It is the equivalent of the periodic table of the elements in the physical sciences. The maturation of production technology and product configuration along with marketing programs proceeds in an orderly, somewhat predictable, course over time with the merchandising nature and marketing environment noticeably similar between products that are in the same stage of their life cycle. Its use as a concept in forecasting, pricing, advertising, product planning, and other aspects of marketing management can make it a valuable concept, although considerable amounts of judgment must be used in its application.

QUESTIONS

1. Smallwood indicates that the product life cycle can be a useful concept for grouping products into homogeneous families. Specifically, how can this characteristic help a marketing manager?
2. The product life cycle concept is applied to major purchases, such as appliances, in the article. Would it be as valuable for other consumer goods, such as grocery products? Would it be as useful for industrial goods? Why or why not? Be specific.
*3. Compare and contrast Levitt's (Reading 15) and Smallwood's ideas about using the product life cycle concept.

A basic requirement for effective marketing decisions is adequate information. The following article discusses the role that marketing information systems (MIS) could play in providing the necessary information. The authors also show that a MIS is an expansion rather than a replacement for traditional marketing research.

---

29. MARKETING INFORMATION SYSTEMS: A NEW DIMENSION FOR MARKETING RESEARCH*

Richard H. Brien and James E. Stafford

BUSINESS ENTERPRISE in the United States is caught in an ironic dilemma: our economic system generates a massive volume of data daily, and the rate of information generation appears to be increasing exponentially; yet most managers continue to complain that they have insufficient, inappropriate, or untimely information on which to base operating decisions.

---

* Reprinted with permission from the *Journal of Marketing*, published by the American Marketing Association, vol. 33, July 1968, pp. 19–23. At the time the article was published, Drs. Brien and Stafford were both Assistant Professors of Marketing at the University of Houston.

In 1958, Adrian McDonough observed: "Half the cost of running our economy is the cost of information. No other field offers such concentrated room for improvement as does information analysis."[1] Today, a decade later, the need for efficient information management is even greater, perhaps especially for marketing management since its job is to match the firm's products with dynamic markets. Marketing is inextricably caught up in the "Communications Revolution." The new era, "The Age of Information," will emphasize the information gathering and processing structure of the organization.

It is the contention of this article that the problem of securing adequate decision information for marketing must, and now can, be seen from a broader perspective than previously has been the case. In seeking to establish a new outlook on a matter it is often helpful to cast the problem in new terms. The new perspective from which this inquiry will be launched is that of "managerial systems." The process of developing timely, pertinent decision data for marketing management can now be characterized more meaningfully, even if somewhat prematurely, as the functioning of a "marketing information system" rather than simply as "marketing research."

THE ROLE OF MARKETING RESEARCH

Where does research fit into the marketing management process? If the marketing concept—with its emphasis on integrated decision-making—were widely accepted and implemented, the answer would be fairly clear. Research would be used to analyze specified relationships in the various functional areas of marketing, but the emphasis would be on its use in a coordinated, systematic fashion in order to make the total marketing strategy of the firm more efficient. (See Figure 1)

Research findings would serve at the outset as a basis for establishing objectives and formulating an apparently optimal plan. At this stage the role of research essentially would be *to predict* the results of alternative business decisions (for example, a "penetration" price versus a "skimming" price, or information dissemination through salesmen rather than through advertising). (See the "A" feedbacks in Figure 1)

If the research effort were extended full cycle, periodic post hoc studies would be conducted *to evaluate* the execution of specific aspects or phases of the marketing program. ("B" feedbacks in Figure 1) In this role, research would provide the basis for control, modification, or redirection of the overall program.

Control and modification (or redirection), in sum, represent *reformulation,* and the "B" feedbacks (evaluative) in fact would become "A" feedbacks (formulative), for the succeeding stage of the marketing pro-

---
[1] "Today's Office—Room for Improvement," *Dun's Review and Modern Industry,* vol. 73 (September 1958), p. 50.

FIGURE 1
The marketing management process and information flow

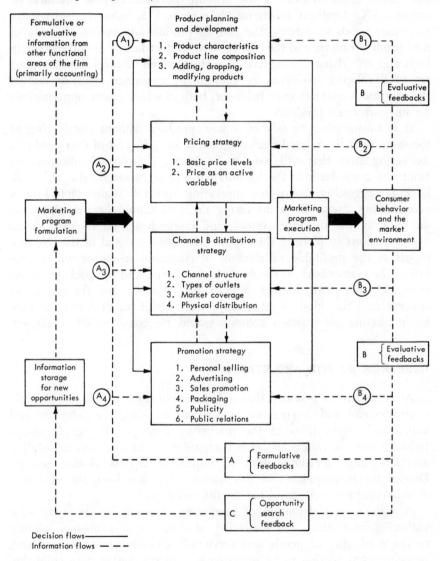

Decision flows————
Information flows — — —

gram. This condition simply underscores the fact that marketing management is an ongoing process, or—in the newer terminology—a dynamic system.

Formulative and evaluative information can also come *from inside the firm,* notably from the accounting department. This information flow typically is not considered part of "marketing research." It is definitely an integral part, however, of a marketing information system.

Under the marketing concept, research should also help to anticipate new profit opportunities for the firm in the form of new products or services. ("C" feedback in Figure 1) In many U.S. industries—especially consumer goods industries—the rate of product innovation, the rate of new product failure, and the cost of new product failure are all extremely high and still rising. To survive in such dynamic markets the firm must try to develop a sensitivity to changes in consumer behavior and in the conditions that influence behavior, both of which create opportunities for successful new products.

It is meaningless to talk of a new product without considering at the same time the related marketing decisions (the rest of that product's marketing mix) that will have to be made. This consideration would bring the cycle back to the formulative role of research (the "A" feedbacks), suggesting again that marketing research really *should be a coordinating agent.* Each marketing decision should be thought of as an input in the dynamic system, and research should be used as an agent to assist in phasing the inputs. The common goal of the decision inputs is the profitable satisfaction of consumer needs or wants; this brings the matter back to the marketing concept, and the package seems reasonably complete. In fact, if marketing research and the marketing concept had this kind of relationship in widespread practice, the case for marketing information systems would be considerably weakened.

RESEARCH BY FITS AND STARTS

A recent survey revealed that unfortunately there is still considerable confusion and wide divergence of opinion regarding the definition and managerial implications of the marketing concept.[2] Especially disappointing was the failure of many companies to cite customer-orientation and integrated decision-making as important aspects of the concept. One of the consequences of this narrow view has been the evolution of marketing research somewhat "by fits and starts."

A widely used definition of marketing research is "the systematic gathering, recording, and analyzing of data about problems relating to the marketing of goods and services."[3] Unfortunately, the research procedure has tended to be unsystematic, to emphasize data collection per se instead of the development of decision-pertinent information, and to concern itself with isolated problems almost on an ad hoc basis. "There is a widespread failure to visualize marketing research as a con-

---

[2] Martin L. Bell, *Marketing: Concepts and Strategy* (Boston: Houghton Mifflin Company, 1966), p. 10.

[3] Committee on Definitions of the American Marketing Association, Ralph S. Alexander, Chairman, *Marketing Definitions: A Glossary of Marketing Terms* (Chicago: American Marketing Association, 1962), p. 16–17.

tinuing process of inquiry in which executives are helped to think more effectively."[4]

TOWARD MARKETING INFORMATION SYSTEMS

The systems approach to marketing management is breathing new life into marketing research. The emphasis that systems theory places on interaction and integration in the decision-making process makes it clear that the particularistic, "brush-fire" approach that has characterized traditional marketing research is rapidly becoming obsolete. What is needed is "a *marketing intelligence* system tailored to the needs of each marketer. Such a system would serve as the ever-alert nerve center of the marketing operation."[5]

The "nerve center" concept is the theme used by Philip Kotler who has drafted a blueprint for a new organizational unit within the firm, the Marketing Information and Analysis Center (MIAC).[6] MIAC represents a complete overhaul and expansion of the marketing research department into a comprehensive executive marketing information service.

Definition of MIS

Despite minor variations in terminology, it is clear that many of the critics of the narrow view of the role of marketing research are advocating a common concept—"the concept of careful search to generate a flow of ideas and information which will help executives make better decisions."[7]

The notion of a sustained flow of decision-information leads to the term, "marketing information system," defined as follows:

A structured, interacting complex of persons, machines and procedures designed to generate an orderly flow of pertinent information collected from both intra- and extra-firm sources, for use as the bases for decision-making in specified responsibility areas of marketing management.

It will be helpful to take a closer look at the essential components of the definition: first, a *structured, interacting complex*. The important notion here is that the marketing information system is a carefully developed master plan for information flow, with explicit objectives and a home in the formal organization. Successful information systems will

---

[4] Joseph W. Newman, "Put Research Into Marketing Decisions," *Harvard Business Review*, vol. 40 (March–April 1962), p. 106.

[5] Lee Adler, "Systems Approach to Marketing," *Harvard Business Review*, vol. 45 (May–June 1967), p. 110.

[6] Philip Kotler, "A Design for the Firm's Marketing Nerve Center," *Business Horizons*, vol. 9 (Fall 1966), p. 70.

[7] Same reference as footnote 4, p. 106.

not evolve spontaneously within the organization, nor will they result if their creation is left exclusively to information technicians. Donald Cox and Robert Good point out that a characteristic common to each of the companies that so far has had success with its marketing information system is the *support of top management*.[8]

A marketing information system is a structured, interacting complex of *persons, machines, and procedures*, requiring the coordinated efforts of many departments and individuals, including:

Top management.
Marketing management, brand management.
Sales management.
New product groups.
Market research personnel.
Control and finance departments.
Systems analysts and designers.
Operations researchers, statisticians, and model builders.
Programmers.
Computer equipment experts and suppliers.[9]

It is clear that in traditional management terms both line and staff personnel inevitably will be involved in any marketing information system. Decision-makers will have to be a great deal more precise in specifying their information needs, and a complete crew of information specialists will be called upon to satisfy them.

What is not clear is the determination of the most effective organization pattern for implementing and administering the system. In fact, the organization problem is probably the greatest deterrent to the more rapid and widespread diffusion of the information systems concept. The question, like many others in the area of organization structure, is not generically answerable; each firm's system will have to be tailor-made.

One of the major factors that makes it meaningful to talk of information systems is the tremendous improvement since World War II in information handling *technology and machinery*. The building of the first primitive computer, only slightly more than two decades ago, has been designated the beginning of a revolution in the information sciences.

There has been some confusion, however, about the relationship between computers and information systems. They are not synonymous; nor is either the sine qua non of the other. The system is the structure and procedure of the entire organization's communicative process; the computer is a processing device that may or may not be included in the information system.

---

[8] Donald F. Cox and Robert E. Good, "How to Build a Marketing Information System," *Harvard Business Review*, no. 3, vol. 45 (May–June 1967), p. 149.
[9] Same reference as footnote 8.

The consideration of the use of computers has, however, forced many organizations to pay explicit attention to their information systems. "The flexibility and power of the new tool, as well as its great cost, has caused many managers to think for the first time of formally planning their information flows and processing functions."[10]

Business information systems include many machines other than the computer and some of them promise to have an impact on future systems that will rival the computer's influence. In particular, data copying, storage, and retrieval machines have greatly expanded management's information processing capability.

It is estimated that in 1966 some half a million duplicating machines spewed out 400 billion copies.[11] At the same time, a new document storage system was developed permitting the storage of up to 500,000 single-page documents on a single 7,200 foot reel of videotape. This means that roughly 20,000 articles or chapters from books could be stored on one reel with a retrieval time measured in seconds.

But the physical capacity to generate and process fantastic volumes of data at very high speed is an asset only if the types of data to be gathered and the sources from which they are to be elicited are carefully prescribed. The definition of a marketing information system alleged that it is *designed to generate an orderly flow of pertinent information, collected from both intra- and extra-firm sources.*

Computer-based reporting systems

Internal information includes fundamental records of costs, shipments, and sales and any analyses of these that can be made to measure the firm's performance (distribution cost analysis, market shares by product and region, and the like). The computer and more progressive accounting departments that see their role as the provision of management information rather than as simply "scorekeeping" have been two of the most important contributors to the integration of such data, on a regular basis, into the marketing information flow.

Many companies are experimenting with "computerized marketing information" in an attempt to shorten the delay between the performance of their products in the market and the receipt of performance reports. In doing so, they stand to sharpen their strategy by gaining valuable lead-time over their competitors.

One producer and nation-wide marketer of consumer goods gets monthly reports on 3,000 key accounts 20 days earlier than before, thanks

---

[10] Frederick G. Withington, *The Use of Computers in Business Organizations* (Reading, Mass.: Addison-Wesley, 1966), p. 3.

[11] E. B. Weiss, "The Communications Revolution and How It Will Affect All Business and All Marketing," a special issue reprinted from *Advertising Age* (Chicago: Advertising Publications, Inc., 1966), p. 22.

to computer-based reporting systems. Each account is compared with its performance at the same point in time during the previous year and with the company's current total volume in the particular market zone. Also provided are gross daily tabulations for each package size of each brand by geographic district.

When the doors open each morning at another company, a major grocery products manufacturer, marketing management has a complete sales analysis and inventory position as of closing time the previous day. The data are fed by teletypewriter from the company's sales offices and warehouses to a central computer which analyzes the day's orders. In addition, each salesman is required to "mark sense" his daily call reports and send them in to headquarters each evening for computer analysis. Once accumulated, these reports on the in-store impact of frontings, shelf positions, and point-of-sale materials provide marketing management with an up-to-date retail product-movement picture.[12]

Integrating research into the MIS

The most important notion in these examples is that a timely, basic data flow has been established to chart the firm's progress and raise warning signals when there is a marketing malfunction. Such a framework will make additional data needs much clearer, allowing special supplementary information to be collected, *as needed,* from external sources through surveys, panels or experiments. At this point, then, the proper order will have been established: *the need for conducting "marketing research" and the technique to be used will be determined in the context of specific managerial information requirements.*

Such an approach will help assure that any data gathered are *pertinent,* another important aspect of the definition of a marketing information system. It is perhaps a more grievous sin to collect unnecessary or redundant information than it is to fail to collect any data at all about a particular matter. Superfluous information costs money to develop and wastes decision-makers' time; it represents a serious misallocation of managerial resources. It must be remembered, the definition asserts, that the data generated are to be used as *the bases for decision-making in specified responsibility areas of marketing management.*

Thus, the questions of the types of data the information system is to generate and the sources from which it is to elicit the data really can be answered only in the framework of a careful designation of the organizational decision-structure and the specification of the information requirements for the decision process. In fact, according to many organizational theorists, information processing and decision-making are inseparable in practice. A decision occurs only on "the receipt of some kind of communication, it consists of a complicated process of combining

---

[12] Same reference as footnote 11, pp. 13–14.

communications from various sources and it results in the transmission of further communications."[13]

Mr. Paul Funk, executive vice-president of McCann/ITSM, contends that marketing information management *is* the basic business of business: "Only by putting together an over-all construction of the total marketing process; only by identifying—and in most instances by visualizing—interrelationships, information flows, concurrent and sequential work patterns and critical decision points can one truly grasp control of the bewildering and complex range of activities engaged in by the present-day major corporation."[14]

The pursuit of marketing information systems, then, really involves much more than expanding and automating the data gathering process. It is an inextricable part of the larger pursuit of more efficient forms and methods of organization for marketing management.

We are running late

There is ample evidence that marketing decision-making is becoming more complex, making the need for a systematic approach to information management all the greater. First, there is a growing complexity of the areas that have to be managed, largely a function of the tendency toward larger scale enterprise. Second, as expanded marketing effort takes the firm across existing environmental frontiers, whether geographic, economic or social (or, more likely, all three), the information needs of the enterprise are substantially compounded. It is highly likely that the most crucial constraint currently imposed on the growth of international marketing, for example, is the dearth of pertinent decision-information.

But perhaps the most compelling argument for marketing information systems is the "Information Explosion" itself. The world's store of knowledge has allegedly doubled during the past decade and is expected at least to double again in the next decade.

Information, including management information, is growing by the microsecond and even nanosecond. We cannot turn off the flow. We had therefore better learn to control it—and we are already running late.[15]

QUESTIONS

1. Define briefly, in your own words, what is meant by a "marketing information system."

---

[13] John T. Dorsey, Jr., "A Communication Model for Administration," *Administrative Science Quarterly*, vol. 2 (December 1957), p. 309.

[14] "Why Industrial Marketers Aren't Using Computers," *Industrial Marketing*, vol. 51 (November 1966), pp. 88–89.

[15] Howell M. Estes, "Will Managers Be Overwhelmed by the Information Explosion?," *Armed Forces Management*, vol. 13 (December 1966), p. 84.

2. Explain how a marketing information system could fit into the marketing management process?

3. How does a marketing information system differ from the traditional marketing research activity of the firm?

*4. Would a MIS have a different role to play in shortage or inflationary times? Explain. (See Readings 14 and 25.)

The contribution approach to cost accounting can relate products, channels, and/or other marketing components to the profitability of market segments. Using the techniques discussed in this article, a marketing manager can plan and control his decisions for the component being analyzed and also make collateral adjustments in other elements of his marketing mix.

---

30. PROFITABILITY ANALYSIS BY MARKET SEGMENTS*

Leland L. Beik and Stephen L. Buzby

By TRACING sales revenues to market segments and relating these revenues to marketing costs, the marketing manager can improve and control his decision making with respect to the firm's profit objective.

First expressed by Smith in 1956, the concept of market segmentation has since been elaborated in many different ways.[1] It has recently been defined by Kotler as ". . . the subdividing of a market into homogeneous subsets of customers, where any subset may conceivably be selected as a market target to be reached with a distinct marketing mix."[2] The underlying logic is based on the assumption that:

* Reprinted with permission from the *Journal of Marketing*, published by the American Marketing Association, vol. 37, July 1973, pp. 48–53. At the time the article was published, Dr. Beik was Professor of Marketing, The Pennsylvania State University, and Dr. Buzby was Assistant Professor of Marketing, University of Indiana.

[1] Wendell R. Smith, "Product Differentiation and Market Segmentation as Alternative Marketing Strategies," *Journal of Marketing*, vol. 21 (July 1956), pp. 3–8; and James F. Engel, Henry F. Fiorillo, and Murray A. Cayley, eds., *Market Segmentation: Concepts and Applications* (New York: Holt, Rinehart and Winston, Inc., 1972).

[2] Philip Kotler, *Marketing Management*, Second Edition (Englewood Cliffs, New ersey: Prentice-Hall, Inc., 1972), p. 166.

. . . the market for a product is made up of customers who differ either in their own characteristics or in the nature of their environment in such a way that some aspect of their demand for the product in question also differs. The strategy of market segmentation involves the tailoring of the firm's product and/or marketing program to these differences. By modifying either of these, the firm is attempting to increase profits by converting a market with heterogeneous demand characteristics into a set of markets that although they differ from one another, are internally more homogeneous than before.[3]

The concept of market segmentation may be used for strategic alignment of the firm's productive capacities with its existing and potential markets. By analyzing market needs and the firm's ability to serve those needs, the basic long-run policies of the firm can be developed. Through choice of target segments, competition may be minimized; through selective cultivation, the firm's competitive posture may be greatly improved.

For both strategic and tactical decisions, marketing managers may profit by knowing the impact of the marketing mix upon the target segments at which marketing efforts are aimed. If the programs are to be responsive to environmental change, a monitoring system is needed to locate problems and guide adjustments in marketing decisions. Tracing the profitability of segments permits improved pricing, selling, advertising, channel, and product management decisions. The success of marketing policies and programs may be appraised by a dollar and cents measure of profitability by segment.

Managerial accounting techniques have dealt with the profitability of products, territories, and some customer classes; but a literature search has revealed not one serious attempt to assess the relative profitability of market segments.[4] Although the term "segment" has a history of use in accounting, this use implies a segment of the business rather than a special partitioning of consumers or industrial users for marketing analysis. Even when classifying customers, accounting classes are formed by frequency and size of order, location, credit rating, and other factors, most of which are related to controlling internal costs or to assessing financial profit.[5]

After indicating the value for marketing decision making, this article will delineate a framework for cost accounting by market segments. An industrial product example is constructed to demonstrate the process

---

[3] Ronald E. Frank, "Market Segmentation Research: Findings and Implications," in *Applications of the Sciences in Marketing Management*, Frank M. Bass, Charles W. King, and Edgar A. Pessemier, eds. (New York: John Wiley & Sons, Inc., 1968), p. 39.

[4] Closest to the present analysis and perhaps the best summary of the state of the art is Charles H. Sevin, *Marketing Productivity Analysis* (New York: McGraw-Hill Book Company, 1965).

[5] Robert B. Miner, "Distribution Costs," in *Marketing Handbook*, Albert W. Frey, ed. (New York: The Ronald Press Company, 1965); see especially pp. 23·17 and 23·32.

and to spell out the features of the contribution approach to cost accounting as applied to accounting for segment profitability. Further discussion extends the concept to a consumer situation and specifies difficulties that may attend full-scale application of the technique. The expectation is that the technique will better control marketing costs and improve marketing decisions.

Market segmentation and its utility

To have value for managerial judgments. Bell notes that market segments should: (1) be readily identified and measured, (2) contain adequate potential, (3) demonstrate effective demand, (4) be economically accessible, and (5) react uniquely to marketing effort.[6] For present purposes, the key criterion for choosing the bases for segmenting a given market is the ability to trace sales and costs to the segments defined. Allocating sales and costs is the most stringent requirement and limitation of profitability accounting as used to support marketing decisions.

Among the many possible bases for market segmentation, the analysis can be accomplished using widely recognized geographic, demographic, and socioeconomic variables.[7] Many of these, such as geographic units and population or income figures, provide known universe classifications against which to compare company sales and cost performance. Other bases of segmentation such as buyer usage rate, expected benefits, or psychological or sociological characteristics of consumers typically require research to match their distribution, directly or indirectly, with company sales and costs.

Given proper segmentation, separate products (or channels or other elements of the marketing mix) can serve as the primary basis for cost and revenue allocation. Knowledge of profit by segments then contributes directly to decisions concerning the product line and adjustment of sales, advertising, and other decision variables. The process is illustrated in the following industrial example.

A matrix system can be developed as part of marketing planning to partition segments for profitability analysis.[8] A company with lines of computers, calculators, and adding machines might first divide its market into territories as in the upper section of Figure 1. The cell representing adding machines in the eastern market might next be sorted by product items and customer classes. The chief product preference of each com-

[6] Martin L. Bell, *Marketing: Concepts and Strategy*, 2d ed. (Boston: Houghton Mifflin Company, 1972), p. 185.

[7] See William M. Weilbacher, "Standard Classification of Consumer Characteristics," *Journal of Marketing*, vol. 31 (January 1967), p. 27.

[8] See William J. E. Crissy and Robert M. Kaplan, "Matrix Models for Marketing Planning," *MSU Business Topics*, vol. 11 (Summer 1963), p. 48. The matrix "targeting" treatment is also familiar to readers of basic marketing texts by E. J. McCarthy or G. D. Downing.

pany class is noted by an important benefit segmentation within the cells of the lower section of Figure 1.

FIGURE 1
Matrix breakdown by products and segments

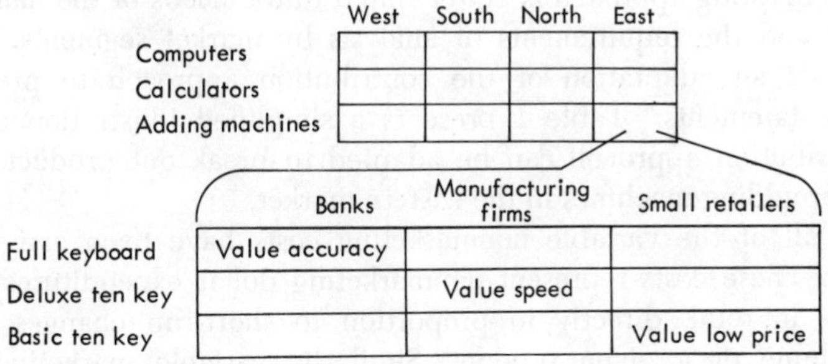

Since the segments react differently to product variations and other marketing activities, it is advantageous to isolate profit by product for each market segment. Using this information, the marketing manager can specifically tailor product policies to particular market segments and judge the reaction of segments to increased or decreased marketing efforts over time. Decision adjustments and control of marketing costs interact to improve product line management directly and other decisions indirectly.

In theory, segment profitability analysis is worthwhile only where decisions adjusting the marketing mix add incremental profits that exceed the costs of the extra analysis. In practice, information concerning the profitability of marketing decisions has been so sparse that the analysis is likely to be profitable where allocations to market segments are approximate and fail to approach theoretical perfection.

Marketing cost analysis

In its simplest form, marketing cost analysis relates the cost of marketing activities to sales revenues in order to measure profits. A profit and loss statement must be constructed for any marketing component (e.g., product, channel) being analyzed. The approach consists of dividing the firm's basic costs (e.g., salaries, rent) into their functional categories (e.g., selling, advertising). The functional category amounts are then assigned within the appropriate marketing classifications.

The actual form of the profit and loss statements will depend upon the nature of the company being analyzed, the purpose of the marketing analysis, and the records available. The form of statement will also depend upon the accounting technique used to assign costs to the marketing components under study. One might use a full-cost approach,

assigning both direct and indirect costs across the marketing classifications on the best available bases. Alternatively, one might use a direct-
cost approach and assign direct costs only, avoiding arbitrary assignment
of fixed or overhead costs. Most marketing sources have utilized the
full- and direct-cost approaches.

A third costing approach is better suited to the needs of the marketing
manager and the requirements of analysis by market segments. Essentially, it is an adaptation of the contribution approach to preparing
financial statements.[9] Table 1 presents a simplified illustration of how
the contribution approach can be adapted to break out product profitability for adding machines in the eastern market.

First, all of the variable nonmarketing costs have been assigned to
products. These costs represent nonmarketing dollar expenditures which
fluctuate, in total, directly in proportion to short-run changes in the
sales volume of a given product. Similarly, variable marketing costs
have been deducted to produce variable product contribution margins
identical to those which would result from a direct costing approach.

The remaining marketing costs have been broken down into two categories—assignable and nonassignable. The assignable costs represent
dollar expenditures of a fixed or discretionary nature for which reasonably valid bases exist for allocating them to specific products. For example, the assignment of salesmen's salaries in Table 1 might be based
on Sevin's recommendation to use "selling time devoted to each product,
as shown by special sales-call reports or special studies."[10] The marketing
manager's salary could be assigned on the basis of personal records
indicating the amount of time devoted to the management of each product. Product advertising would be assigned by reference to the actual
amount spent on advertising each product.

The use of the actual dollar level of sales was purposely avoided
in choosing the allocation bases for the assignable costs in Table 1.
Horngren, among others, has stated that when dealing with fixed or
discretionary costs, "The costs of efforts are independent of the results
actually obtained, in the sense that the costs are programmed by management, not determined by sales."[11]

The nonassignable marketing costs represent dollar expenditures of
a fixed or discretionary nature for which there are no valid bases for
assignment to products. Consequently, institutional advertising has not
been assigned to the products to avoid confounding the product profitability margins which would result from the arbitrary allocation of this

---

[9] See Charles R. Horngren, *Cost Accounting: A Managerial Emphasis*, 2d ed.
(Englewood Cliffs, New Jersey: Prentice-Hall, Inc., 1967); and Ralph L. Day
and Peter D. Bennett, "Should Salesmen's Compensation be Geared to Profits?"
Journal of Marketing, vol. 26 (October 1962), pp. 6–9.

[10] Same reference as footnote 4, p. 13.

[11] Same reference as footnote 9, p. 381.

TABLE 1
Product productivity analysis—contribution approach

	Company total	Full keyboard	Deluxe ten key	Basic ten key
Net sales	$10,000	$5,000	$3,000	$2,000
Variable manufacturing costs	5,100	2,500	1,375	1,225
Mfg. contribution	$ 4,900	$2,500	$1,625	$ 775
Marketing costs				
Variable:				
Sales commissions	450	225	135	90
Variable contribution	$ 4,450	$2,275	$1,490	$ 685
Assignable:				
Salaries—salesmen.	1,600	770	630	200
Salary—marketing manager	100	50	25	25
Product advertising.	1,000	670	200	130
Total.	$ 2,700	$1,490	$ 855	$ 355
Product contribution	$ 1,750	$ 785	$ 635	$ 330
Nonassignable:				
Institutional advertising	150			
Marketing contribution	$ 1,600			
Fixed-joint costs:				
General administration.	300			
Manufacturing.	900			
Total.	$ ·1,200			
Net profits	$ 400			

cost. Since the primary purpose is calculating marketing related product contribution margins, the remaining nonmarketing costs can be taken as a deduction from the total marketing contribution margin to produce a net profit figure for the firm.

Although the preceding example was purposely simplified, the framework is sufficiently flexible to handle different objectives and more complex problems. If the firm in Table 1 were a single product firm, for example, the three customer classes (banks, manufacturers, and retailers) could easily be substituted for primary emphasis in place of the products. The analysis would differ only through variations in the treatment of fixed, variable, and assignable costs required by the new objective. That assignability changes with objective may be illustrated by the fact that product advertising costs can often be assigned to products but rarely to customer classes.

To aid in handling more complex problems, a discussion of common bases for assigning a wide range of marketing costs may be found in Sevin.[12] In some instances, the approach can be further improved by application of mathematical programming to assign costs to the marketing

---

[12] Same reference as footnote 4, chapter 2.

components.[13] Budgetary data and marketing lags could also be introduced to upgrade the analysis.[14]

Costing by segments

In particular, the framework of the contribution approach may be applied to costing by segments. Table 2 extends the product analysis of Table 1. Recall that the segments are partitioned by territorial, customer class, and product benefit criteria although the primary customer class names are used to identify segments in the table. Instead of tracing the sales of each product to all three customer classes, one simplifying device is to identify the primary benefit sought by a customer class as segment sales and to combine sales of the given product to the other customer classes as nonsegment sales. For example, sales of the full-keyboard adding machine to banks become segment sales, while sales to large manufacturing firms or to retailers are nonsegment sales. This device is appropriate where nontarget sales are expected to be minimal; otherwise more columns can be added to the table.

Where sales revenues can be traced directly to customers, customer classes, and territories and where marketing costs can be similarly traced, the analysis is straightforward. Where the less tangible benefit segmentation is used, sales analysis or marketing research must measure the degree to which benefits are related to each customer class. If sales analysis shows that banks purchase 75% of the full-keyboard sales because they value accuracy while manufacturers and retailers account for the remaining 25%, both revenues and sales commissions may be prorated accordingly. This allocation is employed in Table 2.

To illustrate a few marketing implications, it might be noted that over one-half of the full-keyboard profit contribution actually comes from nonsegment sales rather than from the primary target segment. The nonsegment profitability results in part from low personal selling and absence of advertising costs. An opportunity possibly exists in further promotion, perhaps to large manufacturing firms. Had the table completed the analysis for purchases of full-keyboard machines by manufacturers and retailers, the actual segment of opportunity could be pinpointed. If institutional or other possible sales proved substantial during further classification, a new segment of opportunity might be identified.

Quite obviously, the eastern banking segment has a low profit contri-

---

[13] William J. Baumol and Charles H. Sevin, "Marketing Costs and Mathematical Programming," in *Management Information: A Quantitative Accent*, Thomas Williams and Charles Griflin, eds. (Homewood, Illinois: Richard D. Irwin, Inc., 1967), pp. 176–190.

[14] Richard A. Feder, "How to Measure Marketing Performance," in *Readings in Cost Accounting, Budgeting, and Control*, 3d ed., W. Thomas Jr., ed. (Cincinnati, Ohio: South-Western Publishing Co., 1968), pp. 650–668.

TABLE 2
Segment productivity analysis—contribution approach

	Company total	Full keyboard		Deluxe 10-key		Basic 10-key retail seg.
		Bank seg.	Nonseg.	Mfg. seg.	Nonseg.	
Net sales	$10,000	$3,750	$1,250	$2,550	$450	$2,000
Variable manufacturing costs	5,100	1,875	625	1,169	206	1,225
Mfg. contribution	$ 4,900	$1,875	$ 625	$1,381	$244	$ 775
Marketing costs						
Variable:						
Sales commissions	450	169	56	115	20	90
Variable contribution	$ 4,450	$1,706	$ 569	$1,266	$224	$ 685
Assignable:						
Salaries—salesmen	1,600	630	140	420	210	200
Salary—marketing manager . . .	100	38	12	19	6	25
Product advertising.	1,000	670	-0-	200	-0-	130
Total.	$ 2,700	$1,338	$ 152	$ 639	$216	$ 355
Segment contribution	$ 1,750	$ 368	$ 417	$ 627	$ 8	$ 330
Nonassignable:						
Institutional advertising	150					
Marketing contribution	$ 1,600					
Fixed-joint costs:						
General administration.	300					
Manufacturing	900					
Total.	$ 1,200					
Net profits	$ 400					

bution considering the level of marketing effort expended. Table 2 deals with one sample area and product class, and a comparison with other area banking segments might prove enlightening. Perhaps marketing costs could be reduced in the eastern segment if sales were up to par. Or if sales were comparatively low, marketing effort (price, personal selling, advertising) could be reallocated to meet competition more effectively.

Similar analysis can be applied to the manufacturing and retailing segments of Table 2, and to the territories and products not incorporated in the present illustration. The advantage over standard sales analysis is that a profit rather than a volume measure is applied and that variations in marketing costs and sales response are taken into account.

Marketing productivity: Consumer segments

The previous example has been simplified so that minimum tables serve to explain the technique. Segment analysis becomes complex as more than two or three criteria are used for partitioning and as additional criteria are considered for different classes of marketing decisions.

A further example adds realism and extends the concept to a consumer situation.

A company that sells snowmobiles is likely to have some special channel problems. To control channel management, meteorological data permit primary and secondary snow belts to be mapped across the U.S. and Canada. Sales analysis or research could show how to allocate purchases among consumers in major metropolitan, city, town, and rural areas. Further analysis could determine patronage among department stores, automotive dealers, farm equipment dealers, marinas, and other classes of outlets. Sales to resorts for rentals might be included as a segment or analyzed separately. Finally, the several analyses could map sales into geographical units. Segmenting by snow conditions, population density, outlets patronized, and dwelling area and then allocating revenues and costs to the segments would point outlet selection and channel adjustments toward the more profitable outlets in favorable population and snow-belt locations.

By collecting and analyzing warranty card information, snowmobile purchasers could be classified as to family life cycle, social status, or other variables. This data would probe the profit potential of appealing to young families, selected social classes, or possibly even to hunters, sailing enthusiasts, and other outdoors people. Dates on the warranty cards would help adjust the timing of promotions in advance of the snow season or to balance the pre-Christmas advertising in line with purchase habits of its customer segments. Having targeted promotion on the basis of past data, current warranty card information, and revenue and cost information, the profitability of each target segment could be determined.

Analyzing the profitability of advertising or price decisions involves special problems in tracing sales and costs. If segments have been defined on tangible bases, say area and dealer patronage, the difficulty might be overcome by setting up an experiment.[15] Variations of advertising messages, local media, and possibly price would serve as treatments in segments matched to control other variables. Recording segment revenues and treatment costs would constitute a profit measure of selected advertising and/or price decisions. Experiments may thus be used with segment cost analysis to plan corporate marketing programs.

Managerial implications

Given responsible means of partitioning market segments, major elements of the marketing mix may be segregated for analysis using the contribution approach to cost accounting. An example has been employed to show how segment profitability can be measured for items in a product line thereby contributing directly to product management

---

[15] Same reference as footnote 4, chapters 6, 7, and 8.

decisions. By analyzing the profit and loss statements for the costs of other marketing efforts, additional adjustments can be made in other decisions such as personal selling and advertising. A further example has indicated how channel and other marketing management problems can be similarly gauged by a profit measure for a consumer product and consumer segments.

Several major problems have to be met in applying costing techniques to market segments. One difficulty is choosing productive bases for segmentation, and limiting analysis to a manageable number of bases is another. Although some bases are obvious from experience, they remain product specific, and criteria for choice are not fully developed. Another major problem is obtaining data for the less tangible modes of segmentation, particularly data that permit assignment of sales revenues and costs in accord with each base used for segment definition.

Recognizing and solving problems, however, often leads to further improvements. For example, many of the behavioral applications to marketing imply use in segment analysis but are difficult to relate to other marketing variables on any basis other than judgment. As limitations of source data are overcome, profit accounting by segments may add to the marketing utility of behavioral advances.

Costing by market segments promises improvement in marketing efficiency by way of better planning of expenditures and control of costs. Upon documenting reasons for today's soaring marketing costs, Weiss comments over and over that marketing costs are resistant to sophisticated cost analysis and that marketing cost controls are inadequate in modern corporations.[16] Although not calculated to stem such pressures as inflation, cost accounting by market segments can control selling, advertising, packaging, and other marketing costs in relation to profit potentials. Perhaps even greater value stems from the potential ability to fine-tune product offerings and other marketing decisions to the requirements of well-defined consumer segments. As part of the material regularly supplied to marketing managers, market segment profitability analysis could easily become a key component of marketing information systems of the future.

QUESTIONS

1. Briefly explain the authors' procedure for calculating the profitability of market segments.
2. Could the process discussed by Beik and Buzby be used to help select target markets? Why or why not?
° 3. Is the Beik and Buzby approach really any different than the "total cost approach" discussed by Lewis (Reading 21)? Explain.

---

[16] E. B. Weiss, "Pooled Marketing: Antidote for Soaring Marketing Costs," *Advertising Age*, vol. 43 (November 13, 1972), pp. 63–64.

This article discusses how to conduct a marketing audit. This is still an "art," requiring much judgment. But an organized approach can be helpful, and Grashof presents a checklist of factors to consider and some forms which can help organize the evaluation process.

---

31. CONDUCTING AND USING A MARKETING AUDIT*

John F. Grashof

OVER THE PAST several years, many firms have come to realize the necessity of "keeping tabs on" and evaluating various functions within the firm. These control efforts often take the form of audits. For example, many firms conduct management audits to assess their management structures and the strengths and weaknesses of their managers and other employees. The accounting profession conducts audits of financial records for purposes of internal control as well as for the protection of outside investors and lenders. And, during the last couple of years, increasing attention has been given to the social audit, an evaluation of the firm's social responsibility.

With the increasing recognition of marketing, and particularly marketing strategies, as central to the success of all businesses more attention has been given to the evaluation of this category of a firm's activities. In response to the need for evaluation, more and more academicians and practitioners are calling for marketing audits.[1] "A marketing audit," suggests Martin Bell, "is a systematic and thorough examination of a company's marketing position."[2] More formally, Abe Shuchman defines a marketing audit as:

. . . a systematic, critical, and impartial review and appraisal of the total marketing operation: of the basic objectives and policies and the assumptions which underlie them as well as the methods, procedures, personnel, and organization employed to implement the policies and achieve the objectives.[3]

---

* An original contribution. At the time of writing, Dr. Grashof was Associate Professor and Chairman of the Department of Marketing of Temple University.

[1] Philip Kotler, *Marketing Management: Analysis, Planning and Control* 2d ed. (Englewood Cliffs, N.J.: Prentice-Hall Inc., 1972), p. 774.

[2] Martin L. Bell, *Marketing: Concepts and Strategies* 2d ed. (Boston: Houghton Mifflin Co., 1972), p. 428.

[3] Abe Shuchman, "The Marketing Audit: Its Nature, Purposes, and Problems," *Analyzing and Improving Marketing Performance*, Report no. 32, (New York: American Management Association, 1959), p. 13.

MARKETING AUDITS: WHY, WHEN, WHAT AND WHO

Are marketing audits really necessary?

Marketing audits are necessary for a number of important reasons, not the least of which is the complex and continually changing environment of the modern corporation. As the marketplace, the competitive scene, and the economic and political climates change, the firm should study its marketing activities to determine what, if any, changes should be made.[4] The marketing audit can be a viable approach to structuring the evaluation of strategies in a meaningful way. By examining the firm's strategies relative to its competitors and the market, and with respect to internal consistency, the audit can highlight strengths and weaknesses.

Audits are typically evaluations of past behavior and present practices, and marketing audits do perform this function. However, marketing audits can reveal not only present weaknesses, but also may identify potential problems and, thus, may play an important role with respect to future planning.[5] Marketing managers are typically more concerned that the goals and directions of their marketing efforts are correct than they are that their past performance has been good.[6] Through a critical evaluation of the objectives of the firm, and the plans and programs designed to meet these objectives, the marketing audit serves a role similar to a pro forma or forecasted income statement.

How often should a marketing audit be conducted?

Most authors suggest that audits be conducted on a periodic basis. The length of time between audits may vary among firms, but audits should be a routine part of the planning process of a firm. Audits, in addition to those normally scheduled, may be conducted as desired by management, but such additional audits should not replace those regularly scheduled.

Shuchman suggests that audits can be profitably conducted in extremely good times, and may be absolutely necessary in times of crisis.[7] For example, American bicycle manufacturers were largely unprepared for the sudden upsurge in sales that occurred in the early 1970's. The combined impacts of increased concern for physical fitness and the growing environmental problems led to the rediscovery of the bicycle by many adults. Failure to anticipate the increasing sales trend left the industry saddled with a child-oriented product line and insufficient production facilities. Thus, the door was opened for an influx of foreign

---

[4] Shuchman, p. 15.
[5] Shuchman, pp. 12–14.
[6] Bell, p. 429.
[7] Shuchman, pp. 15–16.

imports. Apparently, the U.S. firms had been lulled into complacency by years of steady, profitable sales. Had these firms been conducting periodic marketing audits, it is likely that they would have been better prepared for the rapid increase in sales.

What is the best way to approach a marketing audit?

There are a variety of approaches to conducting a marketing audit. One decision that must be made is whether to examine generally the whole range of marketing activities or to look at one section in detail. Richard Crisp defines these as the horizontal and vertical audits:

> The *horizontal* audit examines all of the elements that go into the marketing whole, with particular emphasis upon the relative importance of these elements and the 'mix' between them. It is often referred to as a 'marketing mix' audit. The *vertical* audit singles out certain functional elements of the marketing operation and subjects them to thorough, searching study and evaluation.[8]

Which approach is best for a particular firm at a point in time must be determined by that firm. The choice will depend on a number of factors, including where the firm is experiencing success and where it is having problems. However, in those cases where the firm selects a vertical audit it must not completely ignore evaluation of the mix aspect of its marketing program.

Who should conduct the marketing audit?

The selection of an individual or team to be responsible for conducting the marketing audit can obviously have a significant impact on the quality of the completed evaluation. The auditor should be unbiased, experienced, and knowledgeable about the company and industry. Crisp lists six alternative sources of auditors.

1. *Self-audit.* A company can ask the executive who is directly in charge of an activity to appraise its strengths and weaknesses.
2. *"Audit-from-across."* A company can assign persons in a related activity on the same functional level to prepare an audit of the neighboring activity.
3. *"Audit-from-above."* The audit can be conducted by the executive to whom the manager reports.
4. *Company auditing office.* The company can establish an office with the responsibility for conducting all company marketing audits.
5. *Company task-force audit.* The company can appoint a team of company executives with varied backgrounds and experience to conduct the audit.
6. *Outside audit.* The company can hire an outside individual or agency to conduct the marketing audit.[9]

---

[8] Richard D. Crisp, "Auditing the Functional Elements of a Marketing Operation," *Analyzing and Improving Marketing Performance,* Report no. 32, (New York: American Management Association, 1959), pp. 16–17.

[9] Crisp, pp. 41–44.

Crisp feels that the sixth alternative, the outside audit, is usually the best choice. The outside agent is able to be more objective since he is not examining his own or a co-worker's performance and since he is not so likely to be subjected to pressure from superiors or co-workers.

CONDUCTING A MARKETING AUDIT

Conducting a marketing audit and the subsequent strategy evaluation is a three-step process, as outlined in Figure 1. Step 1 consists of the accumulation of a great many facts concerning the firm's marketing program. Step 2 is the evaluation of the information gathered in Step

FIGURE 1
The marketing audit process

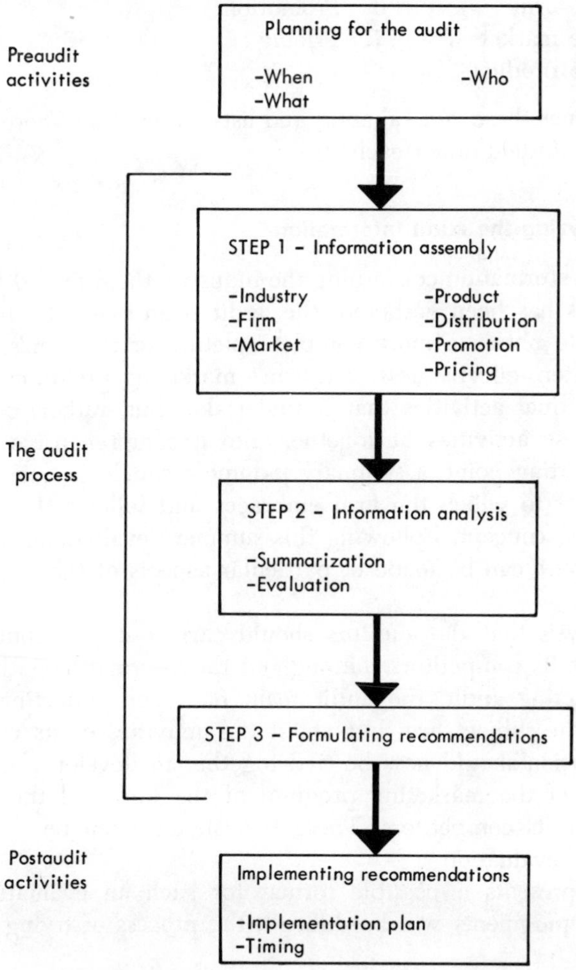

Preaudit activities

Planning for the audit
-When   -Who
-What

The audit process

STEP 1 - Information assembly
-Industry   -Product
-Firm   -Distribution
-Market   -Promotion
               -Pricing

STEP 2 - Information analysis
-Summarization
-Evaluation

STEP 3 - Formulating recommendations

Postaudit activities

Implementing recommendations
-Implementation plan
-Timing

1 with respect to the firm and its competition and the internal consistency of the firm's marketing program. The third and final step is the development of a set of recommendations based on the analysis conducted in Step 2.

Step 1: Information assembly

The information assembly step of a marketing audit is the most time consuming, and may be the most frustrating. A detailed examination of a firm's marketing program involves a great deal of data, and a comprehensive listing of the information required for a marketing audit would be lengthy. Seven major areas which affect a firm's marketing program need to be examined. They are:

1. The industry   5. Distribution
2. The firm   6. Promotion
3. The market   7. Pricing
4. The product

Table 1 outlines these general areas and lists a few of the more important factors to be studied under each.

Step 2: Analyzing the audit information

Once the information concerning the industry, the firm and its marketing programs has been gathered, the audit team needs to analyze this information to obtain a more complete picture of the firm's marketing activities. Often, effectiveness of a firm's marketing program hinges not on the individual activities that it undertakes but, rather, on the way in which these activities fit together into a comprehensive marketing mix. As a starting point, a summary judgment should be made concerning the extent to which the firm embraces and follows the dictates of the marketing concept. Following this summary evaluation, other, more specific analyses can be made of particular aspects of the firm's marketing activities.

One analysis that the auditors should carry out is a comparison of the firm with its competitors. Throughout the information-gathering step of the marketing audit, the audit team has been collecting data not only about the subject firm but about the activities of its competitors. This information should now be tied together to develop a comprehensive picture of the marketing program of the firm and the marketing operations of its competitors. These two should then be compared in a side-by-side evaluation.

Table 2 presents a possible format for such an evaluation. While some of the judgments will be difficult, the process of trying to accomplish such an analysis will be beneficial to the auditors and the firm. While a firm need not, indeed probably should not, be doing exactly the same thing as its competitors, such an evaluation does point out where their activities are the same and where they are different. Where they are the same, they should be examined for possible changes that would give the firm an advantage over the competitors. Where they are different, each difference should be evaluated to determine whether it is a strength or a weakness. Such side-by-side evaluation can mean much to a firm in identifying competitive strengths and weaknesses and in developing suggestions for ways to make its marketing programs relatively stronger.

In addition to the comparative analysis of the firm's marketing program with that of its competitors, the market offerings of the firm should be evaluated with respect to each market segment it is attempting to serve. In analyzing the market, each segment was identified along with those factors which cause persons in the segment to buy the firm's product versus the product of a competitor. The degree of congruence between the factors which are important in a segment's purchase decision and the marketing offering of the firm should be evaluated. Further, the trends in specific aspects of the behavior of market segments should be evaluated with respect to proposed changes in the firm's market offerings. Such an evaluation will help to insure that the firm is adjusting to the changing needs of the market it serves. For example, a marketing audit might have shown the U.S. auto companies the shift in consumers' preferences toward smaller, more economical cars. Had the strength of this trend been identified earlier, the U.S. companies might not have suffered as much as they did from imported car competition.

In evaluating the firm's offerings to the several market segments it serves, the internal consistency of the marketing mix should be given close scrutiny. While a firm's marketing mix is made up of many different aspects, there are strong relationships among these aspects. For example, products which are considered to be convenience goods in the consumer goods classification system should have intensive distribution, whereas products that are in the shopping goods categories may need only selective or perhaps even exclusive distribution. This was relevant for the Elgin Watch Company, a prestigious manufacturer of high quality men's products. The company suffered irreparable damage when the U.S. Time Company began selling inexpensive Timex watches as convenience goods. A marketing audit could have helped Elgin revise its marketing strategy to compete effectively with Timex. By identifying the shift in goods class of wrist watches for a large segment of the population, an audit might have given Elgin the information necessary to make better decisions.

One approach to such an evaluation is to select several control points

TABLE 1
Checklist of areas to be examined in a marketing audit*

I. THE INDUSTRY
    A. Characteristics
        1. Size (in units produced, dollar sales)
        2. Number of firms
        3. Nature of competition
        4. Geographical concentration
        5. Interaction with other industries
        6. Product life cycle
        7. Government and societal constraints
    B. Trends
        1. Sales volume and number of firms
        2. Geographic localization
        3. Size of firms
    C. Firm's Position
        1. Size relative to industry leaders
        2. Market strength
        3. Leader or follower
II. THE FIRM
    A. History
        1. Growth and expansion
        2. Financial history
        3. Past strengths and weaknesses
    B. Goals and Objectives
    C. Current Strengths and Weaknesses
        1. Market
        2. Managerial
        3. Financial
        4. Technical
        5. Market information mechanisms
III. THE MARKET
    A. General Structure
        1. Number of customers
        2. Geographical spread and/or grouping
        3. Breadth of product use
        4. Urban vs. rural
        5. Demographics of current customers
    B. Firm's Approach to Market Segmentation
        1. Degree to which firm has segmented the market
        2. Degree of specification of target markets
        3. Bases of segmentation used
            a. Socioeconomic and demographic
            b. Psychographic
            c. Geographic
            d. Use patterns
    C. Segments Identified by the Firm
        1. What are characteristics?
        2. Degree of difference among segments
        3. What segments have been selected by the firm as target markets?
    D. Has the Firm Considered Factors Which Affect the Market?
        1. Income effects
        2. Price and quality elasticity
        3. Responsiveness to marketing variables
        4. Fashion cycles
        5. Seasonality

* Source: Based in part on an outline for a marketing audit developed by Professor B. J. La Londe, James R. Riley, Professor of Marketing and Logistics, The Ohio State University.

IV. THE PRODUCT
    A. List the Company's Products
        1. Strengths
        2. Weaknesses
        3. Distinctive features
    B. Competitive Position
        1. Price and quality relative to competitors
        2. Market share
        3. Patents or trademarks
    C. Product Policy
        1. Written or verbal
        2. Product line width and depth
        3. New product policy
        4. Product deletion policy
V. DISTRIBUTION
    A. Channels of Distribution
        1. Description of channel(s) used
        2. Institutions in each channel
        3. Basis for selection of institutions used
    B. Distribution Policy
        1. Extent and depth of market coverage
        2. Role of distribution in marketing mix and marketing plans
    C. Physical Distribution
        1. PD organization within firm
        2. Customer service level policy
        3. Inventory
           a. Number of locations of stock
           b. Type of warehouse (i.e. public vs. private)
           c. Planned and actual inventory levels
        4. Transportation
           a. Product shipment terms
           b. Mode of transportation used
           c. Type of carrier
              (1) Common
              (2) Contract
              (3) Private
VI. PROMOTION
    A. Goals of Promotional Activities
        1. Advertising
        2. Personal selling
        3. Sales promotion
    B. Promotion Blend
    C. Advertising
        1. Budget in dollars and per cent of sales
        2. Tasks assigned to advertising
        3. Evaluation procedures
    D. Personal Selling
        1. Organization of sales force
        2. Sales force management
        3. Tasks assigned to the sales force
VII. PRICING
    A. Goals and Role of Pricing in the Marketing Mix
    B. Approach Used to Set Prices
        1. Basis on which prices are set
        2. Flow of pricing decisions within the firm
    C. Prices Compared with Competitors
    D. Trade Discount and Allowances
    E. Financing and Credit Arrangements

TABLE 2
A possible format for interfirm comparative evaluation

Factors*	The firm's approach	Major competitors' approach	Differences
1. The Market			
Has the market been segmented?.	(Highly, somewhat, or not segmented)		
What is segmentation based on?	(Demographics, psychographics, or benefits; specific attributes)		
Size of market served	(Local, regional or national)		
2. The Product			
Quality level	(High, medium or low quality)		
Width and depth of product line	(Broad, medium, or narrow; deep, moderate, or thin)		
Is the firm an innovator?	(Typically innovator, typically follower)		
Brand strength in market	(Brand unrecognized, recognized, preferred, or insisted upon)		
Market penetration.	(Largest, average, or small market share)		
Goods class of products	(Industrial or consumer goods; subclasses)		
3. Distribution			
Direct or indirect distribution?.	(Direct or indirect; number of intermediaries)		
Type of middlemen used	(Handles own distribution or uses others; specific type of middlemen used)		
Degree of market coverage	(Intensive, selective, or exclusive)		
Service level.	(Best in market, average, poorest)		
Physical distribution system	(One central warehouse or field warehouse system; public or private transportation and/or warehouses)		
4. Promotion			
Amount of advertising.	(Percent of budget; total dollars)		
Target of promotion	(Consumers for pull strategy or middlemen for push strategy)		
Type of appeal	(Factual, emotional, humorous)		
Type of media	(Print, broadcast; local, national)		
Promotion blend	(Percent advertising vs. personal selling)		
Organization of sales force	(By territory, division, product line; company sales staff or manufacturers' agents)		
Functions of sales force	(Technical design, customer systems design, non-technical)		
5. Pricing			
Price level	(High, medium, or low price)		
Terms and/or discounts	(Strict or liberal; better, same or less than industry)		
Use of price competition	(Price major competitive weapon, competes on other bases)		

* The factors listed are suggestions and are not intended to be exclusive or exhaustive. Further, the descriptors for each of the factors are only suggestive.

or factors which have been identified as being critical to the firm's marketing program. Potential control points include product attributes such as quality and number of special features, distribution considerations such as number and type of retail outlets and service level along the channel, promotional appeals used and media selected, and pricing policies. The performance of the firm with respect to each control point can then be evaluated. Deviations should be noted and those that are significant will be points about which suggestions for improvement need to be made.[10]

Evaluation of a firm's marketing strategies can be made even more valuable if the control points selected are tied to characteristics of the target markets selected. Table 3 suggests one approach to such an evaluation.

To be used most effectively, an approach such as that suggested by Table 3 requires that the dimensions of the firm's approach and the target market characteristics be similar. With similar dimensions in both columns, congruence and discrepancy between the firm's marketing strategy and the characteristics of the target market are easily seen. For example, a firm might select as a target market stereo enthusiasts who want good quality sound and are willing to build kits in order to save money (target market characteristics) but offer only poor quality kits that are extremely difficult to assemble (the firm's marketing approach). Listing these factors on a form such as Table 3 would make the discrepancy more obvious.

Step 3: Developing recommendations

Once the analysis of the information about the firm's marketing programs has been completed, the audit team should complete its activities by making specific recommendations regarding the firm's marketing program. The recommendations should be based on the strengths and weaknesses of the firm's activities, as identified in Step 2. If the analysis was done well, such recommendations will often be relatively simple to make because discrepancies become quite obvious.

In making recommendations, the audit should be concerned more with how the firm's marketing program can be modified to improve it in the future rather than pointing the finger at poor performance in the past. While management errors should be identified, it should be done from the point of view of not making the same mistakes twice rather than a "witch hunt" to single out poor performers. This approach will establish confidence in managers concerning the value of an audit and the ability of an audit to help them.

[10] Mark E. Stern, *Marketing Planning: A Systems Approach* (New York: McGraw-Hill Book Co. 1966) pp. 131–36.

TABLE 3
One approach to firm vis-a-vis target market strategy evaluation*

Strategy aspect	Target market characteristics	The firm's approach
1. Product		
Quality level		(The firm's quality level should match that desired by the target market)
Features/options		(Those of the product should be the ones desired by the target market)
Services offered.		(Such as delivery, installation, and repair)
Guarantee.		(Consistent with the desires of target market?)
Selection offered		(Consistent with variability within target market?)
2. Distribution		
Store type.		(Characteristics of retail outlets must be consistent with desires of target market)
Market coverage		(Be consistent with target market's view of product; i.e.–intensive if convenience good)
Channel structure		(Provide services desired by target market)
3. Promotion		
Type of appeal		(Firm's message must be consistent with what will affect the target market)
Media used		(Must be media that reach target market)
Personal sales effort		(Self-service vs. sales aid vs. high pressure salesperson)
4. Price		
Price level		(Consistent with target market; also consistent with product quality and promotional appeals)
Discount structure		(Meet needs of target market; i.e.–quantity discounts if customers buy in quantity)
Price as competitive factor		(Use price if major factor in purchase decision, and vice versa)

* The strategy aspects and characteristic descriptors listed are only examples and are not intended to be exhaustive. The approach is based on the concept of identifying those factors that are determinants of purchase behavior *for the target market selected* and comparing the firm's market offerings to the needs of the target market.

CONCLUSION

A marketing audit is often a time-consuming and perhaps expensive project. However, the benefits which result from such a comprehensive evaluation of a firm's past programs and present activities often more than justify the time and money invested. Further, the insights gained can be profitably applied to future planning of the firm's marketing activities. The improved future planning that can be accomplished as a result of a marketing audit may be just the edge needed to provide a breakthrough opportunity for the firm.

Marketing audits should be a regular part of the firm's planning process. The audits should be conducted by experienced and knowledgeable people who are in a position to be unbiased in their evaluation of the firm and the industry. The firm may choose to examine either the whole range of its marketing activities at a general level or examine part of its activities in depth. In either case, the audit should concentrate on the marketing mixes of the firm with respect to the industry in which it operates, its competitors and, most importantly, the market segment(s) which the firm is attempting to serve.

QUESTIONS

1. What is a marketing audit? Why is it needed?
2. List and briefly explain the three steps that are involved in conducting a marketing audit.
3. Try to complete Table 3 for one of the cases in your textbook. Then make the appropriate recommendations.
° 4. Would a marketing audit be more important during shortage and/or inflationary times? Would the procedures have to be changed? Explain. (See Readings 14 and 25.)

The auto industry was one of the hardest hit by the fuel shortages of 1974. Car sales fell as gasoline prices increased sharply and lines formed to buy decreasing supplies. Even the industry leader, General Motors, was affected. Many questions of marketing strategy are raised in this article and the responses of General Motors and other auto companies are discussed. The article seems to suggest that the auto companies had, or could have had, advanced warning of the "small car trend" but did not adjust to market and environmental changes.

---

32. THE SMALL CAR BLUES AT GENERAL MOTORS*

WHEN THE 1975 automobile model year begins next fall, the Ford Motor Co. will be ready with seven small cars, two of them new, in response to a market trend that President Lee A. Iacocca calls "irrevocable." Chrysler Corp., lampooned widely for picking the current model year to launch a new line of big cars, will nevertheless have 60% of its production capacity committed to compacts. American Motors

---

° Reprinted with permission from *Business Week*, (March 16, 1974), pp. 76–83. © 1974, McGraw-Hill, Inc.

Corp., the only automaker showing sales gains this year, is showing them all on small cars.

And how is General Motors responding to the small car boom? The world's largest manufacturer is rife with confusion, indecision, even panic. "We don't know what the hell is going on," says a frantic middle manager at GM's Oldsmobile Div. "First we were told we were going to shut down our big car lines from April until August, then that it would be for only a month or so this spring. Now I hear that we are going to build X-bodies [compacts]."

GM, the drummer that the industry has marched to for almost 50 years, cannot decide whether to swing heavily into the small cars that the turbulent, tricky market seems to be demanding or to continue to push the bigger cars that deliver the bulk of the company's earnings. As a result, the company that last year amassed 44.4% of industry sales, including imports, has seen its market share drop to 37.5% in the past two months—a massive tumble in the auto business. Sales for the year through March 10 are down a huge 37%. As things stand now, Ford, with two-thirds of GM's sales volume and a traditional quarter market share in autos, will be able to produce more compact and subcompact cars next fall than GM.

Right into this month, GM's chairman, Richard C. Gerstenberg, 64, was indicating that the company would respond to soaring demand for fuel economy ambivalently, with compacts and subcompacts but also with intermediates that do not look much smaller than so-called full-sized models. "We've got some pretty good plans for intermediate cars down the road," Gerstenberg said. They and full-sized cars will represent 60% of production capacity this fall, the company figures.

GM is thus taking a decidedly different tack than its competitors in reacting to a marketing phenomenon that Gerstenberg described to a Chicago audience last week: "Customer preferences which we foresaw for the late 70s have become evident right now, even before the mid-70s." The company had just witnessed a precipitous 42% production decline in January and February, and recent cost reduction decisions point up the company's trouble. It has halted construction of two new assembly plants, a car plant in Oklahoma City and a truck plant in Memphis, and delayed expansion plans for the Oldsmobile and Buick divisions. Last weekend it announced temporary layoffs at 16 of its 22 assembly plants to bring big car inventories in line with sales. It also cut out the second shifts at three plants. To make matters worse, the troubled, super-automated Lordstown, Ohio, plant, GM's biggest Vega assembly facility, suffered a new walkout.

Period of uncertainty

It is conceivable, of course, that time will show GM to have been strategically hedging its bets, straddling the whole gamut of car sizes.

It is uncertain now whether termination of the Arab oil boycott, for example, will sweep away the market's uncertainty and send consumers back to the full-sized gas guzzlers. Ford, American Motors, and Chrysler, however, think that the small car trend is massive and irreversible. Says Arjay Miller, dean of Stanford Business School and former president of Ford, "The energy crisis has had a permanent effect on the mix of cars to be sold." If he and the competition are right, GM faces two or three of its roughest years ever trying to catch up.

GM was headed for trouble well before the end of last year. While 1973 earnings climbed 11% to a record $2.4-billion, they declined 22% in the final quarter. This year, Wall Street analysts think the company will be lucky to earn half what it did last year, and they do not see earnings rebounding to 1973 levels until 1976 or 1977. By midweek, about 70,000 GM workers had been permanently laid off, and dealers were waiting in lifeless showrooms with immobile inventories of 890,000 GM cars, or an 81-day supply, about 30 days above normal. Industry figures for January and February told much of the story. Small car sales were up 2% for the period, but intermediates were off 27%, and full-sized cars fell 50%. The driver waiting in a gas line with a Buick that gave him as little as 10-mi. per gal. was not so sure he would really rather have another Buick.

The opportunity for a major redirection looms later this year with the retirement of Gerstenberg, a financial specialist, and President Edward N. Cole, 64, an engineer. But there is no probable successor who is a product man, like Cole, at a time when product decisions are the most crucial facing management. Nor is there anyone in the wings who is strong enough and young enough to build a new corporate identity and burst through the dull gray managerial mantle that has shrouded the company since the reign of Harlow Curtice, who retired in 1958. Moreover, the financial types who have come to dominate the top executive cadre may have been maximizing short-term profits at the expense of the long-term and product development. It is well known inside GM that Ed Cole's influence has deteriorated over the years. That may lie at the core of GM's delayed response to the small car trend. Some critics say GM now needs a man like John Z. DeLorean, a flamboyant, youthful executive—and potential chief executive—who resigned last spring as head of the Car & Truck Group because he felt frustrated.

Symbol of capitalism

For years, General Motors has been the unparalleled prototype of American capitalism. Few companies could touch its marketing genius, its financial control, its management expertise and facility for breeding new managers, its reputation for citizenship in its communities, its bold if tardy efforts to employ and train minority groups, and its uncanny knack for fattening earnings in defiance of economic laws that say the

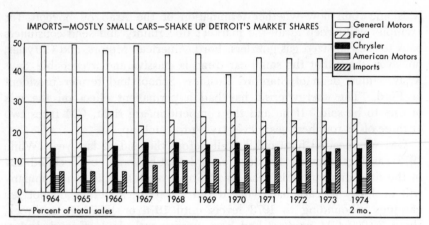

IMPORTS—MOSTLY SMALL CARS—SHAKE UP DETROIT'S MARKET SHARES

Legend:
- ☐ General Motors
- ▨ Ford
- ▓ Chrysler
- ▤ American Motors
- ▩ Imports

Percent of total sales — years 1964, 1965, 1966, 1967, 1968, 1969, 1970, 1971, 1972, 1973, 1974 (2 mo.)

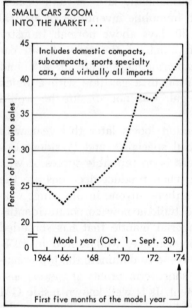

SMALL CARS ZOOM
INTO THE MARKET ...

Includes domestic compacts, subcompacts, sports specialty cars, and virtually all imports

Percent of U.S. auto sales

Model year (Oct. 1 – Sept. 30)

1964 '66· '68 '70 '72 '74

First five months of the model year

. . . AND GM's BIG CAR DIVISIONS GET CLOBBERED

	Unit car sales during October–February of the model year						
	1968	1969	1970	1971	1972	1973	1974
Chevrolet	2,053,417	2,154,970	1,937,592	1,878,009	2,367,781	2,516,864	894,413
Pontiac	866,826	843,610	664,879	576,021	741,691	854,343	232,238
Oldsmobile	607,382	665,833	569,444	550,314	749,018	853,793	238,694
Buick	627,454	685,007	606,532	543,407	666,196	689,757	222,149
Cadillac	220,478	231,488	213,553	202,960	264,559	288,504	106,530

Data: BW and GM

bigger a company is, the slower it grows. In 1954, GM was a giant with sales of $9.8-billion; last year, sales were up to $35.8-billion.

GM is the industry's acknowledged pricing leader. Ford and Chrysler have been forced into embarrassing price rollbacks on new cars after GM announced lower prices. In many ways, GM is also the styling leader, if not the top innovator. After a disastrous styling departure with the fabled "fins" of the early 1960s, Chrysler reverted to GM's basic sculptured design. As Chrysler Chairman Lynn Townsend explained: "GM sells five of every 10 cars, and we sell only two." Chrysler's new big cars are unabashed copies of successful GM products.

Even before the Arab oil embargo, critical rumbles were shaking the GM edifice, no doubt a consequence of being the No. 1 automaker. In an environment where social critics chastized companies for single-minded devotion to profits, consumerists attacked GM for building dirty and unsafe cars on dehumanizing assembly systems, and for blind waste of resources. GM has also been charged with seducing consumers into buying bigger cars than they needed and to trade them in for new ones sooner than necessary.

Some congressmen, notably Senator Philip A. Hart of Michigan, even talk about breaking up GM. One target is the automaker's strong franchise in mass transportation on the grounds that its power could be used to thwart mass transit development. In recent testimony before Democrat Hart's antitrust and monopoly subcommittee, Los Angeles Mayor Thomas Bradley charged that in the early 1940's, GM bought the Los Angeles street car system only to tear it down.

The company makes diesel engines, locomotives, and buses, and in January it formed a transportation systems division. But critics doubt that GM can put its soul behind it. "To the extent that buses thrive, cars don't," says Robert Heilbroner, the New School economist and author. He suggests that GM's bus business might be divested. "Pushing private cars in one case and public transportation in another results in a conflict of interest," he says.

The ailing BOP lines

Most of what ails GM comes down to big and medium-sized Buicks, Oldsmobiles, and Pontiacs—the BOP lines, and to a lesser degree, Cadillac. GM makes its greatest per-unit profit on Cadillacs and the least on Chevies, although Chevrolet is far and away the company's sales leader. The production cost difference between a Chevrolet Caprice and a Cadillac de Ville with comparable equipment is $275 to $300. But the selling price differs by $2,700, giving GM a $2,400 extra gross profit on the Cadillac. GM, unlike the other companies, learned to exploit those differences in the fat medium price range. The profit difference between that Caprice and an equivalent Oldsmobile is $1,200.

Ford and Chrysler's Plymouth have always been able to compete effectively in Chevrolet's market and in recent years, Lincolns and Mark IVs have managed to chip away at Cadillac. But neither Ford Motor nor Chrysler is much of a threat to the BOP market. Ford's worst attempt was the Edsel, a $250-million casualty. Chrysler's De Soto also tried and failed. "GM's strength has been in the full-sized car," says Chrysler's Townsend. "That has always been our weakness." Adds Bennett E. Bidwell, general manager of the Ford Div.: "Before, we never really cut into GM's penetration. They were the Bank of America."

Another critical factor in GM's profitability in recent years has been vertical and horizontal diversification. The company makes some or all of every component it uses except steel and glass. More and more, the company fosters intra-divisional use of standardized engines, axles, transmissions, bodies, and other components to achieve economies of scale. And now the Assembly Div. builds all GM cars not manufactured in the car divisions' home assembly plants. It is no wonder that GM's return on investment—19.1% last year—is consistently the industry's highest and one of the highest for all industrial companies.

Now, in a sense, GM is a victim of its own success. "Other companies don't have the same relative exposure to trouble now because they had to devise strategies in the past that emphasized areas that GM was not strong in," says an auto analyst. GM, by contrast, hesitates to play with a profit formula that works. As a result, Paul W. McCracken, University of Michigan professor and former chairman of the Council of Economic Advisers, sees market penetration shifting around as Ford, Chrysler, and American Motors swing into small cars. "There is more fluidity in how the market penetration will be shaping up here than we have seen since the 1920s," he says.

The 20s were Ford's Waterloo. The market collapsed in 1921 following an extended boom. GM was floundering, hanging onto only 12% of the auto market compared with Ford's 60%. Alfred P. Sloan recalled in *My Years with General Motors:* "Not only were we not competitive with Ford in the low-priced field where the big volume and substantial future growth lay—but in the middle, where we were concentrated with duplication, we did not know what we were trying to do except sell cars which, in a sense, took volume from each other." Ford, meanwhile, was riding high with the plain, black, single-line Model T.

Sloan and GM redefined the niches in the marketplace, made decisive moves in paring the company's automotive operations from seven to five, gave each division operating autonomy, and gave each car a distinctive price and style category in response to a growing consumer demand for diversity. Ford ignored those moves. And ultimately, Ford had to junk the Model T. The penalty was a total shutdown for almost a year as the company switched over to the Model A. But by then, GM was well en route to capturing half the domestic car market.

Lacking the small car image

This time around, the Model T may be GM's. Even as it tries now to expand its small car capacity, it cannot rely on the 70% automatic return business it gets on big cars because driver loyalty tends to diminish as cars get smaller. Further, unlike Ford, American Motors, and the importers, GM lacks a small car image. GM dealers' huge BOP inventories include many unsold smaller cars because shoppers rarely think GM in going out to buy one. Through its strength in compacts and subcompacts, Ford is betting it can extract 5% additional market penetration in the next two years from GM—an astounding achievement in an industry that heralds a 1% gain.

Even for Ford, though, the market today is a can of worms. It is awash with uncertainty, and even the small car market is showing signs of softness. People are depressed over Watergate, inflation, gasoline shortages, and generally bad news, says Jay W. Schmiedeskamp of the University of Michigan's Survey Research Center. This, he says, creates uncertainty. "Uncertainty feeds on itself. The biggest thing that is killing the big car is the uncertainty. The key factor in the energy crisis is the U.S. Government in which people have zero faith." Said Gerstenberg in Chicago: "The public needs to be told, clearly and with consistency, where we stand with respect to gasoline availability."

Schmiedeskamp suspects that if all the uncertainty were to dissipate, the big cars would come back, though not in previous record number. "There is a hard core of big car buyers who are going to give them up reluctantly," he says. "Desired behavior trends tend to change rather slowly. Some of these people are entirely resistant to the small car."

Phenomena far more profound than fears of gas shortages also seem to be wafting through the marketplace. Families are smaller, gas is costlier, parking space is scarcer—factors that stimulate small car sales. Many of those sales have been going to imports, which now hold 15% of the market despite the loss of their pricing advantage. "We are in a pie that is growing bigger," says Norman Lean, Toyota's U.S. sales manager, with great enthusiasm. Ronald Glantz, an auto analyst with Mitchell, Hutchins, Inc., sees an "increasing percentage of Americans who don't want what Detroit offers and specifically what General Motors offers." Harvard sociologist David Riesman perceives a "downward spread of aristocratic values."

"If you visit colleges in non-cosmopolitan areas," Riesman says, "you will still find both faculty and students driving tanks." But, he says, the move to smaller cars is like "the tipping of a neighborhood," in that nothing much happens until a sort of critical mass is reached when things happen very fast. First there is "the realization that whatever the desirability of a big car, it isn't stylish anymore," and second, "the realization that a certain proportion of people are doing something else."

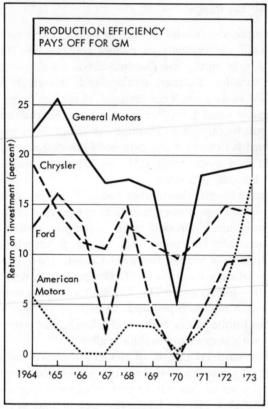

PRODUCTION EFFICIENCY
PAYS OFF FOR GM

General Motors

Chrysler

Ford

American
Motors

Return on investment (percent)

25
20
15
10
5
0

1964 '65 '66 '67 '68 '69 '70 '71 '72 '73

Data: BW

What Riesman calls "aristocrats" have lost their desire for showiness.
And he adds: "Showiness has been so long satirized that it has become
an embarrassment."

A calm public face

Publicly, General Motors executives seem unperturbed by all that
is spinning around them. Pushing a button under his big walnut desk
to close the door, Gerstenberg explains to a visitor: "It is easy to overesti-
mate where that thing [the market] is going because of the situation
we've been in here for the past 60 days. The rules have changed a
little bit. We're down in penetration and we're working hard to get
it back."

Elliott M. "Pete" Estes, executive vice-president, operations-staff,
seemed equally self-assured at a recent Detroit press gathering. "Things
are not as good as we would like them to be," he said, "but they indicate

that we've bottomed out, and I'd have to say that I'm optimistic." The head of the Chevrolet Div., F. James McDonald, is outright bullish. At the Chicago Auto Show a few weeks ago he declared: "We think that 1974 could be our second best year." However, reports from inside GM's massive headquarters on West Grand Boulevard in Detroit indicate that the quiet executive demeanor is a well-staged facade.

Says a Ford man: "While that Olds guy is telling you that big cars are here to stay, he's screaming like hell in those executive committee meetings, 'I've got to have a small car or my dealers are going to take gas.'" Now and then, the confusion surfaces, as it did following a decision to expand 6-cylinder engine production at the Flint (Mich.) plant. One day in Detroit, Gerstenberg was explaining that other plants would also be used for six-cylinder production, while Estes was telling reporters in Chicago that the Flint facility would be the sole source of sixes.

The corporate aplomb breaks down further among dealers. A Los Angeles dealer with enough Olds 88s and 98s to last through the end of the year is bitter. "I'm losing money badly right now, and it won't be too long before I'll have to decide on weathering it out or not," he says. "What it boils down to is that the company has been too slow to wake up to the energy crisis and do what the dealers need."

Labor is just as anxious. "I wake up in the middle of the night and just worry how this thing is going to be settled," says Irving Bluestone, the United Auto Workers vice-president in charge of the GM department. "We've got 65,000 or more members on permanent layoff and thousands more on temporary leave."

GM is, at least, keeping an eye on its flanks. Since the end of its 1973 model run in September, the company has converted one plant from intermediate (112-in. to 118-in. wheelbase) to small car production. It has boosted production of the subcompact Vega at the Ste. Therese, Quebec, plant by 40% and will start tooling up Apr. 5 for Vega assembly at the Southgate (Calif.) facility which had been assembling big Chevrolets, Buicks, and Pontiacs. This spring GM will also switch from building big Chevys to compact (108-in. to 111-in. wheelbase) Chevy Novas and Pontiac Venturas at its Tarrytown (N.Y.) plant. Those conversions will increase GM's small car capacity to 40% of the total by next fall.

That is still far under its competitors' goals. Some critics also wonder whether GM might have missed an opportunity to take advantage of its delays and build a better small car. An equivalent of the German Audi or the Swedish Volvo, for example, would give the company muscle in the high-profit, medium-price market while meeting demand for fuel efficiency. So far, the only such initiative that GM is known to be planning is a scaled-down Cadillac to be launched late next year. But it will be trailing Ford again. In September Ford will introduce two mini-luxury cars—the Mercury Monarch and the Ford Granada—in the $4,000-plus category. Both cars resemble the Mercedes.

Arjay Miller is convinced GM will make the right moves eventually. "There will be some dislocation in the short run because of the energy crisis," he says. "But GM, both the company and its dealers, have the financial resources and the credit, if they need that and I doubt it, to turn it around. You go back through the years and you have a pretty hard time marking GM for not being responsive."

Bigness gets in the way

Still, wherever GM goes with small cars, it will travel a road littered with corpses. Off and on for years, Americans have been offered small cars—the Crosley, the Henry J, the Nash Metropolitan, English Ford's Cortina and Anglia, Chrysler's French-made Simca—all of which have perished or been pulled out of the domestic market. GM's Corvair went down under Ralph Nader's gun. Ford found a successful candidate in the Falcon, but it robbed volume from other Ford lines.

GM may be the worst positioned of any auto maker to move boldly into new products. "Big companies get so diffused by their bigness that they can lose focus," claims Eugene A. Cafiero, Chrysler vice-president for North American operations. Says economist McCracken: "The very characteristics which make for effective low-cost management in a stable market are the same that make it hard to make 90-degree turns." Adds William J. Abernathy, a Harvard Business School professor, who is launching a major government-supported study of the auto industry: "You can't have great efficiency and real innovation. There's no such thing as a free lunch."

That may be a matter of opinion. "I wouldn't agree with Abernathy at all," says Miller, the former Ford President. "A larger company can gamble because it has the money to do so. Look, General Motors put $50-million on the line for the Wankel engine. American Motors could not have done that."

Nevertheless, GM has trailed the industry in recent years in innovation. Ford's original Mustang, this year's new Mustang II, and the Maverick all beat comparable GM products into the marketplace. No auto maker has been able to match the public relations clout of American Motors' Buyer Protection Plan. GM's few notable departures in recent years have been the ill-fated, rear-engined Corvair and the Lordstown plant, an innovation in automation. Lordstown's workers struck last year, however, not over the usual grievances, but over working conditions.

But despite this background—and the shocking sales reports and dealers' wails—many industry watchers are confident that GM will manage simply because it is GM. Dealers, they note, have always cried when sales slipped. "All the resources are there," says analyst Donald DeScenza of Donaldson, Lufkin & Jenrette. "It's just a question of time." Adds

Miller: "GM has the money. They are planning fast. They will be in the finals."

Indeed, new tactics do appear to be poking through the clouds over GM. They include deemphasizing the biggest cars in favor of intermediates, a belated stress on compacts and subcompacts, and loading the smaller cars with high-profit options. Additional subcompacts will be made or imported to round out the lines of Pontiac and Oldsmobile, which do not currently offer such cars. Production of 6-cylinder and smaller 8-cylinder engines to improve the fuel economy of intermediate cars will be increased. And GM may also revive the fundamental divisional and product line identities that were created in the 1920s and 1930s. They were dissipated over the past decade as component and assembly commonality was emphasized.

Restoring the old distinctions would be the most significant. Rationalizing manufacturing has, as intended, buttressed earnings. But it may have stifled earnings improvement in other respects. By reducing divisional autonomy—a cornerstone of the 1920s recovery—the company may have sacrificed intra-divisional competition and the quest for innovation, leading to largely superficial differences among GM cars. Years ago, a buyer could choose among the Buick Dyna-Flow, the Olds Hydramatic, and the Chevy Power-Glide automatic transmissions, for example. Today there is only one. Price distinctions have softened, too. Today a consumer can buy a Buick, Olds, Pontiac, or Chevy for $4,000.

In rounding out the car lines with subcompacts, GM is planning a Vega-derivative for Pontiac, similar to the Pontiac Astre sold in Canada, and is rumored to be scheduling an as-yet-unidentified import for Oldsmobile. "Our best knowledge from Oldsmobile," says Dallas Olds dealer Jerry Freeman, "is that we will have an imported small car by this fall. That's the rumor anyway." Olds may also get the Wankel-powered minicar originally planned for Chevrolet, and Chevrolet is scheduled to get another Vega-like car next year to compete with Ford's Mustang II.

Keeping the dealer afloat

Imports, to be sure, are only a stop-gap, intended to give dealers who are awash with cars they cannot move something to keep them afloat. Further down the road, GM appears to be planning a subcompact for Chevrolet that will be smaller and lower-priced than anything its sister divisions will be selling. Says Gerstenberg: "We're watching what's happening to a couple of small cars in our overseas operations—the new Opel Kadett we introduced in Germany and a new Chevette in Brazil. Where the Vega is 2,300 lbs. to 2,400 lbs., those cars are 1,750 lbs. to 1,800 lbs."

With small cars likely to dominate GM production eventually, observers wonder whether the company should continue to try to support five divisions. Ford and Chrysler each have two car divisions. Says Stuart Perkins, president of Volkswagen of America: "My feeling is that there are too many divisions at GM. They will go through a process of simplification." Adds a GM competitor: "It's got to be a problem. How can they support four big car divisions when there is only one place to go, and that's where Chevrolet is?" Gerstenberg admits that the big car divisions are hurting today, but he denies some Wall Street reports that one or more may be losing money. "I think that every one of those BOP divisions will be viable outfits down the road," he says.

Such optimism has done little to placate GM's strong and usually loyal dealers. Never before have they seen the bottom fall out of their bread-and-butter products so fast or so far. A man who knows GM well sees Ford making hay of the dealers' plight. "Iacocca seems to have made the right moves in adding more small cars to the company's product mix," he says. "Now if you are at Ford, and you are on the ball, you figure how to take 500 BOP dealers for Lincoln-Mercury. If Ford stays tough, the doors are wide open." A Pontiac executive says he faces losing 10% of his dealerships next month.

Jerry Freeman, the Dallas Olds dealer, says he lost $48,000 in December and $12,000 in January. "We don't have a single small car for attracting the public," he says. In Atlanta, Buick-Opel dealer D. L. Claborn says that "it will be rough for the next couple of years." So he is cutting advertising and staff.

Part of the problem is image. People are looking to small car companies for small cars. Datsun, for example, sold almost 34,000 cars in January and February, up 10% over the same month last year. Another problem is that BOP dealers never really had to move small cars. They would use the compact Buick Apollo or Pontiac Ventura to lure customers into the showroom and then super-sell a big car. And then, many of the small cars BOP dealers have on hand feature thirsty V-8 engines. So the compacts the BOP dealers do have are not selling much better than bigger cars. At the end of February, Buick had a 138-day supply of Apollos on hand. Says Edgar Fleck of San Francisco's Lesher-Muirhead Motors, Inc., an Olds dealer: "We think GM's long-range planning has proved unrealistic. It has people working on this who should have come up with the right answers."

Did GM miss the boat?

The right answers may have been two small-car programs that top GM management pigeon-holed a couple of years ago. One was the so-called "K–Program," a far-reaching concept that proposed squeezing all cars, from the intermediate level down, into lighter, smaller packages with smaller engines. The other program called for shrinking the full-sized cars into intermediate sizes. Either approach would have borne fruit by now, and in view of current developments, both are back under review.

George Qua, a Cleveland Buick dealer, says that former GM executive John DeLorean pushed management to adopt smaller cars, including those that would have been borne of the K–Program. But, says Qua, "nobody wanted to call off the party since it was going so good. Guys like DeLorean could see this thing coming, but nobody would listen to them." The company may be learning. In the past year, Chevrolet began an "Alternate Futures" program designed to anticipate rapid market changes and to build enough flexibility into the manufacturing system to respond quickly.

Gerstenberg, nevertheless, sees most of the difficulty in sales terms. "We've got a selling job to do with the dealer," he says. "And he has a job to do with the customer." He doubts that many dealers will drop out. "Oh, I hope not," he says. "They are coming off three awfully good years, and hell, they are good businessmen. They are going to adapt to the needs of the market."

The company is, nevertheless, making things a little easier. It is not forcing big cars on dealers, for example, and in many cases it is offering cash bonuses—$250 at Chevrolet—for selling full-sized cars. They can use it. Some are still stuck with 1973 models. Hansord Pontiac of Minneapolis, for one, started the new year with 350 of last years' cars on hand.

Dealers want more help. They are asking GM to deliver cars on consignment or to extend payment terms from 20 to 60 or 90 days. But Gerstenberg says the company will not consider sending out cars on consignment, and Murphy Wright of Taber Pontiac in Atlanta says: "We have pushed for a 90-day floorplan [inventory and financing], but we have gotten nothing." Says DeLorean: "I think if I were still at GM, I would find a way to give dealers 90-day floorplanning right away."

General Motors Acceptance Corp., the financing arm that bankrolls dealer inventories, has apparently adopted a pick-and-choose policy in assisting dealers. Some Chicago dealers say GMAC lowered interest rates 1% in February, while San Francisco's Fleck says the financing company has not budged a fraction.

General Motors' troubles today come down ultimately to the men in charge, their push for quarter-to-quarter earnings gains, and their devotion to financial control. "The guy who takes a nickel out of a switch around here is a hero," says one GM man. The moves toward consolidating divisions and component commonality certainly had their roots in corporate desires for tighter financial control. And if the finance side of the company takes the credit for GM's earnings performance, it must also take the blame for getting caught short on product innovation and responses to market changes.

The shuffle at the top

With Gerstenberg and Cole retiring, the odds-on favorite to succeed Gerstenberg as chairman and chief executive is Vice-Chairman Thomas A. Murphy, 58, a financial man with some operating experience. For the president's job, neither of the two front-runners has Cole's stature as a product expert. One is Richard L. Terrell, 55, executive vice-president for car and truck-body assembly, who spent most of his 36 years at GM in the non-automotive Frigidaire and Electro-Motive divisions. The other, Pete Estes, had 34 years of divisional experience at Pontiac and Chevrolet. But Estes, 58, is blamed for letting Chevrolet lose market share from 1965 to 1969.

Death and resignation have thinned the top ranks. DeLorean's departure was seen as a serious blow to product development. In 1968, the company lost another top product man, Semon E. "Bunkie" Knudson, who quit after the presidency went to Cole. One promising comer was John Beltz, Oldsmobile Div. general manager, who died of cancer two years ago at 46. Then last December the highly regarded former head of GM in Canada, John D. Baker, died unexpectedly after only two months running Oldsmobile.

There are also signs of conflict. Last year's appointment of Oldsmobile's head, Howard H. Kehrl, to succeed DeLorean as group executive for cars and trucks touched off grumbling among other car divisional managers, all but one of whom had more experience than Kehrl and did not like being bypassed.

Whatever the makeup of GM's next first team, it should find a timely message in words that Alfred Sloan set down: "Even mistakes played a large part in actual events . . . And if our competitors—Mr. Ford among them—had not made some of their own of considerable magnitude, and if we had not reversed certain of ours, the position of General Motors would be different from what it is today."

QUESTIONS

1. Based on the discussion in the article, what was (is) the crucial strategy question facing General Motors? Given the "facts" at the time, what should they have done?

2. Do you think General Motors (and the other auto companies) could have better anticipated the large scale shift to smaller, more economical cars? If so, how? If not, why? (Try to separate a long term shift to small cars from the drop in sales of all cars caused by the Arab oil embargo and subsequent large price increases.)

3. What should General Motors (or any business) do to avoid a repetition of the "oil crisis" problems?

5

Marketing reappraised

MARKETING ACCOMPLISHES a great deal, both as an activity within the firm (micro-marketing) and within society as a whole (macro-marketing). However, marketing has critics who feel that marketing could accomplish more or cost less.

The first two readings in this final section examine some of the fundamental questions raised by consumerism regarding the value and role of marketing. The readings point out both positive and negative aspects of current marketing practice and then make some positive suggestions for action.

The final article of the section, and the collection, is a discussion of the desirability of governmental controls on the economy. Written by the former chairman of the Price Commission, the article argues for a return to a freer market, where a firm's survival is based on its ability to satisfy a market need at a competitive price.

> Consumerism is not a new phenomenon, but Kotler argues
> that the current movement was inevitable and will be en-
> during. Further, it would be beneficial, promarketing, and
> profitable. He feels the real challenge for business is devel-
> oping products and marketing practices that combine short-
> and long-run consumer values. This leads him to advancing
> a new concept of societal marketing to replace the market-
> ing concept.

33. WHAT CONSUMERISM MEANS FOR MARKETERS*

Philip Kotler

IN THIS CENTURY, the U.S. business scene has been shaken
by three distinct consumer movements—in the early 1900's, the mid-
1930's, and the mid-1960's. The first two flare-ups subsided. Business
observers, social critics, and marketing leaders are divided over whether
this latest outbreak is a temporary or a permanent social phenomenon.
Those who think that the current movement has the quality of a fad
point to the two earlier ones. By the same token, they argue that this
too will fade away. Others argue just as strongly that the issues which
flamed the latest movement differ so much in character and force that
consumerism may be here to stay.

In retrospect, it is interesting that the first consumer movement was
fueled by such factors as rising prices, Upton Sinclair's writings, and
ethical drug scandals. It culminated in the passage of the Pure Food
and Drug Act (1906), the Meat Inspection Act (1906), and the creation
of the Federal Trade Commission (1914). The second wave of consumerism in the mid-1930's was fanned by such factors as an upturn in
consumer prices in the midst of the depression, the sulfanilamide scandal,
and the widely imitated Detroit housewives strike. It culminated in
the strengthening of the Pure Food and Drug Act and in the enlarging

* Reprinted with permission from the *Harvard Business Review*, May–June 1972,
pp. 48–57. © 1972, The President and Fellows of Harvard College. At the time
of writing, Dr. Kotler was Professor of Marketing at Northwestern University.

Author's note: I wish to thank Professor Fred Allvine for his helpful and incisive
comments during the writing of this article.

of the Federal Trade Commission's power to regulate against unfair or deceptive acts and practices.

The third and current movement has resulted from a complex combination of circumstances, not the least of which was increasingly strained relations between standard business practices and long-run consumer interests. Consumerism in its present form has also been variously blamed on Ralph Nader, the thalidomide scandal, rising prices, the mass media, a few dissatisfied individuals, and on President Lyndon Johnson's "Consumer Interests Message." These and other possible explanations imply that the latest movement did not have to happen and that it had little relationship to the real feelings of most consumers.

In this article, I shall discuss the current phenomenon and what it portends for business. In so doing, I shall present five simple conclusions about consumerism and largely focus my discussion on these assessments. Consider:

1. Consumerism was inevitable. It was not a plot by Ralph Nader and a handful of consumerists but an inevitable phase in the development of our economic system.

2. Consumerism will be enduring. Just as the labor movement started as a protest uprising and became institutionalized in the form of unions, government boards, and labor legislation, the consumer movement, too, will become an increasingly institutionalized force in U.S. society.

3. Consumerism will be beneficial. On the whole, it promises to make the U.S. economic system more responsive to new and emerging societal needs.

4. Consumerism is promarketing. The consumer movement suggests an important refinement in the marketing concept to take into account societal concerns.

5. Consumerism can be profitable. The societal marketing concept suggests areas of new opportunity and profit for alert business firms.

These assessments of consumerism are generally at variance with the views of many businessmen. Some business spokesmen maintain that consumerism was stirred up by radicals, headline grabbers, and politicians; that it can be beaten by attacking, discrediting, or ignoring it; that it threatens to destroy the vitality of our economic system and its benefits; that it is an antimarketing concept; and that it can only reduce profit opportunities in the long run.

WHAT IS CONSUMERISM?

Before discussing the foregoing conclusions in more depth, it is important to know what we mean by "consumerism." Here is a definition: *Consumerism is a social movement seeking to augment the rights and power of buyers in relation to sellers.* To understand this definition, let us first look at a short list of the many traditional rights of sellers in the U.S. economic system:

Sellers have the right to introduce any product in any size and style they wish into the marketplace so long as it is not hazardous to personal health or safety; or, if it is, to introduce it with the proper warnings and controls.

Sellers have the right to price the product at any level they wish provided there is no discrimination among similar classes of buyers.

Sellers have the right to spend any amount of money they wish to promote the product, so long as it is not defined as unfair competition.

Sellers have the right to formulate any message they wish about the product provided that it is not misleading or dishonest in content or execution.

Sellers have the right to introduce any buying incentive schemes they wish.

Subject to a few limitations, these are among the essential core rights of businessmen in the United States. Any radical change in these would make U.S. business a different kind of game.

Now what about the traditional *buyers' rights?* Here, once again, are some of the rights that come immediately to mind:

Buyers have the right not to buy a product that is offered to them.

Buyers have the right to expect the product to be safe.

Buyers have the right to expect the product to turn out to be essentially as represented by the seller.

In looking over these traditional sellers' and buyers' rights, I believe that the balance of power lies with the seller. The notion that the *buyer has all the power he needs because he can refuse to buy the product is not deemed adequate* by consumer advocates. They hold that consumer sovereignty is not enough when the consumer does not have full information and when he is persuasively influenced by Madison Avenue.

What additional rights do consumers want? Behind the many issues stirred up by consumer advocates is a drive for several additional rights. In the order of their serious challenge to sellers' rights, they are:

Buyers want the right to have adequate information about the product.

Buyers want the right to additional protections against questionable products and marketing practices.

Buyers want the right to influence products and marketing practices in directions that will increase the "quality of life."

Consumer proposals

The "right to be informed," proposed by President Kennedy in his March 1962 directive to the Consumer Advisory Council, has been the battleground for a great number of consumer issues. These include, for example, the right to know the true interest cost of a loan (truth-in-lending), the true cost per standard unit of competing brands (unit pricing), the basic ingredients in a product (ingredient labeling), the nutritional quality of foods (nutritional labeling), the freshness of products (open dating), and the prices of gasoline (sign posting rather than pump posting).

Many of these proposals have gained widespread endorsement not only from consumers but also from political leaders and some businessmen. It is hard to deny the desirability of adequate information for making a free market operate vitally and competitively in the interests of consumers.

The proposals related to additional *consumer protection* are several, including the strengthening of consumers' hands in cases of business fraud, requiring of more safety to be designed into automobiles, issuing of greater powers to existing government agencies, and setting up of new agencies.

The argument underlying consumer protection proposals is that consumers do not necessarily have the time and/or skills to obtain, understand, and use all the information that they may get about a product; therefore, some impartial agencies must be established which can perform these tasks with the requisite economies of scale.

The proposals relating to *quality-of-life* considerations include regulating the ingredients that go into certain products (detergents, gasoline) and packaging (soft drink containers), reducing the level of advertising and promotional "noise," and creating consumer representation on company boards to introduce consumer welfare considerations in business decision making.

The argument in this area says that products, packaging, and marketing practices must not only pass the test of being profitable to the company and convenient to the consumer but must also be life-enhancing. Consumerists insist that the world's resources no longer permit their indiscriminate embodiment in any products desired by consumers without further consideration of their social values. This "right" is obviously the most radical of the three additional rights that consumers want, and the one which would constitute the most basic challenge to the sellers' traditional rights.

CONSUMERISM WAS INEVITABLE

Let us now consider in greater depth the first of the five conclusions I cited at the outset of this article—namely, that consumerism was inevitable. Consumerism did not necessarily have to happen in the 1960's, but it had to happen eventually in view of new conditions in the U.S. economy that warranted a fresh examination of the economic power of sellers in relation to buyers.

At the same time, there are very good reasons why consumerism did flare up in the mid-1960's. The phenomenon was not due to any single cause. Consumerism was reborn because all of the conditions that normally combine to produce a successful social movement were present. These conditions are structural conduciveness, structural strain, growth of a generalized belief, precipitating factors, mobilization for action, and social control.[1] Using these six conditions, I have listed in Exhibit I the major factors under each that contributed to the rise of consumerism.

Structural conduciveness refers to basic developments in the society that eventually create potent contradictions. In the latest consumer movement, three developments are particularly noteworthy.

First, U.S. incomes and educational levels advanced continuously. This portended that many citizens would eventually become concerned with the quality of their lives, not just their material well-being.

Second, U.S. technology and marketing were becoming increasingly complex. That this would create potent consumer problems was noted perceptively by E. B. Weiss: "Technology has brought unparalleled abundance and opportunity to the consumer. It has also exposed him to new complexities and hazards. It has made his choices more difficult. He cannot be chemist, mechanic, electrician, nutritionist, *and* a walking computer (very necessary when shopping for fractionated-ounce food packages)! Faced with almost infinite product differentiation (plus contrived product virtues that are purely semantic), considerable price differentiation, the added complexities of trading stamps, the subtleties of cents-off deals, and other complications, the shopper is expected to choose wisely under circumstances that baffle professional buyers."[2]

Third, the environment was progressively exploited in the interests of abundance. Observers began to see that an abundance of cars and conveniences would produce a shortage of clean air and water. The Malthusian specter of man running out of sufficient resources to maintain himself became a growing concern.

These developments, along with some others, produced major *structural strains* in the society. The 1960's were a time of great public discontent and frustration. Economic discontent was created by steady inflation which left consumers feeling that their real incomes were deteriorating. Social discontent centered on the sorrowful conditions of the poor, the race issue, and the tremendous costs of the Vietnam war. Ecological

---

[1] These conditions were proposed in Neil J. Smelser, *Theory of Collective Behavior* (New York, The Free Press, 1963).

[2] "Marketers Fiddle While Consumers Burn," *Harvard Business Review*, July–August 1968, p. 48.

discontent arose out of new awarenesses of the world population explosion and the pollution fallout associated with technological progress. Marketing system discontent centered on safety hazards, product breakdowns, commercial noise, and gimmickry. Political discontent reflected the widespread feelings that politicians and government institutions were not serving the people.

Discontent is not enough to bring about change. There must grow a *generalized belief* about both the main causes of the social malaise and the potent effectiveness of collective social action. Here, again, certain factors contributed importantly to the growth of a generalized belief.

First, there were the writings of social critics such as John Kenneth Galbraith, Vance Packard, and Rachel Carson, that provided a popular interpretation of the problem and of actionable solutions.

Second, there were the hearings and proposals of a handful of Congressmen such as Senator Estes Kefauver that held out some hope of legislative remedy.

Third, there were the Presidential "consumer" messages of President Kennedy in 1962 and President Johnson in 1966, which legitimated belief and interest in this area of social action.

Finally, old-line consumer testing and educational organizations continued to call public attention to the consumers' interests.

Given the growing collective belief, consumerism only awaited some *precipitating factors* to ignite the highly combustible social material. Two sparks specifically exploded the consumer movement. The one was General Motors' unwitting creation of a hero in Ralph Nader through its attempt to investigate him; Nader's successful attack against General Motors encouraged other organizers to undertake bold acts against the business system. The other was the occurrence of widespread and spontaneous store boycotts by housewives in search of a better deal from supermarkets.

These chance combustions would have vanished without a lasting effect if additional resources were not *mobilized for action*. As it turned out, three factors fueled the consumer movement.

First, the mass media gave front-page coverage and editorial support to the activities of consumer advocates. They found the issues safe, dramatic, and newsworthy. The media's attention was further amplified through word-of-mouth processes into grass-roots expressions and feelings.

Second, a large number of politicians at the federal, state, and local levels picked up consumerism as a safe, high-potential vote-getting social issue.

Third, a number of existing and new organizations arose in defense of the consumer, including labor unions, consumer cooperatives, credit unions, product testing organizations, consumer education organizations, senior citizen groups, public interest law firms, and government agencies.

EXHIBIT I
Factors contributing to the rise of consumerism in the
1960s

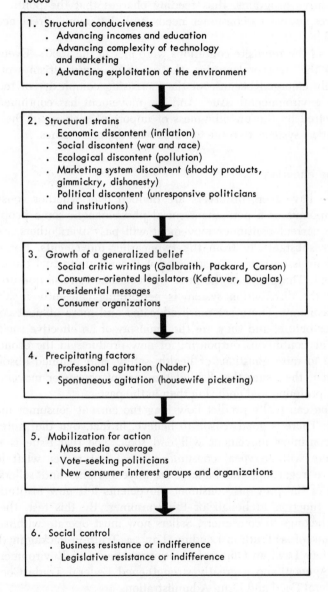

1. Structural conduciveness
   . Advancing incomes and education
   . Advancing complexity of technology
     and marketing
   . Advancing exploitation of the environment

2. Structural strains
   . Economic discontent (inflation)
   . Social discontent (war and race)
   . Ecological discontent (pollution)
   . Marketing system discontent (shoddy products,
     gimmickry, dishonesty)
   . Political discontent (unresponsive politicians
     and institutions)

3. Growth of a generalized belief
   . Social critic writings (Galbraith, Packard, Carson)
   . Consumer-oriented legislators (Kefauver, Douglas)
   . Presidential messages
   . Consumer organizations

4. Precipitating factors
   . Professional agitation (Nader)
   . Spontaneous agitation (housewife picketing)

5. Mobilization for action
   . Mass media coverage
   . Vote-seeking politicians
   . New consumer interest groups and organizations

6. Social control
   . Business resistance or indifference
   . Legislative resistance or indifference

Of course, the progress and course of an incipient social movement
depends on the reception it receives by those in *social control*, in this
case, the industrial-political complex. A proper response by the agents
of social control can drain the early movement of its force. But this
did not happen. Many members of the business community attacked,

resisted, or ignored the consumer advocates in a way that only strength-ened the consumerist cause. Most legislative bodies were slow to respond with positive programs, thus feeding charges that the political system was unresponsive to consumer needs and that more direct action was required.

Thus all the requisite conditions were met in the 1960's. Even without some of the structural strains, the cause of consumerism would have eventually emerged because of the increasing complexity of technology and the environmental issue. And the movement has continued to this day, abetted by the unwillingness of important sections of the business and political systems to come to terms with the basic issues.

It will be enduring

As we have seen, observers are divided over whether consumerism is a temporary or a permanent social phenomenon: some people argue that the current consumer movement will pass over; others argue that it differs substantially from the two earlier movements. For example, the ecology issue is here to stay and will continue to fuel the consumer movement. The plight of the poor will continue to raise questions about whether the distribution system is performing efficiently in all sectors of the economy. There are more educated and more affluent consumers than ever before, and they are the mainstay of an effective social move-ment. The continuous outpouring of new products in the economy will continue to raise questions of health, safety, and planned obsolescence. Altogether, the issues that flamed the current consumer movement may be more profound and enduring than in the past.

No one can really predict how long the current consumer movement will last. There is good reason to believe, in fact, that the protest phase of the consumer movement will end soon. The real issue is not how long there will be vocal consumer protest but rather what legacy it will leave regarding the balance of buyers' rights and sellers' rights.

Each of the previous consumer movements left new institutions and laws to function in behalf of the consumer. By this test, the victory already belongs to consumers. Sellers now must operate within the new constraints of a Truth-in-Lending Law, a Truth-in-Packaging Law, an Auto Safety Law, an Office of Consumer Affairs, an Environmental Pro-tection Agency, and a greatly strengthened Federal Trade Commission and Federal Food and Drug Administration.

It is no accident that such laws and institutions come into being when the demonstration and agitation phase of the consumer movement starts to dwindle. It is precisely the enactment of new laws and creation of new institutions that cause the protest phase to decline. Viewed over the span of a century, the consumer movement has been win-ning and increasing buyers' rights and power. In this sense, the consumerist movement is enduring, whether or not the visible signs of protest are found.

It can be beneficial

Businessmen take the point of view that since consumerism imposes costs on them, it will ultimately be costly to the consumer. Since they have to meet more legal requirements, they have to limit or modify some of their methods for attracting customers. This may mean that consumers will not get all the products and benefits they want and may find business costs passed on to them.

Businessmen also argue that they have the consumer's interests at heart and have been serving him well, and that customer satisfaction is the central tenet of their business philosophy. Many sincerely believe that consumerism is politically motivated and economically unsound.

The test of beneficiality, however, lies not in the short-run impact of consumerism on profits and consumer interests but rather in its long-run impact. Neither consumerism nor any social movement can get very far in the absence of combustible social material. Protest movements are messages coming from the social system that say that something is seriously wrong. They are the body politic's warning system. To ignore or attack protest signals is an invitation to deepening social strains. Protest movements are social indicators of new problems which need joint problem solving, not social rhetoric.

The essential legacy of consumerism promises to be beneficial in the long run. It forces businessmen to reexamine their social roles. It challenges them to look at problems which are easy to ignore. It makes them think more about ends as well as means. The habit of thinking about ends has been deficient in U.S. society, and protest movements such as consumerism, minority rights, student rights, and women's rights have a beneficial effect in raising questions about the purposes of institutions before it is too late.

Beyond this philosophical view of the beneficial aspects of protest movements may lie some very practical gains for consumers and businessmen. Here are four arguments advanced by consumerists:

1. Consumerism will increase the amount of product information. This will make it possible for consumers to buy more efficiently. They may obtain more value or goods with a given expenditure or a given amount of goods with a lower expenditure. To the extent that greater buying efficiency will result in surplus purchasing power, consumers may buy more goods in total.

2. Consumerism will lead to legislation that limits promotional expenditure which primarily affects market shares rather than aggregate demand. Consumer games, trading stamps, and competitive brand advertising in demand-inelastic industries are largely seen as increasing the

costs of products to consumers with little compensating benefits. Reductions in the level of these expenditures, particularly where they account for a large portion of total cost, should lead to lower consumer prices.

3.   Consumerism will require manufacturers to absorb more of the social costs imposed by their manufacturing operations and product design decisions. Their higher prices will decrease the purchase of high social cost goods relative to low social cost goods. This will mean lower governmental expenditures covered by taxes to clean up the environment. Consumers will benefit from a lower tax rate and/or from a higher quality environment.

4.   Consumerism will reduce the number of unsafe or unhealthy products which will result in more satisfied, healthier consumers.

These arguments are as cogent as contrary arguments advanced by some business spokesmen against responding to consumerism. This is not to deny that many companies will inherit short-run costs not compensated by short-run revenues and in this sense be losers. Their opposition to consumerism is understandable. But this is not the basis for developing a sound long-run social policy.

It is promarketing

Consumerism has come as a shock to many businessmen because deep in their hearts they believe that they have been serving the consumer extraordinarily well. Do businessmen deserve the treatment that they are getting in the hands of consumerists?

It is possible that the business sector has deluded itself into thinking that it has been serving the consumer well. Although the marketing concept is the professed philosophy of a majority of U.S. companies, perhaps it is more honored in the breach than in the observance. Although top management professes the concept, the line executives, who are rewarded for ringing up sales, may not practice it faithfully.

What is the essence of the marketing concept?

The marketing concept calls for a *customer orientation* backed by *integrated marketing* aimed at generating *customer satisfaction* as the key to attaining long-run profitable volume.

The marketing concept was a great step forward in meshing the actions of business with the interests of consumers. It meant that consumer wants and needs became the starting point for product and market planning. It meant that business profits were tied to how well the company succeeded in pleasing and satisfying the customer.

Peter F. Drucker suggested that consumerism is "the shame of the total marketing concept," implying that the concept is not widely implemented.[3] But even if the marketing concept as currently understood

---

[3] "The Shame of Marketing," *Marketing/Communications*, August 1969, p. 60.

were widely implemented, there would be a consumerist movement. Consumerism is a clarion call for a *revised marketing concept*.

The main problem that is coming to light rests on the ambiguity of the term *customer satisfaction*. Most businessmen take this to mean that *consumer desires* should be the orienting focus of product and market planning. The company should produce what the customer wants. But the problem is that in efficiently serving customers' desires, it is possible to hurt their long-run interests. Edmund Burke noted the critical difference when he said to the British electorate, "I serve your interests, not your desires." From the many kinds of products and services that satisfy consumers in the short run but disserve or dissatisfy them in the long run, here are four examples:

1. Large, expensive automobiles please their owners but increase the pollution in the air, the congestion of traffic, and the difficulty of parking, and therefore reduce the owners' long-run satisfaction.

2. The food industry in the United States is oriented toward producing new products which have high taste appeal. Nutrition has tended to be a secondary consideration. Many young people are raised on a diet largely of potato chips, hot dogs, and sweets which satisfy their tastes but harm their long-run health.

3. The packaging industry has produced many new convenience features for the American consumer such as nonreusable containers, but the same consumers ultimately pay for this convenience in the form of solid waste pollution.

4. Cigarettes and alcohol are classic products which obviously satisfy consumers but which ultimately hurt them if consumed in any excessive amount.

These examples make the point that catering to consumer satisfaction does not necessarily create satisfied consumers. Businessmen have not worried about this so long as consumers have continued to buy their products. But while consumers buy as *consumers*, they increasingly express their discontent as *voters*. They use the political system to correct the abuses that they cannot resist through the economic system.

The dilemma for the marketer, forced into the open by consumerism, is that he cannot go on giving the consumer only what pleases him without considering the effect on the consumer's and society's well-being. On the other hand, he cannot produce salutary products which the consumer will not buy. The problem is to somehow reconcile company profit, consumer desires, and consumer long-run interests. The original marketing concept has to be broadened to the societal marketing concept:

The societal marketing concept calls for a *customer orientation* backed by *integrated marketing* aimed at generating *customer satisfaction* and *long-run consumer welfare* as the key to attaining long-run profitable volume.

The addition of long-run consumer welfare asks the businessman to include social and ecological considerations in his product and market planning. He is asked to do this not only to meet his social responsibilities but also because failure to do this may hurt his long-run interests as a producer.

Thus the message of consumerism is not a setback for marketing but rather points to the next stage in the evolution of enlightened marketing. Just as the *sales concept* said that sales were all-important, and the original *marketing concept* said that consumer satisfaction was also important, the *societal marketing concept* has emerged to say that long-run consumer welfare is also important.

It can be profitable

This last assessment is the most difficult and yet the most critical of my five conclusions to prove. Obviously, if consumerism is profitable, businessmen will put aside their other objections. It is mainly because of its perceived unprofitability that many businessmen object so vehemently.

Can consumerism be profitable? Here my answer is "yes." Every social movement is a mixed bag of threats and opportunities. As John Gardner observed, "We are all continually faced with a series of great opportunities brilliantly disguised as insoluble problems." The companies that will profit from consumerism are those in the habit of turning negatives into positives. According to Peter F. Drucker: "*Consumerism actually should be, must be, and I hope will be, the opportunity of marketing. This is what we in marketing have been waiting for.*"[4]

The alert company will see consumerism as a new basis for achieving a differential competitive advantage in the marketplace. A concern for consumer well-being can be turned into a profitable opportunity in at least two ways: through the introduction of needed new products and through the adoption of companywide consumerist orientation.

NEW OPPORTUNITIES

One of the main effects of consumerism is to raise concerns about the health, safety, and social worthiness of many products. For a long time, *salutary criteria* have been secondary to *immediate satisfaction criteria* in the selection of products and brands. Thus when Ford tried to sell safety as an automobile attribute in the 1950's, buyers did not respond. Most manufacturers took the position that they could not educate the public to want salutary features but if the public showed this concern, then business would respond.

Unfortunately, the time came but business was slow to respond. Con-

---
[4] Ibid., p. 64.

sumer needs and wants have been evolving toward safety, health, and self-actualization concerns without many businessmen noticing this. More and more people are concerned with the nutritiousness of their foods, the flammability of their fabrics, the safety of their automobiles, and the pollution quality of their detergents. Many manufacturers have missed this changing psychological orientation of consumers.

Product reformulations

Today, there are a great many opportunities for creating and marketing new products that meet consumer desires for both short-term satisfaction and long-term benefits.

Exhibit II suggests a paradigm for thinking about the major types

EXHIBIT II
Classification of new product opportunities

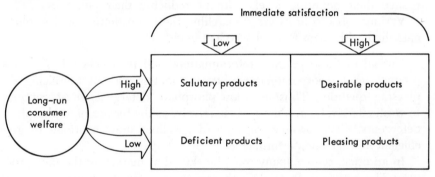

of new product opportunities. All current products can be classified in one of four ways using the dimensions of immediate satisfaction and long-run consumer interests. As this exhibit shows, *desirable products* are those which combine high immediate satisfaction and high long-run benefit, such as tasty, nutritious breakfast foods. *Pleasing products* are those which give high immediate satisfaction but which may hurt consumer interests in the long run, such as cigarettes. *Salutary products* are those which have low appeal but which are also highly beneficial to the consumer in the long run, such as low phosphate detergents. Finally, *deficient products* are those which have neither immediate appeal nor salutary qualities, such as a bad tasting patent medicine.

The manufacturer might as well forget about deficient products because too much work would be required to build in pleasing and salutary qualities. On the other hand, the manufacturer should invest his greatest effort in developing desirable products—e.g., new foods, textiles, appliances, and building materials—which combine intrinsic appeal and long-run beneficiality. The other two categories, pleasing and salutary prod-

358 Readings in basic marketing

ucts, also present a considerable challenge and opportunity to the company.

The challenge posed by pleasing products is that they sell extremely well but they ultimately hurt the consumer's interests. The product opportunity is therefore to formulate some alteration of the product that adds salutary qualities without diminishing any or too many of the pleasing qualities. This type of product opportunity has already been seized by a number of companies:

Sears has developed and promoted a phosphate-free laundry detergent which has become a big selling brand.

American Oil and Mobil Oil have developed and promoted no-lead or low-lead gasolines.

Pepsi-Cola has developed a one-way plastic soft drink bottle that is degradable in solid waste treatment.

Various automobile manufacturers are redesigning their engines to reduce their polluting levels without reducing their efficiency.

Various tobacco firms are researching the use of lettuce leaf to eliminate the health hazards of tobacco leaf in cigarettes.

Not all of these product reformulations will be successful. The new product must incorporate the salutary qualities without sacrificing the pleasing qualities. Thus new low-phosphate detergents must continue to wash effectively, or almost as effectively, as the former high-phosphate detergents. New low-lead or no-lead gasolines must continue to give efficient mileage and performance.

In addition, the company must be skilled at marketing the new products. The company faces difficult questions of what price to set, what claims to make, and what to do with the former product. In the case of low-lead gasoline, initial sales have been disappointing because of several factors, not the least of which is that it was priced at a premium and discouraged all but the most devoted environmentalists from buying it. The environmental appeal is strong, provided that the new product performs about as well as the old product and is not priced higher.

Salutary products, such as noninflammable draperies and many health foods, are considered "good for the customer" but somehow lack pleasing qualities. The challenge to the marketer is to incorporate satisfying qualities in the product without sacrificing the salutary qualities. Here are examples:

Quaker Oats has been reviewing desirable nutrients and vitamins, and formulating new breakfast cereals around them.

Some food manufacturers have created new soybean-based products, in each case adding pleasing flavors that appeal to the intended target groups.

Fabric manufacturers are trying to create attractive draperies out of new synthetic noninflammable materials.

Thus new product opportunities may be found by starting with appealing products and trying to add salutary qualities, or starting with salutary products and trying to add appealing qualities. This will become more important as more people show a concern for their environment and demand desirable products. There is already a sizable market segment made up of environmentalists who are ready to buy any product that has a salutary stamp. The alert company can even specialize in this market by commiting itself to creating and assorting products of high environmental appeal.

Consumerist orientation

A second way to respond profitably to consumerism is to become one of a growing number of companies that adopt and implement a thoroughgoing concern-for-the-consumer attitude. This goes beyond the occasional introduction of a few new products that combine pleasing and salutary qualities. It goes beyond an enlarged public relations campaign to appear as a "we care" company. To be effective, it involves management commitment, employee education, social actions, and company investment. A few companies have moved into a total consumerist orientation and have earned high consumer regard in the process. Here are two illustrative examples:

Giant Food, Inc., a leading supermarket chain in the Washington, D.C. area, actively introduced unit pricing, open dating, and nutritional labeling. According to a spokesman for the company, "These actions have improved Giant's goodwill immeasurably and have earned the admiration of leaders of the consumer movement."

Whirlpool Corporation has adopted a large number of measures to improve customer information and services, including a toll-free complaint service and improved product warranties. According to Stephen E. Upton, Whirlpool Vice President, "Our rate of increase in sales has tripled that of the industry. Our interest in the consumer has to be one of the reasons."

Obviously, such companies believe that these measures will increase their consumer goodwill and lead in turn to increased profits. The companies in each industry that adopt a consumerist orientation are likely to earn the early advantage and reap the rewards. If the profits are forthcoming, others will rush in and imitate the innovators. But imitation is often not as effective as innovation. Consumerism may well turn out to be an opportunity for the leaders and a cost for the laggards.

CONCLUSION

Consumerism was born for the third time in this century in the middle 1960's as a result of a complex combination of circumstances, not the least of which was increasingly strained relations between current business practices and long-run consumer interests. To many businessmen, it came as a shock because they thought the economic machinery, creating the highest standard of living in the world, was beyond consumer complaint. But the movement was inevitable, partly because of the success of economic machinery in creating complex, convenient, and pleasing products.

My assessment is that consumerism will be enduring, beneficial, promarketing, and ultimately profitable. Consumerism mobilizes the energies of consumers, businessmen, and government leaders to seek solutions to several complex problems in a technologically advanced society. One of these is the difference between serving consumer desires efficiently and serving their long-run interests.

To marketers, it says that products and marketing practices must be found which combine short-run and long-run values for the consumer. It says that a societal marketing concept is an advance over the original marketing concept and a basis for earning increased consumer goodwill and profits. The enlightened marketer attempts to satisfy the consumer *and* enhance his total well-being on the theory that what is good in the long run for consumers is good for business.

QUESTIONS

1. Was consumerism "inevitable"? Explain.
2. Evaluate Kotler's view that consumerism:
   a. will be enduring
   b. can be beneficial
   c. is promarketing
   d. can be profitable.
3. Provide a new illustration for each of Kotler's four new product opportunities.
*4. Compare and contrast the societal marketing concept and the marketing concept (see Reading 3).

Greyser feels that some of the gap between business and its critics is caused by different views about how the market works and/or should work. He presents several models to help one understand how he thinks. Then he offers several suggestions for narrowing the gap between marketing practice and the expectations of those making public policy.

---

34. PUBLIC POLICY AND THE MARKETING PRACTITIONER—TOWARD BRIDGING THE GAP*

Stephen A. Greyser

MANY other speakers at this conference are addressing themselves to identifying, describing, and defining the gaps between public policy interests and marketing practice. My purposes are to try to understand what underlies those gaps, and to suggest ameliorative actions on the parts of marketers, public policy officials, and researchers. In so doing, much of my attention will be devoted to issues involving advertising, for this is the area where most of my own research work has been done. Much of the presentation also will focus particularly on what we can logically expect from marketers themselves in bridging the gap.

WHY THE GAP?

The conference "call memorandum" asked why it is that a problem exists if marketing is the practice of varying responses by firms to the heterogenous demands of the marketplace? The matter of trying to understand the conflicts between marketers and critics of marketing has been a long-standing interest of mine. I see three different sets of phenomena involved. One has to do with ways different groups and individuals view the *mechanism of the marketplace,* i.e., the interface between marketers' actions and consumers. (For example, how does advertising work—in terms of the consumer behavior it is intended to affect and how that influence occurs.[1]) A second is the conflict within us (individually and communally) between "citizen" and "consumer," a dilemma for both the *marketer* and *marketplace.* A third is the consequence of the realities of segmentation. Let us look at each in more detail.

---

* Reprinted with permission from Fred C. Allvine, ed., *Public Policy and Marketing Practices* (Chicago: American Marketing Association, 1973), pp. 219–232. At the time of writing, Dr. Greyser was Professor of Business Administration at the Harvard Business School.

[1] For a more detailed treatment of this concept see Raymond A. Bauer and Stephen A. Greyser, "The Dialogue That Never Happens" (Thinking Ahead), *Harvard Business Review,* November–December 1967, p. 2.

Marketplace models

How one views the marketer-consumer interactions as taking place is one's model of the marketplace. And the fact that different people have different models of the marketplace underlies some of the conflict between marketer and public policy groups. In a recent *Harvard Business Review* article, I described three different overall models, and set forth a set of questions to enable one to define his own model.[2] While no single model applies to all situations, one's *basic* view of the marketplace will generally fit one of the following overall models:

1. *Manipulative*—a critic's model that portrays marketing's role as basically that of persuading/seducing less-than-willing consumers to buy. Consumers are seen as pawns struggling in an unequal battle against their adversaries, the marketers, who use advertising as an important and powerful one-sided weapon.
2. *Service*—a pro-business model that (a) portrays as successful marketers only those who serve consumers best and (b) predicts failure for those who do not so serve. Consumers are seen as rather more intelligent and less seduced than in the manipulative model. A credo of the service model is: "Consumers cast their ballots at the cash register every day . . . and besides, we know what they want via market research." Advertising is seen as helping to facilitate choices made by consumers who generally know what they want.
3. *Transactional*—a model derived from communications research that portrays the marketplace relationship in more of a give-and-take fashion. Consumers trade time and attention to advertising for the information and entertainment in the ads; consumers trade money for products that provide them with functional and/or psychological satisfactions. The transactional model posits a somewhat sophisticated consumer, at least in terms of his or her individual buying criteria.

To try to define your own model of the marketplace, let me suggest a self-administered test of your thinking. Thus:

What is your basic view of how the marketplace mechanism operates?
What really constitutes "consumer needs" and "rational" choice?
How intelligent are the choices made by the typical consumer?
Where does the emphasis lie between adversary and friend in the marketer's role toward the consumer?
How does advertising work?
What is the perceived "seduction quotient" in advertising?
How sophisticated or defenseless are consumers in their ability to screen the advertising and its content that comes their way?

---

[2] Stephen A. Greyser, "Advertising: Attacks and Counters," *Harvard Business Review*, March–April 1972, from which the models and questions are repeated.

After you have determined your marketplace model, then ask yourself whether your model grows from your view of how consumers do behave or your view of how consumers should behave. I suspect that how consumers *should* behave is the premise for what most critics of advertising and marketing believe, whereas how consumers *do* behave perforce is the premise for what most marketers believe. From answering the foregoing questions, you should be able to understand why you view certain issues regarding advertising's social impacts as you do.

Consumer versus citizen

Each of us faces a set of moral dilemmas as individuals, the understanding of which may help further to explain the gap. And as a community or society, we face the same dilemmas. For example, as citizens we may want to hold in check the use (depletion) of energy; yet as consumers we may wish to have air conditioners, electric appliances, and the like that consume such energy. Indeed, the Electric Companies of New England have recently been running an advertising program spawned by this dilemma. The ads show "two faces" of the same person debating the personal desire for more appliances and the societal interest in fewer power plants.

Another example is the consumer use of throw-away bottles and the citizen concern for the environment. The extent to which we, as individuals, are willing to trade off additional inconvenience or additional cost (e.g., in cars for safety or anti-pollution equipment) is a measure of our individual resolutions of the citizen-consumer conflict. My impression is that the *citizen* in us is affected first by new directions in broad societal thinking, witness Ford's experience in the 1950's with "safety doesn't sell."

As some speakers here have noted, particularly George Fisk, certain situations seem so serious that societal resolution, affecting us all, is the eventual resolution. Mandatory safety and anti-pollution equipment on cars is one example, as would be a ban on the manufacture of cigarettes. Until such mandatory actions occur, however, the brunt of the dilemma for the typical marketer is far more serious than for the typical consumer. The reason: a marketer typically aims at only *part* of the marketplace; thus he is extremely vulnerable, in serving one subset of heterogeneous demands, to having all his eggs in an unsteady basket. This is not to plead for those marketers; it is to explain in part how voluntary action can go only so far. What, pray tell, would a liquor manufacturer do—by way of voluntary restriction—in the face of arguments to restore Prohibition?

Realities of segmentation

This leads us to the third factor that helps us to understand the gap between practitioner action and perceived community interest, namely the realities of segmentation. That ever more refined segmentation—in products and premises addressed to subgroups of consumers—is the trend seems undebatable. Whether this trend reflects improved marketer *service to* or *power over* consumers is very debatable (based largely on one's view of the marketplace mechanism!)

The realities of segmentation create a host of "fallout" problems. Here are a few illustrations drawn from just one area of marketing, namely advertising:

a. *Irritating advertising*—The current mass media structure represents a relatively narrow channel through which most of the segmented consumer products are promoted to their intended consumer subgroups. Despite the existence of segmented magazines, more use of direct marketing, and some clear audience segmentation in TV (e.g., daytime audiences predominantly women), the bulk of consumer product promotion is done via TV at times when much of the audience may *not* be in the segment being directly addressed. The result is increased annoyance on the part of the *non*-target members of the audience. Further, the apparent acceleration of diversity in life styles within our society, and the vigorous affirmation of that diversity, seems to me to strengthen the likelihood of more such annoyance in the future.

b. *Role portrayal*—How advertising portrays different groups in our society is another "fallout" issue in advertising. The portrayal of women and of ethnic groups in ads has been a topic of concern and complaint. For example, ads in which women are portrayed in a particular manner may individually be defensible in terms of management's view of the majority of its market.

Yet the cumulative effect of all such ads (for a given brand, product, or in general) may not reflect present-day roles of women.[3] Value judgments are again distinctly involved—e.g., should ads show society as it is or as someone (the advertiser?) thinks it should be?

The reality of segmentation here lies in large part in the kind of people to whom the product and advertising are geared . . . and how the portrayal of *these particular people* is perceived by others who *aren't* like them. More on this momentarily.

c. *Miscommunication in advertising*—The broad availability of media advertising, particularly in TV, leads to yet another problem. The *opportunity* for miscommunication—or, better, misreception of intended communication—particularly on the part of a minority of the audience, is enhanced. Our growing societal sensitivity to the importance of such miscommunication and misreception creates a salient new question for advertisers and public policy people: Is there a "normal minimum" proportion of people who take away an incorrect impression

[3] For an analysis of this subject, see Alice E. Courtney and Sarah Lockeretz, "A Woman's Place: An Analysis of the Roles Portrayed by Women in Magazine Advertisements," *Journal of Marketing Research,* February 1971, p. 92.

from marketing communications? (Perhaps rephrased more pungently as "What is the consumer equivalent to the legendary military 10% who 'never get the word'?") Whatever one's view on what constitutes miscommunication (see the section below, "Legal Applications of Consumer Psychology"), this question is relevant.

ISSUES FOR FAIR-MINDED MARKETERS

The above problems have been described in large part from the marketer's point of view. This is not because that is the proper or predominant perspective to take. It is because the extent to which we can expect voluntary action on the marketer's part to help bridge the gap is a chief focus of my presentation.

Let us for the moment posit a "sensitive, fair-minded marketer." This is a marketer aware of changing societal trends and expectations, and interested in being responsive to them even at more than small expense (but not in voluntarily going out of business).

How would such a marketer, in my opinion, react to some major issues (again chosen from advertising) that reflect changing, and rising, expectations for marketing-advertising behavior? In each area, let me try to delineate reactions to the *concept* and to its *implementation*.

1. *Claims substantiation*—The concept of advertising claims substantiation is one that is strongly supported even by the business community. (According to a *Harvard Business Review* survey in 1971, over 85% of the executive community supports the forcing of advertisers to substantiate their claims.) For the fair-minded marketer, the questions are principally those of implementation, in terms of research,[4] along with matters of *modus operandi* for protecting design or formula secrets.

2. *Corrective advertising*—The concept of restoring the state of the marketplace is another that the fair-minded marketer can espouse. For if a marketer has been proven to have advertised deceptively, certainly his marketplace position—and the advertising's impacts on the consumer—should be "rolled back." Again, in my view, the relevant questions relate to implementation: the rather Procrustean initial FTC plan (a fixed percentage of the erring firm's advertising for a fixed period of time) needs calibration. The meaningful research questions here are not dissimilar to those asked by advertisers and agencies themselves about the impact of their ads. Assessing the degree of miscommunication and its consequences at the *output* point (consumers) is to me a preferred place to start the process of remedy. (More focus on the state of the consumer's mind in the next section.)

3. *Group portrayal*—This area, as noted earlier, does involve value judgments more than either of the first two. However, the fair-minded

---

[4] Stephen A. Greyser, "Advertising: Attacks and Counters," *Harvard Business Review*, March–April 1972, p. 26, provides a list of major research questions.

marketer can show sensitivity to issues of portrayal, and (as a number have) make adjustments to overcome inadvertent slips in this area.

However, feasibility can go only so far—depending on the product . . . and the nature of the protest. For example, a recent NOW protest claimed that 43% of TV ads monitored in a two-week period showed women involved in household tasks. But if one were a detergent or floorwax manufacturer, what other major uses of the product are there?

A recent Folger's Coffee commercial shows how the housewife stereotype can be avoided . . . but at the risk of being accused of chauvinistic unrealism; in the commercial, the husband is shown, in an apron, making and praising the coffee.

4. *Counter advertising*—This is an area where I believe the *concept* must be seriously questioned . . . both generally and particularly as viewed by the fair-minded marketer. For the latter would seem to have little alternative other than to restrict or even withdraw his advertising in the face of free counter advertising.

Perhaps even more of a problem—for all advertisers, and for the public—is the prospective chaos that might easily result because almost *every* product, in the minds of *some* group, would have "another side to the story." For example, consider chewing gum's effect on teeth, foreign cars (U.S. unemployment), and liquor (excessive drinking). Illustrative of the realistic extent to which this concept can be taken is an ecologist's argument, reported in the June 12 *Sports Illustrated,* that a false advertising suit be brought against Smokey the Bear because (in the ecologist's view) fires in the forest are largely ecologically sound!

Again let me note that the fair-minded marketer's perspective is not the only, nor necessarily the most important, one to consider in assessing public policy issues such as the above. But the ease with which rational discussion and research may lead to bridging the gap via marketer action is closely and clearly linked to that perspective.

LEGAL APPLICATIONS OF CONSUMER PSYCHOLOGY

A "growth industry" emerging in the wake of increased public policy activity in the marketing field is that of legal applications of consumer psychology. The increasing need for evidence on the "state of consumers' minds" has spurred an interest in this area on the parts of consumer psychologists, corporate lawyers, public policy interest group lawyers, public policy officials, professors of consumer behavior, and marketers. For the consumer's mind is indeed the consequence of much marketing and advertising activity.

General Electric's Dr. Herbert Krugman has been a focal point in this development, and his work has thus far resulted in several informal meetings among members of all the above groups, and a public session on the subject at the recent national American Marketing Association Spring Conference in New York.[5]

Because the field is so new, at this juncture let me only categorize its principal dimensions.

The major areas of effort cluster around three topics. These are *deception, unfairness,* and *remedy.* The first of these involves such matters as defining what deception means, under what conditions, for what kinds of consumers, and the like.

Unfairness encompasses such topics as:

definition for diverse consumer groups (e.g., based on interest in particular products, responsiveness to advertising, etc.);

questions of functional and psychological needs—whether they are separable and if so call for different sets of considerations;

the issue of unconscionability (taking advantage of consumer's gullibility), and whether the reasonable man or the credulous man should be the standard of appraising unfairness.

Remedy includes considerations of restitution and contraception. Most aspects of this area await progress in the first two. All three zones call not only for much research work but for clarification in order to sharpen issues to be researched (or to be declared "unamenable" to measurement).

The foregoing is sketchy . . . but should serve to indicate the broad dimensions of the territory. One specific current research effort is the preparation of a Marketing Science Institute working paper treating the current status and trends regarding the use of evidence from and about consumers in legal and regulatory proceedings regarding marketing activity.

AMELIORATIVE ACTIONS

What can and should marketers, public policy people, and teachers and researchers do to help bridge the gap? My context here is one of amelioration, not solution, because candor compels me to think that the latter is an unrealistic goal. But I believe that there is room for substantial progress, albeit short of solution.

Marketers' actions

What can marketers do? In my view, they must reconsider their view of their relationship with their consumers, and also develop additional criteria for planning and assessing their marketing programs.

---

[5] The session included reports from Herbert Krugman, Charles Ramond, Joseph Smith, and Stephen A. Greyser.

Consumer orientation—The first action I think marketers must take is a mental one. It is to realize that marketers in the 1970's will have to *live* consumer orientation, whereas their counterparts in the 1960's mostly only *talked* about it. What does this change imply? Whether based on perception alone or also on reality, there seems to be a feeling among the public that there is a growing distance between the individual consumer and the impersonal corporation. Thus, individual marketers need to assess this perception in their own situation, and work to reduce the distance by direct and visible actions.

For example, Whirlpool's "Cool-Line"* is a channel for corporate repersonalization in resolving consumer service problems. Stop and Shop's "consumer board of directors" provides direct input from representative consumers to major executives in a regular fashion. Various firms have "offices of consumer action" and the like as a conduit and contact for consumers with the company.

In terms of both consumer *input to* and *feedback on* marketing actions, marketers must ask "where *is* the consumer on our oganization chart?" Another aspect of this reorientation is that efforts to reach, and be reached by, consumers must be genuine and serious. *Cosmetic consumerism* is worse than none. This is particularly true when a company wants to advertise its consumer orientation. When, as one automobile firm did, a company advertises "its man" at headquarters as a hub for consumer contact, the man and his staff not only need to be there, but need to be able to take action.

An interesting sidelight to the matter of "action" comes from the consumer affairs executive of a major airline, whose department was dubbed the "office of consumer action." He preferred to name the department more modestly—the "office of consumer affairs"—until it had demonstrated that it *could* take action.

Yet another element of "living" a consumer orientation is to recognize that there are merchandising opportunities in the "land of public policy." As has been seen in the supermarket field, there are opportunities to "bridge the gap" at a competitive advantage. For example, the supermarket companies which first espoused unit-pricing, open-dating, and nutritional labeling have generally been able to use these to competitive advantage in their market areas.

Marketing programs—Additional areas of marketer action lie in the realm of marketing programs themselves. For example, in product planning, new product introduction, and promotion—to cite just the most obvious zones—new questions must be added to those management should ask.

More specifically, in product planning and introduction, consideration of a product's *environmental implications*, its *safety* and *reliability*, and

---

* *Editor's Note: This is a free telephone service enabling consumers to talk directly to the manufacturer if satisfaction cannot be obtained locally.*

the company's ability to provide adequate *servicing* must all be reexamined in light of the public's changing (rising) expectations of product performance in these respects.

In the promotional area, the new questions that must be asked concern the substantiability of advertising claims, the extent of potential miscommunication in advertising messages, and the ways in which various groups are portrayed. The implications for creative work and for copy testing are direct, and major.

Other actions—Two other areas of action and sensitivity warrant at least brief mention. First, that marketers should support research efforts to learn more about the effects of marketing programs on the public, in the latter's twin roles of consumer and citizen alike. The Moss bill to create a national institute for the study of marketing is of particular potential usefulness in this territory. And—if a brief "commercial" be permitted—the work of objective but knowledgeable research organizations in the field of marketing, such as the Marketing Science Institute,* warrants strong support from the marketing practitioner community. Second, marketers—whether they like it or not—must become more accustomed to living with criticism. Business, particularly marketing, seems to be bathed in the spotlight of substantial critical attention. Not only will marketers have to become more tough-skinned, but they will be spending more time on public policy/legal issues than ever before.

Public policy people's actions

What steps toward "bridging the gap" do I suggest should be taken by public policy people? My recommendations fall into four zones of inquiry and thought.

1. Ask "why" more often—Marketing and advertising students are taught to ask about the objectives of a program or campaign—why a marketer is doing what he is doing—before appraising the program. Similarly, this should be a more frequent activity in the public policy field than my experience indicates that it is. Sometimes marketers are unwise or even incorrect, from a marketing viewpoint, in their work; very few are deliberately malevolent. My impression is that the former is occasionally mistaken for the latter by regulatory and legislative officials. Their own understanding might be enhanced, and their perspective somewhat modified, if they stopped long enough to ask questions such as:

what was the marketer's aim?
to what kind of people was that ad addressed?

---

* *Editor's Note: This is a non-profit research group supported by business firms with the view to better understanding and improving both micro and macro marketing.*

in what way was this marketer trying to have his own product viewed versus competition?

Similarly, the "why" behind public policy proposals might be explored. The objectives—in terms of consumer and marketer behavior—and the likely impacts (including the important *secondary* effects) of such proposals should be probed.

2. *Marketing education*—My natural prejudice for education is already betrayed by the paragraphs above. But I strongly believe that regulators (particularly) should know more about the activities and phenomena they are regulating than many marketing regulators have evinced. The need for more understanding of marketing and of consumer behavior on the part of the FTC staff has been underscored by no less than FTC Commissioner Mary Gardiner Jones herself, in calling for both additional trained staff people and more assistance from trained academic researchers.

My own urging for increased knowledge of marketing and consumer behavior carefully delineates *education* from *indoctrination*. The fact that professors of marketing and marketers themselves may be among the principal sources of information and knowledge does not mean that indoctrination is my aim. Far from it. Education here, as I view it, not only takes no particular "party line" about what is known about marketing, but also focuses on what we *don't* know. And "don't know" includes what public policy officials don't know, what marketers don't know, and what even professors (!) don't know . . . about marketing and its impacts on consumers.

3. *Listen to consumers themselves*—If the voice of the consumer is sometimes not fully heard by marketers, to me it seems at least as often not fully heard by public policy people. Both marketers and regulators need to listen more.

The voice of the consumer, I would argue, is not solely transmitted through consumer organizations, which act (and appropriately so) as pressure groups more often than as representatives. In terms of both the *importance* of certain issues, and the *postures* on those issues, more input from the public itself is a vital and needed ingredient in public policy making. The emergence of the field of legal applications of consumer psychology is to me a positive sign that the "state of the consumer's mind" will be playing a greater role in public policy decisions than heretofore.

4. *More concern for marketplace pluralism*—Marketers almost by definition strive for pluralism in the marketplace through their efforts to differentiate their products from those of their competitors. This pluralism in product offerings, and all that accompanies them, is paralleled by growing pluralism among the consuming public. Interest and concern

in preserving pluralism would seem to serve both the public and marketers.

That pluralism is obviously impinged upon as successive legislative and regulatory steps are taken. (Robert Moran has characterized the profession as moving from *laissez-faire* to *anti-fraud* to *prescribed information* to *product performance standards* to *design standards*.)[6] My suggestion is not to stop what seems to be a continuing movement along this spectrum as legislators and regulators interpret the needs of our society regarding marketing activities. But I do urge that the maintenance and enhancement of pluralism in the marketplace be a strong criterion in considering and assessing public policy proposals.

Teachers' and researchers' actions

Teachers and researchers can be of considerable assistance to public policy-makers, also to marketers, and to consumers.

For public policy-makers—Already cited is the need for more education about marketing-advertising-consumer behavior on the part of public policy makers. By dint of their own training and inclination, faculty people can do this best, via seminars, meetings, and the like. Such activity *should* be undertaken.

Research guidance and advice is the other way in which professional researchers can help. This is particularly so in the case of interpreting consumer behavior. I see them offering independent and experienced insight into the relevance and meaning of consumer evidence in particular cases. For example, in the FTC hearings in the Wonder Bread case, the Commission staff used data from a consumer study showing nutrition to be the reason for purchase expressed by about 20% of respondents. They failed, however, to note that this percentage came from a forced choice question with four reasons, and that an open-end question in the same study showed less than 1% of the public said they bought bread for reasons of nutrition. Separately, other staff analysis of the data failed to look at cross-tabulation responses from consumer subgroups whose reactions would lead an experienced researcher to different conclusions.

Of perhaps even greater assistance than at the final litigative stage is advice and involvement *preceding* that point. Involvement *before* positions harden may save valuable time and money on the part of regulatory staffs. Going even further, at the stage of pre-analysis of regulatory and/or legislative proposals, professional consumer behavior researchers may serve to alert people on all sides as to strengths and

---

[6] Robert Moran, "Formulating Public Policy on Consumer Issues: Some Preliminary Findings," Marketing Science Institute Working Paper, 1971.

weaknesses to help focus and sharpen debate . . . and perhaps even reshape the proposals.

For marketers—Many teachers and researchers have long helped marketers by serving as consultants regarding marketing programs. This assistance needs to be extended into the public policy zone in two ways. First, research is needed to study the tradeoffs between citizen and consumer interests. For example, a current Marketing Science Institute exploratory study is examining the relationships between *pleasantness* and *effectiveness* in advertising.

A second kind of help is that involving better understanding of the implications of public policy actions and proposals for marketers. My colleague Robert D. Buzzell has suggested that marketers must reconsider all elements of the marketing mix in terms of such implications—a "revised marketing mix," so to speak.

For consumers—If teachers and researchers can succeed in making contributions to public policy makers and marketers, then by that very fact two kinds of value can come to the public. From the former comes better value for his or her tax dollars spent on the public policy apparatus. From the latter comes better value for dollars spent in the marketplace. Hopefully both can result.

CONCLUSION

These remarks have deliberately sought to cover a rather wide territory within the public policy field. Let me try to restate my principal observations:

1. The gap between marketing practitioner actions and public policy desires is unlikely to be bridged in full. To try to narrow the gap, however, we should first try for better understanding of why there is a gap. The latter particularly involves recognizing that:

different basic models of the marketplace tend to characterize marketers and public policy people

the consumer and the citizen within us, individually and communally, are in frequent conflict regarding marketing and public policy

the realities of segmentation suggest an irreducible minimum in such conflict.

2. While marketers should hardly be the sole or even the central focus of public policy considerations, the question of "what would a fair-minded marketer do" in response to given public policy proposals is one important element in appraising them.

3. The field of legal applications of consumer psychology is a "growth industry," and reflects a need for more input from consumers themselves in the adjudicative process. Knowing more about the "state

of the consumer's mind" is an important element for marketer and public policy maker alike.

4. Ameliorative actions to help bridge the gap (*not* solutions) are urged upon marketers, public policy people, and teachers-researchers. Marketers, in terms of both marketing programs and sensitivity, will have to *live* the consumer orientation their colleagues of a decade ago could afford just to *talk about.* Public policy people should make a priority of learning much more than they now know about the how and why of marketing and consumer behavior. Teachers and researchers can aid in this educational process, and can also provide useful research insights on public policy issues, preferably by involvement *before* positions harden on a particular proposal or case.

QUESTIONS

1. Describe your own model of the marketplace.
2. How would a critic with a "manipulative" model react to the four suggested actions of a "sensitive, fair-minded marketer"? What model does this hypothetical marketer seem to have? Explain.
3. Evaluate Greyser's suggestions for "ameliorative action" for:
   a. marketers
   b. public policy people
   c. teachers and researchers.
4. How should we determine what the consumer-citizens want, i.e., "the state of the consumer's mind"? Who should speak for them?
°5. Are Greyser's and Kotler's (Reading 33) suggestions consistent? Explain. Is Alderson's thinking (Reading 5) relevant or useful in this "debate"?

For years, some economists and historians have been predicting the eventual collapse of capitalism in the United States, and the emergence of a perfectly-planned government-regulated economy. We have already reached the stage where private enterprise has surrendered many of its freedoms to public authority. And, with the aid of inflation and price controls, we may be approaching the point where it will be too difficult either to give up the controls or to manage the economy that has been created. Our free-market system may simply collapse. Grayson argues that this should be a concern not only for business and labor leaders, but also for each individual who wants to preserve a way of life that is worth caring about.

35. LET'S GET BACK TO THE COMPETITIVE MARKET SYSTEM*

C. Jackson Grayson, Jr.

FOR ALMOST 15 months during Phase II of the Economic Stabilization Program, I served as the chairman of the Price Commission. Exercising control over most of the nation's price system, I saw this complex, capitalist economy from a most unusual observation post.

From this experience, and from what has happened since, I am personally convinced that our economic system is steadily shifting from a private enterprise, free-market economy to one that is centrally directed and under public control.

Price and wage controls such as we have experienced in Phases I through IV have helped to extend the degree of public control and to accelerate the rate of change. At some point—and I predict that, at the present rate, this point may be reached in about 15 to 20 years—the essential characteristics of a competitive, private enterprise system (nonregulated prices, profit motive, risk taking, collective bargaining) will no longer make up the economic engine that drives our system.

I am not saying that there is and will continue to be public regulation of the private enterprise system. Since 1930, we have had that—a mixed public-private system. But, in the 1970s, the pendulum of the mix has been swinging further, and faster, toward central control.

Call it what you will—managed capitalism, socialism, a planned economy, a postindustrial state—the end result will be the virtual elimination of the free-market system as we now know it. There will be no signposts or traffic lights. We will simply shift over to another kind of system.

The resulting system will probably not have widespread public ownership of production and distribution; but it will have public control. General Motors will not die; but neither will it remain a capitalistically motivated and directed enterprise. Rather, it will operate as an organization designed to implement *public* economic, political, and social policy.

Impetus for this trend has not come from a group of revolutionists, and only partly from leftists, liberals, youth, intellectuals, and socialists. Instead, it has come from the public at large, from the Congress, and,

---

* Reprinted with permission from the *Harvard Business Review*, November–December 1973, pp. 103–12. © 1973, The President and Fellows of Harvard College. At the time of writing, Dr. Grayson, former Head of the Phase II Price Commission, was Dean of the School of Business Administration of Southern Methodist University.

perhaps most surprisingly, from the actions of many labor and business leaders.

I feel that this current threat to our free, competitive economy should seriously concern us, not only because I strongly believe in that system, but also because of the effect its loss would have on the social character of the United States.

In this article I attempt to identify what the current shifts away from freedom are and why they are a cause for alarm, and to suggest courses of action that businessmen, labor leaders, and legislators could take to help reverse the clear and present trend.

WARNING SIGNS

The trends I see can be summarized as follows:

Business and labor are too often seeking to reduce rather than to encourage competition in their markets.

Continuing price and wage controls are leading the public to believe that central planning and control are superior, mandatory, and desirable.

Americans, in distrusting the market system, are demanding more economic benefits from the federal government and are seeking ways to insulate themselves from the impact of economic change.

In addition, international economic interdependencies are complicating our privately controlled market system. As recent balance-of-payments and exchange-rate problems demonstrate, closed economies are a thing of the past. Inflation can be exported and imported, increasing the call for more centrally coordinated economic policies between and inside nations.

Business seeks protection

Consciously and unconsciously, businessmen themselves are adding to the probability of greater centralization of economic control by seeking ways to reduce market competition—the very keystone on which the capitalist system rests.

Normally, competition is curtailed either by private monopoly power or by government protection. It is still unclear whether large corporations have sufficient power to control markets, reduce competition, and "administer" prices. Our internal studies at the Price Commission did not provide any evidence that prices were being administered by corporations. But, clearly, we did not have sufficient time to make a full study of this issue.

We did have time, however, to observe innumerable instances in which business turned to government to seek forms of assistance which, in effect, would reduce competition—for example, asking for imposition of subsidies and tariffs, occupational licensing, fair trade laws, and import quotas.

Excerpts from letters written to me at the Price Commission by businessmen serve as illustrations:

"I do not advocate any program of isolation, but I do think it is good business for us to protect our national economic situation in the face of stiff and competitive foreign trade." (A steel company)

"We need government protection because we can't compete against the big companies." (A consumer goods company)

"If you break our fair trade laws, the market will be chaotic." (A cosmetics company)

"We can't survive if you let cheap products in from foreign countries." (A shoe manufacturer)

"We must have minimum milk prices if we are to have an orderly market." (A dairy products company)

"If we allow liquor prices to fluctuate freely, competition will be ruinous and the Mafia might move in." (An alcoholic beverages company)

Another way some businesses are hampering the free-market system is by not using the age-old competitive tool of reducing prices as a way to increase their sales.

Again, to quote from my 1972 mail:

"In all my years in business, I have never reduced prices to hurt a competitor." (A retail food supplier)

"Why did I raise my prices? My competitor did. I always go up when he does." (A chemical company)

Of course, this attitude is not shared by all businessmen. After the Price Commission authorized a cost-justified price increase, one businessman told me, "You gave us a price increase. I wish the market would."

My point, however, is that far too few companies are exploring market flexibility by reducing prices. And yet, when we ordered some companies to reduce prices because they had violated regulations, several reported that they experienced increased volume and a higher total profit.

But the reluctance to reduce prices is also understandable. Several heavy-industry companies reported that they feared competing too aggressively on price because they would capture a larger market share, drive out smaller companies, and be subject to Justice Department or competitor antitrust suits. Efficient stevedoring companies argued they would drive out smaller businesses if they held prices down. And after the Russian wheat sale drove flour prices up, small bakeries urged us to force large bakeries to raise their bread prices.

The threat of continuing price controls has compounded the price-reduction problem. Many companies report hesitancy to reduce prices for fear of being caught with a low "base price" in future freezes and phases. This was clearly demonstrated in Phase III, when freeze "talk" actually accelerated price increases.

Finally, I was surprised to find that the majority of businessmen with whom I talked wanted Phase II controls continued. The most commonly stated reason was fear of union power. The argument was that the balance of power has swung so far toward the unions that businessmen feel they can no longer negotiate successfully. Accordingly, they choose price controls over wage disputes; they prefer regulation to the problems freedom poses.

So does labor

In the model of the free market, it is axiomatic that competitive behavior is required not only of business but also of labor. There must be competition in wages as well as in prices. More and more, however, it's not turning out that way.

Like big business, big labor tries to use government or private power to protect itself against such natural effects of competition as layoffs, dislocations, wage reductions, and advancement by competition.

Whether labor has too much power was not an issue we studied at the Price Commission during the control period. But many instances in which noncompetitive labor practices were driving costs up were reported to us as justifications for price increases—featherbedding in railroads and docks, restrictive work rules in construction and shipping, and rules barring more efficient methods in construction and printing.

An October 1971 staff report of the Bureau of Domestic Commerce estimates such extra costs in construction at $1 billion to $3 billion annually, in railroads at $700 million to $1.2 billion, in printing at $400 million to $600 million, in supermarkets at $250 million to $400 million, and in trucking at $275 million to $400 million.

These restrictive, noncompetitive work practices are usually defended by labor on humanitarian grounds. Without judging the merit of that position, I can definitely say that these practices drive costs up and usually result in higher unit labor costs, higher domestic prices, and reduced competitive abilities abroad.

Just as business often does not see price reductions as necessary and competitive, so labor does not see wage levels as connected to successful or unsuccessful competition in the free-market system. Nor does labor see the natural relationship between productivity and the wages that a company can afford to pay. Companies report mounting pressure from labor for increased compensation, regardless of the productivity of individual workers or of the nation as a whole. Labor's typical demands include increased minimum wage levels, "catch-up" wage increases, fixed productivity rates, tandem wage agreements, and annual pay increments.

For example, in late 1971, workers in the coal industry, which has had productivity decreases in recent years, received nearly a 14% wage increase settlement. The Price Commission, in one of its most important decisions, ruled that this practice would lead to further cost-push inflation and, despite the 14% wage settlement, allowed the coal industry to submit only a 5.5% wage cost as justification for price increases. This practice was then followed for all companies throughout Phase II.

As a result of this "5.5 rule," two things happened. Some companies suffered reduced profits. But other companies bargained harder at the table because they knew they could not "pass on" more than 5.5%. In fact, some companies reported privately that they were pleased with the rule because it gave them a bargaining weapon greatly needed to withstand labor's pressures.

There is little question that if labor settlements, on the average, rise faster than overall productivity, the result will be inflation, unemployment, or both. Our 5.5% limitation was an attempt to crack into the wage-productivity imbalance by forcing price increases to reflect no more than the long-term national productivity gain of 3%, plus a 2.5% inflation goal. The 5.5% was a national procrustean bed that served a crunching purpose in the short run.

We've also heard arguments by labor that economic justice demands wages be increased—a growing egalitarian ethic that wages be based on need rather than on competitive reality.

But those who argue this line sometimes end up taking contradictory positions, as was illustrated during the debate over the minimum wage. At the same time that many labor leaders and members of Congress were loudly protesting price increases in Phase II, they were also fighting equally hard for increased minimum wage levels and extended coverage. Without entering into the merits of the economic justice argument, the commission computed that the various proposed bills on the minimum wage before Congress in 1972 would have increased the Consumer Price Index anywhere from 0.3% to 0.8%. Since no productivity gains would have ensued, the increased costs would have either come out of profits or been passed on in prices.

In summary, I can only point out to labor and to business that any time they seek, through private market power or government help, to reduce the effects of competition, they invite the danger of permanent central control over the economic system. Without competition, public controls may become, not an option, but a necessity.

Wage-price controls distort

True, wage-price controls help attack inflation in the short run by (a) reducing inflationary expectations, (b) intruding on discretionary market power of business and labor, and (c) influencing the timing of price and wage decisions.

But, by their very design, such controls interfere with the market system and hasten its move toward a permanent central one. I can spot seven ways this occurs:

First, wage-price controls lead to distortions in the economic system, which can be minimized only in the short run. The longer controls are in, the harder it is to discern real from artificial signals. No matter how cleverly any group designs a control system, distortions and inequities will begin to appear. It happened in European control programs; it was beginning to happen in Phase II.

For instance, lumber controls were beginning to lead to artificial middlemen, black markets, and sawmill shutdowns. Companies trapped with low base-period profit margins were beginning to consider selling out to those with higher base periods, sending their capital overseas, or reducing their efforts. Instances of false job upgrading—which were actually "raises" in disguise—were reported on a scattered but increasing basis. To keep away from profit-margin controls, companies were considering dropping products where costs, and thus prices, had increased. And shortages of certain products (e.g., molasses and fertilizer) were appearing because artificially suppressed domestic prices had allowed higher world prices to pull domestic supplies abroad.

Exceptions and special regulations can handle some of these distortions, but the task grows more difficult as each correction breeds the need for another.

Second, during controls, the public forgets that not all wage-price increases are inflationary. In a changing, competitive economy, wage and price increases occur because of real consumer demand shifts and supply shortages. The resulting wage and price increases signal to business, "Make more"; or to labor, "Move here"; or to the public, "Use less."

Controls interfere with the signaling mechanism. A good example of how an artificially suppressed price-signal leads to eventual shortages is natural gas. Similar examples can be found in labor where suppressed wages do not attract labor to areas in which there are shortages of skills or of workers.

But with wage-price controls in place, the public believes that all increases are inflationary—almost antisocial—and the clamor is for no, or very small, increases.

The sense of the statement, "You can eliminate the middleman, but not his function," applies equally to our economic system. We live in a world of scarce resources, and, as much as some would like to repeal the laws of supply and demand, it can't be done. Some system must allocate resources, we hope to the most efficient use for society. If wage-price controls, other government regulatory rules, or business labor monopolies prohibit the price system from performing its natural function, then another rationing system (central planning and control) must be used. You can eliminate the price system, but not its function.

Third, during a control period, the public forgets what profits are all about. Even before wage-price controls, the public believed profits were "too high," even though they have actually declined in the past few years, from 6.2% of GNP in 1966 to 3.6% in 1970, and increasing only to 4.3% in 1972. And, with profit increases raised to the top of the news during the recovery of 1972 and early 1973, the negative public sentiment against profits increased. Why? The control system itself heightened the public's negative attitude toward profits at a time when capital regeneration, the fuel of the capitalist engine, was already alarmingly low.

Fourth, wage-price controls provide a convenient stone for those having economic or political axes to grind, particularly those interested in promoting a centralized economic system. For example, in 1972, Ralph Nader argued that automobile companies should not be allowed to raise their prices to reflect style changes. Others argued that price increases should not be given to companies that employ insufficient numbers of minorities or pollute. Nor should wage increases go to uncooperative unions.

Fifth, wage-price controls can easily become a security blanket against the cold winds of free-market uncertainties. They tell people what the limits are; they help employers fight unions, and union leaders to placate demands for "more" from their rank and file. The controlled tend to become dependent on the controllers and want regulations continued in preference to the competition of a dynamic market. At the same time, the controllers themselves can become so enamored with their task that they also don't want to let go. The public begins to fear what will happen when controls are ended, and seeks continuance. Witness the recent fears of moving from Phase II to Phase III, and the public (and Congressional) pressure for the freeze to replace Phase III. Even Wall Street seems terrified at the thought of returning to supply and demand in the market. All of this proves that it is much easier to get into controls than to get out.

Sixth, under controls, business and labor leaders begin to pay more attention to the regulatory body than to the dynamics of the marketplace. They inevitably come to the same conclusion, summed up by one executive: "We know that all of our sophisticated analysis and planning can be wiped out in the blink of a Washington controller's eye."

Seventh, and most dangerous, wage-price controls misguide the public. They draw attention away from the fundamental factors that affect inflation—fiscal and monetary policies, tax rates, import-export policies, productivity, competitive restrictions, and so on. The danger is that attention will become permanently focused on the symptom-treating control mechanism rather than on the underlying problems.

The public voice

The public is also adding to the probability of more central control of our economic system. I can cite several basic attitudes at work to explain this phenomenon:

Increasing loss of faith in the ability of both business and labor leaders to operate our economic system.

Increasing expectation of greater economic benefits.

Intensified search for stability and egalitarianism.

In recent years poll after poll has quantified the growth of these trends in public opinion. For instance, over the last seven years, Louis Harris and Associates has been asking the public about its degree of confidence in the leadership of our institutions, and has made these discoveries:

Corporate executives share with bankers and educators the largest loss in public respect, declining from 55% in 1966 to 27% in 1973.

Confidence in labor leaders shrank from 22% to 15% in the same time period.[1]

And a 1971 Opinion Research Corporation study revealed that 62% of the public favored governmental controls over prices, 60% of all stockholders believed competition could not be counted on to keep prices "fair," and fully one third of the public believed that Washington should set ceilings on profits.[2]

In general, my personal mail and my experience in numerous interviews with newspaper editorial boards and others confirmed that the public feels there should be more, not less, control of business and labor. And Congress reflects this mood in asking for more controls, tighter regulations, and more public agencies. Time and again, when I was testifying before congressional committees, I was told that we had to have more controls because the private enterprise system "didn't work." Such a sentiment does not make me optimistic about continued public support for our free enterprise economy.

Nevertheless, the growth in the public's disenchantment with the private enterprise system has been matched by an increase in the public's

[1] Louis Harris, "The Public Credibility of American Business," *The Conference Board Record,* March 1973, p. 33.

[2] Thomas W. Benham, "Trends in Public Attitudes toward Business and the Free Enterprise System," *White House Conference on the Industrial World Ahead* (Washington, Government Printing Office, February 1973).

demands on that system. The public wants, for instance, higher pay for teachers, policemen, and women; a clean environment; better schools and medical care—and all without increases in prices or taxes.

At various Price Commission public hearings and in meetings with public groups and congressmen, I heard demands for increased pollution controls but, at the same time, for lower transportation prices, increased health benefits but lower hospital costs, increased mine safety but lower coal prices, decreased insecticide usage but lower food prices, protected forests but lower lumber prices, and so on. The demands are outrunning what we, as a society, can afford.

We cannot have it all ways without increased productivity. And, more and more, the public is not willing to wait for the market to provide remedies but is seeking centralized solutions to obtain the desired benefits now.

Finally, the move toward a central system is being aided by the public's desire to make people the same, both in ability and in susceptibility to economic change. The market system is conceived on the concepts of competition, monetary reward, excellence, and change. The current attitude stresses stability, cooperation, egalitarianism, and income equality enforced by a central authority.

"Can we be equal and excellent too?" queries John Gardner in the subtitle to his book *Excellence*—a question which he discusses extensively but does not answer.[3] Everyone might like both, but the competitive system is built on the notion that those individuals and institutions outperforming others are not and should not be rewarded equally. But now, more people are seeking and getting protection, through tax reform income redistribution plans, promotion by seniority, and so on, against "differences" generated by the operation of the competitive system.

And society's insistent cry for economic stability poses two dilemmas for our capitalistic system.

First, if the business cycle can be sufficiently dampened by government policies to avoid the unpleasant by-products, we might also run the risk of removing some of the essential features of capitalism, principally the ability of the capitalist system to adapt to changing circumstances and to encourage risk taking. That is, if we remove the valleys do we not also remove the "mountains of incentive" for risk and change?

Second, the goal of "maximum employment" has been interpreted to mean low unemployment, and the arguments have centered on definitions of "low" (3%, 4%, 5%) and "unemployment." But stimulating demand to achieve low unemployment risks inflation. And moderating demand to reduce inflation risks high unemployment.

This unemployment-inflation trade-off is becoming more difficult to manage centrally. If low unemployment is government's primary goal,

---

[3] New York, Harper & Row, 1961.

as it has been in recent years, inflationary pressures are created and fixed incomes become vulnerable. In turn, there are more cries for wage-price controls and greater planning.

Central economic planning holds a great deal of logical appeal for many economists, intellectuals, and businessmen. They conclude that, if businesses plan, governments should—or that somebody should be in charge of the economy.

While their arguments are appealing, to date no one in any society has been able to come up with a central planning model that is more efficient and effective than the seemingly uncoordinated actions of the marketplace. I do not believe it is possible to construct one. In the Price Commission, almost every time we tried to adjust our economic system to correct one problem, two or three more were created, and the more we felt the temptation to "control."

In the end, I believe that any extended control system would disrupt the free-market system. At worst, the market would break down; at best, it would be highly ineffective and subject to bottlenecks, quotas, and black markets. The trade-offs in our extremely large and highly interdependent economy are too complex to be done efficiently on a centralized basis. And then there is the question of who would supply the value judgments for the operations of such a system. Why not return to the one planning system we have that *works*—the price system.

POINT OF NO RETURN?

What does this all add up to? Where are we headed? Is our private enterprise system actually doomed?

There are many who have said *yes*. Karl Marx predicted that capitalism would destroy itself; Joseph A. Schumpeter flatly stated that capitalism cannot survive;[4] and Robert L. Heilbroner concluded: "The change [away from capitalism] may require several decades, perhaps even generations, before becoming crystal clear. But I suggest that the direction of change is already established beyond peradventure of doubt."[5] Even 'Adam Smith' observed in *Supermoney* that "the consensus is moving away from the market as decision maker and from the business society."[6]

Clearly, the factors I have cited *are* carrying us further and further away from the market system and toward a central economic one. I cannot prove we have gone or will go "too far," but I can point to figures substantiating the trend: our national income accounts show a shift in governmentally directed expenditures from 15% in 1930 to about

---

[4] *Capitalism, Socialism and Democracy*, 3d ed. (New York, Harper & Row, 1962), p. 61.

[5] *Between Capitalism and Socialism* (New York, Vintage Books, 1970), p. 31.

[6] New York, Random House, 1972, p. 266.

40% today. And the federal proportion has risen from 5% to 26% in the same period.

I am *not* saying, however, that the private enterprise system is doomed, nor that continuance of the trend toward central control is inevitable and irreversible. Nor do I feel that government has no role in the economic-allocation system. It clearly does and should. I believe, rather, that we are very near the point where further centralization will change our present system into one that can no longer perform its function efficiently.

I view this trend with alarm because I favor retaining the very powerful features of the market system. I hold this position, not out of blind faith in an ideology, but for these reasons:

Demonstrated economic superiority—The economic record clearly reads that the U.S. free-market, private enterprise system has produced the highest standard of living in history and has demonstrated a remarkable ability to adapt to changing conditions.

Political freedom—The principles of democracy and personal freedom are most compatible with a decentralized market system.

Personal experience—I have witnessed the difficulties of trying to allocate resources by centrally directed price controls. These difficulties have convinced me that it is impossible to improve on the system in which billions of daily market decisions by the public determine our resource allocations.

Before some brand me a chauvinistic throwback to Social Darwinism, let me quickly add these points.

I am aware that our present system has competitive imperfections on both the price and the wage sides. It has never been, and never will be, as theoretically competitive as Adam Smith's description. Government vigilance and action are required to prevent the natural monopolistic tendencies of the system.

I am also aware that there are social problems and inequities in our present system which need correction, and that the central government should play a role in this task.

The difference between the centralists and myself is that I do not think the best solution is always to increase the size of the central system. *Rather, it is in a better functioning of our private competitive system and a better quality, not quantity, of public control.* The question remains: How can this be accomplished?

Backing up

It is obvious from the foregoing that I strongly believe the trends toward a centralized, or government-controlled, economy should be halted. I believe the survival of almost our total economy is at stake.

Businessmen, labor leaders, government legislators, and administrators have the power to slow or alter the trends I've cited. By doing so, we may be falsely labeled right-wingers or reactionaries, but we should not be daunted. If a goodly number of us do not try to stop the present trends, we may, even within this decade, end up with an economy we cannot manage.

Recommendations on how to halt the present trends are discussed below. I do have one comment that applies to all of them. I do not believe, as some free-enterprisers do, that any of the suggestions I make should do away with the social achievements of the past 40 years. I believe that much, if not most, of the social legislation passed by the U.S. Congress protects the unprotected and provides social equity in economic terms that are consonant with the spirit of our political life and the protection of the individual by law. I deeply believe in equity.

I do not believe, however, in inequity. It is the inequities, rigidities, bureaucratic stiflings, and actual absurdities that we must attack. But again it is a question of how.

Selective deregulation: Obviously, not all regulation in the public interest should cease—for example, in the areas of safety, product quality, pollution, and health. But many economists can make a good list of those regulations that are interfering excessively with the competitive model, such as subsidies, quotas, tariffs, and competition-limiting labor and business practices referred to earlier in the article.

Monopolistic vigilance: Both business and labor have innate tendencies to seek monopolistic positions, and therefore they must be restrained. The same message also goes for professions (e.g., medicine and law) and trades (e.g., accounting and investment) that build up anticompetitive practices in the name of "professionalism."

The Sherman, the Robinson-Patman, and the Clayton acts, all designed to bring about these goals, were written many years ago. Each needs continued enforcement and should be examined for revisions and oversights in its application.

Three-branch overhauls: Just as physical systems need periodic checks and overhauls, so do our social institutions. Government is no exception. Many of our procedures and institutions at the local, state, and federal level were designed for an agrarian society with slow communications and an isolated domestic economy.

At a minimum, I suggest a regularized public review, say, every three years, of the organizational and administrative procedures of government.

Political involvement: We live not just in an economy but in a *political* economy. Our economic system does not operate according to the classical laws of supply and demand but through the interaction of power and politics with economics. If business and labor leaders wish to steer the system in the direction they believe best, they cannot simply deplore, fume, curse, and hire a Washington lawyer or lobbyist. They must get directly involved by holding public office, personally visiting regulatory bodies and Congress, participating in citizens' affairs groups, and allocating time for employees to participate in local, state, and national politics.

Public advocacy: Related to the need for political involvement is the need for public advocacy of all views about our economic system. Those supporting increases in government's role are currently more vocal than are the advocates of the private enterprise system. The reason, I suspect, is that advocacy of private enterprise is often ridiculed as mossback in viewpoint, anti-intellectual, socially insensitive, and on the side of vested interests and "fat cats."

Nevertheless, those believing in the private enterprise system must speak out, not bombastically but intelligently. Every avenue should be utilized—speeches, articles, participation in local affairs, appearances at schools, employer-employee discussions, and so forth.

Economic education: If people are to make intelligent choices about the nature of our economic system, they must understand more economics. My experience at the commission has convinced me that economic understanding in this nation is low, much lower than it should be for people to make wise choices.

Education to promote understanding should begin with our young people and extend through adult life, emphasizing not a partisan view but a clear presentation of various economic fundamentals and systems.

Better economic tools: The economic policy tools of taxation, budget, and monetary supply, by which government manages the overall economy, are very crude and require overhauling. The econometric models are weak, the implementation process rigid, and the needed data often not available. For instance, decisions were made in Phase II with a frightening paucity of economic information. At the very least, this situation could be corrected by funding the many excellent economic research organizations to enable them to come forward with recommendations for the Congress and the President.

Business schools: Business schools should turn out students who understand both the strengths *and* the weaknesses of the private enterprise system, as well as its responsibilities to society. Too often, technicians are being graduated who are narrow professionals and blind ideologists.

One particular recommendation is that more schools encourage entrepreneurs. The entrepreneur is the lifeblood—the innovator, creator, pusher—of the private enterprise system; without him, the system will tend to become change-resistant and bureaucratic.

Department of Economic Affairs: Part of President Nixon's proposed departmental reorganization program is the creation of a new Department of Economic Affairs. In the Price Commission, we saw numerous instances in which the dispersal of economic policy matters in various parts of government inhibited the formulation of an integrated and consistent program.

I support the proposed new department, which would gather together under one head the economic branches of various departments and agencies, e.g., Transportation, Commerce, Labor, the Small Business Administration, and others.

Productivity: A strong, increasing productivity is one of the best preventives against inflation and one of the strongest assets of a private enterprise system. Therefore, business and labor must work together to shore up our lagging productivity, particularly as we shift to a more service-oriented, and hence lower-productivity, economy. Government can also help in this area through policies that stimulate capital investment and R&D.

In addition to the National Commission on Productivity in Washington, there should be a private sector productivity institute, like those in Japan, Germany, and Israel, which would be a clearinghouse of information and source of help and education.

A DIFFERENT KIND OF ROAD

My recommendations advocate continuation of a private enterprise, free-market system with these essential features:

The price system.
Private ownership.
Collective bargaining.
The profit motive.
Freedom of entry.

Capitalism is more than a system of economic voting by buying a can of peas. It is also a system of values and attitudes, a way of life that permits individual motivation, excitement, personal freedom, variety, and excellence. I do not see these attributes flourishing in centrally planned and controlled systems.

Yet I am not denying a role to central government. Government can help to ease transitions caused by change through stimulating or contracting the economy and informing the public of the cost and benefits of various alternatives, e.g., pollution control versus higher prices, caribou protection versus energy supply, unemployment versus inflation. Government also has the extremely important function of setting and monitoring the rules of the economic game through antitrust laws, product-quality standards, pollution controls, and so on. These restrictions are set principally to keep competition alive and to protect the general public.

The key issue is at what point do such activities and restrictions on the private enterprise system inhibit it to the point of rendering it effectively inoperative?

The tug between laissez-faire and state regulation has been going on for centuries. They are contradictory, but both are valid approaches and applicable under appropriate conditions. Yet neither is of universal application for all purposes.

We seem to advance by overaccentuation of one principle at a time, like a sailing vessel that is first on one tack and then on another, but is making to windward on both. It is important, therefore, not to hold too long on the same tack, not to believe too strongly that either principle is absolute and universal.

For the real danger is that people will strive for the triumph of a particular philosophy and will refuse to consider the limits of proper application of their particular point of view. In the heat of debate, the advocate often asserts extreme opinions and demands action more drastic than he would call for if he reflected more calmly.

I submit that what we must do is seek the balance between these opposing principles, realizing that it is almost as impossible to frame a comprehensive and universally applicable economic system as it is a political one. In making our Constitution subject to amendment, our forefathers showed they were aware that the best solution will not be found in one principle but in a set of ideas determined by experiment and observation of practical results. And it is extremely likely that the chosen path will not be the same forever, but will shift from time to time.

Phase IV could be a return trip to the relatively free-market system and, I hope, a reversal of the trend I have observed. It could be an opportunity for labor and business to demonstrate that the private sector can manage the market and fight inflation without further government intervention. If not—then I don't think that either labor, business, or the public will like the controls that will be imposed on our freedoms in the future. And we will have helped to build our own cages.

This is not a pessimistic view, for, as Schumpeter stated, a report that a ship is sinking is not defeatist. It is only defeatist if the crew sits and drinks. They can also rush to man the pumps.

In every sense it's up to each of us.

QUESTIONS

1. Why does Grayson feel that we should "get back" to a competitive market system? Who and what forces are pulling the other way?

2. Would the changes suggested by Grayson be a step forward or backward toward meeting the societal goals of the United States? Whose goals?

3. What impact would Grayson's suggestions have on the relative importance and use of price in marketing mixes? Is this wise from a profit point of view?

*4. Is Kotler's proposal for a more socially responsible marketing concept (Reading 33) compatible with Grayson's position?

*5. How would Grayson be classified in Greysers' framework (Reading 34)?